INSIDE RACING TECHNOLOGY
DISCUSSIONS OF RACING TECHNICAL TOPICS

PAUL HANEY • **JEFF BRAUN**

This book was first published in 1995 by *TV MOTORSPORTS*, 1829 Brewster Av., Redwood City, CA 94062.

The information in this book is true to the best of our knowledge. All recomendations are made without any guarantee on the part of the authors or Publisher, who disclaim any liability incurred in connection with the use of any information presented here.

We recognize that some words, model names, and designations mentioned in this book are the property of the trademark holder. We use them for indentification only.

Tables, diagrams, and graphics in this book are either original work created by the authors, images used with permission, or common knowledge in the community.

COVER CREDITS:

Cover design by William Nagel of Redwood City, Calif., who also consulted on the layout and design of the body of the book.

The yellow car on the cover comes from a photo of an Indy car turning into the Corkscrew at Laguna Seca Raceway. The photo on the previous page was taken at the same place. Those two photos and the three on page 60 by Bob Gularte, Sunnyvale, Calif.

Contents

PREFACE

In the many conversations Paul and I have had during the development of this book, I kept telling him that race engineering "is not magic." This is an important point. Race engineering is not magic, it's just basic engineering applied to a very narrow set of conditions. It is actually very low-tech. The concepts are basic. The implementation is straightforward.

What makes one car or team better than another is how the team applies the basics to the particular conditions on the day, how quickly the team adjusts to changing conditions, how well they are able to tune all the components of the car to work together, how well they record and use their data, and how well the individual team members work together and understand each other. It is a thousand small details that make one team win and the rest of the teams lose, not one magic trick possessed by only one team.

There are no magic tricks in this book. What I hope the reader gets from the book is a basic understanding of the engineering principles involved. I think that through the interviews and stories presented here, you will get an insight into how engineers and designers currently apply the basic principles.

Racing is more about people and what they are doing than about machines and what they do. If the rules required us to race wheelbarrows, racing would be just as much fun and just as competitive. We would all still be working to have a better wheelbarrow than the next guy. We tried to show this side of race engineering in addition to the nuts and bolts.

I hope you have half as much fun reading this as I had helping Paul put it together.

Jeff Braun, Ovalo, Texas, May 1995,

Jeff Braun

I met Jeff Braun, pronounced brown like the color, in 1991. Both of us are intensely curious about all things technical, especially racing. Jeff and I both have mechanical engineering degrees, and this gives us a common language during the long phone conversations we have when Jeff is answering my dumb questions. I remember saying to him during one of our hour-long telephone conversations that there are probably people out there who would like to hear what we were talking about. I began to include Jeff's explanations in my newsletter, *TV MOTORSPORTS*, and it wasn't long before we were talking about "doing a book." Jeff has helped me understand much more about racing than I ever thought I would learn.

The technical information in this book emphasizes racecar aerodynamics and shock absorbers because that's what matters on modern racecars, and also because there hasn't been much written about either one. The use of computers in racing is also a major part of this book because so much of the performance and safety improvements made in racing in the last 20 years came about because powerful computer hardware and software tools have become widely available.

Mainly, this book is about people. I hope the stories and interviews give the reader a chance to get to know a few racing people. There is no magic and no free lunch. Successful race teams result from smart, competent, highly motivated people responding to leadership and direction. All the neat, techie stuff comes from the minds of these people.

I want to thank all the people who have tried to answer my questions about racing. I even learned from the few people who didn't want to tell me anything. I knew it was important if they wouldn't talk about it, so I asked other people the same questions. Like Carroll Smith says in the last interview in the book, "Motor racing is full of very, very nice people." I've found that if you're not too demanding and you ask enough people the right question, you'll get useful answers.

My wife, Pat, has read this whole book at least once, and I could not have done it without her proofreading and general support.

Linda Mansfield edited the copy. She did a great job and finally taught me what to do with most of the commas.

Bill Nagel designed and laid out the color cover and advised on the overall book design. The professional appearance of the book is mainly due to his efforts.

The following people read a draft and gave me invaluable feedback about the concept and contents: Carroll Smith, Sam Garrett, Chris Andrews, Jack Calaway, Bob Gularte, and James Braun.

Bob Lesnett took that horrible picture below. I couldn't find another one. Thanks Bob.

Personal computers make it possible for an individual to publish a book like this. I use a 486 clone running PageMaker and Word for Windows under MicroSoft Windows 3.1. The graphs and sketches were created in CorelDraw and the printer is a Lexmark Optra R.

Paul Haney, Redwood City, Calif. May 1995.

Paul Haney

CHAPTER 1

RACECAR AERODYNAMICS

Aerodynamics has always been a mystery science. Like electricity, it's tough to visualize. And, at speeds close to the speed of sound, compressibility effects complicate things. Aerodynamics has, however, become extremely important in racing and, as always, benefits discovered in racing trickle down and improve the performance of our road cars.

Racecars have to travel over a surface and through the air. The relationship the tires have with the track surface and how well the shape of the racecar deals with the air flowing around it are the two major factors that determine the success of any racecar design. Engines used to be the focus of racecar tuning, but are now considered to be a standardized, predictable component like a wheel or coil spring.

At any speed, engine power output is pitted against the rolling resistance offered by the drive train and tires as well as aerodynamic resistance resulting from movement through the air. When a car is going as fast as it will go, all the available engine power is being used to overcome rolling and aerodynamic resistance. Rolling resistance (all resistance to motion other than aerodynamic drag) is usually estimated at about 15% of engine output. At any speed less than the top speed, there is excess power available for acceleration.

In the 1980s, radial tires, better bearings and gears, and lighter lubricants decreased rolling resistance in racecars. These improvements pale, however, when compared with the benefits in performance gleaned from aerodynamic improvements. Millions of dollars have been spent building aerodynamic test facilities, mainly by Formula 1 teams. The data from wind tunnel testing backed up by on-track testing with data acquisition has resulted in aerodynamic drag reduction, increases in downforce, and better stability in almost every type of racecar.

What racecar designers continue to do is reduce aerodynamic drag and increase downforce. Drag reduction causes an immediate increase in top speed, leaving more power available for acceleration at lower speeds. More downforce increases braking and cornering performance.

We'll show you that although wings create a lot of drag, the resulting downforce decreases lap times in spite of hurting top speeds. We'll explain ground effects and look at data from full-size and scale-model wind tunnel testing of an Indy Lights Lola. We'll also look at the only state-of-the-art wind tunnel in the United States.

WINGS ON RACECARS

The first time I saw a racecar with a wing on it, I thought it was dumb. It was 1966 and a guy at work (Pratt & Whitney's Jet Engine Development Center near West Palm Beach, Fl.) took me to a local dirt track race after hearing me talk about the infamous Devil's Bowl track in my hometown of Dallas. I had just been graduated with a mechanical engineering degree, and I thought I knew everything. "That wing couldn't be doing any good," I said to my smart-ass self.

But, thinking about it later, I realized that racers are practical people in a very competitive environment. If those wings didn't do any good, they wouldn't be using them. So, I sat down with a couple of the books I was supposed to be familiar with and tried to figure out why those silly looking wings made any difference.

What I finally figured out was that those upside down wings provided additional force down on the tires in excess of the weight of the car, allowing the tires to produce more grip. Wings on an airplane generate an upward force that's called lift. If you turn the wing upside down, mount it on a car, and move it through the air you get negative lift which we call downforce. More force pressing the car down with no extra weight on the car makes the car brake, accelerate, and turn better. We'll explain the difference between the weight of the car and downforce later on. Right now, let's look at wings on racecars.

SLOWER TOP SPEEDS BUT FASTER LAPS

Done properly, aerodynamic improvements to racing cars are almost free performance improvements. For an open-wheeled car, especially, the tires produce a huge amount of aerodynamic drag. If a clever designer is able to reduce this drag by cleaning up the flow over the bodywork and around the tires, wings, and other downforce-producing devices can improve the car's performance with little or no penalty. Even when added aerodynamic devices produce some drag along with downforce, the car can turn faster laps. The car can actually have a slower top speed due to increased aero drag and still turn faster laps because of more downforce.

You can see a good example of how wings hurt top speeds, but still lowered lap times, by looking back to the early '70s when Indy car designers first began to learn about wings and downforce. Here's a table from the book, *Indy Car*, by Roger Huntington, showing the increase in speeds for the fastest two cars at the Brickyard in 1971 and 1972. The tremendous increase in the average lap speed came about because the United States Auto Club (USAC) liberalized the rules for the 1972 Indy 500, allowing much bigger wings than in 1971. Mark Donohue and Bobby Unser were the fastest qualifiers at the 500 in those two years. The table shows how speeds in the turns went way up due to downforce while the drag from the wings actually lowered top speed on the straights. Since, at Indy, the car spends a lot of time in the turns, the overall average speed increased 17 miles an hour. In a single year!

| | Speed, Miles per Hour | | |
	Turn	Straight	Average
Mark Donohue, '71	163	217	179
Bobby Unser, '72	183	206	196

When Jim Hall put a wing on the rear of his Chaparral racecar, he made it movable and driver controllable so it could be flattened out on the straights for less drag, when the downforce wasn't needed. That gave him the best of both worlds—maximum speed on the straights and downforce during braking and cornering.

Another feature of Hall's design, mounting the wing directly onto the rear suspension uprights so the aerodynamic forces go right to the tires and not through the suspension, was simple and direct. Unfortunately, some of these wing supports failed, probably due to fatigue failures, causing some scary crashes. For that reason "movable aerodynamic devices" were immediately banned by all sanctioning bodies. From that time on, wings and all other aerodynamic devices have been considered a part of the body work and aerodynamic forces cannot be transmitted directly to the wheels. We'll show later how wings, constrained by these rules, led to ground effects which led to active suspension which resulted in the entire chassis becoming a movable aerodynamic device and forced a new generation of rules. Racecar designers and engineers always seem to stay ahead of rules makers.

HOW WINGS PRODUCE LIFT

The fact that a plane as big as a Boeing 747 can fly seems magical because it looks so slow and ponderous when you see it landing. But of course it's not magic. It's simply natural forces used cleverly. Here's a simple, familiar situation you experience every day that happens because of the same natural phenomenon that gets a 747 off the ground.

When you're driving on the freeway and you open your car window an inch or so, you get a rush of air coming into the car from the air vents. This is the same natural occurrence that allows a wing to generate lift. The air going by the window has to speed up to get out of the way of the car. When air speeds up, it loses pressure. The lower pressure of the air speeding past the car window sucks more air out the window, increasing flow into the car through the vent. An airplane wing has a shape that causes the air going over its upper surface to speed up more than the air going under it. The air on top loses pressure and the difference in pressure top to bottom times the area of the wing makes a huge amount of lifting force.

When a car is traveling at freeway speed air accelerates going over the top and sides of the car, but piles up and slows down in front of the windshield and behind the rear window. The air at the base of the windshield is almost stopped. The air near the side window has speeded up to get out of the way of the car. When you open a side window a few inches, you can feel increased flow coming in through the fresh air vents. Close the window and you can feel the flow get smaller. The slow air at the base of the windshield is at a higher pressure than the faster air outside the window opening, and the difference in pressure pushes air into the grill, through the vent ducts into the interior, and out the car at the lower pressure area of the open window. Fresh air normally enters your car through that grill in front of the windshield and goes out through an exit vent. Cracking the window connects the inside of the car with a low pressure area outside the car. This increases the pressure difference between inlet and exit and so increases air flow. Air, like any fluid, flows toward a lower pressure.

That high pressure area at the base of the windshield is where a NASCAR racecar has an inlet that collects air for the engine. An engine makes more power if it gets its air/fuel mixture at a higher pressure. That's why turbochargers and superchargers boost engine power. If you can put the engine air inlet in the place that has the highest pressure, it's like a free power boost compared to a location where the pressure is lower.

Bernoulli's Theorem

In 1738, Daniel Bernoulli, a Swiss physicist, observed and measured fluid flow behavior, causing him to propose that a fluid loses pressure as it speeds up. Moving air has static pressure and dynamic pressure. The total of the two is called the total pressure and that remains the same whether the air is still or moving. Static pressure plus dynamic pressure is total pressure, a constant at sea level.

Any fluid (air or water, for instance) has no dynamic pressure when still. When a car is motionless, the air inside and outside has no dynamic pressure and the static pressure is the same both places. When you put your hand out the window of a moving car, you feel the momentum of the air as it runs into your hand. This pressure you feel is called the dynamic pressure and it increases the faster you go. You know you feel more pressure on your hand when the car goes 60 mph than when it goes 30 mph.

The air has to give up static pressure to match the dynamic pressure it acquires as it speeds up. At speed, there is a pressure distribution over the surface of the car because air goes different speeds at different places on the car. The difference in pressure between the vent at the base of the windshield and outside the cracked window happens because the still air at the vent is at a higher static pressure than the moving air at the cracked window.

Through experiments, Bernoulli found out that this pressure difference increases with the square of the airspeed. That means the pressure loss quadruples when speed doubles. If you can accurately measure the difference between these two pressures, you can find out how much the speed of the air increases.

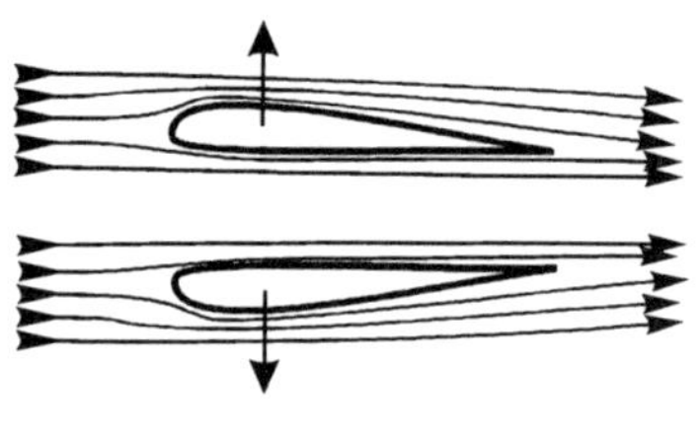

Aerodynamic Force

That lower pressure air going by outside your car window is what causes lift on airplane wings and downforce on racecars. The curved upper surface of the wing (on a plane) makes the air speed up to get around the wing in the same time as the air on the bottom going a shorter distance. This speed difference creates a pressure difference because the faster air on top loses static pressure as it gains dynamic pressure. Remember, the sum of the two pressures has to stay the same. When the pressure on the bottom of the wing is higher than the pressure above the wing, we get a pressure difference and a lifting force.

Turn a wing upside down, put it on a car moving through the air—you get downforce.

How About Some Numbers

It doesn't take much pressure difference to create a bunch of lift. An airplane can easily have a 1,000 square feet of wing area. Let's say the plane is going fast enough to generate an average pressure difference between the top and bottom of the wing of a tenth of a pound per square inch. There's 144 square inches in a square foot, so that's 14.4 pounds per square foot. That pressure difference multiplied times the 1,000 square-foot wing area gives a total lift of of 14,400 pounds. Naturally, there's some drag created when the airplane moves through the air and that's what the airplane engine is for, to overcome that drag.

Lift increases proportionally to the square of the speed. Let's say that plane is going 100 mph when it makes 0.1 pounds per square inch lift. At 200 mph, the lift is four times as big. The resulting 0.4 pounds per square inch now generates 69,600 pounds of lift. You can see how those 747s get off the ground.

A Formula 1 car weighs about 1,500 pounds with fuel and a driver. I've seen estimates of 3,000 pounds of downforce for those cars during early 1994. Even after rules changes that have decreased downforce, they can still "race on the ceiling."

DRAG: YOU DON'T GET SOMETHING FOR NOTHING

Mount a wing upside down on your racecar and, when the car moves through the air, the wing will press the car to the track surface, giving more grip. But it's not free. Just as airplane engines are needed to overcome the drag of the plane, a racecar engine has to overcome the drag of the car, including the wings.

There is a basic equation for the force it takes to push something through air:

Aerodynamic drag = $1/2\ DAV^2$

In this equation, D is the density of the air, A is the frontal area, and V is the velocity.

For real body shapes, air at standard conditions, V in mph, and drag in pounds of force, this equation becomes:

Drag = $1/391\ CdAV^2$

This equation shows that to calculate drag you need to know three things: Cd, the drag coefficient; A, the frontal area of whatever you're driving through the air; and the speed of air past it. This equation shows an important point—aerodynamic forces are proportional to the square of the speed. That means you quadruple the drag or lift when you double the speed.

The drag coefficient, Cd, is important because in concert with frontal area, it determines the power cost of pushing a shape through air at a certain speed. A small, low Cd road car will have a higher top speed than a larger, boxier car with the same engine power.

Here are measured drag coefficients for some basic shapes. These numbers come from tests of shapes with known cross sectional areas. You blow air over them and measure the force on the shape. Notice the difference in the Cd of a long and short cylinder. You probably know that a slippery road car has a Cd of about 0.32. A chunky one is 0.38.

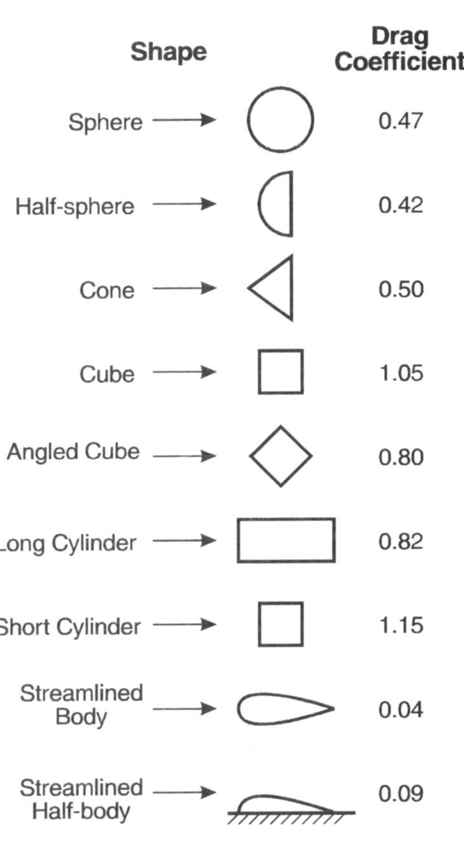

Measured Drag Coefficients

Wings Need Horsepower

Jeff Braun is a full-time race engineer who makes his living chasing the elusive quick lap. Here Jeff tells a story that illustrates what we all know; you don't get something for nothing.

"In 1992, when I was working for Andy Evan's Scandia team running an IMSA Camel Lights car, Mike Lozano was building our motors, "Jeff recalls. "He was making pretty good incremental improvements in power between every race. But, because our car had a lot of drag for the downforce—it was effective but not particularly efficient aerodynamically—we were always looking for ways to increase the downforce. Mike would come to the race all excited because he had found us another 10 horsepower and I'd just tell the crew to crank the wing up another two degrees. We'd go the same speed down the straightaways but the lap times would get better. Andy Evans, the team owner, would come to Mike and say, 'We're not going any faster. Can't you get us some more power?' Mike would tell Andy, 'I keep getting more power but Jeff keeps turning it into downforce.'

"I felt sorry for Mike because it robbed him of the perception of his performance—higher top speeds. The Comptech Acuras would run away from us on the straights and most people would think that our Buick-engined cars were down on horsepower. But, if you really looked, you could see that we had so many wings hung on to the car that it was lucky the car could get out of its own way.

"Phoenix was a good example. In the infield turns, we'd catch up with the Acuras easily and we'd run the same lap times, but they looked like they were running away on the straights. We did our lap times differently than they did, but the times were about the same. That's tough on engine builders. We always take their hard-earned power and turn it into downforce."

ANGLE OF ATTACK

The difference between where the wing is pointed and where it's actually going is the angle of attack as shown in this sketch. The graph below shows how lift and drag changes with the angle of attack for a typical wing design.

Where the curve crosses the Drag axis is where the wing is generating zero lift. Notice the angle of attack at that point is a negative value. That means a typical wing has to point down to get to zero lift. Notice, also, there is some drag at zero lift. There is, truly, no free lunch.

As the nose of the wing turns up, angle of attack increases, and lift increases. Drag goes up also, but not as quickly as lift.

Think about the last time you took a trip on an airplane. During take-off, an airplane builds up to a certain speed and then the pilot "rotates" the plane; that is, the pilot manipulates the controls so that the nose of the plane comes up and, at some angle of attack, the wings generate enough lift to take the plane into the air. Since an airplane wing is fixed to the fuselage, the whole plane has to rotate to increase wing angle of attack. Wings on racecars are fabricated so you can easily adjust the angle of attack, and that's the usual way the crew adjusts a wing to get the amount of downforce they want.

A wing is fairly efficient. You get a lot of lift without much drag—until you get to about 12 degrees angle of attack on this curve. Then drag goes way up, without creating much more lift. As the angle of attack increases from 12 to 19 degrees, there isn't much increase in lift but you have a lot more drag. We say the wing is "stalled" when lift decreases at increasingly higher angles of attack.

The shape of this curve is why you read about airplane crashes during stormy takeoffs and landings. Under conditions of low speed and high lift, the plane is rotated up there near the top of the curve. If the plane has to climb and the pilot tries to bring the nose up, he gets more drag and not much more lift. What he really needs is more airspeed.

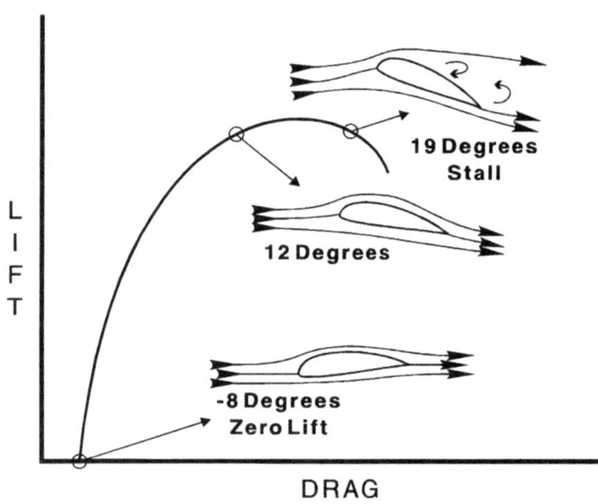

Lift vs. Drag Curve for a Wing

WHAT'S A GURNEY?

If you've watched IndyCar races on TV, you've probably heard a pit reporter mention that a crew member made a change to the "Gurney" during a pit stop. I've heard Gary Gerould, one of the best of the TV announcers, explain that this "Gurney" is a device the teams use to adjust the downforce generated by the wing.

Gerould is correct, of course, but in aerodynamic terms that "Gurney", also called a "Gurney flap" or "wickerbill," is a trailing edge flap. Airplanes use flaps for increased lift during takeoff and landings. Dan Gurney's Eagles were the first to use a trailing edge flap at the Indy 500 in the early 1970s and his name stuck to the device. A trailing edge flap improves the performance of a wing at high angles of attack. Here are some sketches to show what's going on.

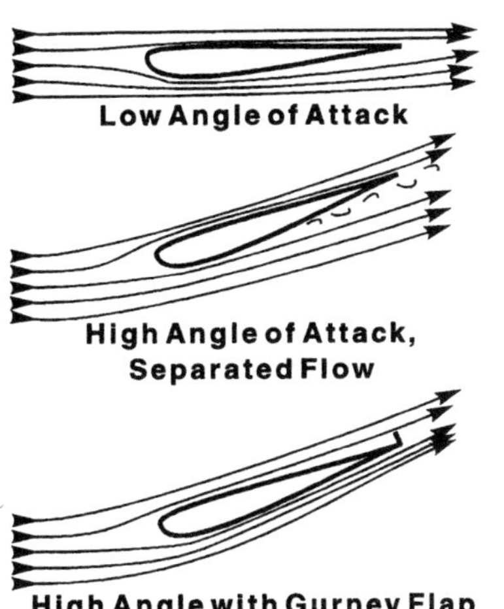

The Effect of a Gurney Flap

The first sketch shows an upside down wing which generates downforce or negative lift as it moves through the air. The air has to accelerate to go around the rounded side of the wing and loses pressure when it speeds up. As you remember, Bernoulli's Theorem says at any place in a fluid, you get the same value when you add up the static and dynamic pressure (what you feel when you put your hand out the window of a moving car). A still fluid has no motion and no dynamic pressure. The slower air on top is at a higher pressure and presses down on the wing surface. The force a wing produces depends on the airfoil shape, the area of the wing, and the square of its speed through the air.

The second sketch is a wing at a high angle of attack. At high angles of attack, air is unable to follow the contour of the lower wing surface and can detach, lowering the efficiency of the wing. As a result, downforce goes down and drag goes up. A small lip on the trailing edge, shown in the bottom sketch, causes a lower pressure just behind it which sucks the lower flow back up to the wing surface. The Gurney flap causes some extra drag, but the wing can be run at a higher angle of attack and produces more downforce.

You can only hang so much wing on a racecar because of rules limiting the number and dimensions of wings or just by running out of room. Those pesky radiators and tires get in the way and they just can't be left out. A designer has to get all the downforce possible out of the wing surfaces allowed by the rules. A Gurney gets more downforce from the allowable wings because you can run them at higher angles of attack.

A Gurney is also used as a quick way to fine tune the force a wing generates in order to adjust the way a car handles. Varying the height of the Gurney adjusts downforce (and drag, of course) and Indy car crews have devised ways of changing the Gurney quickly. L-shaped aluminum extrusions are available in various sizes, and the rear wings are made so these extrusions can be quickly inserted from the side into a groove in the wing during a pit stop. Some teams use lengths of 4 or 6 inch diameter white plastic water pipe with caps on each end to store and transport their Gurneys.

INDY CAR WINGS: SPEEDWAYS VS. ROAD COURSE

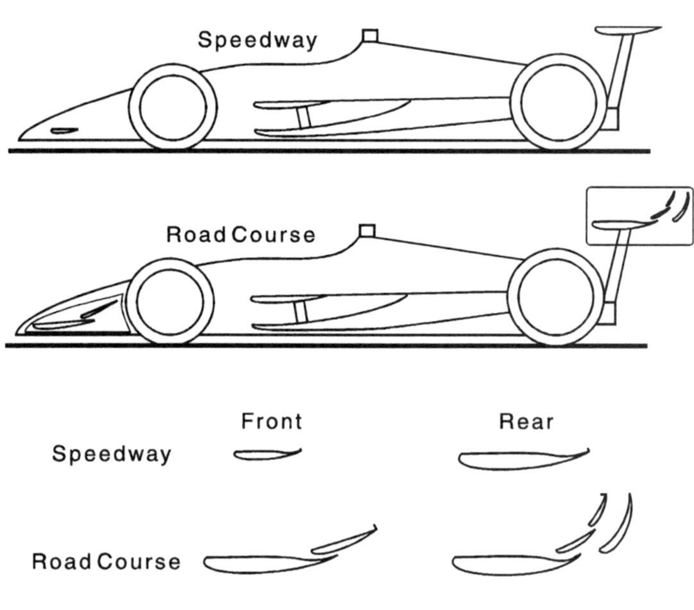

Wing Configurations

Wings are devices that operate efficiently within a small range of speed. That's why airplanes have movable slats and flaps on leading and trailing edges of the wing that, when deployed, increase lift at low speeds so the plane can land and take off slowly. As soon as the plane is off the ground, these devices are stored to reduce drag.

Indy cars compete on three different types of race tracks. There are high-speed superspeedway ovals like Indianapolis and Michigan, 1-mile ovals such as Phoenix and Milwaukee, and road and street courses like Elkhart Lake and Long Beach. Indy cars go more than 230 mph on the straights at Indianapolis and don't get below 200 mph on a good lap. But, on road courses and street courses, the cars have to produce cornering grip at speeds of 40 to 120 mph. They need downforce in both fast and slow corners, but a wing that's good at 220 mph won't do much at 40 mph, and movable devices like airplanes use are not allowed. Indy cars use different types of wings when they compete at different kinds of tracks. Indy car chassis manufacturers like Lola, Reynard, and Penske furnish high and low downforce kits so customers can modify the aerodynamic configuration of the cars depending on the type of track they're running on.

From the sketches above, you can get an idea of the different wings used at different tracks. Indy cars use small, single-element wings on the front and rear at superspeedways. At over 200 mph, a small wing at a low angle of attack produces enough downforce without much drag.

Big wings are needed on road courses at lower speeds to augment the lower downforce generated in the tunnels. As the sketches show, wings for a road course are much bigger and more complex. The road course rear wing shown above has four elements—that is four separate airfoils.

For 1994, IndyCar changed the rules and limited the number of airfoils in the rear wing to three. There are now three configurations allowed, including an in-between wing configuration for the small ovals. Here are sketches of these three configurations.

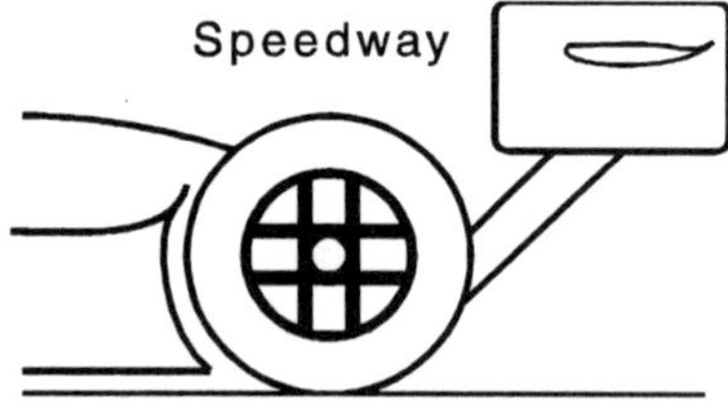

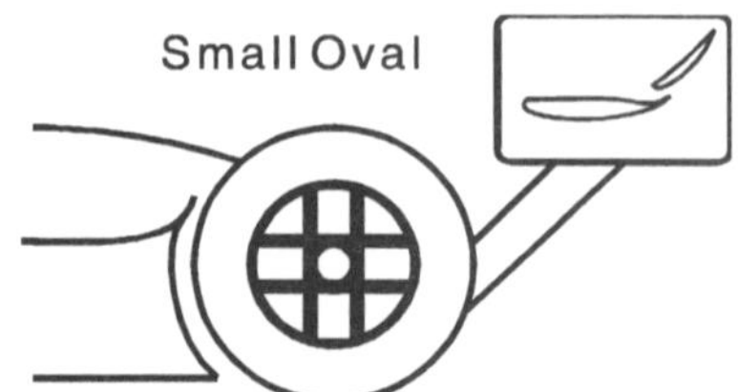

SUMMARY OF BASIC WING AERO

Before we go on to other aerodynamic topics, I'd like to summarize how wings work. It's a simple concept but very important in racing.

Wings have one flat and one curved surface. When they move through the air, there is a longer path for the air over the curved surface than past the flat surface. The air has to go faster over the longer upper surface. Consider two air particles side-by-side at the leading edge of the wing—one goes over the top and the other past the bottom of the wing. Since they started together, they have to finish together or there would be a vacuum created at the trailing edge of the wing.

Bernoulli's Theorem says that the total pressure of a fluid is always the same. Total pressure is the static pressure plus the dynamic pressure. Air going fast has higher dynamic pressure than slower air, but the total has to be the same. So, as the air speeds up, its static pressure goes down to offset the increase in dynamic pressure.

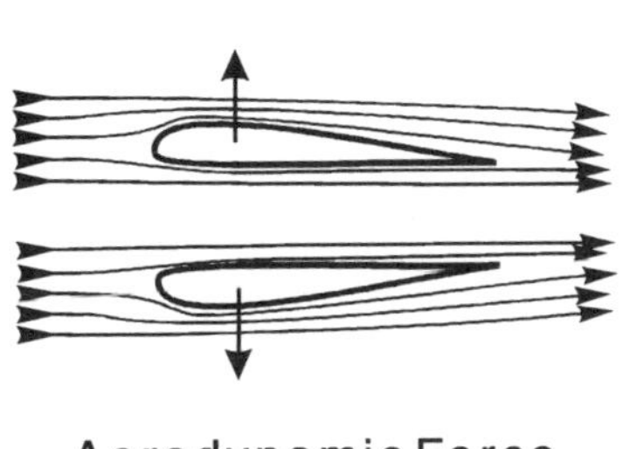

Aerodynamic Force

The faster air on top of an airplane wing has a lower static pressure than the slower air on bottom. That difference in pressure (higher on the bottom) multiplied by the area of the wing is the lifting force produced by the wing. Turn a wing upside down on a racecar and you've got downforce.

Any body that has air flowing past it creates drag. A wing has both drag and lift, and these drag and lift forces go up with the square of the car speed. That means there's four times as much drag (and lift) when the speed doubles from 20 mph to 40 mph.

A wing creates more lift at higher angles of attack. Put your hand out the window of your car at speed, and you can feel the lift and drag on your hand. You can rotate your hand and change the angle of attack. When the front part of your hand is turned up in a positive angle of attack, lift forces push your hand up. Turn your hand down and the force is down.

Turn your palm toward the front of the car. You feel a lot of force. That's aerodynamic drag. Drag goes down as you turn your palm back down because this lowers the frontal area of your hand. You can "fly" your hand up and down by varying the angle of attack. Do you feel the drag changing also as you vary theangle of attack? Are people in passing cars staring at you?

GROUND EFFECTS

Almost every racecar competing today uses some degree of ground effects. Technically, any vehicle moving through air near the ground is a ground-effects vehicle.

Current racecars (F1, IMSA World Sports Car, IndyCar, Indy Lights, Formula Atlantic) use ground effects to generate much of their downforce. We're going to look at how ground effects got started in racing and the difference between tunnels and flat bottoms.

Denny Hulme on McLaren's Accidental Downforce

Maybe most people don't think about technical stuff when they go to the Monterey Historics at Laguna Seca, but I do. I like to look at the basic design and construction of the cars and what type of engines and suspensions were used during various eras of motor racing. Some designs, like the twin overhead cam, four-valve-per-cylinder engine, are not as new as you might think.

At the 1992 Monterey Historics, Denny Hulme was there to drive a 1972 McLaren M-20. Hulme was, of course, Formula 1 World Champion in 1967 driving for Brabham, but is better known in the United States for his achievements in the

Can-Am series driving a McLaren. I wanted to ask him about a story in an English magazine where he had talked about how, in the late '60s, they almost stumbled onto some aerodynamic benefits with the McLaren M8. In that piece in *Racecar Engineering*, Hulme said, "At Goodwood one day, we squared off the bottom of the tub with a piece of aluminum and she picked up some time. We popped it off again and dropped time, so we put it back on. We didn't understand what was happening, but looking back now, technically, I think we got very close to a ground-effects car. We didn't run hard suspension on the McLarens, but it was hard with a full load of fuel. The springs were a joke and the shaft of the shock absorbers had Aeon [bump] rubbers and, with a full load, the car sat solidly on these which meant that there was fixed suspension. The M8 always ran its quickest when you put the 80 gallons of fuel in and jammed it down onto the ground.

"The first couple of laps were always your quickest of the race. We put that down to having new tyres on, but what we totally overlooked was that we had made the car into a ground-effects car and it clamped itself onto the road through running so close to the ground. When you could hear it scrape, you felt the car was going at its best, but we didn't like doing that because we were wearing the tub out. We didn't have rubbing strips underneath, so the grounding was knocking rivets off."

I looked around for Denny Hulme that day at Laguna Seca, and found him standing in the paddock talking to a guy. I waited patiently until they paused in their conversation, and Hulme looked toward me expectantly. He was about 6 feet tall, hefty but not fat, and had that familiar hawk nose and jutting jaw that I'd seen in all those photos in magazines.

I introduced myself and asked if he could tell me more about the ground-effects car that almost happened. "We were there, we just didn't know it," he said. "We had a big radius on the body along the sides of the tub, and we squared that off and it went faster. We knew it was aero, because it went faster in fast corners than in slow ones.

"We had to get to America for the race season and so we stopped. We should have given it to some boffin [that's Olde Country slang for a scientist or engineer] to work up a program, but we didn't. Those cars would have been really fast because there was a lot of body area and lots of power. We should have gone on with it, but we didn't." It was a friendly conversation, and Hulme seemed to enjoy talking about it. Hulme died a few months after our conversation. I'm glad I got to talk to him.

The cars of the late '60s had rounded body work, probably because it looked good, and they thought it was aerodynamic. Actually, the rounded areas under the radiator air inlet on the nose just packed air in under the car and caused lift. The rounded lower corner of the body sides between the wheel wells likewise let air under the car and resulted in more lift. A decade later, race car shapes had changed drastically. Air dams at the front kept air out from underneath, and slab sides with lips on the bottom helped seal under-body areas. As a result, lap times came down, and there was really no penalty for this benefit.

Ground effects enhances the efficiency of a wing because the air under the wing is accelerated by interaction with the ground. Earlier, we gave an example of air flowing past an open window to illustrate how a fluid speeds up and loses static pressure as it gains dynamic pressure. The underside of the racecar drags the air up to speed, creating lower pressure under the car.

The result is phenomenal. Without ground effects, a good racecar, say a Swift DB-1 Formula Ford, can generate 1.2 to 1.4 Gs of cornering force. An object dropped from some height accelerates at 1 G—one unit of gravity. In 1993,

Formula 1 cars routinely generated 4 Gs in medium speed (100-120 mph) corners. Downforce is the reason. Ground effects is a big part of the story.

Colin Chapman: The Creator

In the summer of 1975, Colin Chapman, founder of Lotus and generally recognized as the all-time premier innovator in racing, wrote a 27-page internal paper outlining his ideas for incorporating a wing section into the sides of a F1 car. The layout of the car Chapman proposed was almost identical to that of any modern open-wheeled racecar. It was rear-engined, of course, and had sidepods positioned on either side of a narrow driver compartment. Air inlets in the leading edge of the sidepods fed ducts to oil and water coolers. Lotus had test data from the World War II Mosquito aircraft to help them design that ducting. The Mosquito used a water-cooled engine and had wing-mounted radiators with leading-edge air inlets.

The real innovation in the proposal Chapman wrote was in the way his concept used the air moving under the car to produce downforce. Air entered another duct beneath the sidepod and flowed over the underside of the sidepods which were shaped like an upside-down wing. They started off with brushes on the outer edges of the sidepods, and then developed rigid skirts that rubbed against the track and sealed the underside.

This was the Lotus 78 which took Mario Andretti to four F1 wins in 1977. Andretti is quoted in Doug Nye's book, *Lotus Formula 1 & Indy Cars*, "The 78? Well I'll tell ya — it's just beautiful. It feels like it's painted to the road...." I'll bet it did! Even a few hundred pounds of force would give the car more grip than any of its competitors. As a result Lotus had a definite but short-lived advantage over other Formula 1 teams.

The Lotus 79 was the logical successor to the innovative Type 78. The underwing shape was flattened and moved closer to the track surface. Downforce went up dramatically. The 78 was a wing car, the 79 a ground-effects car. The 79 took Mario Andretti to six Grand Prix wins in 1978 and earned him a World Championship.

What's so hot about ground effects? Well, it's tough to keep air out from under a racecar, so why not use it to your advantage? A racecar has a large area of bodywork when viewed from the top. If you can get the pressure under all that real estate a little lower than the pressure on top, you can suck the car down and make it stick to the track better.

The bottom of the car has to be shaped right, and there is an optimum distance between the bottom of the car and the track surface. This is referred to as ride height, and the front ride height is lower than the rear. That's called rake. This, in effect, makes the entire car act like an upside-down wing, and, in fact, the bottom of a ground-effects car is often called "the underwing." If you can get the rake and ride height stuff right, the bottom of the car generates a lot of downforce with not much drag. It's almost a free lunch.

Today's Indy cars and Formula Atlantics still use these same type of tunnels, but skirts that seal off the sides have been banned. Formula 1, IMSA's World Sports Cars, and Indy Lights use a flat bottom as required by the rules. We'll look at some wind tunnel data later in this chapter so you can get a feel for how critical ride height and rake are in getting maximum downforce from the bottom of the car.

THE UNDERWING

Here is a wing cross section for reference and two sketches showing cross section shapes and rear views of a tunnel car and a flat bottom with diffuser. Indy car sidepods and '95 Formula 1 flat bottoms have 2 inches ground clearance because the rules mandate the bottom of the sidepod at 2 inches above the bottom of the car.

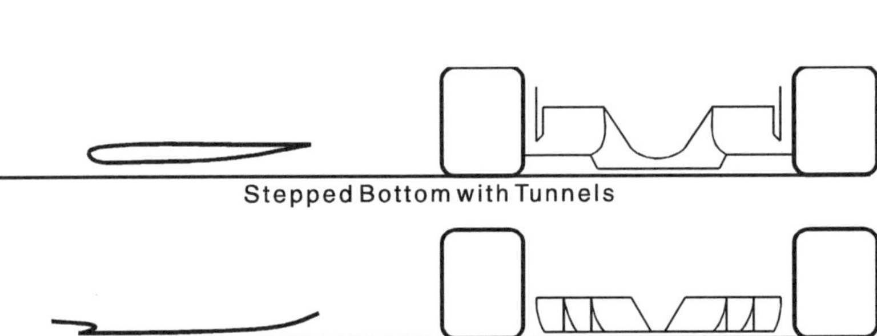

The lower sketch shows an underwing similar to that of a current Indy Lights car and that of an F1 car prior to the "plank rule" created in mid-1994. It's a flat plane starting with a "splitter" and ending in a diffuser section that slows the air back to ambient velocity and pressure with minimum drag. The splitter is a lip at the front of the underwing that causes a clear division of air going under the car and air going around the car. As we'll see later, maximum downforce demands minimum ground clearance for the splitter and a specific "rake" of the flat part of the underwing.

THE DIFFUSER

The purpose of the diffuser is to allow the air that has been accelerated (so that its higher speed can produce a lower pressure) under the car to decelerate back to close to the same speed and pressure it was before the car ran into it. The better the diffuser works, the less drag the underwing produces.

You also see lateral fences or strakes in the diffuser area at the rear of the car. These have been banned from Indy cars (that means they worked), but Indy Lights and F1 cars still use them. The strakes probably do several things, but one of the most obvious is that they prevent low-speed, high-pressure air getting in along the sides of the car from disturbing the flow in the central area of the diffuser.

Indy Car Lola with Vortex Generating Vanes in the Inlet (bottom) and Tunnels at the Exit

Indy Lights Flat-Bottom Undertray with Strakes in Diffuser

Ground Effects Rules

In an attempt to reduce cornering speeds, several race series including Formula 1, IndyCar and IMSA have almost continually changed their rules. Things almost got out of hand in the 1980s when F1 cars developed sliding skirts that sealed the underwing, producing a lot of downforce that went away quickly if the car got sideways or went up on a curb. This lack of stability, a term you'll hear often when people talk about aerodynamics, made the cars dangerous. Rules-makers thought that banning the carefully sculpted underwing shapes would slow the cars and make them more stable. They mandated that the bottom of the car be completely flat.

The designers caught up quickly, however, and by 1993 Formula 1 cars, with the help of controlled ride height and active suspension, generated thousands of pounds of downforce at high speed. What the flat bottom rules really did was discourage suspension travel and make the cars more difficult to drive safely. After the tragic season of 1994, F1 went to a stepped bottom as developed by IndyCar.

Most designers think a stepped bottom is much safer than a flat bottom. The raised sidepods allow air leakage under the car and decrease the sensitivity to ride height and rake. Lower downforce and less penalty for suspension movement tip the scales back toward mechanical grip. As a result, cornering speeds go down and emphasis returns to suspension geometry and damper tweaks.

THE BOUNDARY LAYER

There are several components of racecars that are individually complicated enough that minute-to-minute performance is difficult to predict or even control very well. The driver is prone to emotional and fitness variables. Tires and dampers are also very complicated systems that yield to scrutiny only with enormous amounts of time, money and smarts. Racecars have to move through the air, and air is also a very challenging medium.

To most of us air is just there. Although we can't survive more than a couple of minutes without it, air always seems to be there and we take it for granted. Air, actually, is pretty simple as long as you travel at a walk or a human run or even at the speed of a galloping horse. But, when you want to accelerate quickly to speeds over a hundred miles an hour and go around corners as quickly as possible with limited power, air becomes a big challenge. One of the challenging characteristics of fluid flow is the boundary layer.

The boundary layer is a simple concept—when a fluid flows next to a fixed surface, friction between that surface and the air molecules slows down the molecules that are close to the fixed surface. If you measure the speed of the air right at that surface, you'll find the air is still, its velocity is zero, as in the sketch. If you measure further out from the wall, you'll see increasing speed until it reaches the maximum speed, which is called the freestream velocity. A difference in flow velocity across a fluid stream means there is shear—differences in speeds between adjacent parts of the stream. If the fluid is a viscous material, as all real-world fluids are, then shear means friction losses in the flow and that's where things get complicated.

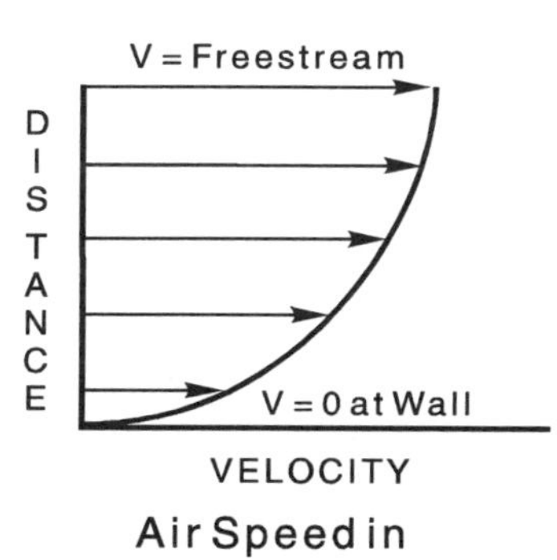

Air Speed in
Boundary Layer

Here's a familiar analogy to demonstrate a viscous fluid boundary layer. Let's say you're driving your car on a crowded freeway with four lanes going your direction. Cars in the left lane are moving at about 60 mph and are spaced out comfortably with six or seven car lengths in between each car. The far right lane is completely stopped because of a crowded on-ramp and the cars in that lane are close-packed bumper to bumper. That stopped right lane slows the lane next to it because drivers aren't comfortable whizzing by stopped cars, and also because drivers in the right lane are pulling out into the second lane in an attempt to make some progress. This drags down the speed of the second lane which, of course, means those drivers try to move into the third lane, which drags down its speed also. If you were to stand on an overpass and get the big picture on this situation you'd see a dense, almost stopped right lane and a loose, speedy left lane. In between, the second lane is moving a little faster than the right lane but is dragging down the speed of the third lane. The reluctance of drivers to travel a lot faster than an adjacent lane is analogous to friction in a viscous fluid.

We talked about Bernoulli's Theorem earlier and observed that a fluid loses static pressure as it speeds up and gains dynamic pressure. The spacing of the cars on the freeway is analogous to dynamic pressure. In the fast lane the cars are strung out but, as the speed decreases in lanes to the right, the spacing closes up just as the dynamic pressure decreases in a fluid. In a real-world freeway situation, a driver in the right lane coming up on an on-ramp dumping a bunch of slow cars into that lane would (if the driver was looking far enough ahead) change lanes to avoid slowing down. The driver senses a pressure increase ahead. If changing lanes is difficult, the driver is forced to slow and now wants to change lanes even more. That's higher pressure.

With air, when a molecule slows close to a stop because it's up against a boundary wall, it might encounter a stopped molecule in front of it at a slightly higher pressure. Air flows away from a higher pressure so the moving molecule moves away from the wall and gets in the way of a molecule going a little faster than itself. The slow, higher-pressure molecules in front may actually move against the flow and reverse direction. This is what causes circular eddies in fluid flow. You can see this in rising smoke and in water flowing around rocks.

As you can see from the freeway analogy, separation is caused by a reverse pressure gradient caused by slowing air. You don't have separation when air is accelerating as on the front of a moving vehicle. It's on the back of the car, where you have the air slowing down, that you get separation and the drag that goes with it.

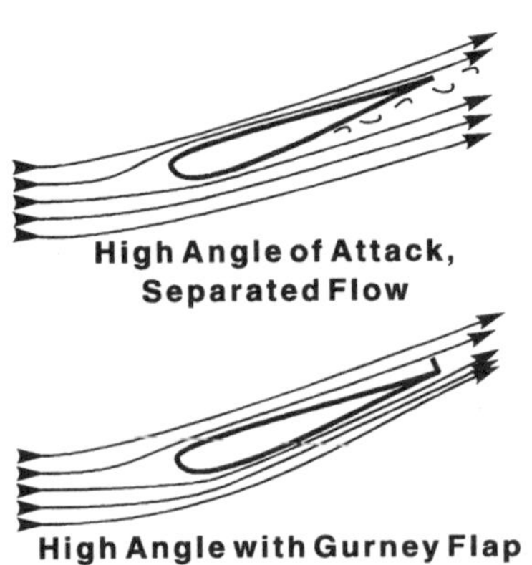

High Angle of Attack, Separated Flow

High Angle with Gurney Flap

Look again at these sketches illustrating what a Gurney does. Air flowing over the bottom of a wing at low angles of attack speeds up over the thick part of the wing and then slows down until, at the trailing edge, it's at the same speed as the air that went over the top of the wing. As the air slows down, its static pressure rises and the boundary layer thickens. At higher angles of attack, the boundary layer can develop well enough to generate eddies and flow separates from the surface. When you have separated flow, as in the top sketch, drag goes up and the wing stalls.

A Gurney flap allows a wing to operate at higher angles of attack than the same wing without a Gurney. Look at the streamlines on the Gurney sketch. You can see the air has to move up to go around the Gurney lip. That creates a lower pressure right behind the flap that translates around the corner to the bottom of the wing. This guarantees a high-to-low pressure gradient along the bottom of the wing and prevents separation.

This same thing happens under a modern racecar. The air entering the tunnel inlet on an Indy car or going under the splitter of a Formula 1 car accelerates because of friction with the track surface, loses static pressure, and creates a low-pressure area under the car. If the diffuser at the rear is designed well and the rake, ride height and speed are in a productive range, the air under the car will decelerate in the diffuser so that it exits at the same speed and pressure as before the car came along, minimizing drag losses in the process. But the air in the diffuser is slowing down next to the surface of the underwing and that's when you get boundary layer buildup. If the air slows too much before it gets to the exit, it will separate just like the wing without the Gurney. This lowers the efficiency of the diffuser, lowers downforce, and creates drag.

Engine Exhaust Can Be a Diffuser Gurney

If you look at most current Indy cars you'll see the engine and wastegate exhaust pipes are flattened and placed just above the tunnel exit. This is not an accident. The hot exhaust gases have enough velocity to speed up the air coming out of the diffuser and retard separation. As Alan Mertens says in the interview at the end of this section, this worked so well on his Galmer design that it disturbed the balance of the car when the driver changed the throttle setting in a corner. It was especially bad at Indy, he says, but it was dynamite on road courses, where traction out of corners is critical.

Fences and Vortex Generators

Lotus first used slim brushes at the outer edges of the sidepods that rubbed on the track surface and kept air from leaking in under the sides and raising pressure under the car. These evolved into plastic skirts that slid along the ground and moved up and down as the car moved on the suspension. These devices sealed the low pressure area under the car and allowed ground effects cars to produce huge amounts of downforce. They were used in Formula 1, Super Vee and sport-racing cars until banned in an attempt to lower corner speeds.

Since then, designers have evolved sophisticated ways of using air to create a "false seal" along the lower edges of the sidepods. You see lips and concave surfaces in these areas to make these false seals more effective. Careful detail design of the front wing can make a huge difference in the aerodynamic performance of a racecar. The fact is that all the air that's going to come into contact with the racecar must first pass by the front wing, so why not use it to make that air do productive things during its travels past the car?

My guess at the general goals in managing airflow around a racecar are as follows: minimum drag; maximum downforce; adjustable balance; engine and brake cooling; cool, high pressure air for the engine; and a low pressure area for engine exhaust. What this means, in general terms, is that the designer tries to provide clean (non-turbulent) air for the cooling inlets, but wants to direct high-energy (turbulent) air along the bottom outside corner of the sidepods. The designer also wants to maximize smooth flow to the rear wing and minimize drag associated with flow off the spinning tires. The designer also tries to put the engine inlet in a high-pressure area and the exhaust in a low-pressure zone.

In 1995, the usual result of all these compromises is a racecar design with a raised nose to allow clean air into the cooling inlets. As the air goes rearward under the raised nose past the splitter or tunnel inlet, the air next encounters a turbulent vortex expanding from vortex generators on the front wing just inside of the front tires. These complicated devices are called "curly Qs" according to John Travis, Lola Indy car design engineer. The "curly Q" creates a swirl of air that propagates back along the lower edge of the side pod on both sides of the car. These vortices keep air from rushing in under the sides and filling in the low-pressure areas under the car. They create a "false seal" and increase the downforce, especially at high speeds. Formula 1 cars have highly sculpted concave areas in the sidepods behind the cooling inlet to give these vortices room to expand. I think these side scoops also keep the flow around the rear tire from disturbing air going to the rear wing. All these complicated shapes are there to accommodate flow fields that started at the front wing.

In 1994, Indy cars and Formula 1 cars sprouted many combinations of turning vanes and fences just ahead of the sidepods. I'm sure these devices do several things, including directing air into the cooling ducts and minimizing the effect of turbulence off the front tires. I think they also help seal the underside of the car. Sometimes there are two or even three fences placed parallel to each other in front of the sidepods. Air that gets under the first fence still has to leak under at least one more fence before it can get into the low-pressure area under the car. The fact that these things change almost every race means that the teams are constantly coming up with new ideas, testing them in wind tunnels, and then trying full-size parts on the racecar itself.

Shark's Teeth

Think back to the boundary layer explanation above and then think about the air flowing under a ground-effects car. When the bottom of the car is close to the track surface, air gets dragged up to the same speed as the car and loses static pressure. As stated before, the purpose of the diffuser is to slow the air back down so it doesn't create a bunch of turbulence and drag at the back of the car. As the air slows in the diffuser it tends to separate from the wall and clog the flow.

Indy car designers use a couple of different devices to get the air swirling as it goes into the underwing inlet. This swirling air retards boundary layer formation and lowers the pressure under the car. If you look at the bottom of an Indy car right at the tunnel entrance, you'll see a pair of vanes on some of the Lolas and you'll see some pointy, shark's teeth-looking devices on most of the cars no matter who manufactured the chassis. Both these devices produce a swirl of air, a vortex, that keeps the air tight against the underwing. The swirling air also produces a low-pressure core inside the swirl that adds to the already low pressures under the car. The bottom two photos on page 60 show Penske and Reynard treatments of shark's teeth in 1994.

All of this aerodynamic stuff was not designed right the first time from scratch. People have spent millions of dollars in wind tunnels with moving belts to simulate the road surface at speed. I've done a little aero testing in my dim past and I'll assure you it is more art than science until you find something that works. Then you can probably explain it. Very small details can produce surprising results, especially at the front of the car. Done well, aerodynamic tweaks on a racecar are almost something for nothing.

A Front View of Shark's Teeth and Underwing Inlet on a '95 Reynard Indy Car.

DIFFERENCE BETWEEN WEIGHT AND DOWNFORCE

You may be wondering about now why, if aerodynamic downforce can increase cornering speed, does a lighter car corner faster? Why is vertical load provided by aerodynamics different than vertical load provided by mass or weight? Those are good questions!

Sir Isaac Newton, 1642-1727, a British philosopher and mathematician, is famous as the discoverer of gravity. The popular story is that he was napping under an apple tree and, when wakened by a hit on the head from a falling apple, came up with the realization that there must be a force on the apple that made it fall toward the ground and clunk him on the head. Silly story or not, Newton formulated some basic relationships between mass and forces and the acceleration of bodies that are the foundation of all the engineering sciences. Isaac Newton is to engineering what Albert Einstein is to nuclear physics.

Newton made the extraordinary observation that a body at rest (motionless) will remain at rest unless some force acts upon that body. That's Newton's First Law of Motion. His Second Law of Motion says that a body will accelerate when acted on by a force. The acceleration is larger if the force is larger and smaller if the mass of the body is bigger. The Second Law of Motion is represented by the equation:

$$F = MA,$$

which reads F equals M times A. F is the force, M is the mass of the body, and A is the acceleration of the body caused by the force. Were it not for the force of gravity acting on the apple, it would have just hung there in the air and not have fallen on the napping philosopher.

So, how does this answer the question about weight, downforce and cornering? It doesn't yet—we have to talk about friction first.

Friction

Consider a block of some material, a cube about an inch on a side. The block is lying on a surface, say a table. The block has some weight because of gravity. We'll call that weight Fv, the vertical force—because it acts straight down. If you push on the block with a force (F) parallel to the table, you can make it slide on the surface. If you push hard, it will slide right off the table. If you push against it very lightly, it won't move.

Intuitively, you know a block of wood will be easier to slide than a hunk of rubber, and also will be easier to push than a block of lead. Why is that?

When you push the block up to some speed, you are actually pushing against two forces—the friction force generated by the block sliding on the table and the force needed to accelerate the mass (weight) of the block. Once you've pushed the block up to some steady speed you're not accelerating it anymore, and the force you're pushing against is friction only. This force needed to overcome friction is bigger if the block weighs more, but it also depends on the properties of the surfaces in contact—their coefficient of friction. The equation is:

$$Ff = CfFv$$

Read that equation: Friction force equals the coefficient of friction times the vertical Force.

You can see from this equation that the friction force is larger when Cf is larger. Cf is why you have to push a rubber block harder than a wood block. Rubber sliding on anything has a higher Cf than wood. Fv is why it takes more force to slide a lead block than a wood one. The lead is heavier and so Fv is bigger than with a wood block. How about some numbers?

Rubber has a relatively large friction coefficient when tested on most surfaces. Let's say it's 0.8. If the rubber block weighs 1 pound, then the vertical force is 1 pound, and it's going to take 0.8 pounds to push the block at a steady speed. That came from this calculation: 0.8 (Cf) times 1 pound (Fv) = 0.8 pound (Ff).

Let's add some vertical force to the block. Let's put an upside down wing on top of the block, blow some air over the wing, and produce a downforce of 9 pounds. Now, Fv is 10 pounds (1 pound of weight and 9 pounds of aero force), and it takes 8 pounds to move the block. That came from the calculation: 0.8 (Cf) times 10 pounds (Fv) = 8 pound (Ff).

You're right, there's some aero drag force too but, since we're in control here, we can rotate the wing and blow the air at right angles to the path of the block. Then, drag forces don't act in the same direction as the friction forces and don't affect our numbers. Anyway, we've got downforce in excess of the weight of the block and gained a lot of friction force without adding weight to the block. What about the weight of the wing? OK, we made the wing out of unobtanium which has no weight.

These calculations show we can add normal force to a racecar with a wing and get more friction force from the tires, but it doesn't answer the part of the question about why a lighter car can corner faster than a heavier car. Let's look at the forces on a car in a corner.

Forces in a Corner

Back to Newton's Second Law of Motion, F=MA. If the mass (M) is going on a circular arc, we can express A as the square of the speed (V^2) divided by the radius of the curve. The equation is now:

$$Fc=MV^2/R$$

The force, Fc, is popularly called the centrifugal force. It's what keeps the string tight when you swing a weight on a string. The force on the string goes up the faster you spin the weight and goes down as you make the string longer. The weight of the car is just like the weight on the string and the tires on a cornering car are holding the string!

Look at this equation, $Fc=MV^2/R$, and think about a car going around a corner. If M gets bigger, Fc has to be bigger so that the equals sign is still right. That means the heavier the car, the more force it takes to hold the car in the arc. The faster the car, the bigger V gets and, at the same time, Fc gets larger for the same arc. A tighter corner means a lower value for R, which means Fc has to be bigger.

This is just a basic equation for what you already know. A lighter car corners faster and a smaller arc (tight turn) is a slower corner. You also know it takes more force to corner faster—you can feel it. Notice that cornering force is proportional to the square of the speed. For the same arc, cornering at 60 mph takes four times the force as 30 mph (60 times 60 =3,600 which is four times 30 times 30 or 900).

These two equations, Ff=CfFv and F=MA, are what modern racing is all about. F=MA or its arc equivalent, $Fc=MV^2/R$, tells you we need a light car with a powerful engine. Ff=CfFv says you need sticky tires, good suspension (to keep the tires in constant contact with the road), and all the downforce you can generate.

AERODYNAMIC FORCES AFFECT SPRINGS

Aerodynamic downforce, generated by wings and ground effects, influence all aspects of racecar design. The heavier springs needed to support the weight of the car plus the extra downforce from aerodynamic devices degrades the mechanical grip the car produces. But, when another 10% downforce lowers lap times by seconds, compromises are gladly made. As Jeff Braun pointed out earlier, the engine has become a power source for the aerodynamic devices. Top speeds stay the same even as lap times tumble because every engine power improvement is used to generate more downforce.

How do springs handle the extra aero load? You have to make them stiffer. Springs are rated by how far they deflect when a known load is applied. If you put a 100-pound weight on a spring and it deflects 1 inch, then that spring is said to have a spring rate of 100 pounds per inch. The coil springs on my Lotus Elan are rated at about 120 pounds per inch. That's very soft. The Elan is a light car that produces no downforce.

An F1 car at 120 mph might produce 3,000 pounds of downforce. If it has 1500-pound springs at each wheel for a total of 6,000 pounds per inch spring rate, that 3,000 pounds of force would lower the car a half inch from where it was when the car was sitting still. I came up with that number by figuring that four 1,500 pound/inch springs is like one 6,000 pound/inch spring and a 3,000-pound force would depress that spring one half inch. In actuality, you'd need even stiffer spring rates to keep the car from bottoming at higher speeds because the car would produce a lot more than 3,000 pounds downforce at its top speed and there will be some bumps that deflect the wheels. Remember that aero forces increase as the square of the speed. So, forces at 120 mph are four times those at 60 mph.

For the sake of simplicity in the explanation above, I've assumed that, when the wheel moves an inch, the spring moves an inch. With modern, pushrod suspension systems, this is never the case. The angle of the pushrod versus the ground plane and the design of the bellcrank between the pushrod and the spring determines the motion ratio of the suspension.

The point here is that downforce generated by the underwing is highly sensitive to ride height and rake. You might be getting tired of hearing this, but it really can't be emphasized enough. Active suspension controlled the relationship between the bottom of the car and the track surface very well. Because ride height is so critical to modern racecar performance and active suspension has been banned in almost every race series, some clever devices have appeared to do the same job.

Here's a story about one such device.

Penske Voodoo: Legal Ride Height Control

The Penske team with drivers Al Unser, Jr., Emerson Fittipaldi, and Paul Tracy dominated the 1994 IndyCar season. Some people don't like to admit to getting beaten fair and square, so a lot of rumors sprang up about illegal or unfair advantages the Penske cars had over their competitors. I call these "voodoo advantages." Webster's definition of voodoo: a class of religious rites—sorcery, black magic or witchcraft.

Just before the '94 Portland IndyCar race, I received a phone call from a guy who said he was a subscriber of my newsletter, *TV MOTORSPORTS*. He asked if I'd mind telling him what racing was going to be on TV the first weekend of July, because he was going out of town and wouldn't get his July issue. I gave him the info and then he said he had a scoop for me. "I'm not going to give you my name, but I work for one of the teams that's getting their butts kicked, and the pit lane gossip is that the Penske cars have a mechanical ride height control. It's within the rules, and it's why they're beating everybody." He suggested I look for this device at the upcoming IndyCar race at Portland.

As I thought about what the guy had said about a mechanical ride height control, I decided it would certainly be an advantage. The tunnels under the sidepods of an Indy car generate a lot of aerodynamic downforce, but are sensitive to ground clearance. They're not as sensitive as flat-bottom cars, but sensitive enough. A car that stays at the optimum ride height generates more downforce and so it accelerates, brakes and corners better.

I wasn't sure how to take that phone call so, when I got to Portland, I looked up Penske engineer, Terry Satchell, also a *TVM* subscriber. Terry was the engineer on the Al Unser Jr. car during 1994. I told Terry about the phone call and asked him what he could tell me about it. "Our power-down [ability of the car to use engine power to accelerate] is not just one thing," Terry explained. "It's a lot of things that we've worked hard on."

I also heard traction control rumors at Portland. I was told that sometimes, when the Penske cars leave their pits, the tire marks are intermittent, possibly indicating an illegal traction control system. Another rumor was that Goodyear had optimized their tires for the Penske chassis. I came away from the Portland race thinking that all these rumors were just good examples of sour grapes and racer paranoia.

A few days later, there was an IndyCar test at Laguna Seca where I talked to more people and heard about "something in the Penske rear suspension under a carbon fiber cover."

"We see them gather round and go at it with spanners [British for wrenches] now and then," said one person. Someone else speculated that this was a droop limiter that prevents the wheel from going down past some adjustable point. This is a not uncommon way to limit chassis roll and control weight transfer.

I also heard of a possible Penske engine power advantage at that Laguna test. I interviewed Teo Fabi (then driving a Reynard/Ilmor for Jim Hall) and he complained of waste gate problems. "Cosworth supplies the waste gate with their engines, but Ilmor leaves it up to the teams," said the diminutive Italian driver. "We've been having a lot of problems, and I'm not getting full boost all the time." Fabi didn't get any more explicit than that, but other people cited rumors that Penske had an electronic waste gate that is more consistent than the one used by most of the Ilmor customers.

I also heard fears that Penske had development engines that put out more power than other users of Ilmor engines. "Not likely," said Don Norton, Ilmor tech support engineer, "We supply the same parts to everyone. Penske builds their own engines and might have an advantage because they can assemble an engine from optimum parts carefully chosen from the pool, but I don't think that would get them much." Don declined to discuss an electronic waste gate beyond saying that it's an idea that's been around awhile.

Cleveland: Voodoo or Reality?

The Cleveland race was two weeks after Portland and, by the time I got there, I had discounted the ride height control story.

It was, however, clear that the Penske cars were fast. This became even more evident after I was shown some lap times taken during the Portland race. Looking at this table of laps driven by Al Jr., Nigel Mansell, and Jacque Villeneuve (driving a Penske, Lola, and Reynard, respectively), I could see that all of them were quicker on fresh tires and all slowed somewhat during the 30 or so laps between pit stops. The lap times showed that Al Jr.'s car was faster almost every lap than the other two drivers, and he won that race going away.

Lap times usually increase as a fresh set of tires "give up" after 10 or 20 laps on the track at speed. The difference is that Jr.'s lap times increased less toward the end of a run on tires than Mansell's or Villeneuve's. Jr. was a couple of tenths of a second quicker than the other two drivers on a fresh set of tires, but he was a half-second a lap quicker on worn tires. Boy, that's really encouraging for everyone. The Penskes were quicker and, at the same time, easier on their tires.

Although I had discounted the ride height control phone call, I was having a lot of fun at Cleveland talking to people about Penske voodoo advantages. Then, during Friday afternoon qualifying, I heard a Penske car leave the pits with a chirp, chirp, chirp noise and, when I looked at the pit lane surface, there were those intermittent tire stripes that some people thought was a symptom of traction control. Now I had seen them for myself, but the cause wasn't at all clear.

By this time I had also heard about the possibilities of hydraulic pumps hidden inside the transaxle cases that could use differential pressure to actuate a limited slip device. After that track session at Cleveland, I asked Chuck Sprague, Penske team manager, about the marks. "Tire chatter's been around a long time," he said. OK, I thought, maybe that's all it is.

Friday afternoon I saw Nigel Beresford, the engineer on Paul Tracy's Penske in 1994, and asked him about the traction control rumors. "It makes me a little hot, actually," said Nigel in his Brit drawl. "People keep talking like we're cheating. I'm not really interested in working for someone who has to cheat to beat their competition. I mean we've talked about ways to use the engine management system that would be within the letter of the rules. There are places on a race track where you know you can't use all the power."

"You could have the computer draw a track map each lap and program it to cut the power at the right places," I guessed. "That's right," Nigel said. "But we don't do it because it's not in the spirit of the rules. Besides that, we don't need to make all this any more complicated than it already is."

On Saturday the Penske crew rolled one of the cars behind the pits to do some work during a track session and, when they removed the engine cover, there was that carbon fiber cover that hides the voodoo device in the rear suspension. I got a good look at it and I could see that the links that usually go straight back to the anti-roll bar angled in toward the centerline of the car and went under the cover before any attachment was visible. So what? I still couldn't tell what it was doing.

Here's the list of voodoo advantages I had accumulated at that point:
1. Mechanical ride height control.
2. Suspension droop control.
3. Something under a carbon fiber cover on the top of the rear suspension.
4. Hydraulically-actuated limited-slip differential.
5. Traction control hidden in the engine management computer.
6. Collusion with Goodyear to develop a tire that works better with the Penske cars.
7. A better turbocharger waste gate—possibly electronic.
8. Newer development engine parts from Ilmor.
9. A pit lane radar jammer.

The last five on the list were surely just talk, fueled by racer paranoia, but I still didn't know what was under that mysterious black cover. That was the only thing on the list I could actually see, so I started to think about it. What would it take to limit suspension travel but still allow chassis roll in corners and let an individual wheel move over a bump? An idea tried to come into my head but it took a while. I made a couple of sketches, and it came together for me. Those links from the dampers go to a linkage or bearing that rotates with chassis roll or individual wheel bump, but is constrained when both wheels move up or down together. A spring or bump rubber could be added to restrain chassis movement when both wheels move in bump—that's what happens at high speed when aero loads try to compress the rear suspension.

My anonymous caller was right! This development allows softer springs which gives more mechanical grip in corners, but keeps the aero forces generated at speed from pushing the car down onto the track.

But this wasn't really a new development. I was told that night in a bar that a similar device was on the front suspension of Mansell's Lola a year before, and Lola was developing a "third spring" that would be a stock Lola part soon available to everyone.

The trick, of course, is to make something like this work out there on the track and during a race. What Terry Satchell told me at Portland was certainly true. It's not just one voodoo doodad that made the Penskes a little faster than everybody else. They've got a lot of smart people working hard. The mechanical device itself is not as impressive as the fact that they made it work reliably.

And they certainly weren't cheating! There's too much at stake. "They're not really cheaters, are they?" said Malcolm Oastler, Reynard designer. "I mean, they'll push it to the limit, but they don't cheat." Bruce Ashmore, technical director for Reynard, agrees. "It's a lot of little things they're doing well. They're doing well now, but we'll come up and beat them. Racing's always like that, isn't it?"

'Third Springs' Control Ride Height

If you look at the front or rear suspension of a modern racecar you'll see two springs with a shock absorber inside each of them. This new mechanical ride height control device or aero helper spring is called a "third spring" because it's additional to those two existing springs in the front and rear suspension systems. The Newman-Haas Lola of Nigel Mansell had one on the rear suspension in July '94 at Toronto, and there was a standard Lola part available to everyone a month later at Mid-Ohio. In addition to the "third spring" on the rear suspension I saw a similar device on the front of Mansell's car at Louden, the race after Cleveland.

A couple of weeks later, at Vancouver, I saw something at the rear of the Reynards driven by Michael Andretti and Jimmy Vasser that looked capable of limiting suspension travel. This device, shown in the picture on the facing page, used bump rubbers and packers, while Lola's had a coil spring. Whatever was under that cover at the rear of the Penske was too small for a coil spring.

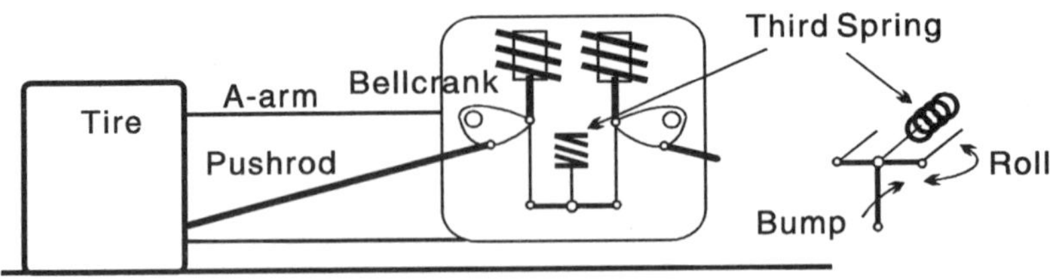

Schematic of Third Spring

Here's a graphic that shows how a "third spring" device works. The left-hand schematic represents the chassis with a tire, A-arms, pushrods, bellcranks and spring/dampers in a typical racecar suspension. The drawing on the right shows the "third spring" mechanism in more detail.

You can see in the drawing that, when a bump moves the wheel up, both pushrods move toward the chassis and turn the bellcranks, compressing the springs and dampers. In a turn, the chassis rolls and the pushrods move in different directions. In each case, it's the same springs and dampers resisting suspension movements. Adding the third spring decouples bump and roll and creates another spring to resist movement in the bump direction.

The links going down from the bell cranks would usually go to a sway bar, but now they go to what I call a T/swivel that moves fore and aft when both pushrods move in the same direction and twists when they move in opposite directions. There is a bearing that allows the T to rotate and the T is also hinged at the bottom mount to allow it to swing fore and aft. There has to be an adjustment in there somewhere for some freeplay in the fore/aft direction so that small bump deflections don't engage the third spring. When the car accelerates up to a speed that generates aero forces enough to compress the springs acting on the bell cranks, the car settles down through the freeplay and engages the third spring. Any additional aero force or bump force has to overcome all three springs.

In general, softer springs help mechanical grip, but you need high spring rates to keep the car from bottoming at high speeds, when the underbody and wings generate a couple of thousand pounds of downforce. This is the problem: Hard springs necessary to keep the car from bottoming at high speeds reduce mechanical grip in slow corners, where the aero stuff isn't producing any downforce. What you'd like, obviously, is soft springs working at low speeds, when the car rolls, and also some help for those springs as speed and aero forces increase. This so-called "third spring" is that aero helper spring.

These "third springs" allow the best of both worlds. When both wheels want to move up together, as happens when both tires hit a bump or aero forces increase with speed, those forces have to overcome all three springs. In cornering, however, the T/swivel mechanism twists and doesn't move the "third spring." Only the coil spring/dampers work in roll and, with a "third spring" you can soften those spring/dampers, which increases low speed mechanical grip. With a third spring you can also run the underside of the car closer to the track without bottoming. Lowering the car increases downforce generated by the underwing.

I'm told that Formula 1 cars progressed during 1994 from third springs to "fourth springs." They put a second spring/damper unit on each suspension rocker so they are able to adjust free play and spring/damper forces on each wheel individually. With two spring/damper units on each suspension rocker, suspension movement due to chassis roll and movement due to aerodynamic forces can each be independently adjusted. Progress marches on.

The 'Third Spring' in this '95 Lola Indy Car Front
Suspension Is Inside the Black Can between the Links.

NASCAR AND AERODYNAMICS

Aero Gets Blamed for Crashes

If you were watching the Daytona 500 in February 1992, you probably remember there was a big crash that took out all of the front runners except eventual winner Davey Allison. The TV announcers talked about aerodynamics as the cause of the wreck. "You just can't run three abreast," said Ned Jarrett or Benny Parsons. They were right about that, and the discussion they had among themselves on the air about aerodynamics shows they were doing their homework.

Shortly after that race, I had a phone conversation with Don Hayward, then a program manager in Ford's Special Vehicle Operations Division. Don is an aerodynamics specialist and was involved in aero testing of NASCAR racecars before going on to become Ford SVO's IndyCar program manager. "The act of passing in NASCAR racing on a superspeedway is a thrilling experience," said Don. "A car trying to pass another car goes through some amazing force reversals."

Don explained to me that he had been involved in some wind tunnel testing with 40% scale model NASCAR racecars, and the data showed the wild ride a passing car gets. In the first place, the drag on each car when there are two running side by side is 40% more than when a car is alone on the track. So, when the passing car pulls out from single file, he better have some momentum or a lot of power to pull off the pass because he runs into "a wall of drag," according to Don.

But worse than the increased drag are the changes in aero forces at the rear of a car as it passes another. "In about one car length," said Don, "the rear of the car goes from 100 pounds of downforce to 50 pounds of lift, then to 450 pounds of downforce before returning to 100 pounds again. That's equivalent to a weight change of 15% on a 3,400-pound car. And there's some big reversals in side forces going on at the same time."

The car following behind encounters less drag than the leading car, so the trailing driver can maintain position with only part throttle. In the classic "slingshot pass," the second car drops back a few lengths, opens the throttle and accelerates past, pulling into line ahead of the former leader, who now has less drag acting on his car. On long, high-speed tracks, before the engine-inlet restrictor plates, you could sometimes see two slingshot passes per lap.

What we have to recognize is the cars in that Daytona race didn't have the horsepower they did even just one year earlier. Yeah, restrictor plates hurt but, up until that year, there were some tricks the motor builders had that retained a lot of power in spite of the restrictions. Gary Nelson, the new NASCAR technical director, outlawed most of these manifolds and other magic doodads. Nelson also decreed bigger rear deck spoilers that increased drag and lowered top speed. Nelson had been a NASCAR crew chief and knew all the tricks. Talk about putting the fox among the chickens! After these modifications, the cars had less power and couldn't pass as easily. They no longer had the power to make an easy "slingshot pass" out of the draft.

When a car pulls out to pass, it hits that "wall of drag" and then gets hit with the force reversals Don Hayward mentioned. If the car is already in a turn and the tires are even close to their traction limits, all this jerking around is going to cause the car to spin.

What happened at Daytona occurred after a restart, when the cars were bunched up close, nose to tail. To Junior Johnson's delight both his cars were on the front row—Bill Elliott on the outside and Sterling Marlin on the inside. Just back of Sterling was Ernie Irvan. Ernie was running part throttle because he was in the lead pair's wake. He floored the throttle and pulled out of line inside of Sterling. But it was a restrictor plate race and Ernie didn't have the power or the momentum to get by. The increase in drag slowed him down quickly. If he couldn't get back in line right then, he would have been forced to drop back to the end of the pack before anyone would let him back in line. So he pulled to the right, hoping Sterling would let him in. But Sterling couldn't do anything. There were cars right up under his spoiler at the rear and Bill Elliott was on his right, up against the wall. The result was the wreck you saw. Ernie came up the track to force his way into line, but couldn't make it. His right rear clipped Sterling's left front and cars went every-which way. Davey Allison got by and went on to win.

There was a lot of griping about the aerodynamic rules changes and some people blamed those new rules for the wrecks, but it's the driver that's controlling the car.

Keeping NASCAR Race Cars from Flying

If you look close you'll notice some funny-looking rails on the NASCAR rear windows and deck lids. They're about a half inch high. Don Hayward told me they accomplish the same lift reduction task as the roof rails that have been on the cars for several years. "The fences on the roof kill the lift of the car when it gets sideways at high speed," Don said. "They keep the car from flying off the ground. But the rear of the car still generates lift, especially when the car is going not quite straight backwards. It's worst when the car is sliding at an angle of about 45 degrees. The car cross section acts like a long wing when it's sliding backward at that angle. It generates a lot of lift. The fences on the rear window and deck lid kill some of that lift."

The new roof flaps have solved the problem these cars had getting airborn. These roof flaps were developed by Jack Roush's engineers with help from Gary Nelson and Louis Duncan, an aerodynamics consultant who works for Ford. Low pressure on top of the cars is what gets them up off the track, and that pressure forces these flaps open and stops the car from flying. Two flaps measuring about 6 inches by 14 inches are set into an insert manufactured and sold exclusively by Rouch Racing. The cost is about $1,000 per car.

WHAT CAUSED THE CRASHES AT THE '92 INDY 500

It usually takes more than one problem to cause a disaster. When a plane crashes, the investigation always reveals several failures that combined to produce the event. If any one of those problems hadn't happened, the tragedy would not have occurred. That's what happened at the 1992 Indy 500. Cold weather, blown motors, eager drivers and unbanked corners with close walls combined to create a disastrous event.

Air Density

My original opinion was that the increase in air density caused by unseasonably low temperatures caused these crashes. Air density affects aerodynamic forces, engine power, brake performance—anything that depends on air. Cooler air is more dense than warmer air. Air density is inversely proportional to absolute temperature, which is degrees Fahrenheit plus 460. You can calculate the percentage difference in air density between a 90-degree day and a 40-degree day by dividing the 50-degree (90 - 40) difference by 550 (460 + 90) and multiplying times 100 to get 9%.

I'm assuming atmospheric pressure stays the same. Atmospheric pressure also affects air density. The city of Denver is more than a mile above sea level, and the air there is about 15% less dense than sea level air at the same temperature. That's why you saw bigger brake and heat exchanger ducts when the Indy cars raced there. They needed to flow 15% more air to the brakes or radiators for the same cooling effect as air of the same temperature at sea level. Aero forces and engine power also go down proportionately in the thinner Denver air.

For jet engine designers, "Hot Day Denver" is a worst-case engine design point. An engine has to have some reserve thrust so it can still power a plane to a takeoff under "Hot Day Denver" conditions. Both the engine and the wings are performing under par by almost 25% due to hotter, lower-pressure air. The entire engine has to be designed with extra thrust and higher temperature capability because of the "Hot Day Denver" takeoff requirement.

At the '92 Indy 500, the air temperature was about 40 degrees and the racecars produced 9% more downforce and drag and also 9% more horsepower than they would have if the air had been 90 degrees. The increase in horsepower could make up for the increased drag, giving the car the same potential top speed and leaving the 9% extra downforce to benefit cornering speeds.

How could that cause a crash? The extra downforce compresses the springs a little more, pressing the car closer to the ground. If the ground clearance is already set at a very small value, that extra downforce can make the car bottom severely.

Let's say the car is set up for a minimum ground clearance of a tenth of an inch. If the car is producing 3,000 pounds downforce, 9% more is almost 300 pounds. If the car has an overall total spring rate of 3,000 pound per inch, that extra 300 pounds presses the car down another tenth of an inch and it's scraping the ground. When the car bottoms, weight comes off the tires and it can slide out of control. Several drivers complained of bottoming during the race.

I called some people to see what they thought of my theory. Once again Don Hayward of Ford Special Vehicle Operations gave me some valuable insight. Don was in Michael Andretti's pit during the 1992 Indy 500. "It was wonderful for awhile, when it looked like he was going to run away from everybody," Don said. "In the end it was horrible, with Michael's motor problem and all the crashes."

But Don didn't buy my air density theory, "You're right about the change in air density with temperature, but I think it was cold tires and blown engines that caused the wrecks. Some of the cars that crashed were still coming up to speed and weren't at maximum downforce yet. I looked at the videotape pretty hard, and I think there was oil in the fourth turn laid down by guys with blown engines coming into the pits. If it had been warmer, that oil would have evaporated and the tires would have been better. I don't think anyone realized just how cold the tires could get going down those long straights."

Ken Anderson didn't agree with my air density theory either. Ken is an engineer who was with Penske Shocks and then went to Europe to work for the Ligier and Onyx Formula 1 teams. He worked for Tony Bettenhausen's IndyCar team as engineer on Stefan Johansson's car in 1994. "The cars at Indy are usually set up with a quarter-inch clearance at the front and a half-inch at the rear," Ken said. "An increase in air density wouldn't lower the car that much. It was mainly cold tires. Ambient temperatures were lower than anyone had ever seen, and the tires cooled off a lot on the straights. If the tires get below 200 degrees, they don't stick near as good. Drivers were going too fast before the tires were up to temperature."

OK, so maybe it wasn't air density that caused all those crashes, but I got to explain air density, didn't I?

WIND TUNNELS

Swift Wind Tunnel

There is only one state-of-the-art racecar wind tunnel in this country and it's at Swift Engineering in San Clemente, Calif., an hour south of Los Angeles. Late in 1992, Alex Cross, vice president at Swift, showed me the pair of modern buildings under construction at that time and talked wistfully of the wind tunnel they would put in the smaller of the two. In November of '94 I got to see the finished facility, and it's a stunner.

You recognize the name Swift from the race cars of that name designed by David Bruns. The DB-1 (DB for David Bruns, of course) is the sleek, wide-track Formula Ford that dominated that class for 10 years. Think of that! Bruns sat down and designed a racecar that went totally unchallenged for more than a decade!

Bruns' Sports 2000 car, the DB-2 and later DB-5, were also dominant for almost that long. Formula Atlantic racers know the DB-4 that appeared in 1986 and still wins occasionally in that very competitive class. The DB-3 and DB-6 are Formula Ford 2000 variants of the DB-3 and were also very successful racecars. In the early '90s, Bruns and the other guys at Swift wanted to design a "Big Car" and needed a wind tunnel to do that.

David Bruns would really rather be designing and building racecars, but instead he's had to plan, design, build, and now develop a wind tunnel so he can get back to his chosen craft. "It's like deciding to build a house and then spending two years making a hammer," he told me. In November of '94, they were almost there. I spent a day watching them install a model of a '93 Lola Indy car during the final stages of the calibration of the facility.

It had been a wet winter in California, and it had rained hard in the Los Angeles area the day before my visit to Swift. As a result, the smog had cleared, and you could see a cap of snow on top of Mt. Baldy, one of the mountains that rim the Los Angeles basin.

It was about 9 am when I went into the huge building that houses the wind tunnel. Bill King, ex-Goodyear Racing PR guy now working the NASCAR scene with Cotter Communications, met me in the lobby and introduced me to Doug Smyth, the aerodynamicist Swift hired to run the wind tunnel. We went through some offices and then out a door onto the floor inside the building. The tunnel itself looks like a huge heating duct suspended off the cement floor on steel posts. Everything, including the floor, was freshly painted just like in any good race shop.

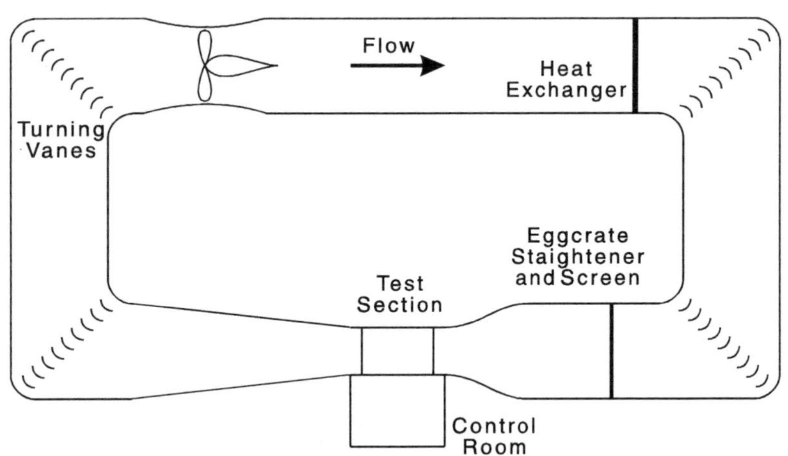

Schematic of Swift Engr. Wind Tunnel

A wind tunnel is a precision measuring instrument like a fine chronometer, dial caliper, or stellar telescope. This diagram shows some of the basic elements. A 15-foot diameter, five-bladed fan driven by a 500 hp electric motor pushes the air around the circuit. The fan and motor also add heat, so a heat exchanger cools the air to 70 degrees, just like the air conditioner in your home or car. Turning vanes in each corner keep the air from piling up on the outside of the path. A honeycomb flow-straightener followed by a fine-mesh wire screen conditions the air just before the test section. The tunnel narrows right in front of the test section and this accelerates the air from about 30 mph to the 140 mph maximum speed in the test section. The inside dimensions of the flow path vary from a 15-foot diameter tube at the fan to a 19-by-20-foot rectangle at the flow straightener. The length of the full path in the middle of the duct is 318 feet with long sides of 134 feet and short runs about 25 feet on each end. It's big!

Nothing I've described so far is very trick. If you were going to hang a model airplane in the middle of the test section, you wouldn't need much more than I've just described, but a car is different because it rolls on the ground and the air flowing around and under the car is affected by the ground surface. There's no use testing a model that doesn't act the same as the real thing.

Why a Scale Model?

Why test a model anyway? Why not test a real racecar? Aren't you trying to improve how a racecar performs on a real track?

A racecar is too complicated to allow detailed testing of individual components right on the car. Performance gains are too small. That's why critical components are tested by themselves. You have engine dynamometers to test engines, shock dynos for dampers, brake dynos, tire testing machines, and wind tunnels. People conceive and implement small, incremental changes to these components, and test them by themselves to see if there is any performance or reliability improvement. The final test is putting an improvement on the racecar and seeing if lap times get quicker.

A racecar is very complicated aerodynamically. The surfaces on the front end of a car are critical, because they influence the air flowing over all of the rest of the car. If a car has wings on the front, they can't be too big or you'll mess up the flow to the radiators or to the ground-effects area under the car. You'd like the air inlet to the engine to be in a place where air pressure is maximum, and you want the exhaust in a low-pressure area. Air cools the brakes, electronics, engine and drivetrain as well as the driver, so there are ducts that need to flow the right amount of air without adding a lot of drag. A rolling tire has a large flow field of its own that can interact with airflow to or from other components. The flow around a modern ground-effects racecar is very complicated, and the downforce and drag produced depend on how all the components work together. Development testing in a wind tunnel is very important.

OK, so we know we have to test components, but why miniature ones? You dyno a real engine, so why not put the whole car in a wind tunnel? The answer is money. Even engine research is often done on single-cylinder test rigs and the changes that work there get tested again on real engines. A properly designed model in a wind tunnel allows the testing of many different changes without renting a race track and running a racecar with a crew and all the other costs.

But the real answer to why aero testing is done on models has to do with the fact that the ground moves under the car, and simulating that with a full-size car costs too much. Modern wind tunnels like this one at Swift Engineering have a moving belt under the car (called a moving ground plane or rolling road) that allows the air to act almost like the air under a real car on a real road. I don't know of a wind tunnel anywhere made to test a full-size car on a moving ground plane. They're all made to test scale models.

Formula 1 constructors Williams Engineering has a 50% rolling road wind tunnel. Many state-of-the-art tunnels can test one-third (33%) scale models. I've read that All American Racers, Dan Gurney's group which designed and built the Toyota-engined cars that dominated IMSA GTP racing, used a 10% scale, open tunnel (straight-through flow instead of recirculating) up until 1994 when they installed a 40% open tunnel to use in their Indy car project. I'm told AAR still uses both tunnels and each of them has a moving ground plane.

The reason why you need a moving ground plane has to do with the boundary layer that we discussed earlier. When air moves next to a wall, or boundary, friction drags down the air molecules right next to the wall, and they just sit there getting in the way and slowing things down. If you're blowing air down a wall at 50 mph it really goes that fast some distance from the wall from the wall, but it slows as it gets close to the wall, and the airspeed is actually zero right at the wall. Under a car you'd have a boundary layer next to the car as well as along the ground, and things would tend to get clogged up toward the rear.

When a car goes through still air, the individual air molecules are pretty much stationary, and the car is moving past them. Since the air isn't moving relative to the ground, there is no boundary layer at the ground surface, but there is on the car's surfaces. A wind tunnel can't exactly simulate this condition because it uses a stationary car and blows air past it. So you have to do a bunch of tricky stuff to get rid of the boundary layer on the floor of the tunnel in the test section. Having a moving belt under the model going the same speed as the air prevents a boundary layer building up. There is, however, a boundary layer in the duct ahead of the test section, and you get rid of that by putting a slot in the floor right ahead of the belt and sucking the boundary layer down into a machine like a big vacuum cleaner, so that the air next to the belt is going full blast.

The reason why so few wind tunnels have a moving ground plane is the complexity it introduces. There is a metal platen under the belt to provide support. Modern ground-effects racecars, the testing of which is the reason for this kind of precision wind tunnel, produce a low-pressure area underneath which can suck the belt up off the platen. The solution is a pattern of holes in the platen and another vacuum machine to generate a countering low pressure between the belt and the platen. To further complicate things, friction between the belt and the platen creates a lot of heat, so you have to cool the platen with water.

Doug and Bill took me under the control room and showed me the mechanism that controls the belt, on the condition that I not write about it. There are several rollers and a hydraulic tension mechanism designed by Bruns that is unique and very simple.

The belt needs to run straight on the rollers, so an optical sensor looks at the edge of the fiberglass-reinforced belt, and the control system keeps it tracking to within a sixteenth of an inch. The belt is slightly conductive electrically so it doesn't accumulate a static charge.

Into the Control Room

Dirk De Beer in the Swift Engr. wind tunnel with a
40% Scale Model of a 1993 Lola Indy Car

We went up the stairs into the control room and there, behind a glass wall on the far side of the room, was the test section and a model of a '93 Lola Indy car. The belt is a medium gray, and the walls are stark white. The black model looked surprisingly large and purposeful—not toy-sized as I'd expected. A long mirror behind the model lets you see the back of the model from the control room. They built the control room so the ground plane is at waist height. Dirk De Beer, a South African aerodynamicist hired by Swift to supervise the "commissioning" of the tunnel, is a tall guy, and he looked even bigger hunkered down by the 40% scale model. Part of the glass between the control room and the test section slides to provide access to the model and instrumentation.

The room is about 20 feet wide and 15 feet long from entrance door to the glass wall. The left side of the room was lined with tables cluttered with papers and blueprints and books, including one about South African flowering plants. A big color computer display and keyboard sat on some tables toward the right front of the room. In a corner on the right near the entrance stands a standard electronics rack about six feet high that holds the Hewlett-Packard workstation computer and the interface boards for all the electronic signals coming from the model and also coming from sensors that monitor tunnel parameters.

Data is what testing is all about, and making sure that data is right is a big part of designing and building a wind tunnel. The model is suspended from above on a streamlined pylon that is structurally isolated from the rest of the tunnel. There is a device inside the model called a balance which measure forces on the model and sends this data through the pylon to the Hewlett-Packard workstation. The pylon support cage on the outside of the tunnel doesn't touch any other structure and sits on its own foundation blocks. This prevents any movement or vibration from the tunnel mechanisms from corrupting data from the model. The control room also has a metal mesh built into the walls. This is called a Faraday cage and it keeps stray electrical signals away from the model and computers.

Up into the Test Section

They encouraged me to climb up into the test section and look at the model up close. The test section is 9 feet wide by 8 feet high by 22 feet long. As soon as I got comfortable in a cross-legged sitting position I realized my black shoes had put smears on the new belt. I felt like a little kid who'd just tracked mud onto his aunt's new carpet.

I crawled around some and looked at the model. There are small holes all over it to measure pressures on the body. The wheels and "tires" have been carefully machined from plastic. The wheels are not actually attached to the model but are supported from the sides of the tunnel by horizontal struts that have sensors to measure forces on each wheel and tire. Simulated suspension members jut out from the model, but they don't quite touch the wheels. You want the wheels to roll like on a real car, but they might put some extraneous mechanical noise into the model, so it's better if they're not attached. Bruns and De Beer were adjusting the position of the wheels so I got out of the way.

The guy who will be responsible for operating the tunnel is Doug Smyth. Swift just hired him from McDonnell Douglas Corp. where he worked as an aerodynamicist for 35 years and contributed to the design of the MD-90 and MD-95, airplanes that you and I are likely to fly in. Doug told me he and Bruns had worked together on some projects over the years, but that he really didn't know much about racing.

About 10:30 Bruns and De Beer climbed down out of the tunnel and got ready to fire it up. I was fascinated and excited to be there. Bruns opened up a panel under the glass doors and crawled in under the platen to check some air valves. Doug explained to me that the platen vacuum system has several zones that can be controlled separately. I guess you'd like just enough suction so that the belt doesn't fly up, but not too much. The 100 hp motor driving the belt can actually stall if there is too much friction.

The Software Guy

While final adjustments were made I talked to Jim Smith, a Brit who wrote the control and data acquisition software and also wired this whole system. This was his last day here at Swift on this trip, the third during the three months of installation and calibration of the system. Jim got started in the music industry working at recording studios. He's done work with several Formula 1 wind tunnels.

Jim Smith is in his thirties I'd guess, and he looks slim in jeans and T-shirt. What hair he has is short and brown, as is his close-cut beard. He proudly showed me the electronic cabinet in the corner, removing a panel and pointing out the racks of data acquisition and processor boards inside. A neat and tidy bundle of small gauge wires comes into the cabinet and snakes to a huge number of individual terminations. "About 500," was Jim's answer when I asked how many wires. "We've done some work with Benetton and Ferrari, too," Jim said. "This is as good a wind tunnel as I've seen. The attention to detail here is the best I've seen. This model is good."

"I've heard that some of the models used by the F1 manufacturers are really trick," I said. "Supposedly, they use heated radiators and simulated engine inlet and exhaust flow."

"I haven't been to all of them so I can't say for sure," said Jim. "I've heard that same stuff but, typically, everyone is so desperate for data that they don't get that detailed. Simulating those flows is tough. They don't have time for basic research so they're usually working on fundamental engineering problems. Even in F1, not very many people have a really accurate test setup. Their main concern is the L/D [lift over drag] of a specific change. They want more downforce and less drag, and they're in a hurry because the next race is coming up and the other teams are all testing improvements at the same time."

"What about computer flow models?" I asked. "Is anyone using software simulations to tell them what they should be testing?"

"They're a mile away from flow simulation," Jim said, grinning. "They should be doing that but they're not. I think they should spend more time developing a basic model and understanding the data, but they really don't have the time. Racing is not like the aircraft industry where they spend years designing a plane and then carefully develop it for 10 or 20 years. There you've got whole groups of people generating and analyzing data. But racecars change every season and sometimes even during the season. Every four to six months you've got data for a new model. The typical F1 design cycle is aero model testing in October and some track testing to roughly confirm the new bits, and then into production in December, if they're lucky. I don't know anyone in racing who has the time or money for a detailed basic research program."

"Isn't it unusual for the guy who writes the software to also wire up all the hardware?"

"If you don't know how each component works, how can you write the program?" Jim answered. "You have to know where the data's coming from and you have to prove to the aero guy that the data is right. You have to understand it. I'll also be here when the first customer uses the tunnel to make sure there's no question about the data."

"Are you a racing fan?" I asked.

"Yeah, I watch on TV," he said. "We get NASCAR and IndyCar on the telly and I watch F1. I've driven some. In England we have a stock car class that races American Chevys and such on quarter-mile dirt and paved ovals. I'm not a great driver, but it's a lot of fun. Pushing on the other cars in the corners is a big part of it." His grin was huge.

While we were talking, the tunnel airflow had been started and stopped several times as Bruns continued to tweak the belt suction system. Doug Smyth said this was the first run with the wheels attached. Around noon Bill King went for sandwiches and, when he got back, they took a break.

After lunch there was a long run at speed, and Bruns used a strobe light to see if the wheels were rotating at the right speed. Dirk De Beer was operating the tunnel, watching info posted on Jim's Windows-style software, and using the computer keyboard or a mouse to enter commands. He told me his job was almost finished and he was leaving in a couple of days. "I'm an independent commissioner," he said. "It's my job to certify that the tunnel meets all the basic requirements. The boundary layer removal equipment works well. You can put a pressure probe as close to the belt as you can get it, about two-tenths of an inch, and it will tell you that the air is moving 99% as fast as it is out in the middle of the airstream. The test section is almost completely free of swirl. Maximum cross-flow angles are less than three-quarters of a degree. And there's uniform flow in the test section. You measure less than a quarter of a percent velocity variation across the section. People who have wind tunnels of this quality don't let anyone else use them. This is the largest and fastest commercially available moving ground-plane wind tunnel in the world."

I watched the goings-on and talked to people until 3 o'clock, when I began to get antsy about getting to the Los Angeles airport through rush-hour traffic. I thanked everybody and left. I learned a lot about wind tunnels that day.

A Few Words About Scale

When we talk about a wind tunnel we say something like "40%, rolling-road" to describe it. The 40% obviously says that the dimensions of the model are such that it is four-tenths the size of the real thing. But the Swift wind tunnel has a test section 9-feet high by 8-feet wide by 22-feet long. You could put some full-size racecars in there. Why a model?

It has to do with how much the model blocks the cross-section area of the test section. Air flowing over a car changes direction to go around the car and, if the walls of the tunnel are close to the model, they interfere with the flow and affect the data. An Indy car has a frontal area of about 12 square feet and 40% of that is about 5 square feet. The 9- by 8-foot Swift test section is 72 square feet in area, so a 40% Indy car blocks 7% of that. Five divided by 72 equals 0.07, and that's called the blockage ratio. A number less than 0.1 is considered good for this type of tunnel.

Indy Lights Wind Tunnel Data

When Lola first introduced its Indy Lights car, the Lola T93/20, it provided wind tunnel data to teams that bought the cars. The data said the car produces 2,300 pounds of downforce at 150 mph in a high downforce configuration and 1,850 pounds with low drag settings. I'm guessing this comes from tests run on a scale model in a rolling-road wind tunnel, probably a model of the Lola F3000 racecar that was modified to become the Indy Lights car. Later, someone tested an actual Indy Lights car in General Motors' full-size wind tunnel and distributed that data to the Indy Lights teams. The Lola data shows almost twice the downforce as the full-size test, and I think it's because Lola tested the scale model in a wind tunnel with a moving ground plane which the GM tunnel does not have.

I've been told that the GM tunnel and the full-size Lockheed tunnel in Georgia do what's called "blowing the boundary layer." They have nozzles at ground level in front of the test section that direct compressed air downstream in an attempt to get the boundary layer air up to free-stream airspeed. There are people who think this technique doesn't give good data. The data may give good relative results; that is, changes in wings and ride height might produce changes that are proportionally correct, but the absolute numbers are not exactly correct. A ground-effects racecar is particularly sensitive to a ground-plane boundary layer because the bottom of the car is very close to the ground.

This GM wind tunnel data is interesting because it shows the effects of wing angles and Gurney flaps and ride heights on drag and downforce. I'm going to present some of the full-size data and then some Lola data which is much less complete. Then I'll make some calculations using track data that will give us an idea how much downforce an Indy Lights car and an Indy car actually generate in race trim. This will show which set of data is more likely to be correct.

Full-size Car in GM Tunnel at 150 mph

This first table shows how downforce (negative lift) changes with ride height. This is a relatively high downforce setup, using the front wing in hole number nine with a quarter-inch Gurney and the rear wing in hole number 15 with a three-quarter-inch Gurney.

Front R. H. in.	Rear R. H. in.	Drag lbs.	Lift lbs.	% Front Lift
0.38	2.00	685	-1,304	40.0
0.50	2.00	681	-1,323	40.6
0.50	2.25	684	-1,303	40.9
0.50	2.50	691	-1,243	40.9
0.75	2.25	684	-1,241	40.5
0.75	2.50	692	-1,216	41.1
1.00	2.50	692	-1,094	39.7

This test shows maximum downforce at a front ride height of 0.50 inch, and rear at 2.0 inch. Although the data at three-eighths of an inch ride height shows a little less downforce (negative lift) than at a half-inch, I'll bet that in a rolling-road tunnel and certainly on a smooth track, downforce is actually higher at the lower ride height. I believe the lower ride height didn't show up better here because a boundary layer blocked the flow under the car.

Although good data is hard to come by, I've been told that on an oval like Phoenix, total suspension travel on an Indy Lights car is less than a quarter of an inch. They set the cars as low as they can, limited only by bottoming. If you ever see a practice session for Lights cars, notice that one member of the crew looks at the bottom of the car every time it comes into the pit. He either get down on his belly or he uses a mechanic's mirror to look for scrape marks. In between sessions, when the crew is back in the paddock, they touch up those marks with black paint so they can see the fresh scrapes during the next track session. The point is that with flat-bottom cars, ground clearance is critical and the optimum ride height is close to zero!

The next table shows the effect of changing the ride height and the height of the rear wing Gurney flap. The front wing has a quarter-inch Gurney in all these tests; the front wing is set at hole number five; and the rear wing is in hole number eight. This is a low drag configuration as it might be on an oval like Phoenix International Raceway.

Test No.	Rear Gurney Ht.	Front R. H. in.	Rear R. H. in.	Drag lbs.	Lift lbs.	Lift/Drag
1	0.00	1.00	2.50	611	-866	1.42
2	0.00	0.75	2.25	602	-1,014	1.68
3	0.00	0.50	2.00	600	-1,095	1.83
4	0.50	1.00	2.50	646	-928	1.44
5	0.50	0.75	2.25	637	-1,076	1.69
6	0.50	0.50	2.00	635	-1,157	1.82

There are several things going on here, but you can see that the closer you get the car to the ground, the more downforce generated and the higher the L/D. Look at the lift and drag numbers for tests three and six. With the addition of a half-inch Gurney, downforce went up 62 pounds and drag increased 35 pounds. The L/D, the ratio of the downforce and drag, of the change from test three to test six is 62 divided 35 or 1.77. Calculating the L/D of a change is a good way to evaluate how much difference that particular change makes. You can't use this calculation to evaluate the ride height changes shown here because drag goes down as you lower the car, and the L/D of the change is meaningless. But when the drag goes down and you get more downforce as you decrease the ride height, you know you're going in the right direction.

The data below is representative of a high downforce configuration as at a road course like Laguna Seca. The front wing is in hole nine for all tests. For these data points, ride height is varied using rear Gurney heights of 0.75 and 1.00 inch.

Test	Rr. Wing Hole #	Rear Gurney in.	Front R. H. in.	Rear R. H. in.	Drag lbs.	Lift lbs.	Lift/Drag
1	12	0.75	1.00	2.50	685	-1,096	1.60
2	12	0.75	0.75	2.25	676	-1,244	1.84
3	12	0.75	0.50	2.00	674	-1,325	1.97
4	15	0.75	1.00	2.50	692	-1,093	1.58
5	15	0.75	0.75	2.25	684	-1,241	1.81
6	15	0.75	0.50	2.00	681	-1,323	1.94
7	15	1.00	1.00	2.50	698	-1,093	1.57
8	15	1.00	0.75	2.25	690	-1,241	1.80
9	15	1.00	0.50	2.00	688	-1,323	1.92

The test that gave the highest downforce and lowest drag is the one with the largest L/D—test number three. You have to remember, however, that this test was run at a simulated speed of 150 mph. An Indy Lights car never gets up to that speed at Laguna Seca, and you'd like to have more downforce in the 80 to 100 mph corners that dominate this race track. Test number six or nine is probably closer to a road course setup.

Lola Scale Model Data

The data Lola provided is in a different form. It gives a baseline setup with resulting downforce and drag numbers, and then shows the effect of changes from that baseline setup. The airspeed was 150 mph, same as in the full-size test.

The high downforce configuration:

Front Gurney = 0.75 inches.
Rear Gurney = 0.75 inches.
Front ride height = 0.875 inches.
Rear ride height = 1.625 inches.
Front wing hole = 7.
Rear wing hole = 15.
Downforce = 2,300 pounds.

Change No. 1: Minus one hole on the rear wing = 23 pounds less downforce and 9 pounds less drag.

Change No. 2: Two holes less on front wing = 100 pounds less downforce and 10 pounds less drag.

Change No. 3: A quarter inch less ride height at front = 110 pounds more downforce and 3 pounds more drag.

The low drag configuration:

No Gurney flaps.
Same ride heights.
Front wing hole = 3 or 4.
Rear wing hole = 7.
Downforce = 1,850 pounds.

Change = 0.75-inch Gurney flap front and rear = 120 pounds more downforce and 54 pounds drag.

This Lola data is not very useful to a race team, which is probably the reason for the GM wind tunnel test. The big question, however, is whether the actual downforce generated by the racecar at 150 mph is the 1,300 pounds measured in the GM tunnel or the 2,400 pounds from the scale-model Lola test?

1,300 or 2,400?

I asked around looking for data that I could use to figure out the downforce of an actual Indy Lights car on an actual racetrack. Ideally, I wanted some speed and/or lateral acceleration data in a flat corner of known radius. Then I could make a calculation using the equation for centrifugal force:

$$Fc = MV^2/R.$$

As we explained before Fc is the lateral force the tires generate to keep a racecar that weights M at velocity V in an arc of radius R. This is the equation that gives you the tension in the string when you swing a weight tied to that string fast enough to make it stand out parallel with the ground.

Turn 4 at Laguna Seca is a flat corner, and the track map says the radius is 200 feet. I found data for a mid-pack Indy Lights car that shows 99 mph and 2.0 G lateral acceleration in that corner. I also found out that a slow Indy car, a '93 Lola at the back end of the grid in the 1994 race at Laguna, goes 105 mph in that same corner. So, if I can figure out the weight of these cars, I can calculate the lateral acceleration of the Indy car and make some guesses about the downforce both cars produce.

The IndyCar rule book gives dry weights, and I can add the fuel and driver myself:

Weight, lbs.

	Indy Lights	Indy Car
Car	1,370	1,550
Fuel	20	20
Driver	140	140
Total	1,530	1,710

Now, using the $Fc = MV^2/R$ relationship, I can calculate lateral force in a 200-foot radius turn and divide by the car's weight to get the lateral acceleration in Gs (units of gravity) in that corner at that speed. First I have to change the miles per hour numbers into feet per second.

R=200 ft.

	Indy Lights	Indy Car
Speed, mph	99	105
Speed, ft./sec.	145	154
Lat. Force, lbs.	5,009	6,597
Lat. Accel, Gs.	3.3	3.7

But this calculated lateral acceleration of the Indy Lights car is way more than the 2.0 taken from on-board data acquisition. Something's wrong!

I worried around on this and finally figured out that the radius of the path of the car is probably a lot bigger than the radius of the pavement that was shown on the track map. Turn 4 is a right-hand corner and, obviously, a driver starts from the left side of the road, cuts close to the berm on the inside of the curve, and exits out on the left side again. I fiddled around with the radius until I got a lateral acceleration close to 2, the measured value. That turned out to be 330 feet.

I want to know the downforce the cars produce, but the tires account for some lateral force on their own. Again, I asked around and several people said that at low speeds with no aero forces, a good race tire will contribute as much as 1.5 G of lateral acceleration. But, as force on the tire goes up due to weight transfer and/or aero forces, lateral force falls off, so I've used 1.2 Gs tire contribution for the Indy car and 1.3 for the Indy Lights. I could use the same value for both cars, but the Indy car weighs more and generates more downforce.

R=330 ft.

	Indy Lights	Indy Car
Speed, mph	99	105
Speed, ft./sec.	145	154
Lateral Force, lbs.	3,036	3816
Lateral Accel., Gs	2.0	2.2
Tire Accel., Gs	1.3	1.2
Aero Lateral Accel.	0.7	1.0
Aero Force, lbs.	1,047	1,764
Aero Force @ 150 mph, lbs.	2,408	3,528

So, what I've done here is estimate the downforce produced by these cars at 150 mph. I started with the measured speed and lateral acceleration of an Indy Lights car in a known, flat corner. I used that data to calculate the actual radius of the path of the car and then calculated the lateral acceleration of the Indy car. Using an estimate of the lateral force due to the tires alone, I subtracted that number from the calculated lateral acceleration to get the cornering force due to aerodynamic downforce. That aero cornering force in Gs times the weight of the car gives us the downforce at that cornering speed. To get the downforce at 150 mph, in order to compare with the wind tunnel data taken at that speed with the forces we've calculated at the cornering speeds of these cars, we have to multiply by the ratio of the squares of the speeds.

The Indy Lights calculation is: 150 x 150 divided by 99 x 99 = 2.3 x 1,047 = 2,408.

The Indy car calculation is: 150 x 150 divided by 105 x 105 = 2.0 x 1,764 = 3,528.

It looks like the Lola scale-model data was right and the GM tunnel data, although it showed the relative effects of changes, did not measure correct absolute values for downforce and drag.

As I said at the start, the corner speed data did not come from the fastest car in either the Lights race or the IndyCar race. The Lights info used here came from a lap of 1:19.6. The car on the pole in October '94, driven by Andre Ribeiro, lapped at 1:18.3. The Indy car that went 105 in this corner lapped at 1:13.2 while the pole time for that race, Paul Tracy driving a Penske/Ilmor, was 1:10.1. Let's look at how the downforce numbers we have above would change if the Indy car was five mph faster and ten mph faster in this corner.

R=330 ft.

	Indy Car	Indy Car	Indy Car
Speed, mph	105	110	115
Speed, ft./sec.	154	161	169
Lateral Force, lbs.	3816	4,190	4,580
Lateral Accel., Gs	2.2	2.4	2.7
Tire Accel., Gs	1.2	1.2	1.2
Aero Lateral Accel., Gs	1.0	1.2	1.5
Aero Force in Corner, lbs.	1,765	2,135	2,525
Aero Force @ 150 mph, lbs.	3,528	3,970	4,300

This table estimates what downforce an Indy car would have to generate to go through that corner 5 and 10 mph faster than the Indy car we started with. All these cars have accelerometers and on-board computers reading them during every lap they're on the track. Someone with access to that data could look at this table and say whether I'm in the ballpark or not. The point is not being exactly right, but to show that anyone can do a few simple calculations and figure out some interesting things.

An Actual Wind Tunnel Test

Jeff Braun tells how he planned and executed a wind tunnel test.

"I've been involved in several wind tunnel tests and they've all been with actual racecars in full-size wind tunnels rather than scale-model tests. The one that happened the way I think it should be done was at the end of 1992, when I was working for Andy Evan's Scandia IMSA team. We did a full-scale wind tunnel test on the Scandia Camel Lights car. This was a Kudzu chassis with a Buick V-6 engine.

"In '92, IMSA had allowed Camel Lights cars to run biplane wings at the rear and dive planes at the front and all these weird aerodynamic devices. We had developed those on the track during '92 and the car made more downforce. For 1993, IMSA outlawed the biplane wing. They were too expensive they said, or something. We were trying to figure out how we could recapture some of the benefits we found with the biplane wing using a single-plane rear wing. Andy said he wanted a big effort on that because the biplane wing was a big improvement, and he didn't want to give that up.

"We set up a wind tunnel test program that included a track test previous to the tunnel test. We had two objectives. I was the race engineer and Sam Garrett was the design engineer. Sam was looking at this test from a design standpoint. He was looking at different wing positions or changing the bodywork or whatever he had to do to the design of the car to get this lost downforce back. I was the race engineer, and I wanted some practical data that I could use at the racetrack to tune the car with a single-plane wing. I needed to know what each little wing position change or each bodywork change would do to the car at the racetrack.

"The problem was, and it's always the problem with a wind tunnel test, how do you relate the wind tunnel numbers to what is actually happening at the racetrack. Andy agreed to do a test at a racetrack with the same parts and pieces that we were going to try in the wind tunnel. That way we could directly correlate those changes. We'd run the changes at the racetrack and then go right to the wind tunnel and test the same parts and pieces. Then we'd have data to directly correlate the effects of the changes.

"Sam and I got a list together of all the items that we wanted to try. Then we consolidated that list. We knew we had 10 hours in the tunnel, and we knew we could do about four changes to the racecar every hour. That's about the quickest you can do it because it takes some time for the air to come up to speed in the tunnel and to slow down after the run. So we could only test 40 things. We talked about it and cut our list down to 40 items. Then we built the parts we needed to do those 40 tests. There were about 20 items that needed to be made. We built the pieces, and we really didn't spend much money doing that. A lot of them were cardboard and duct tape kind of pieces.

"First we went to the racetrack. We went to Phoenix using the road course inside the 1-mile oval. We instrumented the car with static pressure taps in the underbody and hooked those into our normal data acquisition system. We put sensors on the shock absorbers so we could measure ride height. We were at Phoenix for two days. The first day we ran rake and ride height tests. We varied the rake and ride height and recorded all the data from the pressure taps and shock sensors and the drivers' comments. The drivers got bored out of their minds. They'd just drive around. We'd say do three laps and they'd go out and do it and they'd come back in and we'd raise the back of the car one turn and they'd go out again for three more laps. We were just collecting data.

"The second day we went through all of our test parts. We tried different wing shapes and different wing mounts and end plates. We tried end plates that went all the way to the ground. We had made end plates that were 4 feet high and went down right behind the rear wheels to about 2 inches above the ground. The big trick back then with those cars was trying to manage the air coming out of the tunnels using the wing. The advantage of the biplane wing was that the lower element increased the draw on the tunnels so they worked better and lowered the pressure under the car. We had lost that when the biplane wing was banned, so we were trying to use the air as best we could to keep the tunnels working as well as before. We tried everything we could think of trying to do that.

"When those two test days were done, Sam and I got together again and looked at the data. There were some things we'd tried that we could throw out right away. Some things just hadn't worked at all on the racetrack, and there was no use wasting our time in the wind tunnel testing those things. We did a list again and we put all the tests in order based on how fast we could make each change. We had two noses for the car, so we'd use one nose during a test while the other nose was being modified for the next test. We worked out the logistics of the test so the wind tunnel operators were never sitting there waiting for us. The tunnel cost about $20,000 a day to run and that's $2,000 an hour. You can't stand around wondering what to do at that rate.

"So we got our list together in the right order and everything, and we went to the Lockheed full-scale wind tunnel in Marietta, Ga. They call it the low-speed wind tunnel. We think 150 mph is fast, but the airplane guys think that's slow speed. We got the big tour of the facility, which was neat. It's a closed-loop tunnel and it's huge. It's giant. You walk around in this dark tunnel where there's only enough light to see. They do a walk around every day before they start testing to make sure there isn't any debris in there that might come flying through the test section. They're more worried about their fan blades than hurting our car. The fan section is giant. The guy told me that the problem they had when they were first calibrating the tunnel was they had to worry about the fan blade tips going supersonic and generating shock waves. You could see the turning vanes at every corner. It made me realize that if you want to build a wind tunnel you don't just go hook up a big attic fan.

"The boundary layer control is pretty crude. A guy walks out into the test section with a big box of pipe fittings. They've got a bunch of 90-degree fittings they screw into the floor about 10 or 15 feet in front of the nose of the car. These fittings blow compressed air toward the car down at the level of the floor. The compressor is controlled so they're blowing air at the same speed as the air in the tunnel. This is supposed to reduce the boundary layer. That's what they claim.

"We unloaded the car and the first thing they do is put lights in front of the car so a shadow is cast on a white screen. They take a picture of the shadow and digitize it so they know what the frontal area of the car is. This is very accurate. If you know the frontal area and the aerodynamic forces, you can compute the drag and lift coefficients.

"Then the car goes into the test section. The balance looks like four scales the car sits on. They tie the car down very tightly. The don't want it coming loose and blowing back into the tunnel, and they don't want any movement either. They tie it down to the pads with tie straps, almost like tying a car down on a trailer.

"These pads look almost like scales, but they're a lot more than that. Under the test section, the balance is two more floors of structure with strain gauges that measure the forces. This is how they measure the yaw, drag, and lift forces.

"A Lockheed guy comes to inspect the car before the test to make sure there's nothing that's going to fly off it. They're very careful about safety. They don't like tape on the car. They don't want any rags left in it. They check it carefully.

"Then they close the big door to the tunnel, and an electric solenoid locks it. A flashing red light comes on, and they start the wind. The first run they do is a velocity sweep. They ran the wind up to 70 mph and took a reading, and then they did 90, 110, 130, and 145 mph. That's to see whether there's a big change in the center of pressure. You don't want a big change in center of pressure. You'd like the car to be stable at all speeds. They do that one time to see if there's anything weird about your car.

"Then they get it at 145 mph and do a yaw sweep. The whole car is on a rotary turntable. They push a button and the car turns at increments of 5 degrees while the wind's blowing. They took data at 5, 10, and 15 degrees, both left and right, to see that the car is behaving predictably. They don't want any surprises.

"During testing, before each run, just before I went outside the tunnel, I'd start the data acquisition system on the car—the same system and sensors we'd used at the racetrack. I'd start the system, run out of the wind tunnel, and they'd start the test. After each run they'd shut the air off, and that solenoid on the door opened when the air got slow enough for you to go into the tunnel. I'd rush into the tunnel and it was still kind of windy. You're kinda hanging on to things while the wind is slowing down. We kept stressing to all the crew guys that this was expensive, and we've got to get in there and get the change done.

"We had our list and the crew guys would have the parts in their hands. We even practiced changing these parts in the shop a week before we went to the test, so they could do it quickly. We had the tools laid out and they'd rush in there with their tools and parts and I'd rush in there with my laptop computer and download all the data from the on-board system on the car.

"Sam was looking at the preliminary data coming from each test we did, and I would quickly look at the data from the car while the crew was making the change. Then the doors would close again and they'd fire up the wind again. Sam and I tried to see if we were getting results similar to what we expected. There were some times during the test that Sam and I would see it wasn't working like we thought, so we'd decide to drop a test and bring in a different test.

"We ran through all the tests, and we got data from the car and from the wind tunnel. The amount of data we were getting was way too much to go through right on the spot. We had to make some quick judgments. We tried some things that seemed kind of silly, but were really useful. One thing we tried was some inserts inside the tunnels that changed the shape and angle of the under-wing. We built up some very thin fiberglass inserts that we slid under the car and taped into the tunnels. During one of those runs, we started to see pieces of fiberglass flying out the back of the car when the air got up to about 100 mph. They shut it down and what had happened was the insert wasn't strong enough and it was breaking up. They made us take that out. But we saw some interesting things.

"There are windows into the wind tunnel, and you can look directly down on the racecar as it's running at almost 150 mph. It was interesting to see what was moving on the car. We saw the doors bulging out at the top where the roof and doors come together. The door was pulling away from the roof and causing a gap. We taped those doors down and we expected the drag to go down because the doors weren't flapping in the wind. What really happened was more rear downforce. It became obvious, when we looked at what was happening, that the door gap was right at wing level and the air coming out of the cockpit was screwing up the air to the rear wing. The rear wing worked better when the gap was taped over. I think we gained about 50 pounds of rear downforce by taping that gap. That was totally unexpected. Later we stiffened up the doors and made sure they would stay closed. The gap was only an inch or so, but it made a big difference.

"We went through all the tests and, when the whole day was over, the wind tunnel guy gave us 200 pages of data. It was balance data, yaw moment data, pressure data plus drag coefficient, and lift coefficient numbers that the computer automatically calculated. And I also had data from the on-board system. We loaded up the trailer and the guys headed back home.

"Sam and I had to sift through all that data. The big question for me, the race engineer, was, now I know numbers for changes in rake and ride height and all these new pieces we tried, but how does that relate to the racetrack? What I had now, for example, was a change in rake that made an extra 80 pounds of downforce on the front axle, and it moved the center of pressure so many inches forward. I took that data and compared it to that same change on the racetrack. We couldn't measure downforce at the track test, but we could measure center of pressure. What I could see was that the pressure changes underneath the car in the wind tunnel test were much reduced from the pressures we saw at the track test. A change in rake on the track showed much more dramatic results than a change in the wind tunnel. Anything we did underneath the car was not as pronounced in the wind tunnel as it was at the track. I attribute that to the problems controlling the boundary layer in the wind tunnel.

"But the absolute value of the numbers didn't matter to me that much. There is a big debate about wind tunnel testing, and some people say you can't learn anything in a full-scale tunnel because it's not a rolling road. Maybe that's true and maybe that's more of a designer thing. For what I need, the test was great. The amount of difference between the wind tunnel data and the track data was consistent. It always seemed to differ by a certain percentage. I don't remember the exact number. On the underside of the car, it was always the same percent error. That's good data for me.

"Let's say we're at the racetrack and we make a change and I see the pressures. I can say, if we were in the wind tunnel, here's what the pressures would read, and I can correlate the two directly. So now, my wind tunnel data may not be exactly accurate, but I know what it's going to be. I can tell you what the racetrack data would be if we were in the wind tunnel. That way I've got real numbers. I can say, 'If I change this, it will help the front downforce by X % and hurt the rear downforce by this other amount.' If I need absolute numbers, I can come pretty close whether I'm at the track or in the wind tunnel. I know the relationship between the two situations. To me, as a race engineer, this is more important than the debate about whether one is better than the other. I proved to myself that I can correlate track data and wind tunnel data, and that's all I care about.

"Sam used a lot of the data to design different wing shapes and mounting spots. The wind tunnel was very accurate when it came to changes on the top of the car because there are no boundary layer problems there. So, when we changed wing shapes, it was a pretty accurate representation of what was really happening. Where we ran into problems was when we changed wing position and got it closer to the tunnel exits. Then the correlation between the wind tunnel and the racetrack became worse. That's when we started to get interaction between the wing and the underside of the car and the boundary layer problem jumps up again.

"This test program was a great opportunity to see how that all works and how all this interrelates. It proved to me that if I was going to do another wind tunnel program on a full-scale car, I'd make sure I did a track test before the wind tunnel test. You can't just go and test in a wind tunnel. You'd miss half the importance. You have to consider a couple of days at the track as part of the wind tunnel program to get the most out of it.

"I'm not sure the track test has to be done before the tunnel test. Maybe it could be after the tunnel. The way we did it, we were able to eliminate some of the changes at the track and didn't need to test them in the tunnel. When you get down to it, it's probably cheaper to test at a track than in a wind tunnel. But, if we had done it the other way, we would find some things that didn't work in the wind tunnel and not have to test them at the track. I'm not sure there's an advantage one way or the other. It was scheduling that decided how we did it. The only day we could get the wind tunnel was December 24th. We were testing on Christmas Eve. That's how that all worked out."

ALAN MERTENS INTERVIEW

Alan Mertens

I first spoke to Alan Mertens in 1993 at an Indy car test at Laguna Seca. I caught him walking back to the pit lane from the bathroom and introduced myself and asked a couple of questions. Mertens is almost 6 feet tall—slim and fit-looking. He wears glasses over steady, blue eyes. Under a hawkish nose is a brown mustache. His light brown-with-gray hair is cut short and close. When I see him at work in the pit lane, he looks intense and thoughtful enough that I don't want to interrupt. But in that conversation at Laguna he was friendly so, when I saw him at Vancouver later that year, I asked if I could tape an interview, maybe at the Laguna race in October. He said sure, just look him up.

I did find him at Laguna but, although he said he'd be available, I never caught him when he wasn't in a crunch. I'm probably not insistent enough, but I know these guys are busy and don't want to get in the way.

At the Indy car race at Phoenix in April 1994 I saw him again and he said he'd have some time Saturday evening after final qualifying. "Just come round to the trailer," he said. It was about 6 o'clock when I caught his eye, and he waved me into the back of the PacWest semi-trailer. We went forward and stepped up through a door into a comfy-looking cubicle with gray carpet on the floor and walls and gray Formica workbenches along both sides. He said pull up a chair and I did, setting up my recorder and getting out my yellow pad. I passed him my list of designer questions (page 188), and he began by responding to the first line about personal background.

"Well, this is Alan Mertens, co-owner of Galmer Engineering in England, Bicester, which is based out of the old March Engineering premises, and co-owner of the PacWest racing team in the IndyCar series. Obviously you can tell by the accent on the tape, if not necessarily by the written word, that I'm English. [While editing the interview I've tried to maintain the accent as much as possible—PH] I was born in London...birth date is 6/4/50. My parents moved out of London when I was quite young and went into one of what they used to call the new towns which was to catch the overspill from London. My father got a job at De Haviland which went on to be called Hawker-Siddley and became British Aerospace.

"When I left school I followed my father into the aerospace business and actually got my mechanical engineering degree by getting a scholarship from British Aerospace, along with an engineering apprenticeship. I went through the various aspects of mechanical engineering: design, production, materials, etc., etc. during the course of that apprenticeship. I ended up in the drawing office working as a design draftsman/engineer. I found the work, albeit interesting, was not really stimulating enough to hold my attention.

"Quite late in life I guess, relatively speaking, when I was around 20 or 21, I suddenly discovered motor racing and attempted to do it myself. I drove a Formula Ford in England for about three years and won one of the many national championships in England in '73 and won a full sponsored ride in Formula 3 for '74. But then, over the winter period, was when the fuel crisis came and there was a big cutback in motor racing activities for '74. The sponsorship that I won through winning the Formula Ford championship was from Shell and they cut back their involvement in motor racing drastically and withdrew from the series. So I lost what was going to be my ride.

"Instead of turning professional in motor racing, I decided to do the next best thing. After a year or two in the doldrums, I used my engineering degree and my now obvious enthusiasm for motor racing in a different way and decided to get in as a designer. I went to March Engineering in '75-'76 as a rookie motor racing designer and worked my way up through Formula 3 and Formula 2 and did Formula 1 for March for some years."

PH: "Did Ian Reed tell me he hired you at March?"

AM: "Yes, he did. In the latter part of the '70s and early '80s, Ian Reed and I kinda split up 'cause I went off to do a project for Robin Herd which was a Formula 1 car for what was, at the time, March Grand Prix."

Someone poked their head in the door and Mertens asked if they could fetch him a coffee, please. He asked if I wanted one and I said no thanks. "Just a coffee and a couple of creamers," Mertens said, and went on talking into the recorder.

"I did the Formula 1 car which was the '80 March Formula 1 car. It was a kind of March, but it was a separate entity from actual March Engineering itself. It was actually run by John McDonald and it later became RAM and went through a number of name changes. I wasn't very comfortable with that arrangement and I asked Robin if I could go back to March Engineering and work on that. Ian Reed had just handed in his notice and was going off to America to work for Doug Shierson. Ian, at the time, was heading up the engineering side and his leaving left a vacancy, so I took over for Ian Reed in sort of late '80, early '81. From there on in I was the chief designer and ran the design department for March Engineering until I left in December '87.

"At the time I went back to March Engineering they were looking to expand their interest in motor racing and we took the Formula 1 car that I had just done for Robin and we converted it into an Indy car. That became the 81C and started the ['Thanks,' he said to the guy bringing him his coffee.] generation of March Indy cars which took them up to whenever they quit, when the Porche program quit.

Anyway, I left March in December '87 kinda disillusioned at the way things were going and turned to the Galles racing team with Al Unser Jr. at the beginning of '88 and ran the last March that I was responsible for, the 88C. We went on to win four races that year and come second in the championship and we created Galmer. I then spent six years building up Galmer and running Al Unser Jr. with Galles until we all split up and went our own separate directions at the end of '93. Which brings us right up to date with where I am and what I'm doing now. But, of course, in '92 we fielded our own Galmer car which Jr. did very well in up till the last couple of races of the season. I think we ended up finishing third in the championship. We won the Indy 500."

PH: "I read about awards that car won."

AM: "Yeah, it won the Schwitzer Award at Indy." [The Louis Schwitzer Award given by the Society of Automotive Engineers for engineering excellence at the Indy 500.]

PH: "I read that there were some innovative things about that car. Was it just a little smaller? What were you trying for with that design? What was achieved with it?"

AM: "We were essentially trying to achieve the same things as any other designer or racecar manufacturer tries to achieve, just optimize all of the features which are properly regarded as being the important ones or the important criteria of designing a racecar. You make it as efficient as you can mechanically and aerodynamically. We tried very hard to do that, drawing from our collective experience we gained over the years.

"I think one of the most innovative aspects of the car which we tried to do was on the back end of the car, in the way in which the rear of the gearbox was styled to extend the underwing as far back on the car as we could do. Whereas the regulations specifically stated that the underwing has to effectively stop at the centerline of the rear wheels, the gearbox was an extension of the underwing and the way it was profiled and shaped. And also the turbocharger had twin inlets on it, one on each side of the engine cover high up. The idea behind that was we were trying to encourage the flow of air over the back of the engine cover to clean up the air going over the rear wing as much as possible.

"At the same time, the overall inlet area to the turbocharger was greater. The combined inlet area of the two was greater than the old-fashioned single inlet so that there was no restriction at all into the turbocharger so it never starved itself. Because the individual inlets were smaller, we could put them up higher on the engine cover and that kept them away from the hot radiator exhaust to try to keep the plenum temperature down and keep the charge temperature down to maximize engine efficiency. Because of the way we'd oriented the turbocharger in the car to do that, we also gave it twin exhausts instead of what was popular, a single exhaust, and twin wastegates. We had twin exhausts from the turbo-charger and twin waste gates so we 'blew' the exit of the tunnel to re-energize the air coming out of the tunnel to make the tunnel more efficient, as well as to create more downforce."

PH: "That's something I've been chasing. I see some designs incorporating the engine exhaust into the underwing and some not. You just said 'energize the airflow.' I wouldn't have thought the exhaust was going that fast. But it is?"

AM: "Yeah, it is. I think the mistake we made was that it actually worked better than we thought it was going to. We always had a problem with that car pushing. That exhaust and a mechanical reason encouraged it to push as well. The car's Achilles heel was almost definitely on ovals. If we were able to get the push out, it's, generally speaking, because we had to run too far forward center of pressure with the front wings. Around an oval the tires tend not to get any rest at all and we could never achieve a good, consistent balance on the mile ovals with the car.

"There's two reasons we knew it worked. At the Speedway, if the driver would breathe the throttle at all and the gas velocity in the exhaust changed, the balance changed instantly on the car in the middle of the corner, which was unsettling and made it very difficult to maintain a consistent balance at the Speedway. The other thing is that we couldn't really quantify, to the degree we'd like to have done, how successful that was because, in the one-third scale wind tunnel model, we couldn't move the air quick enough through the air movers in the model to simulate the real velocity the gas was actually going on the car. We couldn't create the suction in the model inlets the same as the engine was creating and couldn't recreate the exhaust gas velocity coming out, so we never really knew how efficient it was until we got it on the track and then it kind of bit us in the ass. Every time we tried to increase the velocity in the wind tunnel model by using more pressure, the lines used to freeze up. They just couldn't cope with it."

PH: "So it's actually adding velocity to the gas in the tunnel. It's adding mass and velocity?"

AM: "We're not allowed to do it through the tunnel like Formula 1 cars do, so you have to do it on the trailing edge of the tunnel. There are two things. First of all we didn't quite direct the flow in the right direction because we had no means of generating the sort of flow we needed in the wind tunnel model to be able to visualize it in some way as to which way the converging gases and the tunnel exit air was going. Like I said, we underestimated how much was coming out. As the air from underneath the tunnel comes out the back of the tunnel and starts to expand, it starts to get tired and give up. The air in the tunnel almost gets pulled out by the engine exhaust."

PH: "That's almost like a Gurney?"

AM: "Yeah. That's right. The idea was the exhaust gas re-energized the air to give it more energy to pull it out the tunnel just that bit quicker and then the tunnel air got caught by the uprush of the rear wing which pulled it out even more and evacuated the tunnel and created even more downforce. We were trying to bridge the gap between the trailing edge of the tunnel and the upwash from the rear wing."

PH: "You had already extended the tunnel some anyway?"

AM: "Just the center span of the tunnel, using the end of the gearbox and the tunnel strakes."

PH: "I didn't think there was enough energy in the engine exhaust to use it like that. I guess what you'd really like is a long slot for the exhaust exit. That would really help."

AM: "It was a slot because the combined turbo exhaust and the waste gate exhaust, when you actually got them down to the section they needed to be to fit between the trailing edge of the underwing and the driveshaft, they virtually traversed the whole width of the exit of the underwing. So we did have, in fact, two very long thin slots on the top of each tunnel exit."

PH: "I'll be darned. I never read anything about that feature of that car's design."

AM: "Nobody's ever asked me before. [We both laugh.] That's true. Nobody's ever asked me or showed that much interest in depth about what we tried to achieve. They said, 'Oh yeah, that's a neat idea,' but never really followed up. I honestly thought we were going to do a '93 car. We'd learned a lot by our mistakes on the '92, so I wasn't that keen on explaining it anyway. But then the '93 car never happened and there's no '94 car and we don't know if we'll ever produce another one. Lola has also cottoned on to it this year. They've actually done it, albeit with their single turbo exhaust. They realized that it happens, not that they've tried to take as much advantage of it as we did. But you can see someone there has thought about it, the way they've curled up the exhaust at the end to get it pointed more uphill toward the rear. It's not just pointed straight back so, when the air from the tunnel comes up, the exhaust would get in the way."

PH: "The Indy Lights Lola has the exhaust through the diffuser and it goes straight in. That probably messes up the flow in the diffuser."

AM: "I'm not sure about that. That's a flat-bottom car and the whole flow field underneath might be completely different than it is in an Indy car. I've got no contemporary flat-bottom experience at all."

PH: "So, with your '92 Galmer, it turned out that blowing the tunnel exit worked but it wasn't stable because the driver was on and off the throttle. That just compounds the weight transfer problem you've got when the driver is on and off the throttle."

AM: "That's right, but it was great on street circuits and road courses. 'Cause just when you want to get after the gas to get out of a corner, you'd pick up a bunch of rear downforce. Traction was beautiful. And, when you get off the throttle going into a corner and you want a little weight transfer on the front so you can stand on the brakes, it was great. We were quick on all the street courses. Al Jr. was on pole at the first race in Australia. We were first and second until it rained. We were first and second at Long Beach until Danny took Jr. out. Danny went on to win the race anyway. Jr. won Vancouver."

PH: "Vancouver is definitely a grip track. I'm glad I asked about that. I've been trying to find out more about how the engine exhaust is used to affect the diffuser. I think in F1, McLaren has been on and off about blowing exhaust in the diffuser. It must be a mixed blessing."

AM: "This is purely speculation and not based on any facts at all, but knowing the problems we had, it makes you suspect that when they had active suspension it was great because the whole of the ride characteristics and the pitch and heave of the car could be controlled by the computer. Throttle and engine rev response could be an input and then you can really make it work in harmony with the vehicle dynamics and the underwing aerodynamics."

PH: "So the computer could read throttle settings and engine revs and determine how much exhaust gases were coming out the exhaust and how that would affect diffuser performance and downforce. That's interesting. That's some great insights I hadn't thought about. So you've been involved heavily in motorsports. You were a driver before you were a designer. Was that fun? Did you enjoy the engineering as much as the driving?"

AM: "It took a long time to get the driving out of my system."

PH: "So you were a frustrated driver for a while?"

AM: "Yes. There's no doubt about that. But then, like most other young men, you've got an ego that makes you believe you're always going to make it and you're the guy that's going to get to the top. But very quickly after I became an engineer in motor racing, I started working with top drivers and I knew that there was no way in hell I was ever going to make it to the top. Once I started working with world-class drivers, you knew that you never quite had the temperament and skill and tenacity or that last little bit of will that was going to get you there.

"I would hope that Jr., [Al Unser Jr.] for example, wouldn't contradict me and I don't think Scott [Sharp] would, that when I did drive, albeit nowhere near to the same extent they do or with the same sort of equipment, that there's enough of that basic instinct there that gives me the ability to communicate with them better and relate to what their problems are and then equate them to pure technical engineering aspects of the racecar.

"If I get a good driver that's got good feedback, and Jr. and Scott Sharp have got very good feedback, I can kinda get inside their heads and I can almost graphically visualize what it is they're going through and then, because of my engineering background, I can equate it in terms of the magnitude and resolution of forces and dampers and springs and aero or whatever. I think that helps me on one hand to explain to them what I'm doing because I can talk to them in sort of their language. It also helps me to help them sort the car out because I can interpret what they're telling me into engineering terms."

PH: "What an amazingly complex athletic task, driving a modern racecar. It's mind boggling. The more I know about it the more complicated it seems."

AM: "Yeah. It is an amazing athletic task to do. I love it. These armchair enthusiasts sit there and say, 'Well, shit. Anybody can drive a car around a racetrack. Damn it, I drive a car back and forth to work every day.' It's not until you work with a driver and you can see the way he breathes, the way his voice quivers at times. You can see the way he's covered in sweat and you can see when he's as white as a sheet when he's just scared the shit out of himself, you know what it is they're going through and the good ones are going through something which is almost super human.

"It is actually unbelievable what they can do and they make it look so goddamn easy at the same time. Some people don't even realize the physical exertion that's required to drive a race car and they sure as hell don't even come close to understanding the mental stress it takes to drive those cars. Anybody in their life that's gone through a period when they've had to use their brain real hard—now that's just as physically demanding as exercise. The degree of concentration that they require and the focus that they need to do that job is incredible. If they're going to put it all together, I mean not just racing, but put it altogether to even get to the point where they can race competitively and test and help you sort out the car, just keeping everything just so all the time. Particularly places like this, like Phoenix, on a mile oval, when they're going to be running with 28 cars. The driver gets no rest at all. Most of them will be physically tired by the end of the race, but I imagine most of them will be totally mentally drained."

PH: "They seem to keep getting faster here and that makes the drivers busier and busier. For some reason the Nazareth telecast last year seemed to capture that more. Maybe it was the in-car cameras."

AM: "Frantic is what it is. Of course, you know the more accomplished the driver gets and the more experienced he is, he keeps control of the situation a lot better and mentally slows it down. He's got to make everything happen in slow motion to be able to cope with it, really. The drivers that get out of control are the ones that get behind, always one step behind what their machinery's doing. They're never really on top of the job. It's really tough and sometimes they get it with experience and sometimes they've got it because it's a natural gift."

PH: "So you've been a driver and then you've also been an engineer/designer and now you're a racecar engineer. I'd think that designing a racecar and developing a racecar are two different things."

AM: "When you design a racecar, I guess, if you're lucky enough to have the budget and the time, we start with a blank sheet of paper, which is more demanding than having a factory racecar and developing it. There's obviously more to designing a part than developing an existing product. Sometimes it's actually more difficult to develop something. There may be something you want to achieve, but there's a limit to how far you can go that's dictated by the base product. You know what I mean? They might have configured the package in such a way that you can't practically do what you want to do without starting with a clean sheet of paper.

"I don't do a lot of designing now. Galmer still does a lot of development. My own chief engineer now, Andy Brown, does most of the work and carries most of the responsibility. I'm the echnical director. I get the final say on things. If necessary, I'll arbitrate and still contribute, hopefully, quite a lot of ideas to the program. What I'm trying to do is bring my overall experience as a designer, as an engineer, as a race engineer, as an ex-driver and all the things I've learned over the years. I try to bring all of those to the table as a library bank, as it were, for the use of all the drivers and engineers on the team.

"I do miss designing quite a lot. You can argue whether I'm good at it or not. I do actually like the challenge of having to come up with innovative ideas in a given time scale. That, in itself, generates a lot of pressure. I quite like that and I like that feeling of accomplishment when you go through a number of iterations to a design till you've finally got it right when you think it's going to do all the things you expect it to do and encompass all the other little functions that it needs to provide as well as its primary one.

"But I'm also a stickler for detail. Even the process of actually producing the drawing, whether it be manually on a drawing board or with the CAD system, you get some sense of pride even in the artistry of it. Of course there's no real artistry in CAD drawing 'cause it's all done for you. But there's a funny sort of thing. There's artistry on the drawing board. I kind of guess I always had a bit of artistic flair and I used to enjoy drawing and put as much emphasis into the pictorial representation of drawings as the technical content.

"There's also another funny challenge with a CAD system which is very difficult to describe. It is actually like a young kid playing on a Super Nintendo or video game. You do end up competing with the machine. Like when you're on a drawing board and you're designing things, the speed with which you put your ideas on the paper is limited by your own ability to draw a line and you can think, hopefully, quicker than you can draw. In a sense, while you're drawing, half your brain thinks about what you're putting on paper and the other half thinks about the next steps.

"You actually get into a competitive element with a CAD system whereas the CAD system can actually create what you're thinking quicker than you can think and you end up competing with the CAD system and you can get quite intense sometimes because you're trying to beat it."

PH: "I know what you're talking about. To explain some of the things I'm trying to explain in the book and the newsletter I've had to learn CorelDraw, which is not like a CAD system but you still have to figure out how the software works so you can do what you want to do. Computers are fun because there's a combination of play and competition. I'm learning and it's a great tool."

AM: "That's right."

PH: "How do you know when to freeze a design? I guess time and deadlines do that for you."

AM: "Yes, that's right. Of course it depends whether you're working for March or Lola or Reynard. Then you're building 12 or 25 or whatever number of cars so you pretty much know what the customer base is and when they expect to take delivery of cars so they can do their winter testing and you freeze the design in time for your manufacturing departments to produce the product. The designers always push it to the limit because they'll always argue that the later they leave it, the better the product they'll produce. They always leave the guys on the shop floor with the shitty end of the stick. They're the guys who have to work day and night to get the cars out on time. Quite often the designer is right. The designers always leave it to the last minute, but the factory guys always manage to get the cars out on time. They do, usually, when they get into a rhythm, produce a better car this way. If you stop the design a month early just to give the guys in the shop an easier time you've actually given away a month of additional development. It's as simple as that. I'm not saying the guys in the drawing office get it easy.

"When I was at March and when we produced the Galmer, I was quite often, during our peak periods, working from 8 in the morning to about 11 at night. We very rarely did all-nighters, whereas guys in the shop floor quite often do all-nighters to get cars out. When you're actually trying to generate ideas and designs, you get to the point where you're brain-dead and you can't work all night anyway. You just sit there staring at the drawing board or the computer screen and you're just over-stressing yourself and pushing yourself and not producing anything because you can't think anymore. I don't mean to suggest that the shop guys don't think, but it's a different kind of work."

PH: "If you were going to design another car starting the project now, what do you start with? Is it track data, wind tunnel data, does the driver feedback count? How do you prioritize things? What's important in modern racecar design?"

AM: "First of all you've got to insure that the designer's already involved in contemporary racecars, so that he's got a running database that is never-ending. He's got opinions and ideas all the time which are reasonably fresh. And the opinions and ideas are new, based on what they're doing at that time. I've never had to start a project designing a racecar without knowing what the hell I was getting into. When I first started working at March, I only got the bits and pieces to do. That built up my product knowledge in the formula that they were involved in. By the time you were given the responsibility to do the overall design or concept of a racecar, you had good knowledge of the product. So I've never been in a situation... like, if you were to say to me, 'Now here's umpteen million quid, go and design a Formula 1 car,' I'd say, 'Holy shit, where the hell do I start now.' Do you know what I mean? It's been more years than I care to remember since I was involved in Formula 1. So the first thing I'd do is go out and hire a couple of good Formula 1 guys and let them do the donkey work to get the thing off the ground."

PH: "What about Indy cars? You've designed one of those. What are the design priorities?"

AM: "Well, without question in my mind, the design of the car will be dominated and dictated by the wind tunnel, by aerodynamics. The ergonomics are pretty straightforward. Even the packaging of the car with the major components is pretty straightforward because that's been predetermined years ago by the car regulations and that's kinda just the way it's done. The last time anybody tried anything really radical was the Porsche thing and they put the turbo between the engine and the chassis. The result of that kinda speaks for itself, you know what I mean. I don't know why it didn't work but it clearly didn't. I don't know if it was the fault of that particular idea or something completely different. But nobody thought of it previously and nobody's done it since.

"So the general packaging you already know. You know the car's response for a given center of pressure and the tires work with a certain weight distribution and you know that between full and empty tanks you want the minimum amount of weight distribution change, all this sort of nonsense. And you know basically what surface area of the radiators is needed to cool the car. You know how big the exhaust headers are going to be and you know you've got a lump of a turbocharger which you can't really put anywhere else, with the Porsche exception, except where it is being put on all the Indy cars at the moment. So your one-third scale scheme or concept drawing of the car is really quite straightforward.

"So you've got a lump which represents the wind tunnel model and you don't draw that as a homogenous piece. Obviously, it's like a three-dimensional jigsaw puzzle and then you'll refine it. You'll thin it here and stretch it there and squish it and squash it and move it around a bit. And you'll keep pinchin' this and repackagin' to squeeze it up as small as you can and whatever. Of course you'll already have what constitutes a contemporary racecar. You've got 5,000 pounds of downforce to equal or beat. You know what sort of drag figures you're trying to equal or beat, etc., etc. You get an idea what sort of pitch sensitivity is tolerable and heave sensitivity, etc., etc. And you just kinda take it from there.

"With the current regulations, it's been refined to the point where it's very difficult, unless they change the regulations and everybody starts all over again. It's like a pyramid. When they first conceive of the regulations you're on a flat line. There's quite a lot of things you can do. But over the years, as the designs evolve and everybody refines the cars to the letter of the regulations, you get to the point at the top of the pyramid and each gain that you make is a very small incremental gain. So you're lookin' for very small changes and you're lookin' for a number of them just to find one big leap that you think's going to destroy the opposition.

"And that actually is very, very difficult now. You've got to the point now where the quality of the model making, the accuracy has to be very, very good to know whether you've made a gain or it's experimental error. The magnitude of gains you're lookin' for are that small. Some people have tried seven-sixteenth wind tunnel models but they're prohibitively expensive and there's not actually many rollin' road tunnels that you can actually get that size of model in without the performance of the model being disturbed by the size of the working section of the tunnel—the out wash of the wing hitting the roof of the working section and all that sort of nonsense."

PH: "Are you going to visit the Swift wind tunnel next week?"

AM: "No. It's not convenient for me to go and see it and the geographics of the way we run our program means that it would be very difficult for Galmer to do a wind tunnel program at arm's length, on the other side of the world."

PH: "What tunnel do you guys use?"

AM: "We've used three. We've used MIRA, which is the Motor Industry Research Association. We've used the Brackley tunnel which is the ex-March wind tunnel. And currently we're using the Footwork Formula 1 tunnel."

PH: "I've heard that Footwork tunnel is a state-of-the-art tunnel. The Swift guys looked hard at that tunnel when they were designing their new wind tunnel and the same people who did the instrumentation in the Footwork tunnel put in the instrumentation in the Swift tunnel. The Footwork tunnel is a 40%, rolling-road tunnel, right?"

AM: "It may well be but we still only use a third-scale model. I have no idea what Footwork uses. I think they're called Arrows now.

PH: "Getting back to racecar design, the major source of research is the wind tunnel model and the aerodynamics. Is mechanical grip passé now?"

AM: "No. Mechanical grip is real important. But you get your space envelope first from the wind tunnel model and then you package all your mechanical aspects inside it and your front and rear suspension which dictates geometry which dictates the mechanical grip. And then, of course, you get the inevitable argument between the aerodynamicist and the mechanical designer, as one wants some bit here and the other one doesn't, and the other one screams and shouts, 'You can't do this.' Each one thinks he's right and the other one doesn't. There's usually a series of compromises and the quickest cars are the ones that produce the least amount of compromises, basically. And the way you arrive at the least amount of compromises is with the ingenuity of your designers, because they don't compromise. They find a solution without having to compromise. You know, it's like race drivers, you've got some good designers and some bad designers."

PH: "With suspension geometry, you can't get everything you want, so what are your priorities? What do you need to get right first?"

AM: "Well, generally speakin', depending on whether it's a street course car or an oval car and if you've already pre-determined the wheel base, we'll just concentrate on the swing axle length and the roll center height and the roll center movement first. Thing's like you've got written down here like caster and Ackerman are pretty much a movable feast even after you've locked into the design of the suspension. It's not that difficult to change the caster and it's not that difficult to change the Ackerman.

"The actual position of the roll center is quite important. Whether it moves laterally a lot is important and whether it moves up and down through the ground plane is important. Your roll axis, which it describes, is important. It's difficult to sum up what that importance is or how to define it in a couple of sentences. Again, that's something that's evolved over the years with the sort of cars we're runnin' and the level of grip they generate with the sort of mass of the cars and with the characteristics of the tires, and the tire design, etc., etc."

Mertens pauses here and seems to struggle with how to go on with a description of a very complicated process.

"It makes it sound like history has predetermined all that for you and you don't have to think much about it, but it's not really true because we find, whether we've done our own car or we're runnin' a March or a Lola, we take the stock package and... You know IndyCar is kinda unique in a way because it runs street courses and road courses and mile ovals and superspeedways. I can't remember a year yet when we haven't finished up with probably a total of between 15 and 20 suspension variations during the course of the year, some of which don't work and aren't worth a shit and some of which we change depending on the track we go to."

PH: "Last year Al Jr. won at Vancouver, which is a mechanical grip track and the Lolas were really struggling there. Nigel Mansell didn't do very well there."

Mertens looks around me to Andy Brown, his designer, who had slipped in next to me earlier and had been working quietly.

AM: "Didn't I do something special for Vancouver last year? That was something of a breakthrough, wasn't it?"

Andy Brown: "I thought we did that at Toronto. We put the shorter swing axle on it."

AM: "Oh, yes, that's right. We changed the rear suspension geometry at Toronto. Didn't quite get it all together."

The tape ran out, so I took it out and turned it around.

PH: "After mid-season in '93 I began to hear about several Lola teams changing suspension geometry."

AM: "Well, yeah, that's true, whether they did their own thing or copied what we did. That sort of thing happens. There's no secrets at all.

"Let's see, I think I read something on your question sheet here. What people or designs have influenced your work? Well, any designer who is being honest with you won't actually say that he does his own thing; know what I mean? Anybody who says, 'Nobody influences me. I do my own thing and everything I do is unique,' is full of shit. We all copy each other's work and we all pay keen interest in what each of us is doin'—whether it's good, bad, or indifferent. We don't want to copy what we think other people have done wrong, but we'll be the first to copy what other people have done which we think is right. Sometimes we directly crib other people's ideas. Sometimes you take something less and maybe we think we can do it a little bit better. And some of the time, we come up with our own ideas but nobody in this business is ashamed of copying something that works or is ashamed of avoiding something that doesn't."

PH: "Dan Gurney told me a month or so ago that Colin Chapman, when he was the absolute best designer in the eyes of everyone in racing, still walked around and watched everbody's cars coming off the trailers."

AM: "Oh, for sure. I'm sure he did."

PH: "What about the lift/drag ratio, L over D? Is that an efficiency number you work with when you're doing aero work? Can you give me an idea what kind of numbers you get with these cars?"

AM: "Andy? Have you got the basic L over D figures for road courses? Just the generic figure? Ask me another question while he's lookin'."

PH: "Talk about balance vs. ultimate grip. Isn't that kind of an ongoing battle?"

AM: "The ongoing battle is balance. You want ultimate grip, but grip is actually not somethin', unless it's excessive changes in grip levels, that drivers really respond to. They'll go quicker or they'll go slower depending on whether they've got more or less grip but, in terms of refinin' the car or makin' it work better, what the driver can really respond to and feel more graphically than anything else is balance changes. And, if you're trying to improve grip, you still tend to end up talking about balance, because there's nothing more scary than havin' a perfectly balanced car which is too slow. You think, 'What the hell do I do now?' You see, you still have to break it down to balance. You say, 'Well, one end must be givin' up. What is the balance like?' And then, finally, after intense interrogation or after a long run or you wait till the thing's on its last legs and gasping for breath and you've worn the tires out, one end will go away sooner or later. You say, 'Right.' So then it's a balance problem, right? And they say, 'Well, yes.' Well, what is it? So they say it's either pushin' or it's loose. So if it's loose, then you've lost grip, so then you try and get the grip back, but you always seem to work on it in terms of balance. So, once you've got the balance back, you've obviously, by definition, got grip back in the rear and you've gained grip overall. If you gained a lot of grip it's going to push and you got a balance problem again.

"Now, you give the driver a hard time and you say, 'Well, all right, the thing's pushin' a bit, might be just a scrub-push.' So then if you improve that, you've gained grip and you've raised it to the next level. It's not very often that you talk in terms of just grip, whether you've got it or whether you haven't. I don't think I've ever had a car which has had no side-bite at all, i.e., no grip, that hasn't had a balance problem. There's always going to be a bit of a balance problem.

"Like with Al Jr. driving—I'd say to Andy, 'I want to run 30 pounds more downforce.' So we go up a quarter on the rear Gurney and half a turn on the front wings or something. You do it and he might go quicker but, if the balance hasn't changed and it was well balanced before, Jr. won't feel it. It'll be quicker on the clock but he'll say, 'Well, I can't feel that.' The balance hasn't changed. Drivers are very susceptible to balance changes but not overall grip level unless it's a big difference.

"Like 'round here [Phoenix] in the old days, for example, going from a three-element rear wing to a cascade rear wing where there's a big increase in downforce. As long as you can give him that increase in downforce and keep the balance the same, that was a big enough difference that he would say, 'Oh wow, that stuck pretty good,' you know what I mean? But generally speakin', with the level of drivers we work with that are up there and runnin' quick, you're always workin' on balance."

Having finished that thought, Mertens reads another question off my sheet.

AM: "How do you size components? Do you use finite element analysis? We don't do that. That requires a lot of computing power and the facilities we've got at Galmer aren't that lavish or that expensive to get into full finite element analysis, etc., etc. We've got very good computing programs that, if you put a lateral load into a car, it will give you the forces through the suspension components and the engineers can do the detail stress analysis on the highly loaded points. Then, when we produce a car or even if we buy somebody else's product, we usually rig test most things. Not because we don't trust our own stress calculations, but because we feel very strongly about stiffness and efficiency."

PH: "So you're not just talking about fatigue tests. You're testing how much the component gives under a given force. I guess stiffness is important because of the small amount of suspension movement in modern racecars."

AM: "There's a lot of suspension movement in Indy cars. That's where the mechanical grip comes from. That's why I raised my eyebrows and you got that shocked response when you asked if mechanical grip still counts. In Indy car racing, it does a lot. On street courses, for a car that weighs 1,550 pounds dry and 2,000 pounds with fuel and driver, it can produce between 4,000 and 5,000 pounds of downforce depending on what kind of wing configuration you're usin'. You'd be amazed at some of the wheel rates that we run, how soft they are for such a heavy car that's got that much power to try to create mechanical grip."

PH: "All I've seen is Indy Lights data ,but here at Phoenix the suspension movement is on the order of a quarter of an inch total."

AM: "Well, I can tell you that the typical ride height of an Indy car around here might be something in the region of about an inch at the front and one and three quarters of an inch at the rear. Dynamically, the thing's still rubbing on the ground and, without lookin' at the data acquisition system, I can't tell you how much of that's tire squash and how much is suspension movement."

PH: "That's a lot more than a Formula 1 car, isn't it?

AM: "That's right, but we don't have flat bottoms. We've got the 2-inch rule and we've got tunnels. If we had flat bottoms, you would have to run that low like a Formula 1 car. Or, if we didn't have the 2-inch rule, we'd run a lot stiffer because the aerodynamic gain would be greater than the mechanical loss. It's like runnin' it like a roller skate."

PH: "That's why F1 is running so low and so stiff. You don't have to do that because you've got the step in the middle and you've got real tunnels that aren't as sensitive as a flat bottom."

AM: "They're not as sensitive but, of course,... It's a bit of a contradiction here. We do generate a lot of downforce. Right? So we have to run a quite high static ride height to compensate for the fact that, when the thing's out there runnin', it's goin' to get sucked down quite a lot. But, because of the 2-inch skirt gap, you can't run enough downforce to run the car stiff enough to run a low static ride height, so the dynamic ride height we run gives good mechanical grip. Mechanical grip still is just as important on Indy cars as aero grip is."

We were interrupted as one of the crew members came in with a problem. Mertens said, "Excuse me but I've got to handle this. If you'd like to hang around, we can continue later." I had just about run out of questions, so I excused myself with thanks.

Mertens Interview Epilogue

I didn't see Mertens again until the race at Milwaukee in early June. I gave him the approval copy on Friday and then saw him again the next morning in the coffee shop of the motel where we were both spending the weekend. "I read some of that yesterday," he said. "And I have to say I kinda enjoyed it. I actually felt proud of some of the things I told you I had done. Come 'round later and I'll give it back to you. I made a few little changes."

I didn't see him that day, but the next morning, Sunday, the day of the race, my team had a full car and I had to scrounge a ride out to the fairgrounds. I went into the coffee shop looking for someone I knew and there was Mertens having breakfast. I asked if I could get a ride with him to the track and he said, "Sure. Have you had your breakfast yet?" I sat down and had another cup of coffee and we talked about racing just like any two racing fans would talk.

"What do you think about Mansell going back to Formula 1?" he asked and we discussed that topic. Later, stuck in raceday traffic in his Lincoln Town Car, he talked about his son's go-kart racing and how amazingly natural it was for a youngster to steer into a slide.

When Mertens returned the corrected interview copy, he said again how much he enjoyed reading it. "At cocktail parties and family things, people ask me what I do and I'm always at a loss to explain. Maybe I'll get some copies of this and then I can just hand it to them." He was all smiles and I felt great.

Nigel Mansell in a'94 Lola at Phoenix.

Al Unser Jr. in a '94 Penske at Phoenix.

Michael Andretti in a '94 Reynard at Phoenix
All Photos by Bob Gularte.

CHAPTER 2

RACING TIRES

The next time you watch a tennis match on TV, notice how the best players pay very close attention to the balls they're using. During a match tennis balls undergo considerable changes in the way they bounce and how fast they go through the air. These changes are different depending on how the balls are manufactured and the type of court surface in use. Balls pick up moisture on a grass or clay court and fluff up, getting slow and heavy. Asphalt and concrete hard courts wear the nap off the ball, making them progressively lighter and faster in the air. In professional tournaments new balls are put into play about every 10 games, and the difference is so important to the players that the server holds them up as a courtesy to his opponent, so the new balls won't be a surprise. On an important point you'll often see a server look for a particular ball to use in order to gain a slight advantage.

Professional race drivers are just as discriminating about their tires as professional tennis players are about the balls in use. Everything the driver feels and every action the driver takes to control the car goes through the tires. During a track session or a race, tires change just like the tennis balls mentioned above. In this section we'll look at some of the basic characteristics of tires.

AYRTON SENNA QUALIFYING STORY

Bill King told me this story while he was manager of press relations for Goodyear's Racing Division. Bill is a great guy, and he always has a good story for me. This is one of his best.

One of those years when Ayrton Senna was qualifying his McLaren-Honda quicker than everyone else by one or two seconds, Pirelli decided to get back into Formula 1 racing in competition with Goodyear. This was during the time when F1 cars qualified on special gumball tires usually referred to as "qualies." Tires made specifically for qualifying are designed to give a lot of grip and have very soft rubber in the tread. They also generate a lot of heat and are good for only one or two laps.

At each race Senna had been consistently quicker than everyone else by at least a second, even though all the drivers were on the same Goodyear tires. The Pirelli qualies, however, proved to be pretty good right out of the box and the few drivers using them began turning in times better than all the Goodyear drivers except Senna, and they were nibbling at his advantage too. This produced a frenzied study by the Goodyear engineers to find out why Pirelli had been able to produce a good qualifying tire so easily.

It took a while, but what they came up with was pretty simple. It turned out that Goodyear molding operators were using a mold release agent that contained a silicone lubricant. This is the same stuff available in spray cans that you and I use as a dry lubricant on hinges and between plastic parts in our car interiors to stop squeaks. The operators sprayed the molds before the tire assemblies were loaded so that, after molding, the tire was easier to pull out of the tooling. The silicone lubricant stayed on the surface of the tires, making the tire a little less sticky for a lap or so before it wore away.

As soon as the Goodyear engineers identified the problem they quickly changed the process to eliminate the silicone material. Afterward, although Senna was still quicker than everyone else, the margin was narrower, but the Goodyear qualies were clearly better than the Pirellis. According to Bill King, Ayrton Senna told the Goodyear people he wished they hadn't changed things, because it had given him an advantage. Senna didn't elaborate, but the point is that, given a situation that spelled trouble for most drivers, Senna figured out how to turn it to his advantage.

I can only guess, but I'll bet that like the tennis players mentioned earlier, Senna was an avid student of the tires he used. He probably felt what was going on with each tire on each corner of his car on every turn of every lap. He was aware of changes due to the rapid temperature rise as the tires work the car around each corner. I'm sure he could also feel the tires change as they accumulated laps. He probably knew each tire as an individual with its own tricks and quirks.

When Senna was out there qualifying for a race, he felt those silicone-coated qualies changing during the first lap as the slicky stuff wore off. He probably tried different tactics and gradually learned what he had to do to get them in the optimum condition for that one hot lap that regularly won him the pole position by a large margin. Maybe he had to use the front tires especially hard or use the throttle to spin the rear tires, and get that silicone lubricant off. He had to do it carefully because overheating the tire would ruin it. Whatever he was doing, it was effective. Think how many other components on a racecar he was probably using in that same superior way. If he could do it with the tires he could use the engine, the gearbox, the dampers, the data-analysis software, or any number of important components to his advantage. I think that's what made him faster than most other drivers day in and day out.

TIRE CHARACTERISTICS

Slip Angle: Where the Rubber Meets the Road

A vehicle turning a corner is actually accelerating toward the center of the arc of its path. It takes a force to accelerate an object that has some mass (weight), and the tires are the source of that force. The cornering force that tires generate is called lateral force or side force.

A tire can't produce the lateral force needed to turn the car without slipping and a slip angle. The slip angle, shown in the sketch below, is the angle between where the tire is pointed and where the car is actually going. The tire tread actually deforms as it rotates through the contact patch area and then recovers as the car's weight comes off the contact patch. The force needed to deform the tire is what produces the lateral force needed to change the path of the car.

Let's try to visualize what's going on where the rubber meets the road. When you turn the steering wheel to make your car go around a corner, you point the tire away from the steady-state direction of the vehicle and create a slip angle. The tire deforms at the contact patch and recovers as it rotates past that point. In the area of the contact patch the tire resists deformation by pushing against the road surface. That resistance to deformation generates the lateral force.

This lateral force, at the front tires only at first, wants to rotate the car around its center of mass. If the rear tires were on casters they would swing away from the corner, and the car would spin in its own length. The rear tires, however, are not on casters, but are attached so they are parallel to the centerline of the car, and they react to the tendency of the car to spin around its center of mass with a resisting lateral force and a resultant slip angle of their own that may or may not be the same as the slip angle at the front.

Do you see that? You turn the steering wheel which turns the front wheels, creating a slip angle between the tire heading and the car heading. The slip angle results in a force that wants to turn the car around its center of mass, but that's resisted because the rear tires are fixed in the direction of the centerline of the car. The resistant force of the rear tires gives them a slip angle similar, but not necessarily identical to, the front tires, and the car travels in an arc around the corner until you change the steering angle again.

All this doesn't happen instantaneously. After a steering input it takes from one-half to one full revolution of the tire for the full slip angle to develop, depending on the construction of the tire. A passenger car tire with tall and relatively weak sidewalls will take longer to develop full slip angle than a racing tire with a short, stiff sidewall.

Look back at the sketch to see what's going on at the contact patch. Visualize this tire rolling on a glass road and you're below the road watching. The car is traveling on a curved path, and the tire is pointed slightly inside that path. As the

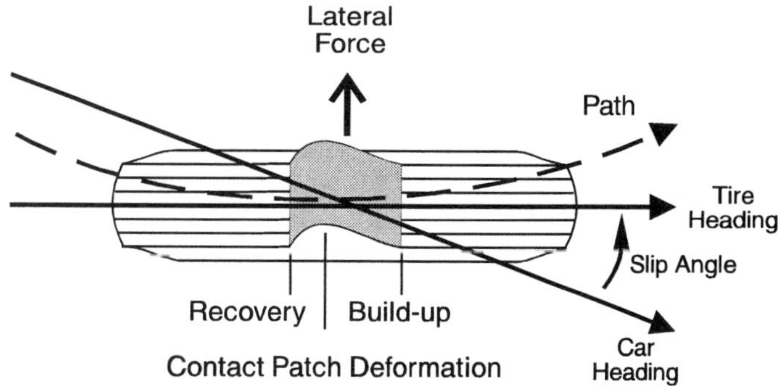

tire rotates, segments of the tread come in contact with the road surface, and have to deform elastically to continue in the direction of the car. Friction between the tire and the road surface prevents the tire from sliding against the road until near the end of the contact patch, when the car's weight begins to come off that end of the patch. Slippage near the end of the contact patch allows the tire to recover to its unloaded condition. When the tread segment first comes in contact with the road the deformation is slight, but it builds to a peak just before it starts the slip-and-recover section. All the time the tire is deformed it's trying to recover, and it's exerting a force on the road. This is how the tire develops the force necessary to turn the car.

Side Force Vs. Slip Angle

The graph shows the general relationship between the lateral force a tire generates and the slip angle of the tire. Each tire design, including carcass construction and rubber compound, has a characteristic curve similar to this one that shows how much side force the tire will produce at a given slip angle. A tire does not generate side force until it assumes a slip angle. The shape of this curve is a specific characteristic of a tire design—the result of the geometry and materials used in the construction and materials in the compound of the tire tread.

Different tire designs produce different curves. We'll look at some characteristic shapes shortly. For now, notice that the curve has a straight section at small slip angles where an increase in slip angle gives a proportional increase in lateral force. The slope of this section of the curve is the "stiffness" of the tire. At higher slip angles you get less increase in lateral force as you increase slip angle, and after the curve tops out, more slip angle can actually produce less lateral force.

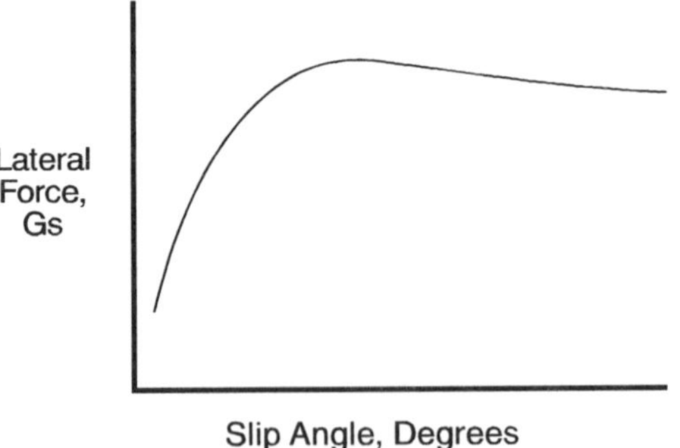

Side Force vs. Slip Angle

Longitudinal Slip

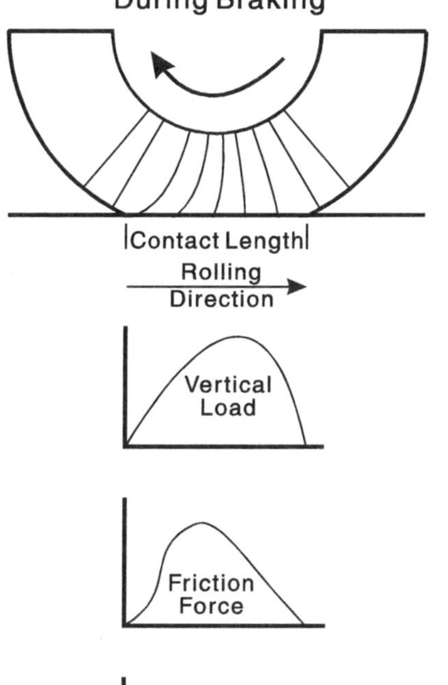

The force generated by tires during braking and acceleration is called longitudinal force. There is no slip angle in this case, but there is longitudinal slip between the tire and the ground. This shows up as a difference between the actual rotation of the tire and the rotation needed if there was no slip. Under hard acceleration the tire turns a little faster, and during hard braking the tire rotates less than it would if there was no slip.

The tire sketch illustrates the buildup of slip in the contact patch. As the tread comes into contact with the ground, slip begins and builds up as the tire rotates. Notice the radial lines on the sidewall show more deflection as they rotate through the patch and then recover straight again. The three graphs show how vertical load, friction force, and relative slip vary over the length of the contact patch.

Vertical load, the first graph, is concentrated more at the front of the contact patch where the tire is first coming into contact with the ground. Why isn't the load distributed evenly over the area of the patch? Visualize the tire tread slapping onto the ground as it comes into contact with the road. The sidewall compresses in this area so the tire tread actually has some relative motion with respect to the ground that adds some force in this area.

The second graph shows friction force. It builds fairly linearly and then falls off sharply as the contact patch gets picked up.

Relative slip, shown in the bottom graph, builds up more slowly and falls off more sharply than friction force.

Sam Garrett: Friction and Wide Tires

Friction between the tire and the road surface is what allows the tire to generate side force. We couldn't walk or even crawl without friction. We talked about friction briefly in the chapter on aerodynamics because we wanted to show that aero forces add to the vertical force on a tire and so increase the cornering force a tire generates. Now we'll use the same equation to talk about tires. Here's the equation again:

$Ff = CfFv$.

Friction force (Ff) equals the coefficient of friction (Cf) times the vertical force (Fv). You can see that contact area doesn't appear in that equation, but our experiences in the real world tell us that brakes and tires work better if there is more material in sliding contact. Bigger brake discs or drums seem to work better and wider tires certainly give a car more grip. With brakes that's true because you need a lot of surface area to help dissipate the heat you're producing. With tires it's different, but more contact area is definitely better.

Sam Garrett is a graduate mechanical engineer who designs and develops racecars. One of the people responsible for the Kudzu Camel Light cars that were so successful in IMSA events, he also worked with the Scandia Camel Lights team in 1992. Sam worked near Atlanta, but has now moved to Arkansas. Here's how Sam Garrett explained to me why "more rubber on the road" works.

"When I was a student at Georgia Tech, a physics professor asked our class why we were preoccupied with putting wider tires on our street cars. We told him we wanted to 'put more rubber on the road.' He tried to tell us that friction force is independent of the contact area.

"In most cases he's right. Friction force (Ff) depends on a coefficient of friction (Cf) which is a characteristic of the materials involved and the vertical force (Fv) pressing the materials together: Ff = Cf x Fv. Area doesn't appear in the equation. In the real world, however, this only applies to materials with a 'hard' surface. To understand why that is, you have to look at what happens on a microscopic level.

"All materials, no matter how smooth or flat they appear to our unaided eyes, have small surface imperfections as shown in the sketchs. To simplify the sketch we show points on one side only, but really both blocks have irregular surfaces. When two solid objects touch they have an 'apparent' contact area which is the area you can see and measure, but they also have a true, micro-scopic contact area which may be quite different. But for hard solids, the true contact area remains constant regardless of the apparent contact area. Here's why.

"When two hard surfaces come in contact, they meet at many sharp points or peaks like you see in the sketch. If you apply a force that presses them to-gether, the material actually yields and the peaks flatten out, increasing the actual area of contact. If we increase the size of the parts in order to increase the apparent contact area, we lower the force at each peak because there are more peaks to take the same overall load. With less load on each peak the points flatten out less, and the actual area of contact is less per peak so, overall, the true contact area is about the same as before we made the parts bigger. That's why hard materials don't show an increase in friction forces with an increase in contact area.

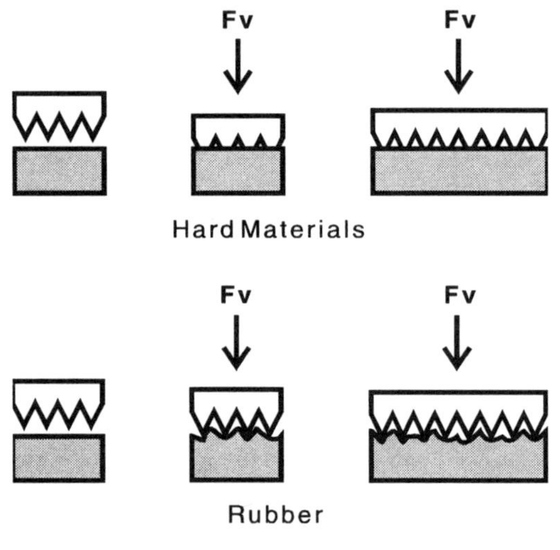

The Nature of Friction

"Rubber is different. Rubber is an elastic solid which 'gives' at a very low stress level. There is no fixed yield point and the deformation is elastic—rubber deforms and recovers. It deforms at low stress levels, and conforms to the microscopic imperfections of a surface with which it comes in contact. You can see in the sketch that more contact area means more imperfections to conform to. With rubber you get more friction force when you increase the contact area."

I think this is a great explanation of one of the characteristics of rubber, which is an amazing material. To sum it all up: hard materials make contact at points of microscopic imperfections which yield when a force presses two surfaces together. If you increase the overall area of contact, the force per point is less, so the points yield less and the actual microscopic contact area stays the same. But rubber is elastic and more contact area means more imperfections coming together, which increases friction.

I need to point out, however, that a wider tire does not guarantee more rubber on the road. The weight of the car (plus aero downforce if there is any) and the air pressure in the tires is what determines the total area of tire contact patch. A 4,000-pound car with evenly distributed weight has 1,000 pounds on each tire. If the tire pressure is 25 pounds per square inch (psi), the contact patch has to be 1,000 pounds divided by 25 psi which is 40 square inches. A narrow tire with a 4-inch wide tread would have a contact patch that is 10 inches long. A tire with an 8-inch wide tread needs a 5-inch long contact patch.

The trend toward larger diameter wheels and wider tires that started in the 1970s began with bias-belted tires. Now we have radials on all our street cars, and they're mounted on larger diameter, wider wheels than in the 1960s. A radial tire with shorter, stiffer sidewalls can have a much softer compound and give the same life. The result is a lower-pressure tire with a shorter, wider contact patch made from softer rubber. That gives us a much better tire and a better handling car.

Graphs Tell the Story

Tires are complicated devices. Several graphs follow that show how tires of different designs differ in performance. The vertical axis of each graph is the lateral force generated by the tire. Lateral force, as you may imagine, is one of the most important characteristics of a particular tire design. We use Gs, the force of gravity, as the units for lateral force. Tire manufacturers don't give out raw data in pounds-force, so Gs is a convenient unit to show some important trends without specific data.

What you notice immediately in these graphs is that race tires develop higher values of lateral force than passenger tires. Street tires need to be bullet-proof, no matter what. Replacement passenger tires are a relatively big expenditure on family cars, so long wear and low manufacturing cost are very important. Racing tires, on the other hand, are made in small numbers for specific races or type of track. The emphasis is on performance and safety while wear is not an issue as long as the tire lasts for a track session, a race, to the next pit stop, a weekend, a season, or whatever interval that race series or racing event demands. The point of these graphs is to show some important aspects of tire performance.

Slip Angle

As you can see, a race tire generates more grip than a passenger tire. The race tire is much wider, and probably has a shorter, stiffer sidewall and a softer compound. Notice the shape of the curves. Each curve starts with an ascending, linear section that rises to a peak and then decreases as the slip angle gets larger. This means there is a slip angle beyond which a further increase in slip angle results in less lateral force.

These curves also show the difference in radial and bias-ply race tires. A radial race tire feels different to a driver than a bias-ply race tire, and needs to be driven differently. We'll look at this in more detail later, so for now, notice that the radial race tire generates more lateral force at smaller slip angles and the curve goes to a higher peak value of lateral force. The radials give more ultimate grip and more grip at smaller slip angles. Notice also the radial curve drops off more after the peak. A radial race tire is less forgiving and harder to drive near maximum grip than a bias-ply race tire. We'll explain that in more detail later.

Notice that the maximum lateral force on the passenger tire curve is about 0.8 G. This is the number you generally see in street car road tests measuring lateral acceleration on a skid pad. Short sidewall, high performance tires on cars such as the Corvette and

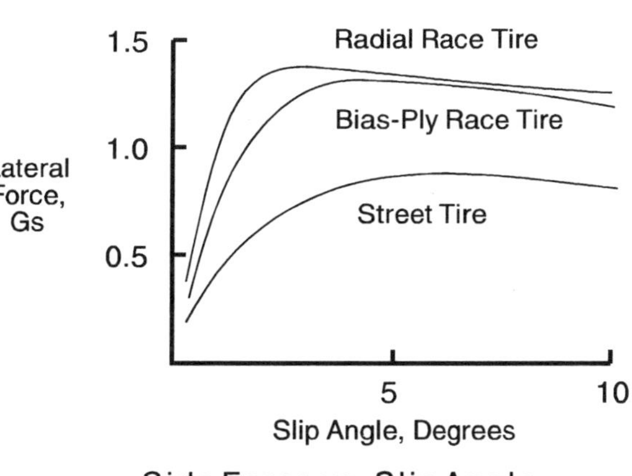

Side Force vs. Slip Angle

Acura NSX are capable of near 1.0 G. The maximum lateral force on the race tire curves is about 1.4 G, and this is representative of racecar cornering forces without aerodynamic downforce.

Tire Temperature

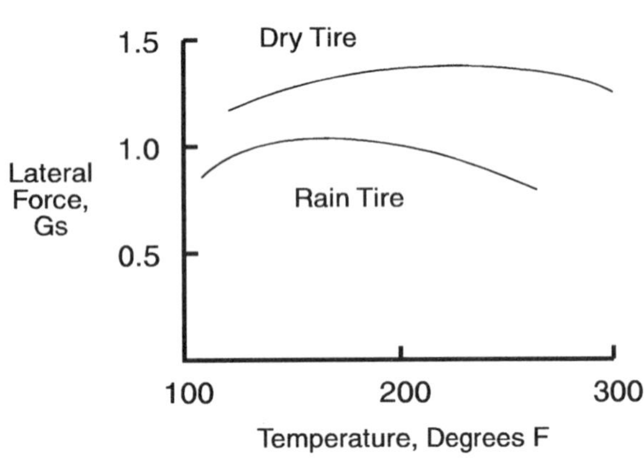

Side Force vs. Tire Temperature

This graph shows that there is an optimum temperature range for a tire. The temperature values on this graph only give a rough indication because the optimum temperature range for a specific tire is a characteristic considered during the design of the tire, and engineers consider operating temperature requirements when they specify the compound and construction of a tire built for a particular application. As you'll see later in this section when we talk about rubber compounding, a racing tire used on a paved oval in the summer in Phoenix is a lot different from one built for a paved oval in the fall in Wisconsin.

Rain tire compounds are optimized for wet grip, and depend on water to keep them cool. They deteriorate quickly at higher temperatures. That's why you see drivers on rain tires looking for puddles when the track begins to dry.

Jeff Braun Talks about Cold Tires

"In 1987 and 1988 I worked with an IMSA Camel Lights team that ran a Ferrari-engined car. Goodyear had just begun to furnish radial tires, and the first examples we got were very difficult to get up to temperature. We crashed the car twice because the drivers didn't have the tire up to temperature. The only way to get them hot enough to have some grip was to abuse them; slide them around. The driver had to be really hard on them by coming out of corners hard on the throttle and pitching the car sideways. It was always dicey because it was difficult to get on the tires hard when they were cold. That's a good way to crash the car.

"The tires are much better now. In the Daytona race that year there were a lot of drivers crashing at the end of pit lane. They'd come in for fresh tires, accelerate out the pit lane and slide into the pit wall before they got back out onto the track. The tires just didn't have much grip until they got up to temperature. I feel that some of that was drivers not paying attention, but some of it was they were caught out because these early Goodyear radials were very hard to heat up quickly."

1992 Indy 500: Effect of Cold Tires

The 1992 Indy 500 was a dramatic example of the effect of cold tires. As we mentioned in the aerodynamics chapter, race day presented an unseasonably low ambient temperature in the 40s. The track was even colder because it hadn't heated up from even lower overnight temperatures. Heat is the usual enemy of tires and Goodyear tends to be conservative at The Brickyard by supplying a relatively hard compound that will stand some abuse with a safety margin. But, given unusually cold temperatures, that same tire proved difficult to get up to working temperature.

Roberto Guererro was the first victim. He spun out on a warm-up lap during a full throttle burst that was supposed to help heat up his rear tires. Instead they grabbed unevenly and thrust him into the wall at a hundred miles an hour.

After the start everything was OK until the first caution flag. During that time at low speeds, the tires cooled off and the first few laps after each restart saw several bad accidents, including Mario and Jeff Andretti, Arie Luyendyk, and Jim Vasser. What the drivers didn't realize was the tires were cooling off during the long trips down the straights, taking several laps to heat up completely instead of just a few corners.

As you can see from the graph, tire temperature is important for proper grip.

Camber Thrust

One of the reasons you see racecars set up with a lot of negative camber (the tops of the tires lean in toward the middle of the car) is that tires produce camber thrust, which adds to lateral force. This is one of the reasons your car darts from side to side when you run along a train track or other road surface elevation change that runs in the same direction as the car. When one side of the contact patch is deformed more than the other, there's a force toward that side.

Bias-ply tires have stiffer sidewalls than radial tires and produce more camber thrust than radials. That's why radials are more forgiving when you run your street car along a train track. This is also the reason you see racecars with more static camber when they have radial tires. The radial tire needs the extra camber to get the same camber thrust that the bias-ply race tire gave at lower camber angles.

You can go too far with camber, however. You don't want the tire running on its inside corner because you're not using all the available tread, and local heat buildup can degrade tire performance. Later in this section we'll look at how NASCAR racers changed their cars to take advantage of camber thrust.

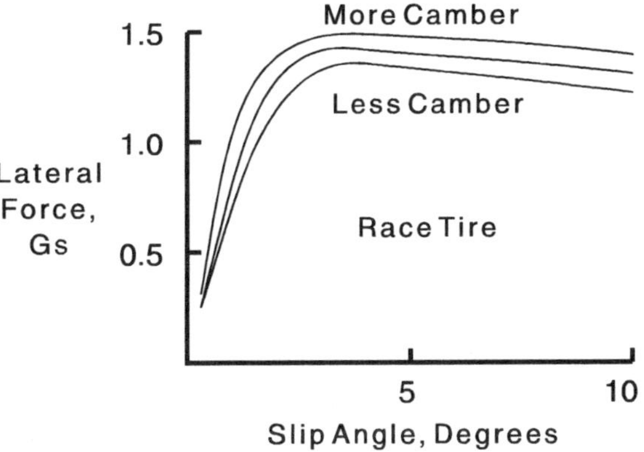

Camber Increases Side Force

Vertical Load

This graph is extremely important because it shows the negative effect of increasing load on a tire. Any car braking or accelerating or cornering transfers load from one side or one end of the car to the other. When a car turns, the outside tires gain load transferred from the inside tires. But this graph shows that lateral force goes down as the vertical load on the tire goes up. That means the outside tires don't gain as much grip as the inside tires lose, and the car has less overall grip.

Weight transfer is bad and this curve shows why. This is why race car designers spend so much time and money making the car's center of mass as low as possible. They try to get all the heavy components as low in the car as they can. NASCAR car builders pay a lot of attention to placing components low, including the driver, and making the overall car very light so they can place big hunks of metal ballast very low in the car. A lower center of mass means less weight transfer.

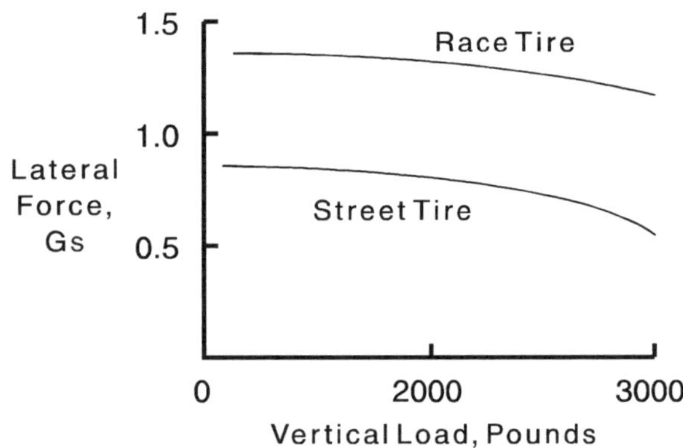

Vertical Load Decreases Side Force

CONSTRUCTION: RADIALS VS. BIAS PLY

Rubber and String

I see a lot of people when I go to IndyCar races. One of them is John Slikkerveer, who was field manager for Goodyear's Racing Tire Division in 1994. John is a tall, serious-looking guy and he always has straightforward answers to my questions. I usually see him standing in the pit lane with a scanner in his ear. John has a tough job, but he always has something interesting to say. Near the end of the 1994 IndyCar season Goodyear was making regular changes in both tire compound and construction. Usually Goodyear tires are very consistent from race to race during a season, and the teams like it that way. The fewer surprises they have the better. Firestone returned to IndyCar racing in 1995, and in late 1994 Goodyear was already beginning to gear up to a more competitive atmosphere.

At the last race of 1994 at Laguna Seca Raceway near Monterey, Calif., Goodyear brought a very sticky tire, and it was causing some setup problems for the teams. I asked John Slikkerveer about the Laguna tire gripes. "It's not a great tire," he said. "It gives up after about 10 laps. We tried something and it didn't work."

"Is this mainly something to do with the rubber compound?" I asked.

"That's right," John said. "We learn all the time and we learned what not to do. We'll fix it."

"At Nazareth [the race just previous to Laguna] there was some griping about too much stagger at the rear," I said. (As you probably know stagger is the difference between the circumference of the rear tires in inches. On a counter-clockwise oval the right rear tire is bigger so, with no differential in the final drive, the car wants to turn left.)

"That's right," John explained. "We work very closely with the teams, so we get feedback about the tires. They said there wasn't enough stagger at Louden so we built in more for Nazareth and went too far. At Louden we had .30 to .31 [inches] and we wanted .35/.36 for Nazareth, but we got .40/.41."

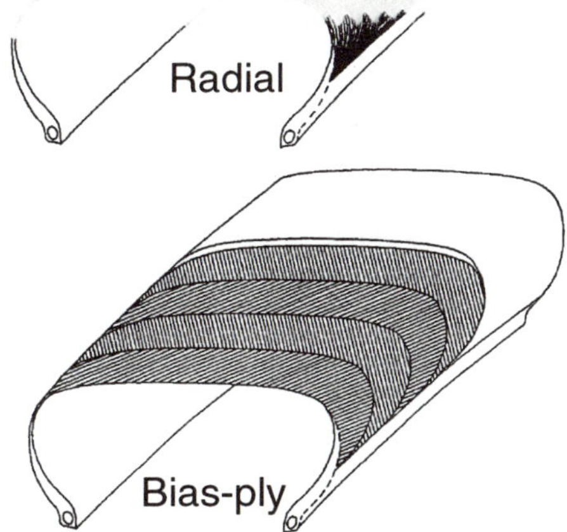

Construction Comparison

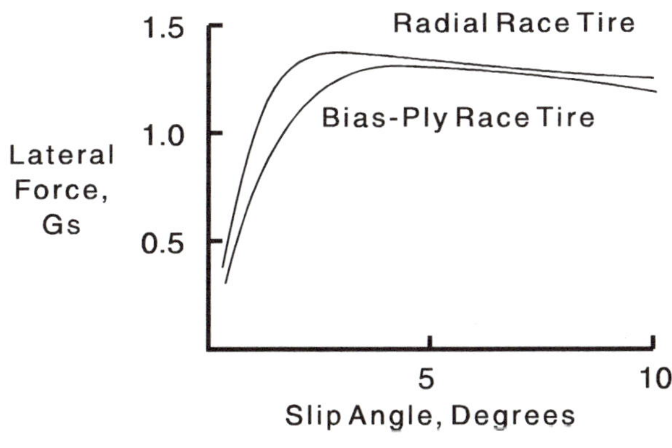

Radial/Bias Ply Comparison

ught you made a mold and got exactly the size you

our manufacturing process," John said. "But there king with rubber and string here." I couldn't help -of-factly and "rubber and string" is such a realistic mplicated device.

ent

of Goodyear) show construction details of a radial e. Both tires are made from layers of fabrics called as nylon, rayon, kevlar, or steel wire. A bias-ply an angle (bias) to the rolling direction of the tire. A ial tire has those fabrics running from bead to d across the tread. In a side view this is the radial dius) direction. A radial tire also has a strengthen-belt around the tire under the tread. The magni-e of the cord angles with respect to the bead and number of the plys as well as the weight and ngth of the fabric materials determines the struction characteristics of the tire.

As you might expect, tires of different construction show different performance characteristics. Look again at this graph of lateral force versus slip angle. The two curves are representative of radial tires and bias-ply tires with similar rubber compounds. The differences in the shapes of these curves mean the tires feel different to the driver. Both curves have a straight, steadily rising shape at low slip angles. As you turn the steering wheel through these first small increments, the side force generated increases in similar small increments. The radial curve, however, is steeper. It generates more side force than the bias ply at a smaller slip angle, so the radial tire feels more responsive to the driver. The radial curve has a higher peak, so it generates more maximum side force.

The radial curve has a sharper peak, too. The radial tire's side force falls off more after the peak than the bias ply. That means its maximum side force is generated over a smaller range of slip angles than a bias ply, and this makes the radial less forgiving than the bias-ply tire. The driver of a bias-ply racecar has a larger range of slip angles to work with at maximum grip. He can turn the steering wheel a little more into the corner if he has to. But, with a radial tire at max grip, if the driver turns the steering wheel more, it's easier to go over the top of the curve where there's less side force and lose control of the car. The driver doesn't have as much time to catch a slide with a radial tire.

What you've got here is a bunch of trade-offs. Tire manufacturers want to supply race teams with radial tires because it's a better tire, and it's the same type of tire they sell to consumers. Radials have a very tough tread belt that resist punctures better than bias-ply tires. Radials are also better race tires because they generate more side force at lower slip angles and heat up less. That means they're more responsive and a softer rubber compound can be used for the tread without increasing wear. Less heat means less rolling friction and therefore better gas mileage and slightly higher top speeds. These are all valuable benefits, but the driver has less margin for error and the car probably wants a different setup. Life is full of trade-offs.

Radial Tires Changed The NASCAR Line Around Sears Point

Sears Point International Raceway is my home track. I don't get to drive on a racetrack much and I'm not a great driver, but I have driven street cars and SCCA Spec Racers at Sears Point. The location is pretty nice, what with San Francisco Bay to the south and the Wine Country just north. The track itself is all turns and is very demanding of both car and driver. There is little runoff room at Sears Point, and any mistake can cost you a bunch.

NASCAR began to race at Sears Point in 1989 and since then the winners have been Ricky Rudd, Rusty Wallace, Davey Allison, and Ernie Irvan. Goodyear supplied bias-ply tires the first three years but switched to radials in 1992, and that completely changed the way the drivers get around this course.

Most drivers looked much smoother on radials in 1992 than they did the year before when the cars were wearing bias-ply tires. Driving on bias plys, the drivers got the car sideways all around the track, including some places where they didn't need to be sideways. A knowledgeable spectator could stand almost anywhere around the course and tell who was going fast by how smooth they looked. Most fans yelled in appreciation when a driver hung it out big in the esses, but really he was just scrubbing off speed. The really smooth drivers like Ricky Rudd looked much less spectacular, but had lower lap times. Rudd qualified on the pole in 1990 and 1991.

Everything changed when Goodyear switched to radial tires at Sears Point in 1992. Since radial tires generate side force at lower slip angles, and the curve falls off quicker after the peak, the drivers can't hang out the rear end like they used to on bias plies. This forced the drivers to use a smoother, less spectacular style. An exception that first year was Darrell Waltrip. He was only slightly slower than Ricky Rudd (fast qualifier once again) and Ernie Irvan, but I don't think he'd caught on to the radials yet. Darrell had an ugly line through the esses. He ran all over the berms trying to straighten out the track, but he had a decent lap time.

I think the switch to radials made watching the NASCAR racers at Sears Point much less exciting. I know they're better tires, but it was fun to watch those guys control the cars at those big slip angles. By the 1993 race everybody had the radials figured out, and the cars all looked the same going through the esses. It just wasn't as much fun to watch!

HOW DO RADIAL TIRES CAUSE BROKEN AXLES?

You may remember that, during the early 1992 NASCAR season, many race winners were late-race survivors after a rash of rear axle failures put the early leaders out of the race. At Martinsville, the last short-track race of the early season, several drivers dropped out, including race leader Dale Earnhardt. All of us watching on TV could see the crews working on the rear axles, and the ESPN announcers talked about drive plate and rear axle failures.

Benny Parsons did a good job of explaining these problems during a report shown on ESPN's *SpeedWeek*. He was taped in Alan Kulwicki's shop showing how camber is easily adjusted on the front of the cars, but not on the rear. The front suspension is a double A-arm type and uses shims to adjust camber, but the rear suspension has no camber adjustment. He said the teams were trying to get some negative camber at the rear of the cars by bending the axle housing, so that the top of the rear tires are closer together than the bottoms. I'd like to expand on that explanation.

Camber

NASCAR specifies most of the parts used to build their "stock cars," and in fact the Winston Cup and Busch Grand National series are successful examples of "spec car" series, which are the future of racing whether we like it or not. The rear axle is a heavy-duty "solid axle." The drive axles run inside a very sturdy housing that firmly links the rear wheels together. If one rear wheel runs over a bump it jerks the other wheel around too. That's the bad news. The good news is a solid axle is tough as nails.

The sketches show a solid rear axle with zero camber and one with negative camber. Positive camber (tires wider apart at the top than at the bottom) is not desirable. Negative camber helps cornering performance. All tires, but particularly radial tires, generate camber thrust, a force in the direction the tire is leaning that adds to the cornering force.

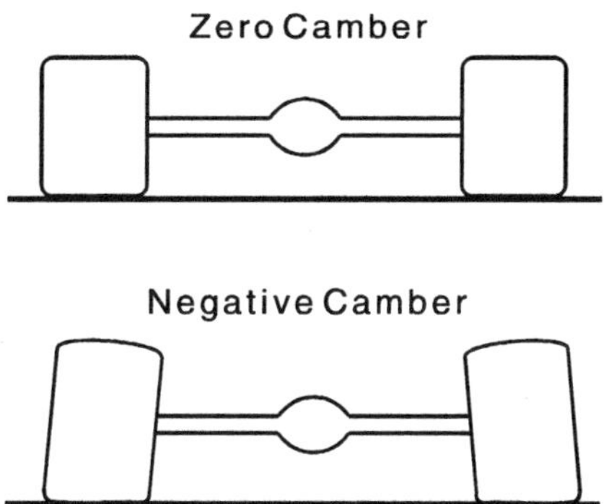

Suspension dynamics, the changes going on during a racing lap, also favor starting out with some negative camber. You can see and measure and adjust the static camber of a racecar when it's sitting still on a level surface. Camber changes during a lap on a track, depending on suspension design and geometry, spring rates, shocks, aerodynamic downforce, track irregularities, and driving style. Tire sidewalls roll under during cornering, affecting tire performance. The combination of all this is to concentrate tire forces on the outside edge of the tire. Under hard cornering the rubber wears more quickly where it gets hot. This is one of the reasons you see crew members taking tire temperatures.

Ideally, you'd like to have the complete contact patch flat on the track when the car is turning hard in a corner. When that happens you're likely to have an even temperature distribution across the tire tread. The outside tires are doing the most work because of weight transfer. If you have adjustable suspension geometry, you make it so the outside tires have some negative camber in a hard corner. Then all the rubber is working, and you get some camber thrust to boot. To make this happen most racecars such as Indy cars and Formula 1 start out with some amount of static negative camber. Static camber and camber change during suspension movement are critical design and development parameters.

Stock car racers have been bending the rear axle housings for years to get a little bit of negative camber. They can get about a half-degree of negative camber pretty easily by using a torch to heat the axle housing at the right place so that, when it cools, the housing has distorted slightly. A half-degree of camber is only about a quarter of an inch difference at the tire tread. There's enough clearance between the splines on the axle and the matching splines in the drive plate so that this small amount of axle housing distortion doesn't cause any big problems.

Radials Like More Camber

Here's another look at the graph that shows the effect of camber on lateral force. Because their sidewalls are less stiff, radial tires need about twice the camber to produce the same camber thrust as a bias-ply tire. That's why, after Goodyear switched to radial race tires in the NASCAR series, the crew chiefs started looking for ways to get more camber at the rear. It was easy on the front suspension because static camber and camber gain with wheel movement are adjustable. It's not so easy at the rear.

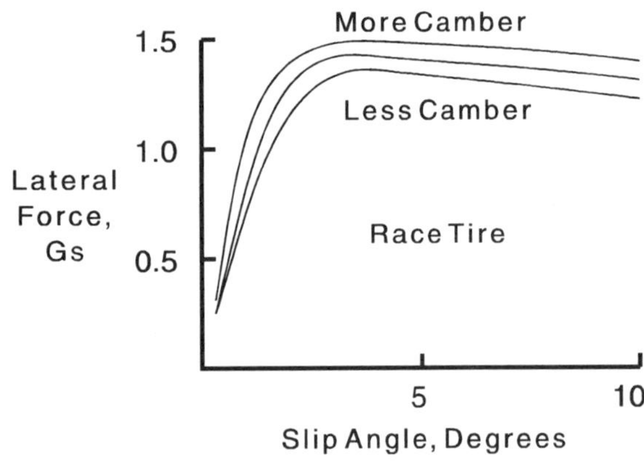

In order to get more than a half-degree of negative camber with a NASCAR rear axle housing, something has to give. The drive plate internal splines and external splines on the axle only have so much clearance between them. These parts transmit more than 700 horsepower from the differential to the rear wheels, and they aren't going to bend just because the axle housing has been distorted! There has to be enough mechanical clearance between the splines to allow the necessary movement.

Benny Parsons explained what was going on during that 1992 TV show. The NASCAR crews ground material from the axle splines so there was some clearance when the splines were misaligned. With that extra clearance they have the effect of a U-joint, but only through a small angle. That way the drive plate, the flange on the end of the axle that drives the rear wheel, can wobble on the axle shaft as it rotates in the plane dictated by the bent axle housing. Some teams were getting as much as 2.5 degrees of negative camber by doing this.

You can visualize this modification by thinking about the ball-ended Allenhead wrenches you can buy in a hardware or tool store. The ball-end wrench is easier to use because it allows some misalignment of the shaft and the bolt you're turning. This is exactly the same concept that the NASCAR guys are using to get controlled misalignment between the axle and the drive plate.

The problem is that grinding on the splines means less material carrying the same drive torque. They don't know they've gone too far until something breaks. Why would they risk axle failure? There is really only one reason—winning. The performance increase due to the increase in negative camber must be substantial for the teams to take the risk of not finishing the race. It's also a measure of just how competitive NASCAR racing is that they would risk axle failure to get this performance edge. Axle failure puts the car out of the race, and it can't be fixed in a few minutes. Winning is extremely important and the teams are willing to try just about anything to increase their chances.

Conversation with Gary Nelson

In 1992, Gary Nelson became the new technical director for NASCAR Winston Cup Racing. Nelson's job is to eliminate the unfair advantage that teams constantly work for, making the NASCAR playing field as fair and level as possible. That's a tough job. The fact that Nelson was a very successful crew chief means that he knows all the tricks of the trade. NASCAR racing is competitive and it doesn't take much of a performance advantage to bring a team from mid-pack to winning races. I looked forward to meeting Nelson when the Winston Cup crowd came to Sears Point in June 1992.

On Friday morning I saw Nelson standing in the garage inspection area. He's in his mid-thirties, has short blond hair, stands about six feet tall, and has a solid, athletic build. His eyes are probably blue, but I couldn't see through the sunglasses. He's a good-looking guy. If he was a driver he'd have a lot of female fans.

I waited my turn patiently as crew chiefs and inspectors came and went with questions and stories. In time, he looked at me and said, "Just a minute" and spoke into a radio briefly. When he was finished, he looked at me again expectantly. I gave my pitch.

"Hi! I'm Paul Haney. I publish this newsletter." As we shook hands, I showed him the June *TV MOTORSPORTS* with the sketches of negative camber and the side force versus slip angle curves. He just listened as I spoke into the sunglasses. "The newsletter gives TV listings for racing and I'm trying to explain technical stuff that I don't see written about in the magazines. I'd like to send you the newsletter, and call sometimes when I have a question."

"Do you charge for this?"

"Yeah, $14 a year."

"Well, I don't think so," he said, and my mouth went dry. "If you send me this for free, then you'd be calling every Monday wanting to know inside stuff."

I was surprised by his negative reaction. I consider my goals to be pretty righteous. Obviously, I hadn't explained things quite right. "I'd never expect that," I protested. "I don't want to know anything you wouldn't tell anyone else. I'm trying to explain some of the technical stuff so racing is more interesting and more fun. But I don't know everything. I need help explaining things."

"I work for these teams," Nelson explained. "I see things that I can't talk about to anybody. If I see Alan Kulwicki [he nodded toward Kulwicki's team working about 20 feet away] doing something that gives him an advantage, I can't tell anybody about it. Like camber; some teams have used that with a lot of success."

"Where did the 1.8 degrees come from?" I asked. After a rash of broken axles, NASCAR came out with a rule limiting rear wheel camber to 1.8 degrees, and I wanted to know why they chose that particular number. "The way we measure it, that's really about 1.4 degrees and some tire stagger," said Nelson. "That's about the most the teams can use reliably with current parts."

"That's the kind of information I'm looking for," I said. "I can write about that, can't I? And I'd like to write about this conversation. This must be a much more sensitive job than I thought for you to have to be so careful."

"Yeah, you can write about that," he said, but he still didn't sound very encouraging. After a thoughtful pause, Nelson said, "Well, maybe I ought to get this thing, so I can see what you're writing. And I'll treat you accordingly."

"Great," I said. "I'd like that. If you give me a card, I'll have your address." He disappeared into the NASCAR trailer and came back with a business card. "OK," he said, still sounding disapproving. "You send it to me and I'll talk to you depending on what you write."

"Great," I said. "Thanks." And I scurried off to get a drink of water to cure my dry mouth. That was a tough sell!

After some reflection, I decided the talk couldn't have gone better. I met the man face to face, got the answer to my camber question, and, more importantly, got some insight into the guy performing one of the most important jobs in racing.

NASCAR Winston Cup is the most successful racing series in the world. It's competitive and exciting, and sponsors aren't hard to find. Creative interpretation of rules is a part of racing and it always will be. In the past, NASCAR officials have sometimes looked silly trying to keep ahead of some of the brighter competitors. I've got a feeling that won't happen as much with Gary Nelson in charge.

Most people agree that Nelson and his staff have kept a pretty level playing field. NASCAR Winston Cup and Busch Grand National racing is the most competitive in the world. What really sets these two NASCAR series apart from all other race series, however, is participants are actually making money. Most racing is paid for by patrons--people with money who spend it on a team or a family member and like to hang around racing. Only the top teams, Penske and Newman-Haas in IndyCar, for example, are actually viable, profit-making businesses. In contrast, many of the Busch teams and almost all of the Winston Cup team owners are making a profit. This, more than anything else, is what makes NASCAR successful.

TIRES ARE SPRINGS TOO

Yes, Firestone is coming back into racing in the IndyCar series. Firestone tested extensively in 1994, and they've begin supplying tires to teams in 1995. Firestone has been a co-sponsor and tire supplier for the Indy Lights series since 1992, and provided competitors in this series with some technical data on the spring rates of their tires.

Front Tire-10.0/22.5R15	Spring Rate, lbs.
Road Course	1,724 lb./in.
Oval	1,786 lb./in.

Rear Tire	Spring Rate, lbs.
Road Course, 14.0/24.5R15	1,724 lb./in.
Oval, 14.0/24.8R15	1,695 lb./in.

This first table shows the spring rate of front and rear tires inflated to 24 pounds per square inch. I assume the data was generated by putting a vertical load on a wheel hub so the tire is loaded the same as it would be on a car. The height of the hub was measured at 500 pounds load and again at 1,000 pounds. The load was divided by the change in height to get the spring rate in pounds per inch. Working backward we can calculate the deflection: 500 lb. divided by 1,724 lb./in. equals 0.29 inches. This says the tire, when inflated at 24 psi, compresses 0.29 inches when the load on it is increased from 500 pounds to 1,000 pounds.

What good is this data? An Indy Lights racecar weighs about 1,600 pounds or 400 pounds per tire with fuel and a driver. In the first section of this book we showed that an Indy Lights racecar generates over 1,000 pounds of aerodynamic downforce at 120 mph. The race engineer wants the car running at optimum ride height and rake when it's out there on course, but the suspension can only be adjusted when the racecar is sitting still on a level surface. The engineer gets suspension movement information from the on-board data-acquisition system. This Firestone data gives the engineer a rough idea how much to allow for tire deflection.

What if you dial a lot of camber into the suspension set-up? Does that make a difference in the spring rate? Yes it does, and Firestone supplied data for that also. The following table shows tire spring rates in lb./in. at three different camber settings and three inflation pressures.

Front Tire, 10.0/22.5R15		Spring Rate, lb./in.	
Tire Pressure	15 psi	20 psi	25 psi
0 camber	971	1,220	1,370
2 degrees	1,063	1,220	1,389
4 degrees	1,000	1,163	1,351

Data for the first table came from a test of the static spring rate with the tire at rest; the data just above came from a test where the tire was rolling at a 3-degree slip angle. That gives you an idea of the kind of sophisticated test equipment a tire manufacturer uses to test tires. The machine necessary for this test has to include a powered roller to drive the tire and against which the tire gets loaded. The part of the machine the tire is mounted on has to be adjustable for camber and include a way to apply and measure the vertical load. It also controls the slip angle and has to be strong enough structurally so it doesn't deflect under any of these conditions.

As you can see, inflation pressure changes the spring rate of the tire much more than camber. Small changes in inflation pressure make a big difference in how a car handles.

Talk With Firestone Tire Engineer Page Mader

At the 1993 Laguna Seca IndyCar event I talked with Firestone Development Engineer Page Mader. Page was working with the Indy Lights teams providing technical support for Firestone race tires. In 1995 Page switched to the Firestone Indy car effort.

PH: "What does a tire development engineer do during a race weekend?"

PM: "Our job is to assist the teams. We answer any questions they have and tell them what we think about their set-up as it relates to our tires. We need to make sure our product looks good. Safety is a big concern. We need to make sure that even a competitor who misses the set-up can run without a tire failure."

PH: "You see each team's set-up. I'll bet you get a lot of racer paranoia. Are they concerned you'll tell other teams what they're doing?"

PM: "Right; that can be a problem. The first year we supplied tires there were some problems. Some people didn't want the tires to change, but later they really liked that we went from 13-inch to 15-inch wheels. Shortening the sidewall makes the car handle better. The teams share info better now. They've learned to trust us."

PH: "Talking about wheel size, CART nixed Firestone's plans to go from 15-inch to 17-inch wheels when they begin to supply IndyCar tires again in 1995."

PM: "Yes, that's too bad. IMSA GTP cars are running 17 and 18 inch wheels, and the tires perform better on bigger rims. It's a political decision, but we have to live with the rules."

PH: "I guess that fits with some of the retroactive technology decisions in racing lately. Racing is supposed to 'improve the breed.' It seems silly to ban technology in racing that's already running on road cars. I can think of ABS, traction control, and active suspension."

PM: "It's too bad if road cars get more innovative than racing."

PH: "Tell me about heat cycles. How many heat cycles do the Firestone Indy Lights tires see before performance goes off?"

PM: "They get four half-hour sessions a weekend. Any tire loses oil as it's run on the track. The oil just comes out of the tires. And heat cures the tire. These tires are pretty stable, but they're fastest when they're new, and then after a few laps the grip falls off slightly."

RUBBER COMPOUNDING

Conversations with Two Compounders

A tire just looks like black rubber that's been molded into a hollow doughnut with a tread on the outside. Believe me, it's much more complicated than that, and the most intricate part of a tire is the compound. Here are conversations with two guys who are responsible for getting the mix right.

Talk With Goodyear Compounder Steve Myers

Steve Myers is Goodyear's chief compounder for race tire programs. He's responsible for determining the mix of materials used in race tires, and he watches over the production and development process. Steve attends races regularly, and when I see him, he always makes time to answer, or decline to answer, my questions.

Steve Myers

"The goal is to develop a combination of ingredients which yields maximum traction while maintaining durability and heat resistance," Steve told me in an early conversation. "A typical compound may have 15 or 20 ingredients, and we make changes in the order of one-hundredth of a part levels, so the difficulty is in trying to find the proper balance of those ingredients."

The main ingredients in the black stuff that makes up a tire, called the compound, are natural and synthetic rubber polymers, curatives, oils, and carbon black, which is what makes the black stuff black.

Polymers need some explaining. For example, polyethylene is a typical polymer that we use as a clear plastic wrap to keep sandwiches or refrigerated leftovers from drying out. Ethane, the monomer of polyethylene, is a fairly simple molecule found in natural gas. It's made up of two carbon atoms bonded to six hydrogen atoms and is the basis for ethyl alcohol, which is the active ingredient in all the alcoholic beverages we drink. Under certain conditions ethane can be made to form long strings of repeating molecules bonded together. The monomer strings together to form a polymer and ethane becomes polyethylene. Natural rubbers, harvested from the sap of the rubber tree, are a complex mixture of polymers. Synthetic rubber polymers are made from specific monomers to form specific polymers such as styrene-butadiene rubber and polybutadiene rubber. Both are used in race tire compounds.

Goodyear produces the synthetic rubbers used in race tires in its own chemical plants. "We don't just buy things over the counter," says Steve. "We don't want other tire companies to know exactly what materials we're using in our tires. Goodyear has the ability through modeling and predictive testing to design custom, specialty polymers with very unique physical properties."

Carbon black is an important component of a race tire compound. It's a filler, but it also adds strength to the compound. The carbon black variables, most importantly particle size, greatly affect the properties of the final compound. "If you have a smaller-particle carbon black, it probably has more surface area and generates more heat than a larger-particle black," says Steve. "Passenger car compounds tend to have lower levels of black and a larger particle size than a race tire or a performance tire because, while smaller particle size and more black gives you more traction, it also generates more heat. In developing a passenger tire or a truck tire, you're looking more for low rolling resistance, but what we want in auto racing, generally speaking, is something that's going to give the maximum amount of traction."

As always, there are trade-offs. "There are literally hundreds of different kinds of carbon black available for use in compounding," Steve says. "Each black, when added to a compound with certain properties, improves traction, adhesion, heat resistance, or wear. So you look at those properties whenever you develop a new compound and find out whether this tire is going to run 10 degrees warmer than that tire, or is this compound going to wear out faster? Will it produce more traction?"

The amount of carbon black mixed into the compound also varies among different applications. NASCAR tires used on superspeedways, for example, may have compounds similar to those found in a softer passenger car/high performance tire. At the other extreme would be a Formula 1 qualifying tire designed to provide maximum adhesion for just a couple of laps. "That's a very unique compound altogether," says Steve, "with very different requirements."

When the carbon black has been chosen the next consideration is the processing oil. Again, there are many trade-offs. These oils can be plasticizers or tackifiers depending on their chemical nature and, when mixed with all the other ingredients, yield specific characteristics in the tire. "If you've got a track up in the Northeast, a short track where they race modified stock cars and they run at night when it's 30 or 40 degrees, you'd use different oils than if you were going to develop a tire for Rio de Janeiro or Sao Paul or Phoenix or some place where it's over 100 degrees," says Steve. "So sometimes you have to customize the compound to a particular track."

A major difference between compounds for race tires and passenger tires is in the amount and number of oils used. A typical passenger car tire might have three or four types of processing oils, but a racing tire will typically use twice as many oils and more of it. Race compounds are very soft and are difficult to mix and process, but the total number of tires produced is not large compared to passenger tires. The cost of the oils and the processing of passenger car tires is very important, and that figures into the choice of oils more than in racing tires.

Another important ingredient in tire compounds is the curatives. Classified as accelerators or sulfurs, the curatives control the rubber vulcanization process and determine the degree of cross-linking in the compound during the molding process. These curatives are largely responsible for the final physical characteristics of the tire.

Goodyear engineers have accumulated an extensive database of these physical characteristics over the years. Each tire's modulus, hardness, dynamic stiffness, and adhesion is carefully measured and recorded. These characteristics are predictable given the compound ingredients and the manufacturing process for each tire.

"The number one thing in racing is the performance," says Steve. "So maybe you can compromise on your output, or the cost on some of the specialty materials that we use that you couldn't justify in other tire areas. We in the racing department have wider capabilities because our quantities are low, and we can use some specialized materials such as special polymers, special oils, and, if it takes longer to produce those and to process those, you can do that if ultimately you're going to have a tire with better performance."

Getting that performance, however, is complicated. There are a lot of choices and trade-offs. "Anything you do to the compound to help grip-wise is usually going to hurt you heat-wise," says Steve. "So you can make changes and add carbon black, you can go to different particles sizes, and you can get more traction and help the performance of the tire, but generally it's going to run hotter. It's constantly a compromise. If you improve your dry traction maybe you give up on your rolling resistance or your wet traction or your handling or your ride. It's always finding that proper balance that's the big challenge in racing."

Dwayne Joyner, Firestone Compounder

I also talked to Dwayne Joyner, a project engineer in the Race Tire Development Group at Bridgestone/Firestone. We started the conversation with Dwayne talking about polymers. "A polymer is like a backbone," he said. "You start with monomers, single-chemical molecules that are all alike. You create a reaction by bringing the monomers in contact with a catalyst and heat. They chain up into big, long molecules like a backbone. This is the first step in making a synthetic rubber or any other synthetic polymer."

PH: "Is cross-linking a part of the curing process?"

DJ: "Yes. Curing the rubber makes it stronger by generating cross-links between the long, backbone-like polymers. If you add sulfur and some heat you can get the polymers to bond together. This is cross-linking. Some types of cross-links are stronger than others and a more complete cure has more cross-links than a less complete cure. The amount of curatives in the compound, sulfur and other so-called accelerants; the curing temperature in the mold; and the time in the mold are variables that determine the degree of curing. It all happens in the mold. Uncured rubber goes into the mold, and heat, mechanical pressure, and time in the mold determine the effect the curing process has on the tire produced."

PH: "What materials do you use in the rubber and how does that and the curing process vary to produce street tires versus race tires?"

DJ: "Materials in the compound are synthetic or natural rubbers, carbon blacks of different types or sizes, oils, and curatives and/or accelerators such as sulfur. Passenger tires are a compromise weighted toward durability, soft ride, traction in a variety of conditions, and low cost. Race tires, on the other hand, maximize traction--that is lateral and longitudinal forces. A race tire runs hotter and sacrifices wear to get traction. Cost is less of a consideration. Race tire production runs are short because a lot of entirely different designs are produced.

"In general a race tire has stronger cross links than a passenger tire. That's one of the characteristics that makes a race tire work at higher temperatures that would hurt the performance of a street tire. Performance tires sold for use on street cars, however, are getting closer and closer to race tires."

PH: "What happens when a tire goes off?"

DJ: "It's overheated, but not enough to blister. If it cools down a little it's OK again. The tire feels greasy when it gets too hot."

PH: "What about heat cycles?"

DJ: "Whenever the car is on the track using the tires hard, they're losing oil and getting harder. Bonds in the rubber break as the tire is used. What we try for is some degree of durability and very good repeatability from tire to tire and session to session until the tire goes off."

PH: "Firestone has been a major sponsor for the Indy Lights series. What specific characteristics did you try for in designing the Indy Lights race tires?"

DJ: "The tire has to be durable for that car on the tracks they run. We take into account the number of sessions during a race weekend, the race distance, the weight of the car, the top speed, the downforce, the lateral Gs the car generates, engine torque, and wheelspin. We also want a limited number of tire options, hopefully only one oval track tire and one road course tire. We came pretty close, but we did have some problems, especially at the first race of 1993 at Phoenix. The Indy Lights Lola car was new, and we didn't have a chance to do any testing. There was some blistering at Phoenix and again at Nazareth. Nazareth is a hard track on tires."

Passenger Tires Don't Always Work Well on the Track

In the late 1980s SCCA Spec Racers, then called Sports Renault, used Goodyear Eagle radial passenger car tires. Drivers had to be careful how hot they got the tires. If they got too hot their color would change from black to steel-blue and the rubber would get noticeably harder. One lap run too fast or several hot sessions on track would seriously affect the tire. It seems, with some tires, there's a total time and temperature threshold that kills them. A short time at a high temperature can do it or a longer time at a lower temperature will take the tire to a higher degree of curing and make it useless for grip. Race tires are usually more completely cured during the molding process and are not as adversely affected by heat as passenger car tires.

Tire technology continues to trickle down to street tires. Performance street tires have steadily become more like race tires. These days, if you autocross your car or compete in SCCA Solo 1 or Showroom Stock classes, you can buy tires that look like street tires and fit your car fine, but are made with compounds more like race tires. They have more grip and can take higher temperatures and more heat cycles.

Jeff Braun on Heat Cycles

"I ran some customers in Sports 2000 a few years ago, and the choice in tires was either Goodyear or Firestone. Goodyear had a good tire, but it was sensitive to heat cycles. It was good for about three heat cycles. The Firestone tire didn't seem to produce quite as much grip as the Goodyear, but was good for 10 heat cycles. I ran my customers on Firestones because, with Goodyears, you'd send the guy out and he'd run one session, and we'd determine what changes we needed to make and go out again and we'd probably do better. The third session there'd be some more changes, and the car was getting better still. The fourth session the car wasn't the same. We'd start changing the car, but really the tires had changed. With the Firestones we could go eight, nine, or 10 sessions, and we'd always make a nice steady progression toward a better setup. When we put new Firestones on the car it didn't change the balance of the car. It had more grip because the tires were fresh. With Goodyears, the tires would go away after three heat cycles, and you ended up with a change in the balance of the car. I'd always prefer a tire that is good for more heat cycles even if you give up a little grip. That way you can work on the car longer without having to buy new tires, when all you're doing is looking for a good set-up.

"That year in that series I chose Firestone, but things change. In 1994 at the SCCA's National Runoffs at Mid-Ohio, Goodyear had the best tire for the Sports 2000, Formula Ford, and Formula Continental classes. Firestone wasn't supplying tires for club racing at that time."

FORMULA 1 MOTORCYCLE TIRES

1994 USGP at Laguna Seca

Laguna Seca is a beautiful racing facility, and for a few years it was the site of the only United States Grand Prix. In the summer of 1994 I was able to spend a day at this amazing event.

Friday morning was the only time I could be there. I got to the track early and was able to talk to a few people and watch one practice session of each class: 125cc, 250cc, and 500cc. One of the things that struck me as I walked through the paddock area was how small everyone was-riders especially, but also crew members. Just about everybody in the paddock was either skinny or short or both. A small rider obviously improves a bike's performance, and I guess most people associated with motorcycle racing are riders or ex-riders or wanna-be riders.

Since tires are probably as important in motorcycle racing as in auto racing, I went to the Dunlop tent and asked if I could talk to an engineer. Somebody pointed to a tall guy with a brown mustache. He said his name was Allan Nichols and he was a service engineer. "I work the pit lane and take tire temps and such. We bring two containers of tires to each race, about 2,000 total. For instance, we have about 15 different types of 500cc rear tires and 15 fronts too. One container comes by sea and the other comes by air."

Allan led me over to the open end of a standard, beat-up, steel cargo container filled to the top with closely-stacked, black, shiny tires. They're a lot skinnier than the tires you see at a four-wheeled race, and the tread area isn't flat. The sidewalls are very short and they transition into curves which meet in a rounded peak on the centerline of the tire. When the bike is straight up, the tire runs on the rounded point, and the contact patch is small. Laid over in a turn, the tire puts down a bigger patch onto the track surface. "Do you bring tires with differences in both compound and construction?" I asked.

"Yes," Allan said in a soft British accent. "And we also bring a small quantity of treaded rain tires and intermediate wets, which are just grooved slicks."

"Are they all radials?" I asked.

"All except the 125cc front tire," Allan answered. "We switched to radials about five years ago. The 125s are on 3.5-inch rims, the 250s 5.5, and the 500cc bikes run on 6.5-inch rims." He picked up a couple of tires and said one had a softer compound than the other. I poked a thumbnail into each of them. My thumb sank easily into the softer one, and the mark recovered slower than in the harder tire.

"Is the recovery rate of that mark my fingernail leaves a good indication of the hysteresis of the rubber compound?" I remembered reading something about high hysteresis rubber compounds having better traction in some conditions.

"That's right," said Allan, "That's a tire we build in the U.K. We also build tires in Japan, and they usually have a more flexible carcass and lower hysteresis rubber, while we make stiffer, higher hysteresis tires in the U.K." I could actually feel the differences he described as I fondled and poked different tires.

"Do the two groups, U.K. and Japan, compete to see who can make faster tires?"

"Yes," Allan answered. "We talk to each other a lot, but we seem to take different approaches to tire design."

"Does that mean that a tire is so complicated that there's just a lot of different directions to go toward making a faster tire?"

"I thinks that's probably right," said Allan, smiling. "We keep making better tires but the bikes aren't going any faster. On most tracks they're slower than they were in 1989."

"Really?" I said, amazed to hear that." Why is that?"

"I'm not sure," Allan said, his grin broadening. "I think it depends on who you ask."

So I Asked Kevin Cameron

My local public library has a large selection of magazines, and I always look in *Cycle World* for Kevin Cameron's column. I think he's the best motorsports technical writer, and I told him so when I found him in the Media Center at Laguna Seca. He was pleased to hear me say I enjoyed his work, as we all are pleased when someone compliments us. Writing, after all, is kinda like spitting off a cliff. You may never know if anyone appreciates your efforts.

Kevin Cameron is probably about my age (49 forever), and has a round face under thinning hair. He wears a full, close-trimmed beard that is dark with flecks of silver. He grins as he talks and his eyes are quick and intense, as if driven by dueling questions and answers. We quickly got into a discussion that taught me a lot about motorcycles. I asked him why the bikes aren't going any faster?

"I think it's poor systems integration," he said. "The tires keep getting better. The engines get better. The suspension people keep making improvements. But all these people work on their own isolated developments. They don't seem to talk to each other. They keep improving their own components, trying to do more of what the riders say they want, but I think these components don't work together well and so the bikes don't go any faster."

Kevin continued to explain. "The tires, for instance, get better, and the engines are up around 200 horsepower now, and they have an amazingly wide power band compared to a few years ago. Coming out of the corners with all that power and a sticky rear tire all planted to the track with a sophisticated suspension results in a huge amount of weight transfer toward the rear. That means that all the weight is on the rear tire, and the front tire just doesn't work. The rider can't steer with the front wheel, because there's no weight on it. The 250cc riders have less power and they can accelerate laid over, but the 500cc riders carry speed through the corner all laid over at part throttle, and then when they're going straight they tilt the bike up and pop open the throttle. Mick Doohan is the only one you'll hear coming out of the corners with big bursts of power. He's the only one that is willing or able to steer with the rear wheel."

"You mean he uses the throttle to slide the rear tire and steer the bike?"

"I guess that's what he's doing," Kevin said. "That's how it's been explained to me. His style is different and that's what it looks like. He's the one winning races."

I was amazed to hear this. I never expected to run into such an interesting situation. If I hadn't talked to Allan and Kevin I would never have noticed anything because I don't follow two-wheel racing closely enough. Even after hearing this explanation I couldn't really see much difference except that Doohan did seem to be on the throttle more and earlier than other riders.

Goodyear (left) and Firestone '95 Indy Car Tires.
Notice the different tread shapes at the shoulders.

The Firestone Indy Car technical support crew at Miami. From the
left it's Page Mader, Debbie Brown's back, Dale Harrigale in the cap,
and Dwayne Joyner in the Sunglasses.

CHAPTER 3

COMPUTERS IN RACING

Computers seem to be everywhere. All new cars now coming out of Detroit and Japan and Europe have microprocessors, and many have digital displays instead of the usual analog gauges. Some computers on-board these cars perform useful tasks and improve performance and drivability. Others are there for marketing reasons.

Without these computer-controlled engine management systems (EMS), modern cars would not be as powerful, easy to drive, or fuel efficient, and would produce much more air pollution. Powerful, inexpensive microprocessors are the heart of these sensing and control systems. Simple tables of numbers called "maps" in these computers precisely control when each fuel injector turns on and off, and when each spark plug fires.

In the last 10 years computers have become very important in racecars. Very sophisticated engine management systems make racing engines more powerful, more fuel efficient, and easier to drive.

Here are a few points I'd like to emphasize about computers.

1. There is no magic. Computers are tools invented, designed, manufactured, and used by humans to do ordinary tasks quicker and easier.

2. Computers do not replace humans. For example, now that data acquisition is a necessary racing tool, every serious team needs at least one new person dedicated to data acquisition.

3. It's the computer software that really matters. Computer hardware, although difficult to keep working in the heat and vibration of the automotive environment, is made up of relatively simple and available components. The software is where the bulk of the human creativity comes to bear.

This chapter is organized so that we talk about data acquisition first, and then Jeff Braun tells us what a racecar engineer does. Next, we give a couple of examples of how on-board computers use acquired data to control critical variables. Finally, Ian Reed tells us about Formula 1 technology in 1994, and how the Ligier team used computers during a tragic and stormy Formula 1 season.

INTRODUCTION TO ON-BOARD DATA ACQUISITION

In addition to engine management systems (EMS), racecar computers also control active suspension systems, gear shifting, traction control systems, automatic braking systems (ABS), clutch engagement systems, launch control, engine throttle position, and data-acquisition systems for both the engine and the chassis. All these control systems need accurate information about the current state of whatever it is on the car they are trying to control. That means there has to be a good data-acquisition system, also called a data logger, to provide that information. So, let's start off with an explanation of data-acquisition systems.

Mario Andretti on Data Acquisition

Mario Andretti talked about racecar data-acquisition systems during a 1991 Indy 500 TV preview show that I captured on videotape. This was during the time that he and his son, Michael, both drove Indy cars for Newman-Haas racing. "Many, many years ago I used to say, 'If I could just tape a little mouse back there on the suspension that could just tell me what's going on in the corners.' We have that now, you see. That little mouse just tells you everything, whatever goes on in the engines with telemetry and a lot of the suspension movements and loadings."

Mario went on, "So we have so much more information, of course, that you're answering a lot of questions that have been just a lot of gray for us in the past. It's still seat-of-the-pants work. The computers are not the ones that ultimately give you the car all set up on the track or anything like that. But, it expedites the set-up situation, the set-up problems, and also it tells you everything about the engines, if you over-rev or where you are through the corners. You can't lie to your crew chief anymore, or your engineer. It's all there in black and white. We have teamwork just like Michael and I. You can superimpose a graph of speed or revs through any type of course, and you know exactly who gains or loses where. So you can really go to the core of the problem pretty quickly. So it elevates the knowledge to the next dimension. Obviously pretty much everyone is using these systems, and so I think it refines the technical side of it all and it's fun in a different way, I suppose. You leave a lot less to chance, if you will."

What Mario is talking about, in his inimitable verbal style, is on-board data acquisition. That means there are sensors on-board the car that are continuously measuring some characteristic such as oil pressure, wheel speed, or suspension movement. The sensors are connected to a computer that reads these devices at a specified time interval, usually every tenth or hundredth of a second. The computer reads and stores this data while the car is being driven on the track.

There are two ways to get the data out of the on-board computer. Most teams transfer the data through a cable to a laptop computer while the car is stopped in the pits. The data can also be transmitted to a trackside computer by radio. The latter, called telemetry, can be broadcast continuously as the racecar goes around the track but, more often, gets transmitted in a high-speed burst when the car is on the track going past the receiver in the team's pit cart. The data is displayed graphically on a personal computer and analyzed by the crew chief or engineer. The results, as Mario says, are not ultimate answers right off the computer screen, but provide information that can be used to determine which direction to go toward a better car set-up or better driver technique.

To use Mario's "little mouse" analogy, an on-board data-acquisition system with telemetry is like the little mouse running around on the racecar as it is being driven, reading strategically placed gauges and immediately relaying that information by radio to the crew chief.

It's Not Magic

Does this sound like magic? Well, it's not. It's not even that new. The NASA manned space program began using transmitted data from satellites and rocket boosters more than 30 years ago. Industrial Data-acquisition and Control Systems, the monitoring and control of entire plant processes, is now a billion-dollar business in the United States alone. The wide availability of affordable personal computers and easy-to-use, flexible application software have made this possible.

In that television interview Mario said several important things about on-board data acquisition, not the least of which is that the driver can't lie to his crew chief anymore. This doesn't mean drivers are liars. Driving a racecar is a very difficult athletic undertaking, and, although Mario can probably recall an amazing amount of data from a practice lap, it's not reasonable to expect him to remember the exact position of the throttle at every moment on every lap. But a computer can record that and much more!

Mario also talked about how information from on-board data acquisition benefits a two-car team. Data from each car can be superimposed on a graph to show where one driver is faster on the track than another. Driver technique or set-up changes can be transferred from the faster car and driver to the slower one. This is one of the major reasons why you see Indy car and Formula 1 teams organized with two drivers. They only have so much time during a race weekend, and they can get closer to the optimum race set-up quicker if they use two drivers going in different set-up directions during each track session and pool the resulting information.

Formula 1 teams have been using on-board data-acquisition systems for more than 10 years. At the 1988 Detroit Grand Prix, I saw a dozen Epson (a Japanese computer manufacturer and team sponsor) engineers supporting the real-time telemetry system used by the McLaren-Honda team. All Indy car teams have data-acquisition systems with telemetry installed in their cars. The larger, more successful Indy car teams have at least one person per car who is responsible for downloading data from the on-board system. Most top Indy car teams have several people working with the data and many have a full-time electronic technician to install and service all the sensors and connectors. Data-acquisition systems are now considered to be tools as necessary as torque wrenches and ratchets.

WHAT IS A DATA-ACQUISITION SYSTEM?

An on-board data-acquisition system is composed of a box containing a microprocessor, some analog-to-digital (read "A to D") signal conversion circuitry, memory (both random access and read-only), a battery or connection to the car battery, and cables linking the computer to the sensors. The sensors continuously measure parameters like throttle position or wheel speed.

Some sensors supply data in the form of continuously varying voltage, while others give voltage pulses. Throttle position data, for example, comes from a linear displacement sensor installed in the throttle linkage, so it moves when the throttle moves. This sensor supplies a varying voltage value from zero to 5 volts as it goes from fully compressed to fully expanded. The computer software changes the voltage values to percent of wide-open throttle. For example, 4.21 volts may correspond to 85% throttle and 3.05 volts to 52%. It's up to the crew to install, calibrate, and maintain the sensor.

The speed of the car comes from a magnetic pickup mounted close to a bolt or a magnet that's rotating on a driveshaft or wheel hub. A voltage pulse appears in the wire to the computer every time that bolt, or any other bolts on that circle, pass by the sensor. The computer has to have a "counter circuit" to capture this data. This counter circuit, maybe a single computer chip, counts the pulses over a specified time period such as one second and places that number in the data.

At selected time intervals (typically one to 100 times a second), the computer reads the sensors or reads and resets the counter chips. As the driver charges around the track, all these sensor readings are stored in the on-board computer's memory. When the car is stopped in the pits between track sessions, the stored data is then transferred to another computer, probably a battery-powered laptop. After the on-board computer is reset, the driver can go back out on the track and gather more data.

A Race Engineer Downloads Data from the On-board
Computer System to a Laptop Computer.

TYPICAL DATA-ACQUISITION SYSTEMS

One of the characteristics of computer systems is that as time passes, they continually get more powerful and less expensive. In 1986 I worked for a company that ruggedized standard commercial computer systems so they could be used in military applications. We bought a computer called a Micro VAX from Digital Equipment Corp. and repackaged it in a stronger box with shock-absorbing mounts and other modifications. The Micro VAX was THE hot system then. It cost a minimum of $30,000 and it performed 1 MIP–that's one million instructions per second. At this minute in mid-1995 I'm working with an IBM-PC compatible computer that cost me about $2,000 and it's rated at 30 MIPs. This trend will continue forever, so the costs of data-acquisition systems we mention in the paragraphs below could change rapidly.

Data-acquisition systems are available right now for less than $1,000. They will sense and record engine rpm and wheel speed. The software that comes with these systems is not as fully featured as software that comes with more expensive systems. For a serious racer on a budget, however, these systems can supply a lot of information that can help tune the car and the driver. SCCA club racers and weekend circle track drivers can benefit, if they take the time to learn how to use the equipment and the data.

At the upper end of club racing and the lower level of pro racing there are systems available for $3,000 to $5,000. A typical setup has six channels, which means it measures six sensors at the same time, and can store up to 30 minutes of data. Those six basic sensors are usually engine rpm, wheel speed, steering wheel position, throttle position, lateral acceleration, and longitudinal acceleration. Exhaust gas temperature sensors are available if engine tuning is important. If a team wants to tune the suspension geometry, ride height, or shock absorbers, a displacement sensor at each wheel gives data about suspension movement. This data isn't any good unless it's read 100 or 200 times a second minimum, and this eats up memory. The software that comes with these systems can be very useful.

Indy Lights and Indy cars come with a built-in digital dashboard and an optional data-acquisition system built by PI Systems in England. A complete system may cost $60,000. Most Indy Lights teams use the six basic sensors and shock travel sensors described above, but Indy car teams use a much more complicated system that usually includes radio frequency telemetry between the car and a receiver in the pit lane.

As we showed in the aerodynamics section, ride height (the distance between the bottom of the car and the track surface) and rake (the angle of the bottom with respect to the track) are very critical to making an Indy car lap quickly. Precise measurements of the car on a level surface when it's stationary in the pits combined with suspension movement data from linear displacement sensors at each damper, allow the software to calculate the dynamic ride height while the car is on course. At the Indianapolis Motor Speedway during practice for the Indy 500, big-bucks teams may use a more direct measurement of ride height, such as accurate but expensive laser sensors.

During a race the two most critical pieces of information to an Indy car team are turbocharger boost pressure and fuel flow rate. The rules say the engine is limited to 45 inches of mercury absolute pressure or about 22 pounds per square inch. Since normal atmospheric pressure is 15 psi, 22 psi represents 7 psi boost. The driver wants the engine operating as close to maximum as possible, so his engine is putting out all the power it's capable of. That's why you see boost pressure numbers shown on every Indy car digital dash.

Because Indy cars are limited to 1.8 gallons of fuel for each mile of the race (except for the Indy 500), the amount of fuel the engine is using during the race is another very critical piece of data. Some years ago vane-type flow meters were used for this measurement, but now the engine management system knows how long each fuel injector squirts and how much fuel that orifice flows at its operating pressure. The EMS adds up every squirt and sends a number for total gallons of flow to the dash and through telemetry to the pit lane. Indy car fuel tanks are limited to 40 gallons, but depending on the design and installation of the fuel system they may not have 40 usable gallons. The teams know just how many gallons they can get out of each car's tank, however, and that number (38.9 or 39.2) is what you see written on tape on the steering wheel. This is a reminder for the driver that he better be stopped in the pit lane before the total fuel flow number on the dash gets to the number taped on the steering wheel.

The data analysis software that comes with these data-acquisition systems is the most important feature by far. A car would be no good at all if the steering wheel was in the trunk. A computer is also worthless unless it has software that does something useful and lets a normal human being operate it.

If you want to know more about data acquisition in racecars you should buy a book called *Data Power* by Buddy Fey. He goes into much more detail than we do here.

JEFF BRAUN, RACECAR ENGINEER

What Does a Racecar Engineer Do?

Jeff explains what he does when someone hires him as a race engineer.

"In simple terms, whether somebody hires me for a weekend or a project or a season, when I come to the racetrack my job is to make the whole team—the car, the driver, everything—work the best it can on that given day. That's my job, all aspects of that.

Jeff Braun talks to a driver at Laguna Seca Raceway.

"If I look around and see a mechanic whose time could be better spent working on the gearbox instead of cleaning out a drain pan from the gear change he just did, I'll clean out the drain pan and let him get to something more important. I'll sweep the floor if necessary. I need to be doing whatever improves the effort, whatever makes the car go faster or the team work better. Whatever I can do to make that happen, that's my job. I go into a job with that theory. It's a whatever-it-takes kind of deal.

"More technically, the race engineer is what in industry would be called a development engineer or a research and development engineer. R&D, that's what I do. The neat thing about racing is the R&D has to be done in about 30 minutes. You don't have three months to research and develop and go back to the engineers. You have to do it all right now. That's what I like about racing. You get instant results. You find out if you're good or you're bad, if you've done good or bad, in 30 minutes.

"I think some people, some race engineers, miss the all-encompassing part of the job that I think is important. The race engineer is there to improve the performance of that vehicle, whatever that means. If it means telling the driver he's the best driver you've ever seen when you think he needs an ego boost, you do it. Or you tell him he's the world's jerkiest driver and can't get out of his own way, if that's what gets him all fired up. If it means sympathizing with the mechanics because they had to stay up all night, you do it saying 'poor baby' and 'that's just terrible' and 'I can't believe they made you guys do that.' That's what you do if it makes the car faster. That's my job—whatever makes the car go faster.

"Some race engineers get caught up in the 'I'm the technical tirector' kind of thinking. They say, 'I just do the esoteric technical stuff. That's all that matters.' I see a lot of people who want to be too technical. There's something missing with that attitude. I know why I think this way, because I've been the team manager, the crew chief, the grunt mechanic. That experience helps me see the whole picture rather than looking at it as a specialty. That's why I like race engineering, because it is all encompassing. You don't get stuck away in some corner like you only have one thing to do."

A Typical IMSA Data-Acquisition System

Jeff describes the data-acquisition systems he used during the 1992 season when he was the engineer on a two-car IMSA Camel Lights team.

"We used a Stack system with a digital dashboard. We recorded engine rpm, axle rpm, steering position, throttle position, longitudinal and lateral acceleration, battery volts, oil pressure and temperature, water temperature, shock travel on each wheel, four differential air pressure values in the ground-effects tunnels, and two brake temperatures, one each front and rear."

As you can imagine, this is a lot of data to read and analyze. Jeff has worked with data acquisition and signal processing software for more than 10 years, and he constantly improves his methods, "I've written some software macros that allow me to display the answers I need right away. When the car comes off the track I plug the cable from my laptop into the on-board computer and start the data download. A few seconds later I unplug and hit one key. By the time I turn around and put the laptop on the pit wall, I've got the answers I need. I can look at the screen, make some decisions, and then tell the crew what changes to make within 45 seconds of the car stopping in the pits."

Does that sound like magic? It's not. Like most of the amazing things in racing, it's just people like Jeff working hard and smart.

A Very Simple Data-Acquisition System

Data-acquisition systems don't have to be high tech. Jeff tells us about a simple system that worked.

"John Brumder drove in Trans-Am in 1990. SCCA had outlawed data-acquisition systems. You couldn't have anything on the car–no computer, no systems at all. Tom Kendall and Chris Kniefel were wining in the Berettas. Everybody was using computers in testing and they were supposed to be off the car for the race. We ran them anyway, as did everybody else.

"But then they really started to clamp down and not let anybody use on-board computers, so we decided to try something that would give similar info but still be inside the rules. We put a video camera in the car that looked out the front windshield just like a lot of people do. There was plenty of room in those cars. You could do this same thing in a Sports 2000, for example, and all sedans.

"They didn't allow any electronic data-gathering devices. So I drew up this little deal that was nothing more than a piece of aluminum with springs and cables and pointers. We mounted this thing on the dash. It had four pointers with springs. One was hooked to the gas pedal with an extra throttle cable. One was hooked to the steering. One was hooked to one front shock and another was hooked to one rear shock. They pulled against the spring on the board and there were pointers and marks on the board for scale. We turned the video camera so it saw the board as well as out the windshield. As John drove around the racetrack the pointers moved up and down as he turned the steering wheel and pushed on the gas and the shocks went up and down. The camera recorded it all on videotape.

"When John came back to the pits, we could freeze-frame the tape just as he was turning in to the corner and see what his throttle position was, see what the shock travel was, see the steering position. We could watch the throttle position coming out of the corner just by watching the pointer move. We could see him turn the wheel the other way to catch an oversteer as these pointers moved. You could see out the front of the car plus all this other data. The whole thing cost about $50 bucks—aluminum, springs, and motorcycle throttle cables. That was a data-acquisition device that cost almost nothing. Every racer who can afford a video camera can afford something like that. People say, 'I can't afford data acquisition.' Yeah, you can!"

Visual Aid for Drivers

On-board data-logging systems provide information that helps drivers improve their lap times. It's better if two or more drivers share data about car set-up and driving technique. In this story Jeff had four drivers to work with.

"I worked for the Scandia IMSA Camel Lights team in 1992. We went testing on the road course inside the oval at Phoenix International Raceway. We used a bunch of segment markers with our data-acquisition system. These segment markers are a light source you put on the edge of the track, and the computer sees them and puts marks in the data as the car goes by. You know exactly when the car goes by each marker. This is great for driver development.

"We had four drivers for one car. One driver was much better going into the fast first turn than the other drivers. The other three drivers couldn't get it right at that first corner. That's where you come down the front straight of the 1-mile oval and turn in left, just before the oval Turn 1. We couldn't tell what the other drivers were doing wrong, but their times in that segment were a half-second slower than the faster driver's times.

"The data pointed out several things. First it showed where everybody was quicker and slower. Then we started looking at all the detail data, and the drivers used that to figure out what was going on. The fast guy was on the throttle much longer on the straight and was turning in to the corner at a different point. The data didn't exactly teach them what to do, but it showed them it COULD be done and why one of them was a half-second quicker. It was all in that one corner. They knew it could be done, and if he could do it they could too. The rest of them got their half-second too. The data made them all better, because they could see it for themselves.

"Later we tested at Road America and it was the same thing. We didn't have all the segment timers, but the drivers started studying the data I was giving them and although each one didn't necessarily want to use the same throttle position or steering position as the other guys, they did want to know where they were slower, so they could concentrate on that. There's so many critical parts to a racetrack that, if the drivers know where to concentrate their attention, they can work on that part and lap times get better.

"Data acquisition for driver coaching does the same as data acquisition for engineering. It points out the weaknesses and strengths so you know what you're doing well and can concentrate on what you can improve. That's what's really nice about data acquisition from both the driver coaching standpoint and the engineering standpoint. It points out where you're good and where you're bad. Sometimes in engineering and driving, that's the biggest problem. Why am I slow? Where am I slow? What's my problem? Defining the problem is sometimes much more difficult than solving the problem once you figure out what it is."

Data-Acquisition Software: What's Important to the Engineer

In this section Jeff tells us about the software he uses, and what works for a race engineer.

"For me, the race engineer, what's important is how quick I can see the data graphed on the screen. In IMSA we had an hour practice session. But in Indy Lights we've only got a half-hour and it's a little harder. It becomes even more important to get the info fast. I need to plug in, download, plug out, and see a screen in 10 seconds. Some software does this and some doesn't.

"Some software is too cumbersome. It might be a 10-minute process to get that first screen. As a race engineer at trackside, I want quick answers. That's what I need. I want to know if that wing change cost us 2 miles an hour, or that the driver's throttle position definitely looks better in that corner after that last change. Or if it's about the same and the change didn't make any difference. I need fast answers so I can talk to the driver when he comes in for a quick stop during a session. I need to tell the mechanics what changes to make in the next few minutes and talk to the driver about what he needs to do different or the same when he goes back out. I'll be looking at the graphs while I'm talking to him and if I see any glaring discrepancies, I'll point it out and say, 'Well you know, you were 4 miles an hour faster in the chicane this time and you tell me it feels worse?' And he goes, 'Well, it's worse. It doesn't feel as good. But if it's faster maybe we should keep that change?' Or maybe he goes, 'Yeah, maybe it's faster, but I'm gonna crash there sooner or later. We gotta get rid of that change.' But I need those numbers right away so I can make those decisions. Twenty minutes later it's no good. For trackside work I like to see the data quick.

"I may want to see something different back at the shop, when I want to look at the shocks or rake and ride height. What's been the rage in data-acquisition software lately is track maps. Wow, the software can draw a track map with all these cute colors and stuff. Personally, track maps don't do anything for me. I can read a graph. I've been looking at them long enough that I can pop up a graph and see these squiggly lines and point right to the middle of Turn 8 and say, 'There, that's the middle of Turn 8.' I can say, 'Here's the end of this straightaway. There's the chicane.' I don't need to see the cursor on a map to tell me where I am.

"For the drivers it's different. The maps are good for driver coaching. The driver can get more of a feel. It's more like driving the car video-game style than the numbers and graphs I'm familiar with. He can actually see himself turning the wheel and where he is on the track and see the throttle and the brake and how he does it. So there aren't data-acquisition software packages you can say are good and others are bad. It depends on what you're using it for. As a race engineer, I need the numbers fast. Twenty minutes later I don't even need the numbers any more.

"Macros [groups of commands programmed to act all at once] are useful. The software needs to be able to handle macros. Say you've got four suspension sensors and want to know dynamic ride height or rake. I can write a macro that will take position data from the four sensors and convert that to rake and ride height. I can have a graph of rake and ride height all around the track for each lap.

"When you measure shocks you're not measuring the velocity, you're getting the displacement. It just records the length of the shock sensor 200 times a second. Most of the time I'm interested in the velocity of the shock. That relates to what I do on the shock dyno. I have to take the first derivative of the displacement, and that's the velocity curve. Some of the better data-acquisition packages do have a suspension macro that gives you chassis rake, ride height, and velocities. It's built in on some software and others don't have it."

Data Acquisition Is 'What Just Happened'

Data is where you find it. Jeff used an unconventional data source in this story.

"Here's another video camera story. John Brumder was at Denver in a Trans-Am car. It was 1992 and the SCCA had absolutely banned data acquisition and was checking every car. They said you can run them if you want, but just write us a $10,000 check after each session. They were checking real hard trying to make some money. We didn't run anything but we had the video camera. John had a handling problem bad enough that it caused him to crash. He turned in for a corner and the car just kind of settled down and lost grip all of a sudden. It did that several times and then John hit the wall because of it. It wasn't understeer. It was massive, instant loss of grip. We could NOT figure out what was going on. Finally, I started looking through the videotapes real slow at that corner. What we were trying to find is exactly the title of this section, 'What just happened.' John didn't know. He was trying not to hit the wall at that part of the course and couldn't remember anything else.

"Watching the video we heard something before we saw it. We could hear a scraping noise, a grinding when John got on the brakes for that corner. Is that the gearbox? We had just put in a Hewland gearbox, and we thought maybe that was what it sounded like but we weren't sure. I looked under the car and yeah, it was scraped, but they all get that way.

"Finally, after looking at the video many times, we noticed the car was shaking, the camera was shaking. We finally decided that the car was settling down on the road and rubbing. At the end of the day we took our scooters out to that corner for a look and sure enough, you could tell just what was happening. Where John was braking was right over the crown in the road and the car was rubbing the chassis so hard that it was taking weight off the tires and killing their grip. We never would have found that if it hadn't been for that video camera."

Simulation Is 'What's Going To Happen'

Like most racers, Jeff has fantasies about tools he needs that aren't available yet.

"Simulation software is a vast untapped area in racing. I hear the Formula 1 teams have it, and a couple of Indy car teams have it. If I could have simulation software, here's what I'd want. I want to download my data, look at my numbers, look at the graphs on the screen, and then I want to type in something like: change fifth gear from a 26/28 to a 26/27. Then I want to hit a button and have a graph redraw the screen as the data would be if that new gear ratio was in the car. I could switch back and forth between the two graphs to see where one was better than the other. And of course I'd have a lap time from the data created by the simulation to compare with the data from the actual lap with the old gear.

"It would be a guess, an approximation, but it might be good enough to help me make the decision about that particular change. That guess would only be as good as the mathematical model being used. Gear ratios aren't too hard. Aerodynamics would be more difficult.

"Ideally I'd like to have a new graph showing me what a lap would look like with 3 degrees more wing. I want to know how much faster I'll be in every corner, and how much slower I'll be at the end of every straightaway. That's very difficult unless you have an accurate model of the aerodynamics and the vehicle dynamics of the car. But I know people are working on this kind of thing and the F1 guys are already using it.

"I have software that lets me do a little of this right now. I use Bill Mitchell's software. I take numbers from the wind tunnel data, the engine torque curve, the gear ratios, and I've got real acceleration data from on-track testing. I fudge the numbers in Bill's program and compare the results with the real data from tests. They aren't the same for several reasons, one of which is that Bill's program doesn't take into consideration inertial losses. The engine rotating mass gains inertia as the engine revs increase, and that takes some power. The car performs a little better in Bill's program than it does in real life. The speeds at the end of the straight are real close, but the time is maybe .3 seconds fast in a 10-second straight. That's only 3% and that's not bad. Sometimes I can get the time to come out, but then the mph won't be the same.

"Maybe I have a situation where I know the engine numbers but not the aero stuff. After some runs on a track I know the accelerations, and I can guess at the frontal area so I can get the drag coefficient (Cd) by guessing at numbers and changing things around, and then I've got a crude simulation that gives me a derived value of Cd. (PH: That's what I did to estimate the Penske Indy pushrod engine horsepower in the aerodynamics chapter.)

"What all this number-crunching stuff does for me is it allows me to predict a lap time when we go to a new track. I get a track map from the people at the track and I look at the turn radii and the length of the straights. I have data from other tracks and I can look for entrance and exit speeds of corners I think are similar to ones at this new track. I know what set-ups have worked on those kinds of corners and at those kinds of straightaway speeds, and that let's me guess at a set-up for the new course. The closer the car is to a good set-up when we take it off the trailer the faster we're going to go that weekend. Like I said, simulation software is an untapped area for somebody to do something really smart."

Percent Full Throttle and Other Tricks

After some years working as a race engineer, Jeff has developed some ways of thinking about drivers and racecars and how to make them faster.

"I started racing go-karts when I was 7 years old. When I first started driving them at a local track my Dad told me I couldn't race, in the real organized races, until I could beat the lap record in practice. It took me a year before I could do that, and I was bugging him the whole time to let me race but he wouldn't do it. He'd say, 'Nah, nah, you're not good enough yet.' I knew I could beat some of those guys. They had a rookie class I could run in, but he kept saying, 'You're not good enough yet. You've got to beat the lap record.'

"I finally did it. He saw me beat the lap record in practice three weeks in a row. I won my very first race, and it felt great. I realized then that's why he wanted me to wait, so I could win that first one.

"Through all that year when I was practicing, my Dad always told me, 'Don't coast. Don't coast.' I heard it till I was sick of it, but he kept saying, 'Either be on the brake or on the gas. Don't coast.' I heard that from the time I was 7 years old. I still hear it now when I race my go-kart.

"Now, as I look at all this data-acquisition info, I still think the most useful thing is the throttle position data. The graph of that data around a track is, to me, the 'Don't coast' graph. My dad was trying to teach a 7-year-old kid how to drive, and still, it's the best advice anybody can give any racecar driver. Don't coast.

"What I'm trying to find out with the data acquisition and talking to the driver is, 'Why is he coasting? Why isn't the throttle on full?' Ideally, you put the gas pedal down all the way, and you run a whole lap without letting up. That's a perfect lap. Anything less than that, something's wrong. That's my thinking. It's my job as the engineer to think, philosophically, that the ultimate lap is possible, and the driver never has to let off the gas.

"Why does he have to coast, or brake? Why isn't he at full throttle? The throttle position graph is the one that tells me the most about that. One of the neat things about some data-analysis software is it has a macro that gives you the percent full throttle for a whole lap. You hit a button and it gives you statistics for that lap. It might say 86%, for example. That says his average throttle position during that lap was 86% of full throttle. That's one of the things I might look at first when the driver pits in the middle of a practice session. If he's up to 87% for that lap, I know the car's better, because the driver can put on more throttle than during the other lap. I can look at where it's better by overlaying the two throttle position graphs for those two laps. Where the lines diverge shows me the difference.

"The software figures that percent full throttle number by adding up every throttle position number it took that lap, maybe 200 of them a second, and divides by the number of samples to get the average. A higher number is better because it means the driver has his throttle down a little more. Like I said, 'Don't coast.'"

Choosing Gears

You might think choosing the gearing for a racecar is simple. Gearing is a critical choice made easier with the right software.

"In 1992 I was working for the Scandia Team running a car in IMSA's Camel Lights series. We were scheduled to run at New Orleans, and we hadn't run there before. Luckily, it was later in the season so I had quite a bit of data from other tracks. I had fudged some aero numbers as I explained in the simulation section. When we got to New Orleans, we got a track map that showed the straights were so many feet long. First, you have to guess the corner exit speeds. I looked at the map, got the radius and looked at data from other corners of that radius. Then you can say, 'OK, the speed there will be 30 or 35 mph.' You can get really close that way, and if you're off a few miles per hour it doesn't make a big difference, because those cars accelerate so fast anyway. OK, you're coming out of a turn at 35 mph and going 1,100 feet down the straight. How fast will you be going at the braking point? You ask yourself that for the longest straight first and use that for your top gear. You know maximum rpm for your engine along with the maximum speed at that rpm, so the gear ratio falls out.

"For shorter straights like maybe one that's only 300 feet long, that's second gear, and I don't want the driver to have to shift to third so I'll pick a second gear long enough to get him through that section. You work the whole track like that and you keep playing with it till you're happy. We'd never been to New Orleans before, but we only made one gear change during that race weekend. I think we changed second or third gear. We hit fifth right on.

"It's not magic. I'd been working on the model all that year. I was pretty confident in the numbers. In fact, we went to a wind tunnel later in the year and the aero numbers I'd derived were very close to what we found in the wind tunnel. But you can't do that with data from just one race. It takes some time and data from several races to get the numbers when you do it that way. You just keep adjusting them until your guesses get better. That's how I use Bill Mitchell's simulation and gear selection programs.

"I do a lot of that with customers that I may only work for at one race. I may be working for a guy with a Sports 2000 going to a new track for that car, but maybe I've been there running a Formula Atlantic car or a Camel Lights car. I can take the gears for those cars that I know and fudge them for the other car."

Evaluating a Change: Is It the Driver or the Car?

The driver is critical in motor racing. In the battle for the fast lap the race engineer has to decide how to interpret feedback from the driver. Jeff tells us about the way he does that.

"This is always a problem. You make a change to the car that you hope will make it faster. You hope the lap time will go down, but most of the time that change produces a small gain, if it works at all, and it's difficult to measure that gain. Maybe the driver just went faster on his own and the change you made didn't help. Maybe the change actually made the car worse, but the driver drove a better lap. Drivers are human and very adaptable. A lot of them drive around the car's handling problems. They can make you look good even when you've screwed up the car.

"This is a problem because the change you make and the result it produces usually shows you a direction to go in and if the result is good you continue to go in that direction until the gain turns bad. If the driver was the reason for the gain, but you think it's the car, you can continue to go in a wrong direction and waste time and effort. You have to know that the gain you made is a result of the change, that the car really is better."

Alan Kulwicki Story

The late Alan Kulwicki, 1992 NASCAR Winston Cup Champion, was a friend of Jeff's and they worked together at various times. Both men were motivated to get mechanical engineering degrees so they could understand more about racing.

"Alan Kulwicki and I grew up together, and I was crew chief for Alan when he was running an ASA car in 1982. We were testing at a track in Montgomery, Ala. We went there three or four days before an event to do some serious testing. One of the things we were testing was Panhard bar location. A Panhard bar looks like a big piece of metal that just holds the diff housing in place laterally, but it's actually very important to the basic handling of a live-axle racecar. It controls the location of the rear roll center.

"Our car had three holes in the Panhard bar bracket. That gives three possible locations for one end of the bar. Alan and I had been having long discussions about the car, and one of the things we had wrangled about the most was the Panhard bar location. We had been having hours of discussions—long, theoretical discussions about every aspect of the car. I remember one time we stayed up all night, till 6 o'clock in the morning, debating front steer versus rear steer on Winston Cup cars. From midnight till 6 o'clock we talked about what they did and how they worked. We didn't argue. We drew diagrams and talked about the theory, and what we had seen and heard. Those were very intense, fun talks and I learned a lot.

"We had talked about the Panhard bar a lot during these sessions, and now we were going to test it. Alan understood this stuff and he wanted to learn more. But he had some strong ideas about what he thought would happen. Some drivers might, consciously or not, make the test come out to support what they thought was going to happen. Alan wanted so badly to learn what was REALLY happening that he set up the test so he couldn't influence it. He said, 'I know what's going to happen. I've got it fixed in my mind what's the best Panhard bar location. That location will be the best no matter what you do because, when I go out there, I'm going to make it the best. Even though I'm not going to try to do that it still could happen. So, what I'm going to do is go in the trailer and you guys are going to put the bar in whatever hole you want. I don't want to know. Then, I'll go out on the track and you can get my lap times and comments. Then, I'll get out of the car and go into the trailer and you can change the location again. Or don't! Leave it where it was if you want. We'll run as many times as you tell me to and I won't ever know which position the bar is in.'"

"We did that and—I think it's funny—I can't remember which position was better, but what stuck in my mind about that test was Alan really wanted to know the answer. He didn't care who was right and who was wrong. Here was a guy who really wanted to know the answer, no ego thing. He didn't care who was right. There are a lot of drivers that won't do that. They may be convinced that there's something they need and they'll argue for that change and they'll make it so they get what they want. The engineer's change just won't quite be good enough for them, but they'll make the car better when they get the change they want. Alan realized that is a basic, human-nature weakness and he would try to take that out of the equation. He knew that he had that same tendency to make things come out like he wanted, and he tried to take himself out of it so he could learn more about what the car wanted instead of just what the driver wanted."

The Stopwatch As a Data-Acquisition Device

Jeff tells us about a simple, reliable device that shows how well a racecar or driver is doing on a track.

"The stopwatch is the ultimate tool for a racecar engineer. Lap time is the only thing that matters. That's what racing is all about. For qualifying it's who can make one lap the fastest, and in the race the winner is the one who can complete the required number of laps the quickest. All the things a racecar engineer does, all the tools he has, are used to make fast laps. That's the ultimate goal.

"My dad and I have been racing together since I was 7 years old, and when I try to impress him with all the trick stuff, the computers and software and all the technology we have available today, he just reaches into his pocket and pulls out his stopwatch and says, 'This is the only data-acquisition device I need. It tells me all I need to know. If you guys are screwing up I know it, because you're slower. If you're doing a good job I know that too, because you're faster.'

"There's a lot of truth to that. Lap time is the most important thing to measure. A stopwatch is also a very inexpensive data-acquisition device. You can get a lot of information from a stopwatch. If you have people in specific corners at a racetrack, you can get segment times. That's the way to find out if your driver is faster or slower than the competition in a particular section of the track. You'll know from the times if your driver is faster or slower.

"I've found that almost never, after a change that made the car quicker according to a stopwatch, does the driver come back in and say he doesn't like the change. The car almost always feels better if the lap time is lower. Very rarely does the driver go faster according to the stopwatch and then says he didn't like how the car felt. The stopwatch is the first indicator of how well you're doing and it's really the only one that matters."

Off-Board Data Acquisition

Here's another piece of equipment Jeff would like to have in his toolbox.

"I wish I had this piece of equipment: a device that I could point at a car while it's on the racetrack, and it would record everything I need to know.

"Data-acquisition systems let you measure anything on your car that you can hook a sensor to. What about the other guy's car? I'd like to know what's going on there too. I want to know what the dynamic ride height is, the rpm, the wing settings front and rear, cornering forces, acceleration forces. I need this to compare with what we're doing so we can tell where we're faster and slower than them.

"One way to do this is with a video camera. A video camera could record all the cars as they come past a certain point. You could use stop motion to analyze what the car's doing. You could see wing angles and ride height. A radar gun built in to the camera could give rate of change of velocity, which is acceleration. After every session we could look at our car, and everybody else's too.

"The operator would pick a spot outside the corner tangent to the apex. The radar gun and video camera could be in one box on a tripod so people couldn't tell what it was. Specific keys would serve as triggers for certain cars. As the car that corresponds to a key comes into the corner, the operator hits that key. The car's number comes up on the video screen with the radar reading, the lap time, and the sound frequency or rpm reading from a microphone on the video camera.

The operator could hit the key again as the car passes an exit spot and you've got a segment time also."

TRACTION CONTROL

Traction control is one of those driver aids that has been banned by most racing organizations. As I've said before, once you have a computer on board a racecar, there are all kinds of things you can figure out for it to do. It's not a great leap to add control to a data-acquisition system. If you have good data about something going on with the car and a way to control that something, you just write software that tells the microprocessor to compare the data it's collecting with a number you want to exceed or not exceed or match or whatever. It's not really that easy, of course, but it's do-able.

Simply stated, traction control uses an on-board computer to vary engine power so that the rear wheels don't spin even though the driver has his foot to the floor coming out of a slow corner. A good driver can apply throttle so the car accelerates without much wheelspin, but the traction control systems used in F1 and Indy cars must have done a better job modulating the throttle than the driver or there wouldn't have been so much time and money spent to develop them.

I think the main benefit of traction control was using lower gears coming out of slow corners so the cars accelerated more quickly without using up the rear tires. In racecars without traction control, the first couple of gears in the transmission have to be higher than optimum because the driver has trouble controlling wheelspin in lower gears. Gears are like levers; the bigger they are the more they multiply the torque put out by the engine.

Traction Control at Laguna Seca

I went to an IndyCar test at Laguna Seca Raceway in September 1992, and one of the things I was curious about was the traction control system reportedly being used on the Penske cars. Early in the day I didn't notice anything different about the Penske cars, but I did hear a buzzing sound from the engine in the Galmer/Ilmor as Al Unser Jr. accelerated out of Turn 11. I asked Ed Nathman, then Newman-Haas crew chief who went to Galles the next year, if that was traction control? "Yeah, it's a part of the Ilmor engine package now," he said.

I began to notice the noise on both the Penske and Galmer cars. It was easy to hear once I knew what to listen for. When the drivers got on the throttle coming out of the slow Turn 11 the engine sounded like it was missing. You could hear it a lot in first gear and less after the shift to second. I had read that the engine management system (EMS) simply skips sending signals to the coils at each spark plug. As a result the spark plug doesn't fire at the time it's supposed to, and that cylinder makes no power that cycle. These spark outages are supposedly rotated randomly around the firing order for smoothness.

The next thing I noticed was that the Galmer/Ilmor car was using lower gears than Michael Andretti's Lola/Cosworth, which did not yet have a traction control system. By counting the concrete barriers, which are 20 feet long, I estimated about where the shifts were made. Assuming the cars are in first gear in this corner, Al Jr. shifted into second at 150 feet, third at 300 feet, and fourth at 600 feet, measured from the apex of the corner. In contrast, Michael Andretti, without traction control, shifted from first to second gear at about 500 feet and again into third almost at Start/Finish about 1,000 feet from Turn 11. Since they're using lower gears, the Ilmor-engined cars are probably getting better acceleration. Like I said, if the traction control systems didn't work, they wouldn't have messed with them.

How Does Traction Control Work?

Three weeks after that test during the IndyCar Toyota Monterey GP weekend at Laguna Seca, I asked one of the Ilmor Engineering field engineers about the traction-control system. He said, "Anything you've read about it is wrong. We haven't released any information at all." I asked him several questions that I thought were general and shouldn't be at all compromising, but he wouldn't comment and looked uncomfortable, so I thanked him and went on my way.

I talked to quite a few technical people during that race weekend, and one of the things I was told was that engine power is modulated for traction control not by spark outages but by "retarding the spark on certain cylinders." So in order to lower engine power and control wheelspin, the spark plug is fired later in the cycle and the pressure buildup due to combustion is wasted as the still-burning charge blows out into the exhaust system and through the turbocharger. That's probably what makes the characteristic engine sound.

One person said, "If this were F1 we could talk about it, but here in IndyCar people are much more secretive. The traction control software we're using now is relatively simple. Next year there will be several control strategies available that will give us the choice to use a certain strategy at a specific track or in a specific situation." By "strategy" I think he meant how, when, and how much the software controls engine power. Do you get an idea how complicated something like this can be?

In F1 the McLaren-Honda had, at that time, an electronic throttle input to the engine management system. A sensor in the throttle linkage produced a voltage signal determined by throttle position. The EMS determined the actual engine throttle position with an electric actuator which could be modulated by the EMS to control wheelspin. That means the actual throttle setting would be determined by the EMS, not by the driver who's got his foot to the floor. The benefit was modulated power for maximum tractive force with no loss of fuel, as happens with the Indy car system.

As I've said before, this stuff is not magic. It's smart people working hard and testing a lot of ideas. I won't get into the controversy over whether all this techie stuff is good for racing. At a press conference before an F1 race in 1992, Nigel Mansell answered the usual question about what he thought would happen at the start of the race. "It's simple these days. If our software is better than their software, I'll get to the first corner in the lead."

Wheel Speed Sensors

How does the engine management system know when wheelspin occurs? They install a magnetic pickup or a Hall Effect device on at least one front and one rear wheel. These sensors produce a voltage blip when a piece of metal, such as a bolt head, rotates by them. Bolts holding brake rotors to the hub are a convenient source that is used to excite these sensors. A counter circuit in the hardware accumulates the number of blips generated in some unit of time, say one-tenth of a second. Then software in the EMS compares these values and cuts engine power when the rear wheel speed exceeds front wheel speed. That sounds simple, doesn't it?

Like most things, traction control is a very simple concept that is probably very difficult to implement correctly. I say probably because I don't have any direct knowledge of the development. But I did put a wheel speed sensor on my Datsun 510. If I describe it maybe you'll have a better appreciation of a part of a traction control system.

The speedometer in the 510 started acting up, so I decided to make a backup. For $100 you can get a magnetic pickup and digital tachometer. A mag pickup generates a voltage pulse whenever a magnet or a piece of steel passes close by. The digital tach counts these pulses and, once every second, sends the total it has counted to a digital display, and then starts counting again. I mounted the pickup on the differential so it would react to the passing of the four corners on a universal joint flange in the rear axle half shaft. Every time a corner of that flange passes by the mag pickup a voltage pulse goes up a wire to a silicon counter chip in the display box, which I duct taped to the ashtray in the dash. The display shows four digits about three-eighths of an inch high. I can see it fine as long as there's enough light.

But how do you get from pulses to miles an hour? It just so happens that four pulses per axle revolution counted for one second is the same number as miles per hour when you've got 175/70X13 tires. Here's the numbers: 60 mph equals 88 feet per second. At 60 mph a tire of 22.5-inch circumference rotates 896 times a minute or 14.9 times a second. Four pulses per revolution times that 14.9 revs per second is 59.6 pulses per second, and 59.6 mph is close enough to 60 for me. So, if I'm going 60 mph, the counter sees almost 60 pulses per second and at 70 it sees about 70 pulses per second. I've now got a very accurate and reliable back-up speedometer. You can guess what happened. The speedometer has worked ever since.

The Wheel Speed Sensing Problem Is Low-Speed Accuracy

In order to prevent wheelspin and still get maximum power through the tires to the track, the computer has to sense the difference in front and rear wheel speeds and change the engine ignition very quickly. This requires an accurate wheel speed measurement as often as five or 10 times a second.

So how many flange corners or bolt heads or gear teeth does that sensor need to see for an accurate wheel speed value? The software can do whatever calculations are needed, while my simple system on the Datsun just displays the number of pulses counted in one second. With good software you can use a large number of pulses per axle revolution by mounting a gear that rotates at axle speed and sensing the passing teeth. A multiplier in the software gives the correct speed if you know the number of teeth on the gear and the diameter of the tire. I wouldn't be surprised if they were mounting a sensor through the transmission case, so it could read a gear with a lot of teeth on it.

Why would they need that? For accuracy! Look at the table below. An Indy car rear tire is 27.8 inches in diameter. That gives 12.45 axle revolutions at 60 mph. If, like my Datsun, they had only four pulses per revolution, that tire diameter would give about 50 pulses per second. If the computer reads the count just before the next pulse happened, the count could be one pulse off. Fifty pulses per second read every tenth of a second is five pulses. One pulse off is one out of five and that's a 20% possible error. They need a lot of pulses for an accurate measurement. This first table gives percent error if the sensor is one tooth off. The accuracy problem is at low speeds, just when wheelspin is most likely to occur.

Speed mph	Speed ft./sec.	Axle rev./sec.	No. Teeth	Teeth/sec.	Teeth/.1 sec	Error (%)
60	88	12.09	4	48.36	4.84	20.68
120	176	24.18	4	96.73	9.67	10.34

These next two tables show the possible error with various numbers of teeth on the sensor gear and two sampling rates. If they need to sample every tenth of a second, they need more teeth.

At 60 mph, 10 samples per second

Number of teeth	4	10	50	100
Teeth/0.1 sec.	4.84	12.09	60.46	120.91
1 tooth error, %	10.34	4.14	0.83	0.41

At 60 mph, 5 samples per second

Number of teeth	4	10	50	100
Teeth/.1 sec.	9.67	24.18	120.91	241.82
1 tooth error, %	10.34	4.14	0.83	0.41

You can see from the table above that the sensor needs to see a lot of teeth going by to have an accurate view of wheel speed. If the EMS needs a sample every tenth of a second at 60 mph to effectively control wheelspin, then they need at least 50 teeth to get better than 1% accuracy.

A modern racecar is a very complicated piece of equipment, and even something as trick as traction control can't make all the difference. Michael Andretti, with no traction control, was the fast qualifier for that 1992 IndyCar race at Laguna Seca and won the race after leading flag to flag.

COMPUTERS IN ROAD CARS; RACING IMPROVES THE BREED

ECU: Ford's EECs

The Monterey Historic Automobile Races at Laguna Seca Raceway would not seem to be the place to go for a technology lesson. At the 1992 event, however, I spent some time in a Ford Electronics display tent and came away with some interesting information I'll pass along. Ford was a corporate sponsor that year because Jaguar, a Ford division, was the featured marque.

Up front in the tent was a Lola Indy car in Target livery with a Ford/Cosworth turbo V-8 installed. Further back sat a Benetton-Ford/Cosworth F1 car with a normally aspirated 3.5-liter V-8. On the back wall of the tent was a display telling the story of the development of the Ford Electronics EEC engine management systems, versions I through IV. This is the computer system that tells the fuel injectors when and how long to spray fuel into the intake manifold and tells the ignition system when to fire the spark plugs.

The display for each computer system included a hardware sample of the system mounted on a pedestal and the following information about each system.

1984/'85 EEC-IV, Phase 1
Size is 10.5 in. x 9.0 in. x 3.0 in. Weight is 9.5 lb.
Used on Ford/Cosworth V-8 3.0-liter Formula 1 engine.
Processor: Intel 8061, 15 MHz.
Sensors: air plenum temperature and pressure, throttle position, crankshaft
    position, camshaft event, coolant temperature.
Controls: tachometer, fuel injectors, ignition, warning lamps, engine kill switch.

1986 EEC-IV, Phase 2
Size is 12.75 in. x 7.0 in. x 3.0 in. Weight is 8.5 lb.
Used on Ford turbo V-6 1.5-liter Formula 1 engine.
Processor: Intel 8061, 15 MHz.
Sensors: air plenum temperature and pressure, throttle position, crankshaft
    position, camshaft event, coolant temperature.
Controls: tachometer, fuel injectors, ignition, warning lamps, engine kill switch.

1988 EEC-IV, Phase 3
Size is 9.0 in. x 6.75 in. x 2.0 in. Weight is 4.0 lb.
Used on Ford/Cosworth V-8 3.5-liter Formula 1 engine.
Processor: Intel 8061, 15 MHz.
Sensors: oil pressure, ambient air pressure, inlet air temperature, fuel pressure
  and temperature, coolant temperature, throttle position, crankshaft position,
  cam event.
Controls: tachometer, fuel injectors, ignition, warning lamps, cockpit display,
  ignition kill switch, fuel micro switch.

1992 Ford Thunderbird Engine Management System
Size is 8 in x 6.125 in x 1.5 in. Weight is 2.2 lb.
Sensors: Supercharger air inlet temperature and flow rate, ambient air temperature and pressure, throttle position, coolant temperature, exhaust gas oxygen
  content, vehicle speed, fuel injector circuit check, exhaust gas recirculation
  pressure, engine knock, ignition profile, air conditioning clutch, octane
  switch, automatic transmission first gear switch, data comm link input, self
  test.
Controls: fuel injector boost pressure, ignition, idle speed, fuel pump, EGR shut
  off, wide open throttle air conditioning shut off, electric fan, air conditioning
  clutch, automatic transmission kick down solenoid, data comm. link output,
  self test output.

As you can see there has been a continuous decrease in size and weight as
well and an increase in function as the system evolved. I'm sure this system could
have been developed without being used in a racecar, but the rigors of racing
surely helped.

NASCAR TV Telemetry

Of course NASCAR doesn't allow data acquisition or telemetry on board a
racecar that would benefit a team during a race, but they do allow an on-board
computer, sensors, and telemetry that provide information for television. This
lets fans at home watching the race view an on-screen display of telemetry data
direct from the car. Ford Electronics is responsible for transmission from the
Thunderbirds and Delco Electronics provides a similar system for GM cars. Like
on-board cameras, this telemetry makes racing much more interesting to watch
on TV.

What we see is a box on the screen with constantly changing numbers
representing engine rpm, racecar speed, what gear the car is in, and a braking
indicator. Sometimes we see throttle position and gear selection also. Again, this
is not magic. Sensors on the car provides data that gets read by an on-board
computer which hands over the data to a radio transmitter. A receiver in a
helicopter feeds the data to another transmitter that sends that same info back
down to a ground receiver. A personal computer processes the data and converts
it to a video signal that we can see on our screen.

The speed of the car is calculated from driveshaft rpm. A sensor is triggered
by teeth on a gear rotating on the differential oil cooler pump driven off the front
of the differential. Software counts the resulting voltage pulses over a given time,
and calculates the speed of the car using the ring and pinion drive ratio and the
circumference of the tire. The engine rpm comes from a pulse counter hooked to
the ignition coil. Micro switches on the transmission and brake pedal take care of
the gear and brake indicators. Throttle position comes from a position sensor
hooked up somewhere in the throttle linkage.

A few years ago a NASCAR crew chief wouldn't have trusted some Ford techie enough to tell him what rear end ratio was on the car. Things have changed. Bob Schultz, the Ford Electronics product design engineer responsible for the telemetry system, agrees. "I'm kind of surprised myself how cooperative the NASCAR teams are. I think we've built up some trust by not telling anybody anything that would compromise that trust."

IAN REED INTERVIEW: HOW F1 USES COMPUTERS

In May 1994 the Benneton Formula 1 team acquired the Ligier team, and Tom Walkinshaw, one of Benneton's owners, sent Tony Dowe and Ian Reed of Tom Walkinshaw Racing USA over to France for an evaluation of Ligier. I met Ian last year and he's been one of my sources for information about Formula 1. Ian is British, married to an American. He was involved in F1 with March Engineering before coming to the United States to work for Indy car teams, so it was an understatement to say he was pleased to get another look at Formula 1 racing.

In September 1994 Ian and I talked on the phone about the state of F1 technology.

IR: "What hits you straightaway is just how high the level of technology is. F1 people think that if they're at a 100, Indy cars are at about 80. Indy car people think that if they're at a 100, F1 people are about 110. In reality, I think, if F1 is a 100, Indy car is 40 or 50. When you have the sort of budgets that an F1 team has, and this is all a function of budget, when you see titanium pit equipment and carbon fiber pit carts...." I interrupted, laughing.

PH: "Is that right?"

IR: "It isn't so silly, because they fly away to 50% of their races, and they have a gross weight limit on all their equipment. So carbon fiber car stands mean something else can go in the box, because weight means as much as volume. Titanium car jacks are the same because they're lighter, and they can get more in the box when they fly to Japan or Canada or Australia.

"When you first see all this you think what a ridiculous way to budget, but then the logistics guy explains it to you and it hits you right between the eyes. When you have to fly, weight is weight, and it's not just the cars that need to be light, but the toolboxes and pit equipment. We did Spain, which was a drive-to race, and then came back and went to Canada. The F1 guys don't even break a sweat. It all happened. It flowed because there's so many fly-away races, and they're geared for it. The European races are just fly-away races without the airplanes. They're still organized the same way. The packing cases are Kevlar, and there's lightweight stuff everywhere. There's a huge budget gone into making everything lightweight. You can really get used to that in a hurry.

"Another example is electronics. Ligier, and they're not unique because the teams are all the same, has the people and the resources to do their own electronics. They've looked at the Pi data-acquisition system that most Indy car teams use, and they're way ahead of Pi.

"The key change was active suspension. Active was like an engine management system. You've got to have good on-board data collection to ever get the thing to work. When they developed active suspensions they developed chassis computer systems that were as sophisticated as engine management systems. Because of the Concorde Agreement they have to do all work in-house. There are some clauses that say how you're allowed to transfer technology from team to team and Ligier does have a Williams gearbox and gearbox control system, but the Concorde Agreement basically says everyone has to do their own thing.

"So Ligier went and hired six postgraduate software engineers. These are very bright guys. Most came from Dassault or Aerospaciale. These companies are great training grounds for racecar personnel. If you give them an idea they just pick up and run with it. They know what they're doing.

"Because everybody developed active suspension and had these superb on-board data-acquisition systems and chassis-simulation systems, there's no guesswork anymore. Before they go to the track the race engineers use the simulations to predict the lap times and the car set-up. When they get to the track the first thing they do is a one-lap check-out and then a five-lap run, and then the car comes in and stops for 15 minutes while everybody jumps onto the computers. They check the car on the racetrack against the simulation. They check the ride height, the rake, the aero loads, and the pitch and roll. They have two pitot tubes (airspeed sensors) on the car because a mosquito could get into one and ruin a run. Back when they had active ride-height control, airspeed from the pitot tube was one of the primary inputs to the system, and a plugged tube would make the suspension go bonkers trying to compensate. That confuses the driver too, because the car's handling goes silly.

"They only get 23 laps of practice now, so they do the one lap to make sure there's no oil leaks or whatever, then a five-lap run, and they stop for 15 minutes. The driver gives his debrief, but the information has already come out of the car and back into the computers round behind the portable screens.

"There's one primary data guy on each car, one guy on the computer box, and a couple of spares. So there'll be about five software guys there. One of the things I did was to create some standard computer screens to go through, so they had the right downforce and the car was the right ride height and the tire pressures were right and the car was within the simulation parameters. They have all these screens and XY plots and data plots and so on. The driver would say he has a bit of oversteer or understeer here or there. There are pre-programmed charts set up so, with data from the car, you can measure understeer and quantify it to 70% or whatever. You look on a chart and you can see, if you change the ride height or any other adjustment on the car, where the car should be quicker at certain places on the course and by how much.

"In F1 you have a 45-minute practice session, a 15-minute break, and another 45-minute session. So you probably won't get your second set of laps in until the last part of that first 45-minute session. You made your first run and then spent the whole middle of that session making sure the on-board measurements were tied to the simulation. Then you make one change and go out and back in and check the results of the change and quantify it all. Then the 15-minute break between sessions lets them drag in any broken cars. The same process goes on during the second session. The whole practice was like an enormous video game.

"Practice is at 11 a.m. and qualifying at 1 p.m., so really you have two or two and one-half hours to go through your four or five sets of data from the morning and talk to the driver. The driver looks at the screens and walks through his best lap, looking at how much understeer or oversteer he had, and it's all quantified in numbers and also the shape of the understeer or oversteer curve—whether it's a snap oversteer or a slow build-up oversteer. The drivers are taught to look at the software on the computer screens and relate that to what they feel in the car. The engineering decisions are not purely engineering decisions. The driver gets into it and helps decide on the trade-offs of a little less understeer in this corner or a little more oversteer in another corner.

"This is just on the chassis side of it. The engine people had a system that was even better. The Renault system was superb. It was a microwave telemetry system, and they had every lap the driver did—every gearshift, all of it. They'd show the driver he's going 292 kph down the straight. They'd say, 'Maybe that's a little quick and you should consider running more wing, because we seem to have the straight-line speed.' Then you run that change through the simulation to see what that does to the lap time.

"You're only allowed 12 laps in a session and only seven sets of tires for the whole weekend. You have to be well-planned and well-organized. What would happen is you look at the track and the weather. You have a weather station there, and you already figured out, by putting the ambient air properties in the simulation, what downforce the car would run against available engine horsepower. The engine guys will tell you how much power you have at this temperature and pressure. If the weather is changing you can tell when to make a qualifying run. Maybe you only have one roll of the dice. You go out and get a time and come in and have a long conference. You have a whole hour to qualify. You look at the computers. Then you go across to Renault and discuss it with them. Then you make a small change to the wing or something and do it again. If you have three sets of tires then you have three chances. At the end of the day you had 23 laps in the morning and 12 in the afternoon and that was it. You had to think very carefully how to use these laps or it would penalize the hell out of you. Then the same thing the next day on Saturday.

"Then, race morning, there's a half-hour for warmup. So one lap to make sure everything works, and then just pound around on a pre-programmed run to see how the car did with a full fuel load and check the brakes and so on.

"Come the race and away you go, but again pit strategy, whether it's two stops or three or four stops, you use computers to help choose. You try and plot the tire degradation. We had an enormous multi-dimensional polynomial equation. You look at the lap time against weight because the fuel load varies, and you can start with different amounts of fuel. The lap times start on new tires with the tires degrading, but weight decreasing so the computer can tell you what happens if you stop three times so you run lighter and you run quicker, and the tires don't degrade as badly. But you have to weigh that against the time it takes to make the stop. This is one of the things you measure off the instrumentation during practice: the time it takes you to come in to the pit lane, pull to a stop, and go out.

"This is why there was a big scene when they changed the pit-lane speed limit during one of the race weekends. Everything the teams had learned about how long it took to make a stop had to be thrown out the window. They had to figure it out all over again.

"It was great fun." We both laughed.

PH: "I bet it was," I said, still laughing. "I remember you telling me last year at Laguna Seca that what you really liked was software development, and it sounds like this is a big part of F1 right now."

IR: "That's right. This is a different breed of driver from a few years ago. The driver now, does two things. First they have to go out and stand on it. There's no warm up or cruising. They go out of the pits on warm tires, and they're up to speed by the fourth or fifth corner. So they come by, and they've got only two timed laps. They'll go at qualifying effort for two timed laps and come in. Then they might be stuck in the pits for a half hour looking at the software. And then they go out and do it again with whatever changes were made to the car.

"Second is the software. You'll tell the driver exactly what difference the change should make and how it will affect him here or affect him there. So you have these drivers that can go out and stand on it. It's unbelievable. Yet they're technocrats. They'll come in and look at the screens and give you value judgments about understeer that, on the screen, looks like 50%, but maybe it really isn't that big a problem. Maybe they're not losing a lot of time in that corner but, if we can fix the traction coming out of that slow corner, then they're going to carry that speed all the way down to the next corner. You have a different breed of driver. They'll go out and stand on it and they're technocrats. They can work with the data acquisition and simulation software.

"I have the greatest respect for Michael Schumacher. At Magny-Cours he had some problem in the morning during qualifying and did only about 10 laps. I think Damon Hill and Nigel Mansell were quickest during early qualifying. Then Schumacher went out of the pits on warm tires and did one timed lap and came back in and sat on the pole for the entire session. He had three laps total. It was unbelievable. I don't see how they do that. They go out of the pits for an out-lap and do the one timed lap and then motor around to come into the pits again. He had to do it early in the session because the temperature was going up and the engine puts out less power and the car also makes less downforce in lower-density air. He only had one chance and he did it."

PH: "Is that Schumacher the athlete, or have all the drivers learned to do it?"

IR: "I don't know how they do it."

PH: "But it's the driver; the cars aren't helping the driver go quickly? Have they learned some new way to set up the cars so the driver can go fast quickly?"

IR: "It's the driver. It was Michael Schumacher that day. There was nobody else who could do that. Michael Schumacher could. I've never seen that in Indy cars ever. I've seen people pound around and put a flying lap in right under the checkered flag at the end of the session and turn in an incredible lap time, but they had three or four laps leading up to it."

PH: "That's pretty amazing that they can go that fast that quickly."

IR: "Senna was the same. He could do the same thing."

PH: "How did that affect everybody? How did his death and Ratzenberger's affect people?"

IR: "Ahh, it was devastating. Devastating.

"And then they changed the rules. When I arrived at Ligier, it was just after Monaco and FISA changed the rules. We had to cut the undertrays off for Barcelona. [The diffusers at the back of the car had to be shortened, reducing downforce and raising drag.] Ligier did some work in the wind tunnel and saw they had lost some downforce. They messed about with the wings and the balance and got it all back. They have a very, very good wind tunnel. The instrumentation is so good and the wind tunnel gives you so much good data.

"And they measure for real the downforce on the car. They go test somewhere that has a long straight, and they measure downforce three or four different ways so there's no doubt about it. They drive up to a speed and they know exactly what the speed is—both car speed and air speed. They measure directly off the car the front downforce and the rear downforce. They know the downforce on each corner of the car, so they know the aero load and the aero balance. They'll reproduce the aero map they got from the wind tunnel using long straights during on-track testing. This shows any errors in the wind tunnel data, because it's a scale model and there'll always be some error.

"During one of these tests Olivier Panis was driving down the straight and one of the wings flew off. He came in without a wing and we went out and got the wing and it looked like it had delaminated. Gerard Decourouge and I sort of shot back to the factory basically to ream out the guy in the composite shop for a potentially life-threatening quality control failure. We went through it with him, he had all his records, and we brought in a guy from Aerospatiale who knew about airplane crash investigations, to have a look. That same design had done two years on the car with no failures. It was one of the lower elements and while we were looking at the problem a second one came off the car, so the team came back from testing and we went through the instrumentation and data very carefully.

"What was happening was the wing had been positioned to tie in with flow off the undertray and, with the shortened undertray, the wing was now in a fluctuating airstream. With the interaction of the wing and the undertray, the center of pressure under the car was going to and fro. In addition to the normal bending load the wing was designed for, it was now seeing a fluctuating torsional load. It wasn't designed for that and it just broke. It took us a few days to get to the bottom of all this, and we had this big panic to redesign the wings.

"They have their own stress analysis capability in-house. They have this tremendous CAD (computer-aided design) system with stress analysis, so they redesigned the wings and laid them up in the shop and worked a weekend and we had everything ready for Barcelona. But it shook everybody rigid. About two days later Pedro Lamy in a Lotus had a big accident at Silverstone where a wing fell off, and I'm sure it was the same thing. It was aerodynamic vibrations.

"The instrumentation we looked at was right, but nobody really believed it. As we painfully built up the evidence it became obvious that the unstable airflow was putting a load into the wing that it was just not designed to cope with, and it had fallen off. We looked at a bunch of new wing combinations. We ran up and down testing until we found one that was stable enough for Barcelona. But we went there with our fingers crossed.

"There was a strike on the first day at Barcelona because the other teams all had the same problems. Some weren't affected because maybe their aero layout wasn't as critical as ours."

PH: "So that's why that strike happened?"

IR: "The strike happened because the safety changes were rammed through and they made the cars more unstable and less safe, because these were major aerodynamic changes with no study given. We were all in trouble and nobody had a handle on how safe the cars were. In fact Benneton sent a letter saying they couldn't guarantee their car was safe. But they were made to back down later."

PH: "So what about 'The Plank'? What was the effect of putting a wood spacer on the bottom of the cars?"

IR: "When you do the aero maps of the cars, you find out straightaway that they produce enormous amounts of downforce when they're in a certain position. With active ride height control you could hold the car in that position the whole time around the track no matter what happens. With active you could, in fact, use very unstable aerodynamic systems and control them.

"With the ban of active ride you can't ever stuff the genie back into the bottle. The knowledge is still there. The people are still there and they're clever enough and there's a lot of them. Ligier had about 30 engineers in various teams. We'd have some ideas about what would make the car go faster and need to prove them on the simulation. These guys could make it happen. It didn't take them very long to come up with some pretty creative things to get around the lack of active suspension.

"You end up with passive cars that try and simulate active suspension. You get third springs [explained in the aero chapter] and things like that. You end up with some very sophisticated ways of doing it. So the aerodynamic instability of the cars hasn't really gone away. The driver's margin of error has been reduced dramatically. The cars are inherently unstable. They can be kept on the race track within a margin of safety by the driver, but if you stray outside that margin you're in trouble. What the drivers were complaining about was that banning active was not the solution. It just made things worse—more dangerous.

"Goodyear is supplying much more tire data than they do in Indy cars, because of past tire wars. We had a Goodyear meeting at each event where they explained what the tires were that weekend and any difference in construction or compound. The software simulation needs tire map information: vertical stiffness, cornering stiffness, braking stiffness, and the braking and turning together. All this was plotted against pressure. We had to run the right tire pressures. All that information was supplied by Goodyear and checked out by the teams. You trust it's correct but you check it out. You've a much closer relationship between the teams and Goodyear. The amount of information was wonderful.

"The tires were factored into the system and the simulation used it to figure ride height with packers and the third-spring devices used to control ride height. There are some very sophisticated devices to do that. The simulation has tire deflections and lateral stiffness and tire pressures all built in."

PH: "So they're using the third springs front and rear just like Indy cars?"

IR: "They've progressed beyond that. They have very sophisticated third and fourth springs—very, very sophisticated ride height and roll control systems."

PH: "So there are ways to connect springs and dampers mechanically that give very good ways to control ride height and roll?"

IR: "Once you've done an active system and you've learned how to program every detail of the system, all you have to do is say 'That's what we want to do, and how do we do that passively?' You can't get all of it, but you work out the key bits. You come out with a passive system that will come pretty close to reproducing an active system. Once again, at the edge of traction, performance drops off drastically, which is why the car's not stable. It's a passive/active system. It's not active but it has the same function. The margin for error is so narrow. If the car gets a little out of shape, it's gone.

"What the plank did is get the cars up a bit and reduced the aerodynamic sensitivity dramatically. Before the plank the optimum setup was at the top of a mountain peak. The best setup was at the top of the Matterhorn, and you just sit there and if you go either way you fall off. With the plank underneath, it rounded the peak off more like a hump so you can make an error and your downforce drops off, but not nearly as much. The plank makes it a lot safer.

"The other thing the plank did was to make it more difficult to get to the top of the hump, because it's not so clearly defined. When you've got a more gentle hump you can be near the top, but not quite on the top and the difference in lap time is only three-tenths of a second. So you need to rely more on the instrumentation to get to the top. The software guys are working on that all the time and they're getting it better and better.

"In the end the plank has desensitized the aerodynamics and put more emphasis on how well the team's run and the software they have. Which is probably, in many ways, more sporting."

PH: "Are they back now to the same kinds of absolute downforce numbers they had before the rules changes?"

IR: "No. The cars are considerably slower. The Barcelona changes lopped about 25% off the total downforce the car made. The plank has taken a bit more off. Lap times are slower."

PH: "What about F1 budgets? Can you give me some ballpark figures?"

IR: "Budgets are very, very high. The sheer numbers of people employed plus the quality of the people takes a lot of money. The Ligier operating budget was in excess of 30 million a year—dollars. That's about 150 people."

PH: "I've heard Williams has about 200 people, and it's equipped like an aerospace research facility."

IR: "Yes, that's exactly what it looks like. Ligier looks the same. Anything you want to do you can do."

"NASCAR is about as major league as motorsports gets in the United States. You don't realize just how major league Formula 1 is in Europe. It's right up there with soccer. You open the sports page and racing is not a footnote like it is here.

Senna's death was front page right across Europe. Racing is a big deal, which is why the budgets are so big."

"The most amazing thing is the quality of FOCA TV available to the teams. In whatever country—Spain, Canada, France, England, different countries, different languages and currency and everything—the FOCA TV produces the same package with the same quality. They have a weather station available and there are monitors in all the pits and garages. You can watch the whole race from within the pits. You don't have to poke your head out. You can't see anything anyway. The cameras follow the cars around the track.

"You press a button and there is the timing and scoring information. Each lap is shown as the car goes by. The last lap and the fastest lap and the order that session. Press another button and it's a weather channel, and there's the humidity and a graph of the temperature and humidity for that day and then a satellite for that part of the world. There's seven channels there.

"Renault would have a bank of computers showing all the real-time info from the car and four TV monitors. Channel one is the continual lap times for each car. Another channel is for session times and one for weather and so on. And the monitors are portable so, when the driver comes in to the pits, he stays in the car and they plop a monitor up on the car in front of him and he can watch what other cars are doing while the engineers are back behind looking at the computers.

"There's nothing like that over here. They need TV because of the language barrier. Everyone speaks a different language. I don't speak a word of French and there I was at a French team. Fortunately they spoke enough English that we got by. Knowing you're in a foreign language, everything gets done on paper and you're very precise about what you want and how you say it because you could be misinterpreted. Once we did that, communication became very easy because it was very clear each way."

PH: "Is English the technical language of Europe?"

IR: "It's universal, especially in racing, even at Ferrari. We were pitted in between Ferrari and Lotus at all the races, and there's a lot of English spoken at Ferrari. They have a Frenchman running it, but they speak a lot of English.

"We ran Renault engines and all the debriefs were in English. Here I was a solitary American-Englishman with four French guys and we're speaking English. One of the French guys laughed and said, 'Why are we speaking English? There's four of us.' That's the way it is. English is the universal language in racing, especially in Formula 1."

PH: "So I guess you thought you'd died and gone to heaven over there?"

IR: "Well, no. The flaws and problems came to the fore pretty quickly and I realized it was a job like anything else. You just have more toys to play with [laughing]. The fundamentals never change. All the usual problems are there. The complexities increased dramatically, but it was nice to have the tools to attack them. The other thing is they all build their own cars. They operate the cars at a very high level but they also build them themselves.

"I was very impressed with the quality of the Ligier factory guys, the composite shop, the factory manager. They essentially do what Lola and Reynard do for Indy cars. They do the wind tunnel models, the whole thing. They build all the components, everything. The manufacturing is quite an interesting part of it.

"Essentially we, Tony Dowe and I, were sent over to Ligier by Tom Walkinshaw. When you buy a company you never really know what you've got. Our first job was to go over and give him a fair and honest report on what they really had. We came back very quickly and said the place is really in pretty good shape, but there are areas that need fixing. We gave our recommendations and the next thing was we were sent back again to get that implemented. Once we came up with a cohesive plan of what had to be done our job was over. Then the real people go in and off they go.

"How often do you get dropped into a Formula 1 team and get to run it for a couple of months? It was total control. It was great. [We both laugh at his good fortune.] Going over there, I had some misgivings being aware of the technology, but it's just real people doing it all, and if you ask them real questions, you get real answers. It didn't take me long to get into it and it is a team, and the language barrier turned out to not be a barrier. It was enjoyable. The place is full of bright, motivated people. All we had to do was get them organized so they pulled together. That really was the main process. It was great to say, 'Why don't we do this?' and have it happen."

PH: "I'm tickled you got the chance."

IR: "It was fun."

PH: "So what are you going to do now? I keep reading about a possible IndyCar team."

IR: "Well, we've got some plans. Nothing I can talk about yet."

Cosworth/Ford XB Indy Car Engine

Ilmor/Mercede-Benz Indy Car Engine

Honda Indy Car Engine

CHAPTER 4
RACING ENGINES

As recently as 10 years ago the engine was the racecar component that got all the attention. Racing fans talked about lighter pistons and bigger valves and better camshafts and stronger connecting rods and porting and polishing of intake and exhaust passages. Tuning carburetors for varying atmospheric conditions was considered a magical art, and successful practitioners earned the same kind of respect our ancient ancestors gave to medicine men and shaman who predicted critical events by studying chicken entrails or the motion of heavenly bodies.

Computer-controlled engine management systems, advanced materials, and computer hardware and software tools trickling down from the aerospace industry have changed all that. Racing engines are now so specialized that they are designed and developed by a small number of organizations inside of or funded by major automobile manufacturers such as General Motors, Ford (Cosworth), Honda, Renault, Peugeot, Mercedes-Benz (Ilmor), Toyota, and Ferrari, owned by Fiat. Even in local dirt track or SCCA club racing, individual competitors now tend to buy their engines from a specialty engine builder. For most racers the engine is now a plug-in, black-box component that is expected to be trouble-free until it's replaced with another identical unit. You'll rarely ever see modern racers tweaking their engines. They have all they can handle worrying about the driving and handling variables.

A few years ago Indy car races were dominated by Cosworth-Ford engines. Then Ilmor began supplying engines with Chevrolet on the cam covers and are now paid to put the Mercedes-Benz logo in the same space. Porsche and Alfa-Romeo made unsuccessful forays into Indy car racing. Honda looked pretty bad in 1994 when Bobby Rahal gave up on them, but were doing much better early in the 1995 season. Toyota will supply an engine to Dan Gurney's All American Racers in 1996. This makes for very interesting racing and a lot to talk about and keep up with.

The last few years I've been able to talk to some of the people involved in supplying engines to Indy car teams. In this section I'll pass on some of what I've learned and share some of the conversations I've had with them.

ROB WHITE AT LAGUNA

I attended an IndyCar test at Laguna Seca in September 1992 and arrived at the track in mid-morning to find Al Unser Jr. testing a Galles/Ilmor-Chevy and Michael Andretti flogging a Lola/Cosworth-Ford. Paul Tracy was also there driving one of the Penske/Ilmor-Chevys.

I saw Ed Nathman, the Newman-Haas crew chief who went to Galles for '93. He recognized me and said, "You want to talk to Michael?"

"Yeah, OK, maybe later," I said. "What I'd really like is to talk to one of the Cosworth guys."

"OK, sure," Ed said. "Hey, Rob." A young guy in a white Cosworth shirt and dark pants came over. He had a dark-brown crew cut and looked slim and about 6 feet tall. I introduced myself.

"I'm Rob White," he said in a clipped British accent. He wore a smile and seemed pleasantly curious, not at all perturbed that I had interrupted his work.

"I've got some questions about engines," I began. "Have you got a few minutes?"

"Ten," said Ed and walked back to the racecar.

Rob and I walked into a shady spot by the trailer, and I told him I had been wondering for some time why, if a V-12 engine was so much better than a V-8, do we see V-8s, V-10s, and V-12s at the front of the grid in F1 races? What, I wondered, are the trade-offs? Rob smiled and started talking. I made notes and asked more questions.

RW: "This is the classic dilemma with engine design. Air is the working fluid, and the more air you get through the engine the more power you can develop. Small cylinders have more valve area, which allows more airflow. The faster you turn the engine the more air flows through it. The limit to engine speed is inertia forces which go up with the square of engine speed. You're starting and stopping a lot of parts—pistons, connecting rods, valve gear. More cylinders with the same displacement gives smaller parts which weigh less and can be jiggled up and down faster without failure. But more parts have more friction surfaces. There's more piston ring length, for example, in a V-12 than in a V-8 of the same displacement.

"More friction with a 12 is a problem but it's more complicated than that. There's at least 50% more parts in a V-12 than a V-8 just because there's 50% more cylinders. But really there's more extra parts than that. For example, a V-12 needs more auxiliary systems, like oil scavenge pumps. You need six on a V-12 versus four on a V-8. It takes power to run these systems. And they add weight and volume. And more parts to break.

"A big problem with a V-12 is the fuel it needs. In F1, you can't refuel [the rules have since changed to encourage refueling] and so you have to start with all the fuel you'll need for the entire race. If you're putting more air through the engine you have to put more fuel through also. The extra friction absorbs some engine power. So the car with a V-12 engine has to start the race much heavier than a V-8 car, and tends to use up the tires early on."

The following table shows some calculations that help illustrate what Rob White was talking about. If we assume a bore/stroke ratio of 0.6 (the stroke is 60% as long as the cylinder bore diameter) and a total displacement of 3,500 cubic centimeters as dictated by the rules, we can calculate these values for bore and stroke. Rob says smaller cylinders have more piston area and you can see a V-10 has 7.7% more and a V-12 14.4 % more than a V-8.

Number of cylinders	Bore in.	Stroke in.	Piston Area sq. in.	% Increase Over V-8	Piston Circum. In.	% Increase Over V-8
8	3.84	2.30	92.6		96.5	
10	3.56	2.14	99.8	7.7	112.0	16.0
12	3.35	2.01	106.0	14.4	126.0	31.0

With a bigger bore you have more room for the valves, and bigger valves get more air/fuel through the engine. A trade-off, however, is friction. If we calculate the circumference of those cylinders we find a V-12 has 31% more length of piston ring, which probably means more friction. I looked in some engine design books, but the graphs for friction all stopped at about 5,000 rpm, and modern F1 engines are turning three times that. So, while the relationships aren't exact indications of the trade-offs, at least we can see that the increase of length of piston ring (friction) is more than the increase in piston area (power). Yeah, a V-12 generates more power, but more of it gets absorbed by internal friction than in a V-8. That's one reason they need more fuel.

Back to the conversation.

RW: "A V-12 is necessarily longer than a V-8 and has less torsional stiffness, like a long tube is less stiff than a short one. All F1 cars these days use the engine as a stressed member, so the V-12 cylinder block may need to be beefed up a little, which makes it longer and heavier unless you're very clever. And the crankshaft of a V-12 twists more for the same reason. But the V-12 has a smaller cross-section, and gets less in the way of the overall aerodynamic package. The V-12 car can have less drag.

"But all this is theory. In practice it's less clear cut. At Ford and Cosworth the success of the V-8 up against engines with more cylinders is due to a lot of people working hard and smart. Theory is one thing, but attention to detail during design and constant development count for a lot. Fatigue is the usual failure mode, so the number of cycles is what matters, not gross over-stressing of parts. With fatigue failures, design details can make a difference. How good your design is determines what breaks. If you do a good enough job with a V-8, maybe it can rev as high as a 12.

"People tend to exaggerate power differences. There's probably only 50 horsepower difference between engines near the front of an F1 grid regardless of the design configuration. Our V-8 is probably closer to the power of the V-12s than most people think."

Ceramics in Engines?

"Are you using ceramics in the engines?" I asked.

"Yes," was Rob's reply.

"Mostly coatings for less heat transfer and less friction?"

"Yes," again.

"Any big pieces like silicon nitride piston-tops or cast-in inserts in the combustion chamber?"

"Can't say anything about that," said Rob.

Although Rob White admitted that Cosworth is using coatings, probably friction-fighting coatings and also coatings which insulate components like valves and pistons, allowing them to operate at lower temperatures, he didn't want to talk about another potential use of ceramics that would get more power out of an engine—using pieces of ceramic material cast into components such as the cylinder head or piston top to insulate each combustion chamber and keep more heat in the gases that expand and push on the piston. I've heard rumors of piston tops made from silicon nitride, and I've also heard of chemical vapor deposition of ceramics to form thermal barriers on engine parts. Why use ceramic materials? The answer is insulation.

You know that ceramics are good insulators because you probably take your hot tea or coffee from a ceramic cup. An ordinary cup is a mixture of sand and clay fired at high temperature, producing a glassy material that is a relatively poor conductor of heat. You can hold a hot cup because the heat doesn't easily soak into the handle. A metal spoon in that same hot liquid can get too hot to touch, because metals are good heat conductors.

The basic principle here is that if you insulate parts of an engine, you keep more heat in the working fluid, the air/fuel mixture. The engine in your car is about 30% efficient, which means that only 30% of the heat generated by the combustion of fuel and air actually gets used to drive the wheels. Twice as much, 60%, goes into the cooling system (and the engine oil) and is dissipated into the surrounding air. You need the cooling just to keep the metal materials in the engine from melting. The remaining 10% goes out the exhaust pipe. If you can retain more of that 60% lost heat in the working fluid, you get a more efficient engine which puts out more power with less fuel. Insulation on piston tops and combustion chamber surfaces keep heat out of the water and oil. If, in addition to more power and less fuel consumption, the engine needed smaller oil and water coolers, then the whole car gets smaller and lighter. Less heat and friction inside an engine is a very big deal in a racecar!

Pneumatic Valve Control

PH: "What about the pneumatic valve springs in the Cosworth F1 engine?"

RW: "Historically, valve spring failure due to surge has always limited the power output of the internal combustion engine. [Valve spring surge, deflection waves caused by the quick opening and closing of the valve, causes overheating and/or fatigue failures in valve springs.] More valves per cylinder in smaller cylinders gets the weight of each valve down so you can rev the engine higher. More valves per cylinder gives more gas flow area also. The end result is more air and fuel through the engine per unit time, which means more power. Metal valve springs have been improved over the years mainly by going to more exotic materials, like special steels manufactured in special ways which raise the fatigue-failure threshold. Titanium valves, retainers, and keepers are lighter and so lower the weight the springs have to control.

"Pneumatic valve springs solve many of these problems, but they are much more complicated than a simple spring. Pneumatic valve springs allow higher engine speeds and therefore higher power outputs, but they are made up of a lot of small parts machined to very tight tolerances and assembled very carefully in near-clean room conditions. If it was easy, everyone would do it.

"Renault has patented a constant pressure pneumatic valve spring. It's a closed cylinder using a gas spring in place of a metal one. In a constant pressure design you'd let the opening valve push the gas out of the cylinder. [Presumably back into the storage reservoir.] The other way to do it is to let the gas pressure rise as the valve opens. We've tested both. We don't know what Renault is using currently, and we won't say what we're using either."

I heard Ed call to Rob, so I thanked him. He graciously said he enjoyed the talk and went back to work. Later in this section there are other conversations with Rob and other Cosworth people.

Penske Indy Pushrod Engine Calculations

After the 1994 Indy 500 and all the hype and speculation about the Penske/Ilmor/Mercedes-Benz pushrod engine, I decided to see if I could figure out for myself how much horsepower that engine generated.

I wanted to know the aerodynamic drag in hp and the equation for that is:

$$hp = 1/146600 \; Cd \; A \; V^3$$

Where Cd is the drag coefficient, A is the frontal area of the car, and V is the speed. If the V you use is the top speed of the car, then the hp calculated is the maximum power of the engine. This is true because, at the top speed of the racecar, all the engine power (except for friction and rolling losses) is going to drive the car through the air.

I asked around and decided to use 12 square feet for the frontal area of an Indy car. I heard all kinds of numbers for the maximum power of the 1994 Cosworth engine, but I thought 800 was too much and 750 was too little, so I used 775. I'm guessing there's about 15% friction losses in the drive train and tires, so net horsepower is 85% of gross horsepower. I didn't know the drag coefficient, but I did know the Cosworth-powered Lolas went about 240 mph at the ends of the straights during qualifying at Indy, so I started with a table that lets me look at what top speeds (Vmax) fall out if I vary the Cd.

Hp (gross)	Hp (net)	Cd	Vmax, mph
775	659	.70	225
775	659	.65	231
775	659	.60	238
775	659	.55	244

This shows the Cd is probably about 0.60. Now we can use the same equation to see what horsepower it would take to get a pushrod Penske, with the same frontal area and Cd, to a top speed of about 250 mph, which was the best top speed I remembered seeing on television during Indy qualifying.

Hp (gross)	Hp (net)	Cd	Vmax, mph
800	680	.60	240
850	723	.60	245
900	765	.60	250
950	808	.60	254

This table says the pushrod Penske had about 900 hp or only 125 more than the Cosworth, but I'd been told that the Penskes were capable of going more than 250 mph on the straights and indeed had done so during secret testing at Michigan. I had heard from several sources that the Penskes were "tire limited." 250 mph was probably nearing the lower safety margin of the maximum design speed of the Goodyear tires and, since the project was so secret that even Goodyear didn't know about it, there was no other tire available. With modern racecars, if you can't use the speed you might as well crank in some downforce, and that's what they did. So maybe the Penske really had a Cd of 0.65. How did that affect the power needed to push the car to a 250 mph top speed?

Hp (gross)	Hp (net)	Cd	Vmax, mph
900	765	.65	243
950	808	.65	248
1,000	850	.65	252

A Vmax of 250 would be in between the two lower calculations, so the pushrod Penske might have had about 975 hp. That was 200 more than the Cosworth at that time. You can see in the table that each 50 hp is worth about 5 mph top speed. The Honda-powered Lola that Bobby Rahal tried to qualify at Indy in '94 was about 10 mph slower in top speed than the Cosworth-powered Lolas. From that you can guess that the Honda engine was less powerful than the Cosworth by almost 100 hp. You can see why Rahal made the last-minute decision to switch to Penske/Ilmors.

More Power Helps in the Corners Too

What about downforce in the corners? Did the Penske/Ilmor/M-B cars have an advantage over the Lola/Cosworths? We can calculate drag at top speed, and we know that drag is proportional to the square of the speed, so we can calculate the drag at any other speed. But how do we calculate the downforce?

L/D, pronounced "L over D," is a common aerodynamic performance factor. L is lift, negative lift or downforce in our case, and D is drag. A wing that has an L/D of 4 makes four times more lift than drag and is more efficient than a wing with an L/D of 3. The only way to get an accurate L/D is in a wind tunnel, which I didn't have, so I asked around again.

In 1993 L/D for the Speedway was about 2 and at road courses the number was 3+. New rules on wings for 1994 cut those numbers to 1 at the Speedway and 2 on road courses. Here's another table that shows calculated drag at top speed and corresponding downforce if the L/D is 1. Of course, V is in mph and Drag and Downforce are in pounds.

	Cd	Vmax	Drag	Downforce
Lola/Cosworth/Ford	.60	240	1,061	1,061
Penske/Ilmor/M-B	.65	250	1,247	1,247

During qualifying these cars were taking the corners at about 220 mph, so I calculated the downforce at that speed to see how they compared. Aerodynamic forces go up with the square of the speed. Downforce at 220 mph equals the downforce at 240 mph multiplied by 220 x 220 / 240 x 240.

	Vmax	Downforce	Vcorner	Downforce
Lola/Cosworth	240	1,061	220	892
Penske/Ilmor	250	1,247	220	966

The designers of these racecars have the data required to make these calculations accurately but I don't, so these numbers aren't exactly correct. They're probably fairly close though, and certainly close enough to show us that the Penske/Ilmor/M-B pushrod cars had more horsepower to push more wing, which gave them more corner speed. They also had more torque coming out of the corners. If they had higher speeds in the corners and more torque coming off the corners, you can see why they passed other cars so easily.

Did Penske use a rules loophole to dominate the Indy 500? Of course not! He used an amazing organization to spot an opportunity, design a sophisticated component to exploit that opportunity, and then execute a manufacture, test, and build schedule that would have been impossible for any other Indy car organization. They deserved that win with no qualifications.

The rule was there and everyone knew about it. Only Roger Penske wanted to win badly enough to make it happen. To show the Indy win was no fluke, they finished first, second, and third at Milwaukee a week later with a regular Ilmor D engine. PEOPLE win races, not rules or money!

Penske Paid For It in 1995

The Penske team with Al Unser Jr. and Emerson Fittipaldi driving weren't able to qualify for the 1995 Indy 500. This was, except for the death of Ayrton Senna, the motorsports story of the decade. I'll list some reasons that contributed to Penske's failure to qualify.

- USAC changed the rules so a non-stock engine no longer had a power advantage in 1995.
- Penske chassis design had followed a trend toward low pitch and roll sensitivity resulting in less downforce, while Reynard went for maximum absolute downforce and let the teams learn how to live with it.
- All that power in '94 masked a racecar that was marginal in aerodynamic performance. Everyone learned about low-downforce set-up in '94 except the Penske team.
- Ilmor spent the winter of '94/'95 designing a new F1 engine and got behind in IndyCar engine development. They were about 20 hp short of the Cosworth and Honda engines.
- Penske didn't switch to other chassis quick enough for their drivers to get comfortable in the new cars.

These are all speculations on my part, but they would have certainly been in much better shape if the engine had been able to produce 20 or 30 more horsepower.

'92 VISIT TO COSWORTH ENGINEERING

During that test day at Laguna in 1992 I wrote about earlier in this section, I was walking along in the pit lane when Michael Andretti made a comment that was not meant to be overheard. He was sitting on the pit wall talking to a crew member and, just as I was walking by, I heard him say in a frustrated, whiny voice, "I bet they never fix that belt problem." He was obviously referring to the problem with his Cosworth-Ford engine that put him out at the 1992 Indy 500 and also that year's Michigan 500.

Michael Andretti was leading both races when his engine died. Sure, he was going to F1 then, but he had never won the Indy 500. Can you imagine what that win would have meant to him? The Indy 500 plus a win at Michigan would also have put him ahead of Bobby Rahal in that year's PPG IndyCar points championship. Those engine failures hurt!

In interviews at that time, Andretti reported loss of fuel pressure at Indy and low oil pressure at Michigan. What happened at both races was actually a failure of the toothed belt on the front of the engine that drives the auxiliary systems—the fuel pump, water pump, and the oil scavenge and pressure pumps.

The Cosworth-Ford Indy car engines are designed and manufactured in England, but are rebuilt at a facility in Torrance, Calif., a Los Angeles suburb. My first visit to Cosworth in October of 1992 started out in Ian Bisco's office. Ian is a Cosworth vice president, and he runs this facility. He's a Brit who's been in the United States since 1978, and with Cosworth since 1980. He's tall, slim, and always professional, with a good dose of humor.

I told Ian what I had overheard Michael Andretti say and asked if the problem had ever been found. "No," he said. "We don't know exactly what the problem is yet. It never showed up in all the dynamometer testing we did or in all the preseason testing we did on ovals and road courses. To make it more confusing, Eddie Cheever, driving a similar car, had no problem at Indy. There were a lot of laps under the yellow flag that year and Michael ran his engine at a higher rpm during those slow laps in an effort to keep it warm. After that failure we thought it was a sustained high-speed problem. Then some things happened that made us think it was a low-speed problem instead. That got us off track. Then it happened again at Michigan, a high-speed track. What we think now is there is an interaction between the chassis and the engine at high speeds. The track at Michigan was very bumpy, and that may have made it worse. We spent a lot of time testing to find out what was going on, but I really can't say we found one single cause."

"What about next year?" I asked.

"The '93 Lola chassis will be quite a bit different and will probably not have the same kind of interaction," Ian replied. "A simple change in the length or diameter of the transaxle quill shaft could make the difference. But we'll make sure there's no problem next year with a design fix. We'll add something to the engine that will absorb auxiliary drive vibrations, and that will solve it."

What evidently happened was, at a certain engine speed and at a specific road speed over a certain-sized bump, a harmonic vibration occured which excited the belt or got one of the driven components moving in the wrong direction. The result was belt failure, it broke. Vibrations are an important part of the mechanical design of any system with moving parts. Every component has its own natural frequency and, when combined with other components into a system, affects the natural frequency of the system.

The classic example of a catastrophic failure due to harmonic resonance is the wine glass shattered by a strong sound at a certain pitch. If you tap a wine glass you hear it ring. That sound is at a frequency near the natural harmonic frequency of the glass. The glass vibrates when struck and drives air waves at a certain frequency that we hear. The shape and thickness of the glass determine the frequency of vibration—the pitch of the sound. A sound at the right frequency drives air which excites the glass, and the resulting deformation of the glass can break it. That's probably what happened to Michael Andretti's engine auxiliary drive belts.

Engine Questions

Over a year later, in October 1993, I visited Cosworth again. Ian Bisco had helped me get an appointment for another interview with Rob White. I spent some time thinking about what questions to ask and came up with the ones below. I sent them to Rob about a week before the trip.

1. Background, personal and professional.
2. Are developmental increases in power planned or serendipitous?
3. What are the sources of power increases? Mechanical improvements vs. software?
4. What are the trends in materials?
   Friction reduction
   Insulating
   Flame or plasma spray? Chemical vapor deposition?
   Metals: titanium, metal matrix?
   Ceramics?
   Carbon fiber rods?
5. How are fuel mileage gains being made?
6. What do multiple injection nozzles accomplish?
7. What are the current limiting factors? Flame travel? Component fatigue strength?
8. What is the weak component at max rpm?
9. Piston trends. Materials? Ringless?
10. What changes are made to engines to maximize performance at different tracks? Fuel and ignition maps? Mechanical parts?
11. Do you have simulation capabilities that work? Design? Dyno?

12. If you have the opportunity to influence chassis design, what do you try to do?
13. What are the trade-offs on pneumatic valve control? Is rising pressure a better choice than constant pressure?
14. Trends in overall packaging?
15. Most difficult/critical component to design/develop?
16. What do you do at a racetrack on race weekends? Technical support? Sympathetic ear? Customer communications?

A Longer Talk with Rob White

When I arrived at the Cosworth shop in Torrance I was greeted by Ian Bisco, and he and I sat down for a talk about general Indy car/Cosworth stuff. Later we found Rob and he and I went into an office to talk. We sat down across from each other at a desk, and I set up my tape recorder. Rob had prepared for the talk by reading the questions I sent and making some notes. He referred to the questions and his notes throughout the talk.

Rob White at Cosworth Engr. in Torrance, Calif.

Rob White is a very likable, university-educated professional engineer in his thirties. Seen in an Indy car pit, Rob seems intensely focused and a little stiff, but when he talks one-on-one his eyes sparkle with enthusiasm and small smiles come and go. Rob has that charmingly-British, disarming, almost-shy, self depreciation that compliments his technical strength and helps him perform what is a very, very difficult task, dealing with Indy car owners, crew chiefs, and mechanics. They expect a lot from a Cosworth engine.

After I got set up, Rob looked up from my question list, grinned and started to talk.

RW: "I anticipated most of your questions, but not the first one [laughs]. The one about how I came to be doing this. It started a long time ago. When I was in school I used to race karts and tinker about with Formula Ford engines in my spare time. When I left school I worked at Jaguar Cars in Coventry, England, and as a result of that they sponsored me to go to University, and I did a bachelor's degree in mechanical Engineering. But as soon as I got my degree I up and left to work for Cosworth. I've worked for Cosworth since 1987, and most of my time at Cosworth I've worked on the Indy car engine. In the early days I worked for Steve Miller, then the chief engineer. It was essentially just the two of us engineering the DFX, which would grow into the DFS. At one point we decided we needed to do another engine, and right from the beginning of the XB engine project I've been in there in the thick of it. After the XB was laid out, designed, and detailed, then I was working directly for Steve and responsible for the performance development of the engine. At the beginning of 1993 I came to Torrance to look after the servicing of the engine and take care of the mechanical spec of the engine as built at Torrance, which is a satellite plant. All the parts of the engine are designed and built in England and serviced in Torrance."

PH: "Where did you go to school?"

RW: "The University of Southampton."

PH: "Was that a theoretical program? Did you get any manufacturing exposure there?"

RW: "There was quite a bit of manufacturing content in my degree courses, but in truth, nothing we could do at school could compare with the practical experience you get when you're doing things for money [laughs]. I learned a lot about that building automobiles at Jaguar, and then, of course, one of Cosworth's greatest strengths is its manufacturing. Even to this day, every time you go into the machine shop you've got to be dumb not to learn something. The place is still very close-knit, and you're perpetually in contact with manufacturing people throughout your working life at Cosworth. The manufacturing process and the discipline it takes is crucial to making this whole thing work. We couldn't work without it."

PH: "Were you a car nut?"

RW: "No, not really. I've never been a car nut. I'm a working mechanisms sort of person. If you can take something apart and put it back together and take out some of the clutter inside, it wouldn't really matter if it was on a car or a boat or an airplane bit. I'm still not particularly interested in street cars. Engines always fascinated me; anything mechanical, clever gizmos and stuff like that."

RW: [starting on the list of questions] "Are development increases in power planned or serendipitous? Bit of both I guess is the answer. About 50-50 [grins]. In the development stage of an engine you have to sort of organize your life. What happens, I suppose, is you plan to go looking for some performance and sometimes you find it and can put a tick in the box and say that was a planned increase. Other times you don't find what you're looking for. I guess it's important to be aware that even if every time you make a change or do an experiment you don't find a big lump of bolt-on power, oftentimes some learning takes place along the way which you can sort of pigeonhole away for next time. Undoubtedly though, there are times when you just get a lucky break, and you stumble over something or you go looking for something and it points the way to something that you haven't anticipated. Probably the best examples of those you can't really talk about, but there have been one or two of them.

"In general, to try and dispel the mysticism that there is out there, most of the performance that you get out of an engine after you move from putting the pieces together for a new design is just a matter of continual optimization, and it comes down to the age-old thing that people have known about engines for probably 80 years ,which is if you want to make more power, you've got to get it to swallow more air, make it breathe better, and run more quickly. So you're into moving closer to mechanical barriers which always exist, or you try to move the mechanical barriers a little bit further away from where you are at the time by making some changes. Everything that we do in the way of performance development is focused on these two areas. Sometimes you find that you're machining big pieces to make a change to make it breathe better, and sometimes you're doing what appears to be infinitesimally small work with, for example, ports or valves or valve seats on a flow bench. Sometimes you're working in thousands of an inch and other times you find yourself sawing a couple of inches off a piece of steel pipe.

"Our goals are similar throughout all that though, and we're always trying to make it use more air. That's because air is the working medium for a reciprocating engine, and it's the stuff that you don't have direct control over. You have direct control over the amount of fuel that you put in and you can basically put in as much fuel as you like. You have to pace that to the amount of air that the engine will swallow. So, when we go to the development phase of an engine, we go after making it swallow more air first off. Then fuel it accordingly.

"The other big path that you follow is reducing mechanical losses. The real big lumps of that come about when you redesign your engine. Most of the mechanical losses that we're fighting against are defined by the architecture of the engine, the layout of the pieces, and based on the base dimensions that you choose for the major components, and so are pretty much cast in concrete as you move into the development phase of the engine.

"There are little things that you can do, and because it's a game of optimization, there's some stuff you can do once you've put your first engine together, things like scavenge pumps. There's a balance between the power consumed in driving these pumps and the power saved by running the crankcase in depression [low pressure], and by completely evacuating the oil from the engine. So you have to balance the two, and somewhere in between there's an optimum speed for the scavenge pumps to run relative to the engine speed."

PH: "When you're designing an engine, what do you work with? Paper, computer, CAD [computer-aided design]?"

RW: "It's a mixture at Cosworth. It's still a very small group of people who actually do the layout of a new engine. For the Indy car engine right now that's Steve Miller, chief engineer; Stewart Groves actually designed the XB engine, but he no longer works for Cosworth. He works at Ferrari.

"The major items are the cylinder heads, block, sump, crank, rods, pistons, and then the cam drive mechanism. The pumps aren't trivial, but they're a packaging exercise most of the time. This is one of the benefits that a company like Cosworth has in that there is a lot of prior knowledge, a lot of information available from previous designs, and, although it's important to assess what you're doing each time you make a new engine, it's equally important to make use of what's available to you from previous times. There are some things which take place in the pumps that make such good sense and get modified only after a lot of soul-searching, and, as a consequence, the auxiliaries themselves give us, typically, [knocks wood, grins] very little trouble. I guess that the cylinder head is the biggest piece in an engine. That's the piece that you tend to guard most jealously.

"Going on down the list, then?"

PH: "That's great."

RW: "Usual sources of power increases, mechanical or software? Almost all are mechanical improvement and very little software. In terms of raw horsepower there's almost nothing you can do electronically or in software to improve the performance of the engine."

PH: "So software has mainly improved the drivability and flexibility?"

RW: "Yeah, and also the thing that's often overlooked in the favor of the electronic stuff on the engine, is the facility it gives you to do mechanical work so easily. Inevitably, when you want to make a mechanical change, you have to make a change to re-optimize fueling, ignition, or injector timing, and, with electronics, you just twiddle a knob or edit a table and you're there. Whereas, in the old days, if you wanted to change the ignition timing, then somebody had to go in there while the engine was running and crank a trigger backwards or forwards or, before that even, crank the distributor backwards or forwards. If you wanted to change the fueling of an engine while it was running, with carburetors, you had to be hauling around choke tubes and emulsion jets and other little pieces of the carburetor. More recently than that and probably even more ghastly, you had to tinker with cams and springs and orifices and restrictors and such things in mechanical fuel injection metering units, all of which would distract you from what you're trying to do, which is investigate a mechanical change."

PH: "Now all that is just a huge waste of time that you don't have to worry about anymore."

RW: "Sure. The electronics greatly increases the amount of mechanical work you can do but, on their own, they're unlikely to give you any power."

"So, I'll go on to your materials question. ['What are the trends in materials?' was the question, and I listed some possible subtopics: friction reduction, insulating—flame or plasma spray; metals—titanium or metal matrix; ceramics; carbon fiber rods.]

"All engineers are interested in materials, and we as much as anyone else. Fortunately, most of the things you have here are either specifically banned or their use is limited in the rules for Indy cars. I guess it's still worth saying that, in modern race engines, the most important materials are still high-strength alloy steels and world-class aluminum castings. There are other materials in there and you try to optimize the materials you use with heat treatments and surface treatments, but the real building blocks of the engines are still relatively traditional materials."

PH: "I've read that Cosworth has a casting process that's better in some way?"

RW: "That's true. I'm not sure of the history, but maybe 15 years ago or so we decided that we should have our own foundry because of the difficulties you have in getting aluminum castings of good dimensional accuracy and good structural integrity. Bottom line now is we have our own foundry with our own unique process that achieves this by a quite novel means.

"The basic difference is that instead of taking molten aluminum from a vat and ladling it into molds, the stuff is pumped out of the vat so you don't have a ladle passing through the scum on the top of the vat or disturbing the stuff on the bottom. You take pure, clean, molten aluminum from the center of the vat and pump it through ceramic pipe with a type of pump that has no moving parts. It's an electro-magnetic device of the type used in nuclear power stations to pump liquid sodium.

"You haul this clean molten aluminum out of the middle of the vat, and you pump it into the mold from underneath. So the mold gets to vent at the top, and you don't have the gas bubbles passing up through the whole melt. It has a clear passage to the outside world. The other thing that's important is that if you maintain a modest pressure on the bottom of the mold until it's solidified, a number of things contribute to the improved integrity of the casting. First is the cleanliness of the material. Second, there is less porosity because there's a good route for the air to get out of the mold, and the pressure helps too. There's another important difference in the process, and that is the sand used in the mold is not the same stuff that's used in a typical molding application, which is usually silicon sand. We use zircon sand. The key feature of zircon sand is that it doesn't have a phase shift close to the temperature where aluminum melts, whereas silica sand does have this phase shift. What happens when silica sand undergoes this phase shift is there is a small volume change which results in a dimensional change to the casting. Fundamentally, the zircon sand gives you a casting which has better dimensional control. The stuff is damned expensive, and the only way you can do it is by recycling the sand. Another part of the process is a novel way of reusing the zircon sand so it's viable. I'm not an expert on the casting process and that's about all I can remember.

"Our basic materials are high-strength steels, good castings, and optimizing surface treatments. We use nitriding on crankshafts, tufftriding on cams and tappets, and plating or vapor deposition processes on titanium pieces.

"Titanium is an interesting material because it's light and very strong. Typically it has yield strengths as good as a reasonable piece of steel. It has several important disadvantages compared to steel, though. First of all, it has terrible properties when any sort of sliding friction is involved. Anytime a titanium piece has to rub against anything else it's bad news. This means that almost any application you can think of for titanium involves a part that's moving, because it's used so you can reduce the reciprocating mass of something. So anywhere you use titanium there has to be a coating."

PH: "You're doing some chemical vapor deposition of materials on titanium to solve this problem?"

RW: "Yes, but most of that is proprietary to a subcontractor. Wherever you have titanium you have to do something to the surface. We've been involved in research to try to improve the surface properties of titanium, but in our engine there's not a single component in the engine that doesn't have some sort of surface treatment on it. And I can't think of a titanium component in anyone else's engine I've ever seen that has been untreated either. Even if it's only anodizing, or sometimes you have to apply a clever surface treatment to the other piece. One example is titanium fasteners. You'll typically use an anodized surface on the titanium and a silver-plated nut for the female thread. Titanium fasteners are not allowed on Indy cars, but if they were that's what we'd have to do. I think I'm right in saying that, in Indy cars, titanium is only allowed for valves and reciprocating parts in the valve gear. Con rods are specifically excluded. Fasteners are specifically excluded. Likewise carbon fiber and ceramics."

PH: "Just a speculation, is anybody using carbon fiber rods now? In F1, for instance."

RW: "I can't imagine anybody who builds racing engines in the fashion that we do, using them. The Mugens, Ilmors, Judds, although I have no idea in truth, but I don't see them being able to do that sort of work. Typically nobody has the resources to devote to high-level research of that type. We'd like to make use of novel materials as soon as humanly possible once they've become established and proven technology."

PH: "So this is probably a much more conservative business than you would think if you believed everything you read."

RW: "There's certainly some truth in that. It's conservative in terms of the materials we use, but the design and the detail design is very adventurous. The performance we achieve is very adventurous despite these largely tried and tested, proven materials."

PH: "I was surprised to hear Eddie Cheever commenting on ESPN's F1 broadcast speculating that the Renault engine might be putting out 100 hp more than the other engines. One percent seems a lot to me."

RW: "It's very difficult to speculate on that, but I would have thought that, for one engine to be more than 3% or 4% up on another engine, is a real big step. Well, let me see, 1% is 7 horsepower so I guess you could be 5% ahead....or behind [laughs]. Depending on your point of view. Yeah, you could be 5% behind in terms of raw horsepower. You're unlikely to be 5% behind in terms of BMEP [Brake Mean Effective Pressure]. The combination of BMEP and the speed you can run the thing, and you might end up being 5% ahead or behind.

[Rob looked down again to the question list.] "How are fuel mileage gains being made? Essentially the same mechanism as for power. It's a matter of optimization. You've perhaps got quite a long way to go in a methanol engine, because you're starting from a position of less knowledge. You're starting with a fuel that's less well understood. You're starting with a fuel that has many endearing properties, but burning well isn't one of them [grins]. I think where we are right now, we run methanol engines far richer compared to gasoline engines of similar technology. Some of this is linked to other elements in the rules package, no intercooler, for example. I think it's fair to say that, certainly in the past, everybody would run rich in order to preserve pistons.

over at hand speed. The thing that really kills them is spring surge, which is the resonance of the valve spring under the influence of the camshaft.

"There are two big elements to the design of the valve gear. One is to make sure that the cam is designed so the valve spring can keep the valve gear in contact with the cam so your reciprocating bits are in control with respect to the rotating bits. We depend on the valve springs to keep the valve in contact with the cam profile. The second and less clearly understood part is making the valve spring survive under the action of the cam irrespective of what the rest of the stuff is doing. You require that the valve spring can conform to what the cam is making it do. If you can imagine the spring in between two surfaces both moving backwards and forwards [Rob uses his hands to illustrate], the spring has to accommodate that movement without getting excited. Typically the spring will resonate, and that's when you get valve gear problems. That's the limit that wire springs still face. It's possible that another way to understand and improve valve gear design will allow us to move valve gear back down to second or third place on the list. Then we'll be limited by con rods or pistons again."

PH: "So when incremental developments improve something, it just shifts the emphasis to the next weakest link. You just improve yourself to a new problem."

RW: "Exactly. Piston trends [the next question on the list] is a similar story. It comes down to detail design. Again, we're very fortunate at Cosworth that we have complete control over the piston. We can design and manufacture every piston for every racing engine that we build. We make our own forgings, and we completely machine them ourselves. The trends are really in detail design. The pieces are getting smaller and lighter the whole time. We're learning things about the details of the piston construction that lead to better fatigue life of the component although we use, at the moment, the same material that we have done for some time. We use a forging alloy that was developed for fighter engines during the second World War.

"Although we're interested in new materials, we haven't yet found one that has the same combination of properties as the one we're using today. In the piston you're looking for a material that combines light weight, high strength, and good fatigue properties, particularly at elevated temperatures. It has to be hot all over, but it's also got to cope with a big temperature distribution. You've probably got 300 or 400 degrees on the piston crown; that's degrees Celsius [400 degrees C is about 750 degrees F], and 150 degrees C [300 F] on the piston skirt. The thing has to be able to cope with rapidly fluctuating changes in temperature. The temperature on the inlet stroke is obviously greatly different than the temperature on the power stroke. It's really detail design that sets a good piston apart from a bad piston.

"You only have to have a look at a Periodic Table of the Elements to decide where you might get a few further improvements. You can look at the light elements up on the left-hand side and start thinking about aluminum alloys that have lithium or magnesium in them, or look at magnesium alloys. We could make pistons from some of these alloys, but I don't think we could use them seriously yet. There is potential for changes in piston material, but I don't think it's imminent.

"We're looking at ways of reducing piston friction. I don't think getting rid of the piston rings is possible at the moment. Most of the work on reducing the friction is getting the skirt shaped right and using the right combination of piston rings and liner materials. Piston rings and liner materials is one place where we will confess to a bit of witchcraft. It's one of the areas of the engine where it's typical to say we're using trial and error techniques and experience rather than first principles. Finding these combinations is sometimes easy and sometimes not so easy.

[Again, Rob looks at the next question on the list.] "What changes do you make to the engines to maximize performance at different tracks? In this series we try to maintain the mechanical spec of the engine as uniform as we can. We try not to have a road course spec or an oval spec. The reasons for this are mainly that nobody has enough engines to be able to manage that type of approach. At the moment, the character of the engine is such that the benefits of doing that would be quite small in any case. You probably wouldn't want to do it.

"Typically, we would be a bit more conservative about the way we use the engine at the Speedway [Indianapolis Motor Speedway]. To go 500 miles, we run the engine a little less quickly and would pay more attention at rebuild to 500-mile race engines. These engines get more new pieces. We have a schedule of replacement, and some parts get replaced every build and others every third build or whatever. A lot of those intermittently replaced pieces are refreshed for a 500-mile race. But in terms of the performance spec of the engine, they're essentially the same for all tracks.

"In terms of software changes, nothing changes. These are not usually driven by a desire to optimize performance for different tracks. They're more driven by a necessity to get the necessary mileage. Fuel consumption is incredibly important in Indy car racing. It's the thing that has the greatest bearing on how you run the race."

PH: "I hate that. I think it ruins the whole thing watching those guys short shifting and waiting until after the last pit stop to start to race. Is that just the alcohol? Would that change if they used gasoline?"

RW: "They could just increase the fuel allowance. That would fix the problem if you thought there was one. You wouldn't have to increase it very much. Of course it's not an issue at the Speedway. Everybody can get all they need there."

PH: "Why do they limit it? I thought it was because people would dump a bunch of fuel in for the cooling effect. Is that right?"

RW: "In our case, it wouldn't do much good. It's probably wrong to have a completely unlimited supply of fuel, but the balance could be shifted in favor of more."

PH: "I guess if the pressure is on and you guys get the baseline fuel mileage up a little bit, then you'd have some to play with. So maybe the pressure for fuel mileage is good?"

RW: "At the moment, you end up running the engines very lean compared with what they need at maximum power. The drivers don't like it. It's kind of worrying because you have to pay phenomenal attention to the accuracy of how you measure the fuel consumption as well as the amount of fuel you have to put into the engine. It's interesting. I quite like it how it is, but I've kind of gotten used to it."

[Rob looks back at the list again.] "Simulation capabilities that work? Yeah, it starts pretty early on and it continues through the development of the engine. Most of the drafting for the engine, most of the layouts for the engine are done on paper, not on CAD. But some of the parts are laid out on a computer. Particularly pieces that change a lot or mechanism sorts of pieces. It can be useful to be able to plot the movement of pieces, and the computer is good at that. It doesn't come under the realm of simulation, but it gives you the data to run in other models and other programs which are simulation. I'm thinking about finite element analysis [FEA] and valve train dynamic models that we have, programs for designing camshafts and examining the influence of valve gear changes on what we do.

"The finite element thing is important to us, but it would be wrong of me to paint a picture of a big finite element model of the whole engine. It's not the case. What we use finite element for is looking at the sensitivity to change of parts that we know to be critical to us. FEA is a great way of looking at fatigue-type problems. It's best suited to the type of problem that doesn't involve plastic deformation; it doesn't involve absolute failure. The type of stresses that lead to fatigue failures are pretty well modeled by even FEA programs that run on office-based personal computers rather than huge mainframe computers. So what we use them for is evaluating different types of detail design on highly stressed bits that we know by experience are prone to breaking. It sort of quantifies the seat-of-the-pants feeling that everyone has when you're putting in a fillet radius or smoothing out a change in section or any of these classic textbook problems. We all know that putting in the fillet radius will make it better. But sometimes the FEA programs are a good way of finding out how much better. And whether it's a change that's going to go far enough to fix the problem, or whether it's only going to stall the real solution while you're doing the experiment to find out.

"FEA is typically done on a piece you're having a problem with or a piece you've had a problem with that you're about to redo fresh. We can see how to improve the part incrementally, quantify that increment, and estimate the cost and benefit of the change.

"We have programs that can more or less design cams on their own, if you know what you want."

PH: "Internally developed?"

RW: "Yeah. Not much you can say about those except if you know what you want, they work. They're always limited by the amount of understanding you had of the problem in the first place when you wrote the program.

"Once you get them up and running, dyno simulations of a racetrack are very valuable. They basically come into two categories, one being performance work and the second being durability work. Performance testing of the engines goes hand in hand with having done a lot of engines for a lot of years. We know a lot about testing racing engines. Although we use typical, standard Heenan and Froude dynos, we just use the big mechanical pieces and the installation and control pieces are designed and built internally. This enables us to make pretty good performance measurements of the engine—steady state performance within 0.5%. That would be a repeatable 0.5%. It's difficult to ascribe an absolute accuracy to it. The absolute accuracy is not really that important as long as you can be honest with yourself when you analyze the results. It's not that often that something happens to change the absolute accuracy of the measurement."

PH: "Are dynamometers accurate one to another? Is there variation from one piece of equipment to another?"

RW: "They should be very close."

PH: "That same 0.5% number?"

RW: "Maybe 1%. There's a lot more difference in test results coming about from dishonesty or different corrections than there is in actual changes in the measured performance of the engine."

PH: "Are all power measurements corrected to standard atmospheric conditions?"

RW: "Yeah. You can get quite big changes if you change what you ascribe to be standard, though. We correct our numbers to 25 degrees C and 66% relative humidity and 45 inches of mercury, which is the nominal boost allowed in the rules. We'll adjust the waste gate so the absolute boost is 45 inches each time and correct the observed power according to the condition of the inlet air."

PH: "In an engine on a track, how close does the boost get to the allowed 45 inches of mercury? How much of the time does the engine run close to the max boost?"

RW: "It depends on the type of track. It's everybody's goal to have the engine at 45 inches of mercury the whole time the driver has his foot to the boards. The whole time the engine's at full throttle, it should be running at 45 inches."

PH: "I guess I don't know how that's controlled."

RW: "There's a pop-off valve that's supplied by CART. That has no influence on boost control. It's the penalty for screwing up the boost control. The rules say we use waste gates that are controlled by the plenum pressure. Essentially, the current arrangement for all the cars that race is that there are two waste gates. The waste gate is a device that measures the boost pressure in the plenum and, according to that pressure, it either spills exhaust gas bypassing the turbo or it forces exhaust gas to go through the turbo. Basically, if the waste gates are open, then there is a direct passage out to atmosphere for the exhaust gases. If the waste gates are shut, the exhaust has to go through the turbo and the turbo will be increasing the pressure in the plenum. When the waste gates are open the turbo will be slowing down and the pressure in the plenum falls.

"Effectively, you match waste gate performance to engine performance using a spring. It can be open or shut or anything in between. Typically, around a superspeedway, the plenum will be at 45 inches all the time. Around a short oval the plenum will be at 45 inches the whole time the driver is on the throttle. He will lift briefly in the corners, but the boost doesn't fall sufficiently far that there is a significant response time when he gets back on the throttle. It's instantly back at 45 inches. On street courses and road courses it's a bit more difficult. There's substantial part-throttle content at a road course. You wouldn't want it to get to 45 inches during the time the driver is at part throttle. At part throttle the turbo slows down and cools down, and when the driver goes back to full throttle there's a response delay before you achieve full boost."

PH: "I hear the drivers blipping the throttle in slow corners. I assume that's to keep the turbocharger spinning?"

RW: "Yeah. There'll be some of that taking place with changing gears and making the car change direction, which some of them don't want to do this year [smile].

"Boost control is a subject all to itself. It's a big part of making the engine work in the car.

"Going back to the dyno, the important thing is the dyno measures the steady-state performance of the engine. It doesn't measure the performance as the driver nails the throttle coming out of a turn. That'll be related to the boost control. There are a number of ways of going after this. We have a performance development dyno in England that's capable of measuring the transient performance of the engine in addition to steady-state performance. There's a big flywheel mounted on the back of the dyno. It sounds simple and looks very scary, with big pieces of metal rotating at engine speed. It's got big railway engine-type disc brakes on it to slow it down. But what it enables you to do is add the inertial load to the hydraulic load on the dyno so you can examine the performance of the engine with realistic rates of change of engine speed which you cannot normally do. Transient testing on a dyno is useful for performance work and durability work.

"The nature of superspeedways is such that you can do a very good simulation with just a regular dyno control. You have to be able to run an engine flat out for a number of hours."

PH: "That'd be scary too."

RW: "You've got to do it. [Laughs with pained expression.] We've learned a lot doing that; bolting the engine down and power testing it in the normal fashion and then doing a superspeedway simulation. You can choose the range of engine speed and cycle it up and down at full throttle. If you have something you're particularly worried about you might have to stop prematurely, but we have one engine which for the last two and a half years has been continuously built and run in this endurance cycle and then rebuilt. This is to find which pieces break."

PH: "So you've got a continuous durability program?"

RW: "It's about the only thing you can do to be able to go into one of these big 500-mile races with the belief that you can finish the race. Sometimes you can have that belief and it still doesn't happen.

"Going back to the questions. If you have the opportunity to influence chassis design, what do you do? The main thing here is making sure the bits that affect the engine work. There's a divided responsibility in putting an Indy car together. Our biggest interest when the chassis is being built is in making sure the systems that interact with the engine do what they have to do without causing performance or durability problems. What we're thinking about here are big mechanical bits. We want to see that the engine mounts are sensible so that the mechanical loads from the car that need to be carried by the engine are being put into the engine in a sensible fashion. And we need to see that all the plumbing is as it needs to be, in particular the oil tanks and the breather systems. They're crucial to making the engine last.

"I guess it's not immediately obvious to someone watching the race on TV that if you're pulling 4 Gs around a turn at a short oval, then the oil that would normally be sitting on the bottom of the tank will be sort of splurged up the side of the tank at an angle of about [Rob pulls out his pocket calculator again.] 75 degrees or something, making it very difficult for the oil tank to cope with the oil being settled on the bottom at one point in the lap and up the side at another. Of course on a road course it can slosh to the other side on another part of a lap. Getting an oil system that works reliably is real important to us all [Rob grins].

"Car designers have these things in their minds but there's other things in their minds as well. Like aerodynamics, they've got packaging goals. They want everything tiny, tiny, tiny. They want it to sit low down. Sometimes these things come into conflict. The engine people just want their engine to live [laughs]. You have to pay attention to a new car when you first test it. If you have a new car and the oil tank doesn't work, you blow some engines up."

PH: "I guess the clutch and gearbox comes in there too."

RW: "The transmission and the way the transmission is attached to the car is not often open to us to have a big influence. In the case with a car that's being laid out and there's fairly close cooperation with the engine manufacturer, then there will be dialog. If there's anything that strongly offends the engine guy, then he's going to tell the car guy what's going to happen because he's interested in the car doing well.

"The other things that are important to us are exhaust layouts and installation and turbo position and installation. The turbo position determines what the exhaust pipe ducting looks like and what the ducting from the outside world into the compressor looks like, and the compressor up to the plenum. All of these factors can affect the performance of the engine so we like to know what's happening there early in the proceedings so we can make changes.

"Likewise the boost control system is an important part of getting the car performance sorted. We like to do more than influence the design of the boost control; we like to control it. We make the waste gates, and we make the boost controller. Although in the past this has been the car builder's territory, we build them. It's one of the things we do to reduce the amount of grief we get at the racetrack. Historically, the boost control has been a gray area, a bit of divided responsibility. The pieces previously would have come with the car, but now they bear more on the engine performance than car performance. The engine person is more likely to understand these pieces than the chassis guy.

"Trends in packaging? [Next question on the list.] The trend in racing the world over is toward smaller, lighter pieces, and to engines that are more greatly integrated with the chassis design. That's become more and more important."

PH: "More integrated in both structure and aerodynamics?"

RW: "Exactly. Specifically, engines have got narrower, particularly in the sump area, under pressure from car designers to give them more space for the diffusers underneath the car. That wouldn't apply to an Indy car because the underside is controlled, but it would apply to a Formula 1 car. Engines have got narrower and could get lower. A recent rule change in Indy cars has perhaps taken some impetus out of repackaging engines, but I don't think they can completely detune us. A new rule controls the shape of the engine covers and is set up around the existing dimension of the Cosworth XB engine.

"The packaging thing is interesting. There's no doubt that if a car designer could convince the engine people of a needed change it would get done, but not if it affected engine performance. You'd only make a change that didn't influence the power because the aerodynamic things can't be measured with the same precision you can measure engine performance, so it would be a fairly risky activity to give away some engine performance in exchange for an aerodynamic hypothesis."

PH: "That's a very interesting point. So the package is important, but you would never sacrifice engine power."

RW: "You'd never give up horsepower. When it comes to horsepower, more is definitely better than less.

"The other thing that's increasingly important to the car people is the cleanliness of the engine. It's becoming the case that they want fewer components external to the engine. So the auxiliary things which used to sprout from engines, things like fuel pumps and alternators that used to be external pieces, are now more integral with the engine. The fuel pump is another example of a chassis bit which has always been built by the engine manufacturer. You can see that engines of today have a much cleaner appearance than engines of 10 or 15 years ago. You can't see through them any more. The space in the valley between the banks is better occupied and there are fewer and fewer external parts.

[Rob again refers to my list of questions.] "The most critical piece to design and develop? Probably all of them [laughs]. It goes, really, back to the bits that are the weakest link. So that it comes down again to the valve gear. The big mechanical bits that people think about when they think about engines are the most difficult to design. The valve gear, the cylinder heads, the block, the crankshaft, the rods, and the piston. The bits that are relatively easy to design and develop are the ancillaries, the pumps and the bolt-on bits on the top. The inlet arrangement might be quite hard, but the design is relatively straightforward. You just do it."

PH: "What do you do on a race weekend? At the Indy car race at Vancouver, Ian said I should try to catch you Saturday afternoon because you might have some time to talk. I hung around, and I watched you in one of the team areas sitting on an electric cart, and there were never less than three or four people there talking to you. What do you do there?"

RW: "It's incredibly difficult to explain sensibly. [Rob shakes his head and we both laugh.] I cannot give an adequate answer to this question no matter how many people ask me, whether it be socially or at work. I have to try to describe what happens at a typical race weekend, and that's very hard.

"Essentially, I'm there to take care of the engines. I'm there to do all of the things that you've suggested in the question here, to give technical support, to be a sympathetic ear, and to communicate with the customer. But the balance or the level of dominance of each of those things varies according to circumstance. Being relatively fortunate this year that the engine has been, on the whole, reliable; we haven't had too many repetitive problems. We haven't had too many common threads running through.

"A big part of my job is to be there to gather information about problems or failures—as early as possible. And try and get information from the teams while it's fresh in everybody's mind and while they're wanting to talk about it. If you don't get the information right away, then it's often lost for all time.

"It's kind of difficult to know how to support the engine in service. We try to maintain very close links between the customers who use the engine and Cosworth, who builds and services the engine. We want to make sure that there's always a channel for communication in both directions just to make sure that if anyone has a problem at a race weekend that they won't think that it's being glossed over. We want them to have confidence that we know about it, for starters, and we want them to have confidence that once we find out about it we're going to get someone to try and fix it. So a big part of my job is information gathering, particularly on problems that exist. If we go to a race weekend and we experience engine failure, then I like to be in there as soon as possible after the fact to try and establish exactly what went wrong.

"Some of the tools that you have in your armory here are the diagnostic equipment that's carried on the engine itself. The ECU [engine control unit] that controls the engine has some diagnostic capability. All of our customers use very good proprietary data logging equipment and we have access to that in order to diagnose what went wrong if there's a failure—temperatures and pressures and the exact sequence in which the traces changed during a failure.

"The failure analysis is important because it enables people to continue through the weekend with some knowledge of what happened rather than continuing in ignorance. If you have to take an engine out of a car, it's good to know if there's a chance of a similar failure with the engine you're about to put in or if it's a random thing that's not likely to recur or if it's a mistake that's hap-pened, which means that it's almost certain not to recur.

"There are times at some of the racetracks where you can influence the performance of the car, where you can work with the customers, making just small changes to things. You're never going to reinvent the wheel on a race weekend, but you can get a little further down the optimization road. You can maybe do something to some elements of the mapping of the engine to contribute to drivability concerns. You can maybe do a small experiment looking for fuel mileage gains. You can't really do any experiment that has a lot of risk attached to it. If you judge the change carefully, then you can go in with an experiment that might get you something back on drivability or fuel mileage or something like that.

"There's a lot of learning to be done about the car systems that we men-tioned earlier. The only real experience that we gain, the real-life performance of oil tanks and waste gates and turbochargers, is during race weekends. For all the work you can do back at the factory on dynos and stuff, you just can't cover the same amount of ground that even one or two cars can cover in a race weekend. Learning the character of these subsystems is very important.

"It's important to keep the customers up to date with what's going on back here, to relay to them the status of any engines they have in work here at the shop, to keep them abreast of any changes in the performance spec of their engine. It's the nature of racing engines that the spec changes quite rapidly. It's a bit of a juggling act. Inevitably you end up releasing parts still with some degree of risk attached to them. So there's an unfolding story really, as you learn about the engines you have in service.

"If you judge it right, what happens is you introduce a change in spec and you try to go in very conservatively. So, shortly after you've changed the spec of the pieces, you can turn the wick up the whole way. When you introduce new pieces, you'd like to think you don't go whole hog when there's still some risk attached to them. For example, you might choose not to run a big rev limiter when you have some new pieces in the valve gear or something like that. Then later on you might learn that all looks good in the engines that you have out in service at the lower limiter, so you can maybe go to the limiter that you thought you should have had all along.

"Alternatively, you might have made a mistake; you might have not been conservative enough. As a result of running some engines with some new pieces in, you might have to do some swift reactionary stuff in order to stop the thing growing into a crisis. It's important to communicate that sort of information as well as gather it. It's got to come back in from the team on one hand, but you've got to be sure you're giving feedback on the other hand or the sources of information will dry up.

"It's particularly the case in Indy cars that even the biggest teams don't employ engine specialists. So you need to be there in order to advise and comfort and just to see that they don't do something inadvertently that will upset the engine."

PH: "That's a big point that's new to me. I didn't know that the teams don't have an engine guy. That's changed. Twenty years ago all they really knew to fiddle with was the engine. They didn't know what the shocks did and not much about the suspension. The engine, now, is a black box that they plug in and out and they don't want it to break and they expect increases in power and they expect someone like you to be right there to make sure all that happens. That's an amazing change in some of the racing series in the United States. Is it the same in Formula 1?"

RW: "Not to the same extent. In Indy cars, Cosworth has one technician with each team, the exception being our two lead teams, Newman-Haas and Ganassi, who have one technician per car. During the race weekend they report to me. They look over each engine every time it goes in the car. They make sure there's no obvious problems. They're there to work closely with the team. They're the primary contact for educating the guys on the team who are maybe dressing the engines. They would deal with most of the mechanical things that would crop up on the engines. The background of these people is that, typically, they've been engine builders. They will also prepare the electronics on the engine for use on the track.

"There are several different features that need to be programmed into the engine, into the ECU. They take care of all that and they will liase with the engineer on the team and decide how lean they're going to run the engine depending on where they are on the weekend. They just check that the car systems are as they should be, and they encourage the teams to pay attention as well. They sort of poke and prod around and ask questions about how much oil the thing's using, and keep abreast of the temperatures the thing runs at. They've only got two feet and they can only get around so far, but the basic idea is they try to maintain an awareness of the needs of the engine. If there's a problem or crisis, then I get wheeled in to find out what's going on.

"It's very difficult to make sense of. Some weekends you'll find yourself lying on your back under a racecar looking at a hole in the side of an engine. Thankfully that doesn't happen very often. Other times you'll be taking somebody's turbocharger or waste gate apart and putting it back together, or maybe you'll spend hours giving yourself a headache over a set of data logger results trying to understand why it's different from the last time at this place or trying to achieve some incremental improvement in some feature like the boost response or something like that. Very, very diverse. The problems of each track are very different. Some places you'll be scratching around the whole weekend looking for how you're going to make it round the track on the necessary fuel allocation. The whole thing is very difficult to describe."

PH: "What parts of your job do you like the most and least? Do you like the race weekends?"

RW: "I like the uncertainty of it. I like the fact that you don't know going in what a weekend's going to hold in store for you. I like the fact that, by our responding quickly to problems, then you can make life better for a lot of people. It forces you to think on your feet. It forces you to assimilate facts very quickly. Hopefully, you don't make too many mistakes. If you react to a problem that you've discovered and you get a fix in place, then you can maybe stop some people from falling out of a race and save some people some money at rebuild. Even if it isn't that clear cut or even if the news isn't good, sometimes you can tell a team they have to change an engine early on and they get it done sooner and they go to dinner earlier.

"The thing I don't like about it? I don't like the feeling of impotence you sometimes have. The feeling you have that the die is cast and you're powerless to do anything about it. I guess the best example of that was during 1992, when we had that auxiliary drive belt problem. We thought we didn't know how to fix it but we knew that until we did fix it we were certain to experience failures. That's a terrible feeling.

"But, likewise, unless you understand the thing, you can't fix it. You have to focus on understanding the thing rather than making up a random change. You couldn't hope it would go away. Although we didn't understand the problem we knew it was something to do with the car and it turns out it probably was, but we still needed to make the engine resilient to this and the change we ended up making was huge. It involved a new front on all our engines. It made half our parts list obsolete overnight. It was a big change and certainly not a change we could entertain without making sure we grasped what was taking place."

PH: "When did you join Cosworth?"

RW: "September 1987."

PH: "How much longer will you be in the United States.?"

RW: "I'm still not sure what I'll do next year. I'm not going to England right after the last race. I'll be here till Christmas time. I'm interested to see what happens the next few months. We'll be testing a new car, the Reynard. Once it gets back over here we'll find out if it's a sinker or a swimmer.

"Would you like a walk around the shop? We're looking at a new location for the shop. This one's too small for what we've done this year. We're hoping to move just down the street."

Cosworth Engineering Shop Tour

Rob showed me around. The shop is neat but crowded, begging the planned move to a larger facility during this off-season. Our first stop was an XB assembly room with a beautiful array of engine parts and assemblies laying around in various stages of rebuild.

I spotted a partially assembled cylinder head and noticed what looked like a moly-type lube smeared on the cams. I asked Rob if that's what it was?

"That's right. We use a bunch of different gunks during assembly, don't we?" he asked, looking at the guy assembling the head. The technician, a mustached guy with a Down-Under accent, said. "Yes, seven or eight different lubes and sealants."

Rob handed me a jewel-like valve machined from titanium. It felt very light and seemed tiny until I noticed how small the piston was. It's easy to forget this is a small engine, only 2.65 liters or 161.7 cubic inches in displacement. The bucket-type cam follower is also extremely light due to a very thin wall. The machining tolerances must be extremely exact. Small and precise-looking also describes the H-section connecting rod. I tried to see the "detail design" features Rob had said make these highly-stressed parts so resistant to fatigue failure, but I just don't have enough experience to see anything significant. "These are just good steel alloys here," said Rob proudly. "Nothing very exotic."

Not so the sump casting. Exotic is the word. Seemingly massive but actually light as well as complicated and, well, beautiful. This cast aluminum component wears a lot of hats. It seals the bottom of the engine, adds considerable structural strength to the engine as a whole and, because the engine is a dry sump design, helps get the oil out. The sump has a closed compartment in the bottom with slot inlets directed so oil slung off the crank goes right in. Rob said there are weirs and baffles inside this compartment that herd the oil toward scavenge pump pickups. The part is all one piece so I assume it's an investment casting and very expensive to make. Oil in the sump getting in the way of the crank is a power robber, and this sump is designed to get the oil out quick.

The cylinder block also looks massive but is actually very light. An open-deck design, the face of the cylinder head seals all the open areas with the help of O-rings. There is no conventional head gasket. The aluminum cylinder liner is "wet," meaning the outer surface of the liner is in direct contact with the coolant. Sealing the combustion chamber/cylinder liner area is always a problem and Cosworth does this with a sealing ring ground to a specific, tightly-toleranced thickness. Selection of a ring of the right thickness for each cylinder ensures the liners seat and seal perfectly at top and bottom. Rob pointed out the oil sprayers that are attached to the block on the underside of the block V. They connect to the longitudinal oil gallery and point around the bottom of the bore, so they can spray oil on the underside of the piston crown to cool this critical area.

The cylinder head is another strong-looking component of surprising lightness. The ports, four per cylinder, are beautifully machined and finished. "It's a bead-blast with baking soda that makes them so smooth looking," Rob said. The combustion chamber recess is very compact for high compression, and has a central spark plug. The valves and seats looked to me like they had a racing-standard three-angle valve job.

The pistons are of an extreme-slipper design that results in not much material in the skirt area and a very short piston pin. Both features lower the weight of this critical, forged-aluminum alloy part. I could see a friction-reducing coating on various surfaces throughout the engine, which I assume is a Teflon material.

Rob picked up a very small part that looked like a water pump rotor and said it was the air/oil separator, a complicated assembly brazed up from several machined components. "There's a lot of air in the oil coming out of the sump," he said. "That mixture comes in here at the center of the separator and the rotation spins the oil out, leaving the air to vent back into the engine."

Our next stop was the dynamometer room, where we saw an engine coming out after a test. I couldn't help noticing fuel lines hooked up near the turbocharger compressor inlet. Rob had said they have to put the methanol fuel in everywhere they could, but I didn't think they'd go that far upstream. This obviously helps with "mixture preparation," as Rob explained during the interview. As Rob said, multiple injection nozzles help engine efficiency (fuel usage per horsepower) and drivability. That means power with good gas mileage, which is what all engine manufacturers strive for.

To keep the testing setup close to the in-car configuration, the dyno includes a Lola spacer behind the engine that houses the turbocharger, just like in the racecar. "This dyno is really overkill for what we need, but we want to have exactly what they have in England, where the engines are designed and manufactured," said Rob. "We can test three or four engines a day here."

An engine sitting outside the dyno room was missing its front cover. This gave Rob the opportunity to show me some of parts that were redesigned as a result of the accessory drive belt failures that may have cost Michael Andretti a couple of races in 1992, including the Indy 500. "It wasn't strictly an engine problem," Rob explained. "An interaction between the engine and the car under very specific conditions of engine speed and track roughness caused a harmonic in the belt drive system. We really didn't know what the problem was, but we redesigned the entire front of the engine so that there are two shorter driven belts now instead of one long one. It's easy to describe, but it was an extensive redesign."

Where's the Crank?

After a tour of the entire shop, Rob escorted me back to the front door and we said our good byes. I promised him a copy of the transcribed text for approval prior to publication. Of course I thought of more questions later and, during a phone conversation with Ian Bisco, I said it occurred to me after the visit that I hadn't seen a crankshaft during the shop tour. "Did I just miss seeing a crankshaft or were they out of sight on purpose?" I asked. "There's one in there for sure," Bisco said, laughing but not confirming or denying a cover-up. "It's a work of art, I'll tell you."

What Does a Cosworth/Ford Engine Deal Cost?

I also asked Vice President Ian Bisco what it costs an Indy car owner to run a Cosworth engine. This was in the fall of 1993, so things might have changed a small amount since then. "A single-car lease, which includes seven new engines, is $900,000 for the first year going down to $700,000 the second year because the engines aren't new anymore," he began. "An average rebuild, needed after 450-500 miles, costs about $25,000. If the team does some testing, they'll need 30-35 rebuilds, so a full season will cost them about $1.6 million. (30 times 500 miles = 15,000 miles or 5,000 laps around a 3-mile track.) We have teams that use as few as 20 rebuilds."

"What about performance upgrades?" I asked. "The TV announcers mentioned an induction system upgrade they said was worth 30 hp. What did that cost the teams?"

"That upgrade cost $14,000 per engine," said Bisco. "That's pretty cheap if you look at the cost per horsepower. We have a team working on performance development all year long, but only about 25% of their time results in something that works. You have to cover your overhead, too."

Saying I was impressed by my talk with the Cosworth people and the shop tour would be an understatement. One of the things that makes racing so special is the competence and professionalism of the people involved.

'94 VISIT TO COSWORTH ENGINEERING

In November 1994 I visited Cosworth again. Since my last visit they had moved down the street to a larger facility. Ian Bisco and I talked about some current IndyCar issues. I asked Ian about Indy Racing League's proposed move to reduce engine size for the Indy 500 in 1996 from 2.65 to 2.2 liters displacement. "I assume it's more complicated than just scaling down all the parts?"

Ian grinned and said, "It's a bit more complicated than that. Someone has to pay for the change, and it's going to be expensive. Basically we've got three choices. We could just destroke the current XB, but that would probably only do for development. We could modify the XB, but that would mean redesigning everything but the block because you have to optimize the bore and stroke and also the valve angles and sizes. So we'll most likely come up with an all-new engine. It's about due anyway, really."

"They say they want to lower costs but I don't see how this does that," Ian continued. "And there are some unresolved issues such as fuel mileage and overall performance. Are they going to stay with 1.8 miles per gallon of fuel? Do they really want a car with 130 less horsepower? Indy car lap speeds need to be fast enough to produce exciting racing. You can't have Indy Lights cars almost as quick, so maybe they'll allow more boost on road courses.

"Less engine displacement and a redesign means a smaller, lighter, higher-revving engine. The chassis can be smaller in the engine area and maybe that will lower aero drag and help the rear wing. Less power means less cooling requirements, so the radiators can be smaller and lighter. Maybe they'll lower the minimum weight."

"Some teams are under minimum weight now," I said. "I know a few are using stainless steel rub plates on the bottom of the cars to lower the center of gravity."

"Right," Ian said. "The chassis rules matter too, and we don't know what they're going to do there. Are they going to a flat bottom? If so maybe the engine shouldn't be an 80 degree V like the XB. Maybe because of the car layout and smaller size you'd want a 90 degree engine. It's not simple."

I asked Ian if Cosworth had looked at a pushrod Indy 500 engine to compete with the Penske/Ilmor/Mercedes engine. "Yes, we had to," Ian responded. "We knew they were testing a big pushrod engine before their announcement. We had to stick with what we had and hope they had reliability problems. Our designers in England spent four or five months working on a competitive pushrod engine for '95 and some of the XB reliability problems we had this year were probably compounded by this extra work that didn't go into XB development."

"What about these new engines from Honda and Toyota?" I asked. "Both those manufacturers have engine groups in Southern California and they're trying to hire people. Have they poached any of your guys yet?"

"No," Ian answered. "Not yet. But it's worrying. There's a fundamental difference between them and us. We need to sell product to make money, and they have big bank accounts from their sponsors. We have good people and we treat them well. These other companies have to see Cosworth as a source when they start hiring. Stewart Groves did the original XB engine design layout. He's a really good guy. Ferrari hired him away two years ago, and now he's gone to work at Ilmor. Mercedes is putting a lot of money into that."

"Does Ilmor have the management depth to grow like they're going to have to grow?" I asked.

"They probably do," Ian said. "And Roger Penske is going to be there to help them."

"Considering Penske's track record in business, that's got to be a big advantage," I said. "He hires good people," Ian nodded and smiled.

Indy Car Engine Tweaks

Ian told me about some of the recent developments. "There are several new features that became available during the '94 season," he explained. "The one talked about most on TV is the pit lane speed limiter. The engine management system senses what gear the car is in. The team has to put in the gear ratios and the tire size, and then the system can calculate the speed of the car and limit engine rpm by not firing the spark plugs. To activate this feature the driver holds down a button on the steering wheel while he's in the pit lane.

"Then there's the auto-upshift. A sensor on the gear lever can tell when the driver starts to select a higher gear and cuts engine rpm enough to make the shift quick and smooth. It only works with up-shifts, but it helps.

"The biggest throttle response improvement we've made is what we call the inlet guide vanes. This is mounted in front of the turbocharger compressor, and it closes off inlet air flow when the driver comes off the throttle. Air can't get into the compressor and so it doesn't lose rpm as quick. If the compressor is still spooled up when the driver gets back on the throttle, power comes on quicker."

"What does that look like?" I asked.

Ian got up and led me out of the office. "Lets go out in the shop. I'll see if I can find one."

This new building is well-lit, clean, and spacious. Ian showed me a parts-cleaning room and a separate grinding room that's carefully isolated so the abrasive dust doesn't get into the engine assembly areas. The dyno operators are cleaning and replacing components, getting ready for a new season. We see a dozen or so engines lined up in rows in a big receiving room, waiting for tear down and inspection, and we walk through several rooms where people are working on various engine components.

"Here's a crank," Ian said. "Last time you were here you said you didn't see one." It looked thick and strong. The throws are short and the counterweights small. It seemed more like a metal sculpture than a crankshaft.

I also see my favorite part, the sump. It's not just an oil pan, but a structural member that stiffens up the bottom of the engine. An aluminum investment casting of some complexity, this sump has cast-in oil galleries positioned to catch oil slung off the crank and get it quickly to the outlets and the scavenge pumps. I just like looking at it. I wish I had one hanging on my wall.

Ian is still looking for an inlet guide vane (IGV). There are nine other throttle plates downstream from the IGV—the usual throttles in each of the eight inlet runners and also a ninth throttle at the plenum entrance. "The regular throttles do what throttles do in any engine," Ian explained. "The ninth throttle keeps the turbocharger from blowing off the pop-off valve in the top of the plenum when the regular throttles close. This maintains pressure in the plenum and helps throttle response."

Ian found an inlet guide vane assembly. It's a ring about an inch thick and 5 inches in diameter. Inside it are four rotating triangular vanes that seal the inlet opening when closed. A toothed ring on the outer diameter engages pinions that turn the vanes in unison. The parts are all aluminum except for the brass pinions. I didn't have time to see exactly how it all fit together, but those vanes need to open completely so that there isn't any flow restriction at wide-open throttle, and then seal tightly when closed. The whole thing has to operate smoothly, so they built an electrically-operated rig to cycle the vanes open and closed using lapping compound on the gears to make sure everything fits perfectly. This is typical of the attention paid to detail here.

TALK WITH PETE SPENCE

On this visit to Cosworth I also talked to Pete Spence, the new IndyCar track support manager who replaced Rob White. Last year Pete worked with the McLaren F1 team and was responsible for the engines in Ayrton Senna's cars. This was his first season managing the dozen or so people who are responsible for the Cosworth engines that Indy car teams depend on. I've seen Pete rushing around at the races this year and he was always friendly but intensely professional and usually busy. Even if people are friendly at the races I feel like I need to let them do their jobs, and carefully pick the time to ask questions. Here, in November in a nice, quiet conference room, it was more like two guys talking about racing. I asked him how he likes what he's doing?

"It's friendly over here and less formal," Pete said in a lilting accent that he said reveals his Northern Ireland background. "People from different teams can talk to each other without getting a stern look from the team manager. F1 can be very secretive."

"What exactly do you do, and what's a typical race weekend like?"

"I look after Cosworth's relationship with the teams," Pete said. "Each team has a dedicated Cosworth technician that stays with the team for the whole year at every test and race. They provide support and advice on engine performance, boost control, and telemetry. They work hard, leaving here on a plane Thursday morning early to get to the track that afternoon, so they can make sure the team has everything it needs. Friday and Saturday means getting there at 7 a.m. and it might be 10 o'clock or midnight before they leave. Sunday is a bit earlier, and they advise on pit strategy depending on the race and the fuel consumption."

"That does sound like a tough job," I said.

"You have to start with good people and then look after them," Pete said. "This next year [1995] will be more difficult because the season is compressed. There's one stretch with six races in six weeks. I'm going to try to rotate some people so they don't have to come back to Torrance between races. When I come back here I might try to stay on East Coast time. Someone told me that helps."

Pete also pointed out another issue if engines shrink to 2.2 liters. "The engines are full throttle now at Michigan and almost full throttle at Indy and Nazareth. With less power we'll surely be full throttle all the time at these tracks. Engine reliability will suffer when we downsize components and turn more rpm, and we'll potentially have fatigue failure problems due to more full-throttle operation."

This visit to Cosworth was, like the other visits, a priceless chance to talk to interesting people and learn more about racing.

MY PLENUM IS BIGGER THAN YOUR PLENUM

Early Saturday morning at the 1995 Phoenix IndyCar race, the Tasman crew was changing a Honda engine, and some Cosworth guys were interested spectators. I asked them what they could see that was different from their own engine. "The plenum looks awfully large," said one. The plenum is an aluminum box on top of the engine that receives the pressurized flow from the turbocharger. The popoff valve that IndyCar uses to limit how much pressure the engine gets from the turbocharger sits on top of the plenum. Intake runners with throttles provide a flow path from the plenum to the combustion chambers in the heads.

"Does the Honda engine have a barrel throttle or a butterfly?" I asked.

"Looks like a butterfly to me, but it's difficult to tell," was the answer. "We also think they're putting fuel in before the compressor, like we do."

The cars we drive on the street have a butterfly throttle-a flat, round, rotating plate that causes some flow restriction even at full throttle. The

Cosworth engines designed for Indy cars and Formula 1 use a barrel throttle similar to a ball valve used in a water line in your home. In the intake runners from the plenum to each cylinder there is a cylindrical "barrel" with machined passages, so that when the throttle is full open there is a smooth path for the air-fuel mixture. The whole barrel rotates to misalign the passage and throttle flow to the engine. This arrangement eliminates the edge-on plate and shaft left in the flow at full throttle with a butterfly system.

The Cosworth engine injects fuel before the turbocharger compressor as well as in the plenum. An engine burning alcohol needs almost four times the volume of fuel than one using gasoline. You know from experience that alcohol absorbs a lot of heat when it evaporates (rubbing alcohol feels cool on your skin). Adding fuel as far upstream as possible allows more fuel to evaporate and gets a more dense charge to the combustion chamber.

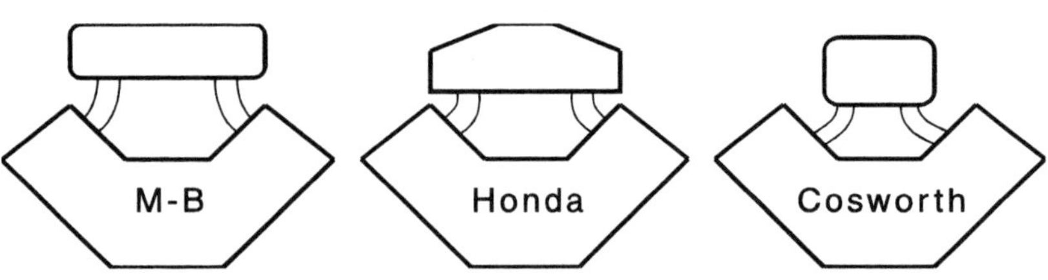

I've drawn engine cross sections to show the relative size and shape of the intake plenums on the three engines. I made no actual measurements, and I've shown a 90 degree V on all three figures. The Honda looks like a 90 degree V, but some racing V-8s are as slim as 70 degrees. The Cosworth is an 80 degree V. As you can see, the plenums are shaped differently and the Cosworth plenum is definitely smaller. I'm showing intake runners from the plenums to the heads, but I really don't know if they look exactly like this.

Rob White was back in the United States early in the 1995, season babysitting the new Series II version of the XB. I asked him about the plenums and, typically, he thought for a bit as he sorted out what he could tell me that was OK to print. "I agree," said Rob. "The Honda plenum looks VERY big."

He paused again and then explained. "There are two schools of thought. A big plenum is safe. If the plenum walls are far enough away that they don't interact with the flow, then it's like the engine is drawing from still air at a higher pressure than outside the plenum. If, however, you think you can use the plenum boundaries to help the flow, you can make it smaller. Plenum design is very important. The rules restrict you to what is actually a box with a hole on top for the pop-off valve. We've spent a lot of time looking at plenum design, but we stick with what we've got now because we haven't got anything better."

During televised coverage of the 1995 Indy 500 all of us could see that the plenum on the Menard V-6 engine was much bigger than any of the plenums I've drawn above. That plenum was so large, in fact, that it earned the car a "humpback whale" nickname due to the required bulge in the engine cover.

Honda Does Add Fuel Before the Turbo

In the section above I learned that the Cosworth guys thought the Honda Indy car engine added methanol at the turbocharger inlet as does their own Cosworth XB. This was confirmed by an odd source. A Honda TV add featuring the Tasman Reynard/Honda Indy car contains a shot where the camera pans across the side of the car and shows a close up of the engine inlet. Sure enough, there in the inlet trumpet are four small pipes arranged at 90-degree intervals around the opening. I'm not sure they are fuel nozzles but what else could they be?

CHAPTER 5
RACECAR HANDLING

We've mentioned before in this book that, until recently, the engine was the component in a racecar that received the most attention. Before 1960 there weren't many people who knew what makes a car go around corners well. Tires were tall and skinny, and the contact patch was so small that the details of wheel alignment didn't seem to matter much.

Grand Prix cars from the 1920s up to the 1950s overpowered their rear tires so badly that the front wheels were given large amounts of positive camber (tops of the tires farther apart than at the bottom) to balance the car. They sacrificed grip at the front so the rear end wouldn't come around when the driver got on the throttle coming out of a corner. Of course that meant that the front tires didn't have much grip in the corners. This is a good example of the balance problem that every racecar designer and engineer fights every day.

The point here is that the engine was the only component that anyone knew how to improve, so road holding was sacrificed to make the car drivable. The focus on engine improvements resulted in more and more power with little improvement in handling. The driver's job was to survive the corners so he could keep his right foot down on the straights. This trend reached a peak in pre-World War II Grand Prix racing when the Auto Unions and Mercedes-Benz teams developed very light cars with supercharged engines running on skinny tires. Pictures of those cars show front wheels with a lot of positive camber. Those drivers were brave!

Things have changed with the growth of the tire contact patch. When you have a wide tire you need to keep the wheel upright so all the rubber stays in contact with the road. Close attention to suspension geometry and spring damping as the car rises and dips over bumps and rolls in corners can help increase overall grip.

The realities of suspension geometry are summed up in one word—compromise. Limiting the total movement of the suspension makes it easier to keep all the rubber on the road, and with less suspension movement the shock absorbers become an important component. Adding large aerodynamic downforce loads to the chassis increases the need to limit suspension movement and dictates higher spring rates and more sophisticated shock absorbers to "stabilize the platform." Now the shock absorber rockets from being just important to being extremely critical to overall racecar handling. That's why most of this section is devoted to dampers—shock absorbers to us Americans.

In this section we'll look at balance, springs, and shocks. You'll see how one big damper innovation came from off-road racing. We'll also explain what a shock dyno does and look at how the now-banned active suspensions worked.

UNDERSTEER AND OVERSTEER

The best way to define these terms is to start with neutral steer. This is the condition where a driver of a car in a corner does not have to change the steering angle when the car changes speed. A neutral-steering car that is not already at maximum grip for that corner can speed up and maintain the same radius path. Extra forces needed from the front and rear tires at the higher speed cause those tires to go to identical but higher slip angles than were required at the slower speed. We say the car is balanced.

Understeer happens when, in that same constant radius turn, the driver has to increase the steering angle (turn the steering wheel into the turn) as the car speeds up. The extra force needed to keep the car at that radius at the higher speed causes the front tires to go to a higher slip angle than the rear tires. Other terms you'll hear used for understeer are push and tight.

Oversteer occurs when, as the car speeds up, the rear tires go to higher slip angles than the front tires. This is not a stable situation, and that's why most street cars are designed with a mild understeer condition. The inherent instability of oversteer is due to the fact that the outward drift of the rear wheels caused by a higher slip angle turns the front wheels further into the corner and tightens up the turn, which increases the lateral forces which increase the slip angles. The result is a tendency toward an inward spiral and ever higher rear tire slip angles until the rear tires go over the side force vs. slip angle hump into decreasing grip, and the car spins out. A car that oversteers is called loose.

Understeer is more stable in the same situation. A driver in an understeering car speeding up in a constant radius turn has to increase the steer angle into the turn so the front tires will turn to higher slip angles and produce more lateral force. The worst that happens is that slip angles increase and the car seeks a larger radius path, sliding toward the outer edge of the road. If the driver is paying attention, there is time to back off the throttle and drive through the corner.

Looking at the more common situation of going into a corner too fast, an oversteering car could swap ends before the driver could correct the steering or the car slows down, while the driver of an understeering car just adds more steering or slides to a bigger radius as the car loses speed. Swapping ends is a less stable situation than plowing to the outside of the curve.

Balance

What you'd really like is a balanced car—one that doesn't understeer or oversteer badly anywhere in the corner. This is, in the real world, only a racer's dream. Actually, a totally balanced car, especially on an oval racetrack, is not desirable. A little understeer helps the driver know where the traction limit is and provides some margin of safety.

Since being able to apply maximum power coming out of the corner is of primary importance, the usual solution is understeer in the middle of the corner so oversteer at the exit is minimized when the power comes on. It's left to the driver to cope with the resulting understeer at turn-in. Trail braking is a solution. The driver brakes late and continues to brake as he turns the steering wheel to start the car toward the apex. This technique increases the weight on the front wheels and gives them enough extra grip to negate the understeer.

Likewise at corner exit, application of the throttle transfers weight to the rear and helps with grip on acceleration. I stood at the middle of Turn 1/2 at Milwaukee and heard Indy car drivers using big changes in throttle to help balance the car. I was told that some of what I was hearing was drivers of understeering cars getting off and on the throttle to get the rear end to come around. I was also told that getting on the throttle can help control the rear end of an oversteering car. It seems to me that would take a massive leap of faith. The driver cannot, however, use these techniques unless the car's suspension is set up to allow the weight to transfer in a way that helps him.

Automatic braking systems (ABS) and traction control on racecars reduce the driving skills necessary for quick lap times. They allow the driver to stomp the brake pedal going into a corner, and a computer modulates the brakes so the tires are almost sliding, but not quite. This helps control turn-in understeer.

Traction control does the same during corner exit. The computer adjusts some engine management parameter (throttle setting or spark advance) for reduced power to keep the rear wheels from going faster than the front wheels, and that helps control throttle oversteer as the car accelerates out of the corner.

Since most of us think that driver skills should be a large part of racing, we applaud sanctioning body efforts to outlaw these devices. Enforcing rules that limit the use of ABS and traction control is not easy. As Ian Reed said in that interview in the computer section, unlearning technology is very difficult.

Jeff Braun: Balance vs. Grip

As a full-time racecar engineer, Jeff fights the balance versus grip battle at every test or event.

"Balance; it's always a struggle. You're trying to do two things. One is to get more ultimate grip than the next guy. More grip than the next guy is always better. The other thing is balancing the car so you don't have a condition where you have too much understeer or oversteer—that's balance.

"The way I approach the whole thing is this—the driver can't drive the car unless it's balanced. Finding a way to get a lot more grip at the front is great, but unless you can find grip at the rear to balance it, it's useless. The car has to be comfortable for the driver; that's the most important thing. An unbalanced car is never comfortable, even if it has a bunch of grip on one end.

"I always work on balance first. I always get the car pretty closely balanced and then, if I have some ideas about how to improve the aerodynamic or mechanical grip on one end or the other, preferably both ends, I start working on those things. Let's say I've figured out something that will improve front grip, and the driver goes out for a few laps and it works. The car is now unbalanced. That's OK because you started with a balanced car, and it's easy for the driver to tell you that it made more grip.

"For example, say you go out at a street circuit and you've got the car balanced. The driver's pretty happy, but he says he needs more front grip. He says it doesn't seem like he's getting enough grip at the front. So you make a change to the camber on the front, and he goes out and the car's loose on corner exit; it's oversteering. Almost certainly, you've improved the grip of the car at the front with that camber change. Now what you have to do is improve the back end of the car.

"I'm of the opinion that you always concentrate on the end that isn't working. If you have oversteer, you work on the back end. There are desperate times; there are situations when you get desperate, and you can't figure out a way to improve the end that's weak, so you actually take away grip from the end that's working best. I prefer that never happens, but there have been times when I've taken grip away from the end that was working because I couldn't figure out a way to improve the end that wasn't working.

"It's balance first, and then we work on grip. Sometimes, with aerodynamics, it's difficult because there are tracks where high downforce works or maybe low downforce works. Sometimes it's OK to give up some aero grip for improvements in lap times that come from lower drag. That's a high or low downforce decision, not a balance decision.

"Sports cars are a unique case. From S-2000s up through GTP cars, the problem is almost always not enough front grip. We can always get more rear grip because of those big rear wings or spoilers. We can always just tip them up to a higher angle of attack and get more downforce and more grip at the rear. The problem is you can only use more rear grip to the point that you can balance the car with front grip. Most designers of sports cars spend their time looking for grip at the front. If you can improve the grip at the front, the balancing grip at the rear is easy. That's why you used to see all those ugly splitters and dive planes and wings between the front fenders on GTP cars. The louvers and reverse scoops you saw on the top of wheel wells were there to generate more downforce at the front. It's similar with the IMSA WSC cars today. The minute they find some more front grip they crank the rear wing up further to balance the car. The result is a balanced car with more overall aero grip."

SPRINGS

A car needs springs to isolate the people riding in the car from road irregularities and weight transfer during changes of direction and speed. The springing medium can be steel, air, fiberglass, or anything that contributes a predictable and repeatable force as the spring deflects through some wheel travel.

Most early automobiles used flat-steel, multi-leaf springs because they were easy to make and had some interleaf friction built in that helped damp out unwanted oscillations. A few manufacturers, mainly Porsche and Chrysler, used torsion bar springs. Air and rubber/air hybrid springs have been tried also, but the most popular type of spring for cars, both racing and street, is the steel helical coil spring.

A coil spring is really a torsion spring wound into a smaller package. You'll see this if you visualize a coil spring during compression. For the coils to get closer together the wire has to twist, just like a torsion spring.

Because an undamped spring tends to oscillate, you've got to have a damper, so why not combine them into one unit, a coil spring with a damper inside? This, of course, is the familiar "coil-over" spring/damper unit that is widely used in street cars and all but universal in racecars. In this discussion we'll talk exclusively about helical coil springs.

You'll see coil-over spring/damper units in road racing applications on both openwheel and stock-bodied racecars. Springs designed for use in coil-over applications come with constant inside diameters of 2.0 inches, 2.25 inches, and 2.5 inches. Some oval track stock cars, including NASCAR, use bigger coil springs of 5.0- or 5.5-inch diameter and don't put the damper inside the spring. NASCAR rules don't allow coil-over units.

Spring Rate

A spring provides a predictable force for a given deflection. That force, called the spring rate, is expressed in pounds of force per inch of deflection, but the inch is generally understood, and people talk about "200 pound" or "1,000 pound" springs.

As pointed out above, a coil spring is really a torsion spring. When you compress a coil spring, the wire twists as the coils move closer together. The resistance to twist is what supplies the resisting force. A common misconception is that a coil spring loses spring rate over time, but a look at the components of the equation for the spring rate of a coil spring will show you that's not likely.

Spring Rate = F/S = $Gd^4/8ND^3$ where:
F = spring force in pounds.
S = spring deflection in inches.
G = torsional modulus of the material. (Steel = 11.5 million pounds per
    squareinch.)
d = wire diameter in inches.
N = number of active coils.
D = mean (average) coil diameter in inches.

The number 8 comes from the basic geometry of a helical coil spring and so is a constant for all springs of this type. If you look at these variables you'll see nothing that's affected by time. The characteristics that affect the spring rate don't change, so a spring can't "go soft" over time.

Having said that, we all know that there are actually springs on certain cars that have sagged, and that's because the spring was designed poorly. If a spring is designed (usually to lower costs) with marginally small wire or too few coils and the spring gets fully compressed, the material is overstressed and doesn't fully recover when the stress is removed. Over time, as the underdesigned spring is repeatedly overstressed, permanent deformation builds up, and we say the spring has sagged.

If we peer at this equation a little closer we can figure out some basic characteristics of coil springs. Look at the variables that are on the top of the division sign on the right side of the equation. Those are the variables that, as they get bigger, make the spring rate bigger. G, the torsional modulus, is a property of the steel used, and we certainly can't tweak that in the garage. There isn't much the manufacturer can do either, except use the highest-quality steel and heat treat it properly and consistently.

You can see that even a small change in d, the wire diameter, dramatically changes the spring rate, because it's raised to the fourth power (multiplied by itself four times). Precision springs have to be made from wire that has tight dimensional tolerances.

Now notice the variables below the division sign. These characteristics make the spring rate go down as they increase. More active coils and bigger diameter coils lower the spring rate.

To summarize: Bigger wire makes a stiffer spring; more coils and larger diameter coils are softer. This is why with some street cars, like my 1972 Datsun 510, just cutting a coil out of the springs helps the handling. Doing that lowers the car an inch or so, and the shorter spring is stiffer. Since the stock 510 has positive static camber at both ends, lowering the car this way gives negative static camber at the rear and less positive camber at the front. With shorter springs the car feels more responsive and has more ultimate grip. Twenty years ago it was a great sleeper street car, and I still drive mine daily.

Progressive Springs

A linear spring is one that gives the same increment of force for each increment of deflection. For a 200 pound per inch spring, the first inch of deflection requires a force of 200 pounds. The next inch of deflection adds another 200 pounds, and now the total is 400 pounds. To deflect that spring three inches you've got to apply a force of 600 pounds.

Maybe you don't want a linear spring. If you want the wheel to feel a stiffer spring as it moves in bump, you have to make a spring built with a variation along its length of one of those characteristics in the spring equation. (There are suspension systems with variable spring rates built into the mechanism or the geometry of the linkages.) You can change the wire diameter along the length of wire used in the spring, and, indeed, that has been done. Porsche has used taper-ground titanium springs in some spare-no-expense racecars for lower weight and a progressive spring rate. Progressive springs are also made from wire that has been drawn so that the wire diameter tapers over the length of wire used in the spring.

A look at the spring rate equation shows that varying coil diameter changes the spring rate, and that's done too. Barrel-shaped coil springs are common in the street-car aftermarket. Since D is on the bottom of the equation, a bigger diameter means a softer spring. The value of D is cubed (multiplied by itself three times), which says a small change gives a large effect. The larger coil diameter section in the middle of a barrel-shaped coil spring has a softer spring rate than the smaller diameter end sections, and will deflect first as load is added to the spring.

The most common way to make progressive springs is to vary N, the number of active coils. A progressive spring has some number of coils that are closer together than the rest of the coils. When weight is applied to the spring, both sections compress. As deflection increases, the coils in the smaller-pitch section begin to touch and go into coil bind. The equation tells us that fewer coils gives a higher spring rate so, as the closer-spaced coils bind, and the spring as a whole loses active coils, the spring rate goes up. If the spring is made correctly the coils lie down against each other gradually, and this smooths the transition from a lower to a higher spring rate. A sudden change in spring rate at one end of a racecar drastically changes the car's balance. It's akin to what happens when the suspension bottoms, and a racecar in a corner doesn't like that.

Here are some force vs. deflection curves for springs and combinations of springs. The force vs. deflection curve of a linear spring (on the left) is a straight line, showing that each incremental deflection requires the same incremental increase in force—that is the definition of a linear spring. Also in that graph is a curve for that same spring (same slope on the graph) combined with a softer tender (auxillary) spring. Both curves are linear, and you have a combined spring rate until the closer-spaced tender spring compresses to coil bind where the line changes slope and the section of the spring left with active coils determines the overall spring rate the wheel sees.

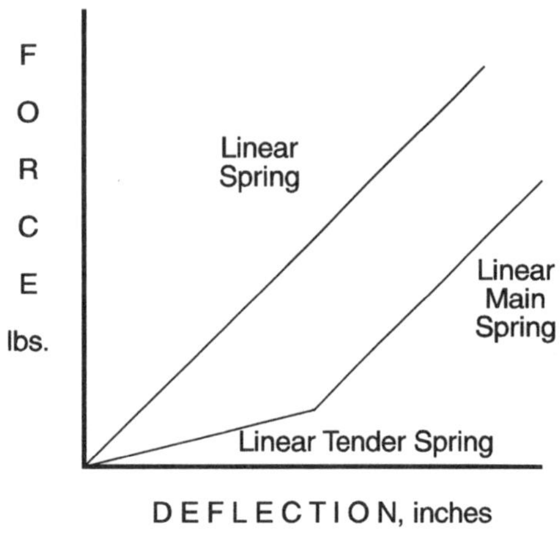

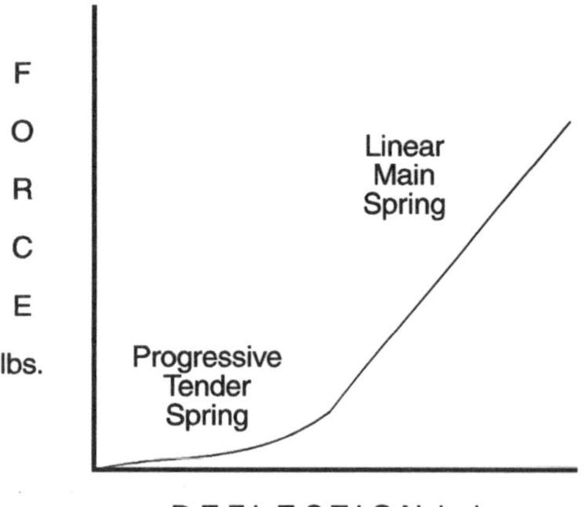

If the tender spring is wound progressively to exactly match the stiffer spring you get a smooth transition, as in this second graph. Instead of being wound with a constant pitch over its whole length, a progressive spring starts at some pitch at one end and goes to another pitch at the other end. One end should have a pitch that matches the main spring. That's how you get a smooth transition.

Why would you want progressive springs? The next section on bump rubbers answers that question in detail. Basically, a usable change in spring rate allows the car to operate with a low spring rate most of the time, with a higher spring rate in reserve for bigger bumps or aero forces. As we keep saying here, modern racecars usually have some aerodynamic devices tacked on that are sensitive to ride height. Progressive springs and bump rubbers are two ways to keep that ride height closer to optimum as aero loads increase.

Bump Rubbers

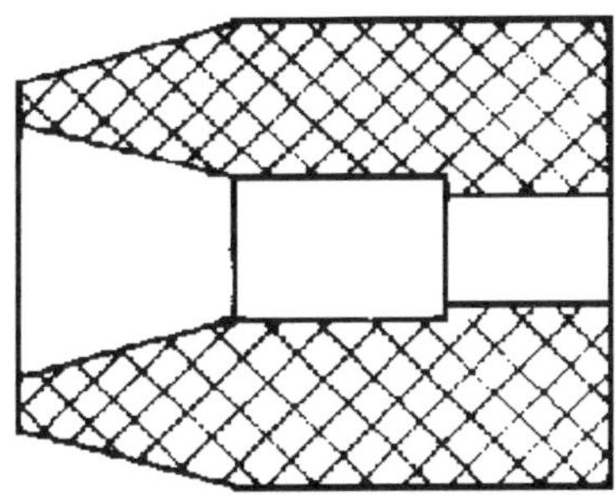

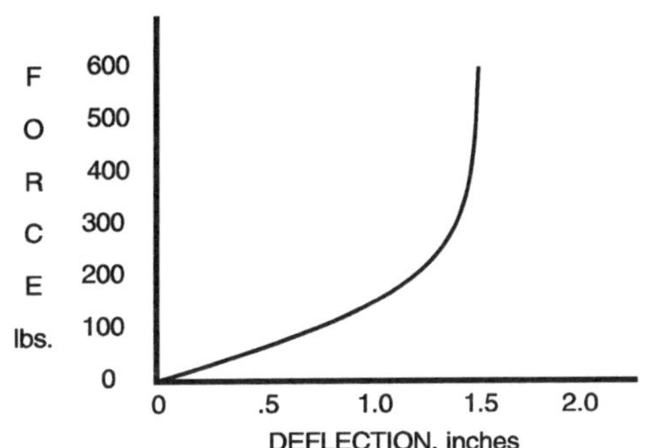

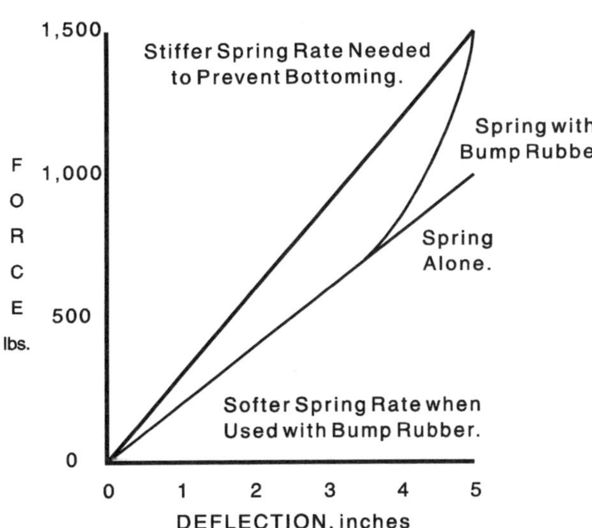

Another way to add to the flexibility of your set-up is to use bump rubbers on the damper shafts to augment the coil springs at full suspension deflection.

Bump rubbers are simple little components that are very useful in setting up a racecar. Originally added to dampers to prevent damage when the damper compresses completely as the car hits a big bump, bump rubbers and their cousin, the packer, become important suspension tuning devices if you need a progressive spring rate similar to that described in the spring section above, but don't have the room for both main and tender springs.

This cross-section drawing of a bump rubber and force versus deflection curve for the same bump rubber are right out of a Koni catalog, but other companies offer similar products. Bump rubbers can be manufactured in any shape that works and from any material that is appropriate. Koni says its bump rubbers are made from a cellular polyurethane. The shape of the device and the material it's made from determines the deflection curve.

This last graph shows why racecar chassis tuners use bump rubbers. Softer springs usually produce better mechanical grip, probably because the tire is able to follow the irregularities in the road with a more consistent vertical load. Most racecar engineers are constantly trying to figure out how they can get to a set-up that uses softer springs.

Combating the constant search for minimum spring rate are the bumps in the track surface and the aerodynamic downforce modern racecars produce. All that downforce compresses the springs and grip goes to hell when a car bottoms out. Dampers help control suspension movement over bumps but, during a long ride down a straight, downforce is at a maximum and it's the springs that keep the car from coming in contact with the track surface, thus the need for a high spring rate.

Think about what happens at a track like Phoenix International, a very fast 1-mile oval with a bump between Turns 1 and 2. An Indy car is going about 175 mph there, and the right side suspension is fully loaded. The car is probably generating more than 2,000 pounds of downforce, more than its own weight. So, just as the car is at maximum grip, and the right-side coil-overs are fully compressed, the car hits a bump. If the car bottoms or the ride height changes drastically, the car could spin. This is a critical test of the compromises that have to be made by the racecar engineer. Proper use of bump rubbers can help.

Tire and chassis stiffness is what determines oversteer and understeer, and therefore balance. Imagine what happens to the balance of the racecar when one corner bottoms out in the middle of a turn. As the chassis rubs on the track, weight comes off the tires on that end of the car. Less weight means the tire generates less lateral force. If it's the front of the car, you get instant understeer. If it's the back of the car, the rear end is going to come right around. Bottoming is bad news.

The top line in this graph represents the force generated by a 300-pound-per-inch spring as it's compressed 5 inches. This line goes from 0 pounds force at 0 deflection to 1,500 pounds force at 5 inches deflection (5 inches times 300 pounds/inch = 1,500 pounds). Let's assume your racecar just barely bottoms out with those springs, but you think it would give more grip with softer springs. If you add a bump rubber, you could use the softer springs (200 pounds/inch) shown by the lower line, and still have the same spring force at the full five inches of deflection.

This becomes really useful in downforce-generating racecars, especially flat-bottom cars like IMSA WSC cars. As we keep repeating, these cars are very sensitive to ride height and rake, and you want the optimum aero configuration in every corner. But how do you do that when the car generates 500 pounds of downforce at 60 mph and 2,000 pounds at 120 mph? Total rear suspension movement for cars like this might be only one inch so you might need some pretty hefty springs, and that might decrease grip on the slow parts of the race-track. How do you handle the needs of slow and fast corners when working with cars that produce aerodynamic downforce?

The answer is, of course, the familiar compromise, but bump rubbers help. Take, for example, WSC cars on the road course at Phoenix International Race-way. PIR has a twisty infield where you need soft suspension for mechanical grip, but half the distance of the course is run on the 1-mile oval and you'd really like a lot of aero grip going into the 120 mph Turn 1. You can set the car up so that downforce during max speed on the oval pushes the suspension down on the bump rubbers, but during the lower-speed infield turns only the springs support the car, and they can be softer than with no bump rubbers. This lets you use softer springs to get more grip in the infield twisty bits and also limits total suspension travel on the high-speed oval section, keeping the ride height and rake closer to the aerodynamic optimum.

The "third springs" we explained in the aero chapter have replaced bump rubbers and packers among many Indy car and Formula 1 racecars during the 1994 season.

Packers

Packers are C-shaped plastic spacers that come in different thicknesses and are the same diameter as the bump rubber. The open side of the C-shape lets packers slide in around the shock absorber shaft under the bump rubber. Packers are used as shims to adjust the point in the suspension travel where the bump rubber begins to add to the spring rate.

During a test like the one at Phoenix we just described in the bump rubber section, a race engineer would add or subtract packers between test laps to quickly vary the bump rubber location in a search for optimum balance and/or grip.

No matter how careful you are with progressive springs and bump rubbers it's very difficult to make the transition between spring rates smooth enough so the car's handling or balance isn't upset when the spring rates change. Racers are using dampers more often where they used to use bump rubbers and packers.

Let's talk about dampers or shock absorbers—whatever you call them.

SHOCK ABSORBERS

At the Phoenix IndyCar race in March 1993, I was talking to Sam Posey, ABC-TV racing analyst, when Ken Anderson, the guru of modern damper technology, walked over to say hello. I introduced them, and Sam admitted that back when he was driving, the engine was the focus of racecar tuning and they only fiddled with the shocks when they couldn't think of anything else to do. "We really didn't know much about what they did or how we could use them to make the car go faster," said Posey.

Today engines are taken for granted and the shocks are the most critical component on the racecar. The mark of a serious racing team is whether or not they have a shock dynamometer in the team trailer. There's been very little written about shocks, and there's a lot of voodoo info out there. Hopefully we can explain a few things about shocks in this section. We'll talk about the history of shocks and why we need them. We'll show you how modern racing shocks work, how the adjustments work, and why a shock dynamometer is so useful.

Why Do We Need Shocks?

Shock absorbers are more correctly called dampers, but I'm going to use the terms interchangeably here. Dampers are one of the most important components on any car because they damp (absorb) suspension movements, improve passenger comfort, and provide a way to control the driver "feel" of the car.

Here's what Jeff Braun has to say about shocks. "To me, the shocks have the single largest influence on the driver's feel of the car. The driver reacts to car movements and the shocks control how that happens. That's why shocks are so important when you're trying to make a car go quickly. It gives the race engineer a great way to control what the driver feels."

Springs are needed to isolate driver and passengers from road irregularities and chassis movements caused by acceleration, cornering, and braking. But springs store energy when compressed and tend to oscillate back and forth unless something absorbs that energy. A well-designed spring/damper system allows the chassis to remain relatively steady, and keeps the tires in contact with the ground despite bumps in the road and forces caused by cornering or changes in the car's speed.

Early autos used stacks of metal-leaf springs which depended on friction between the leaves to damp vibration. In the first decade of this century the hydraulic damper appeared, but most cars used friction dampers until the 1930s when hydraulic shock absorber designs became more sophisticated.

Here's an important point! Dampers are transient devices. They don't do anything on a straight, smooth road. They don't do anything after the car is settled into a turn. They don't do anything when a car is in a steady-state condition.

It takes movement for a damper to create a force, and that force is proportional to the speed of the damper piston. By design, dampers are connected to a car's suspension so the damper shaft moves when the suspension moves. A damper works when a car enters or exits a corner. That's when the driver turns the steering wheel into and out of a corner and the chassis rolls on the suspension. Dampers work when a wheel goes over a road irregularity such as a bump or pothole. Dampers work when the driver brakes and weight transfer compresses the front springs and lengthens the rear springs. Acceleration causes front-to-rear weight transfer, which causes springs to deflect and the dampers work then also.

Dampers absorb energy. They convert kinetic energy to heat energy by working the fluid inside them and raising the temperature of that fluid. Fortunately that heat can be fairly easily dissipated to the air flowing over the damper.

Bump and Rebound

When a car moves over a bump in the road, the wheel moves up with the bump and back down on the road on the other side of the bump. The spring and damper compress as the wheel moves up, and we call movement in that direction compression or bump. After the bump goes by, a correctly designed spring and damper go through some small oscillations tending toward a recovery to their original length, and the car returns to its steady-state ride height until the next road irregularity. Movement in this recovery or extension direction is called rebound. I think the British refer to these movements as bounce and jounce. In this section of the book we'll call these movements bump or compression and rebound.

We just described a simplified, ideal case. What's really happening with any road vehicle in motion is complicated and continuous movement of the suspension components.

The Purpose of Dampers

In the bump direction the spring/damper system mainly controls the movement of the wheel, and its purpose is to isolate the chassis from road irregularities. The temporary resisting force of the damper during bump movement allows the use of a softer spring than would be needed if there were no damper. You can think of the damper as a helper spring during bump.

In the rebound direction the damper absorbs the energy stored in the bump-compressed spring. The classic mouse trap is an example of the deadly potential of a compressed spring. Anyone who's ever fooled with the return spring on a heavy garage door also has some respect for the magnitude of the energy that can be stored in a spring.

The effect of an undamped car spring compressed by a bump is that, during rebound, it will tend to drive the wheel down past its steady-state position and then reverse and compress again, going into a series of oscillations that don't feel good to the passengers and deteriorate that critical contact between the tire and the road. A damper absorbs the energy stored in the compressed spring, giving a more comfortable ride and better traction.

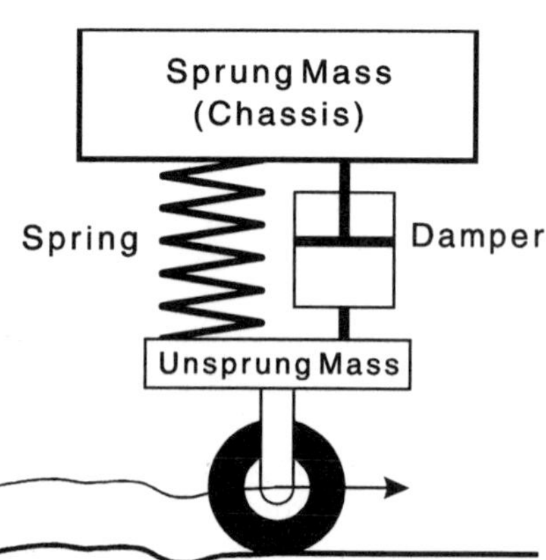

Designers of passenger cars used to be mainly concerned with the first two uses of dampers—spring helper in bump and energy absorber during rebound. More and more, however, designers of our street cars are using sophisticated dampers to control the more subtle transient effects caused by weight transfer during steering, braking, and acceleration and, therefore, fine tuning the "feel" of the car.

This third purpose of dampers, providing a means of adjusting the "feel" of the car, is a big concern of racecar engineers using modern racing dampers. The engineer tunes the racecar for maximum grip and best balance—not too much understeer or oversteer. But the engineer also knows the driver has to be able to drive the car at max grip and feel somehow that he is near max grip, so he won't go farther and lose control. That's the driver's job, but the engineer wants to make it as easy as possible.

If the racecar designer creates suspension geometry that provides the basic conditions for acceptable driver feedback, the racecar engineer can use the dampers to fine tune the car's grip and "feel" in a turn. The damper controls car feel at turn-in and exit when there are braking, steering, and throttle transients which transfer weight laterally, longitudinally, and diagonally. In a long corner that has a mid-turn, the car is probably in a steady-state condition, and the dampers don't have as much influence.

Dynamics of Spring/Damper Movement

There is a basic difference between spring forces and damper forces. We've covered this before, but it's an important point. It takes a specific amount of force to deflect a spring through a given displacement. For a linear (not progressive) coil spring with a 100 pound/inch spring rate, it takes 100 pounds to compress the spring and it takes another 100 pounds for every additional inch you move it. We call this displacement sensitivity.

Dampers, however, are velocity sensitive. If you put a tiny bit of force on a damper it will move slowly but steadily until it reaches the limits of its travel. But moving the damper quickly can take a lot of force, as you'll see later.

If that same 100 pound/inch spring is hooked up with the right damper, that damper will help the spring absorb the energy of a big compression input (bump) and, when the spring is fully compressed and exerting maximum force for this deflection, the damper resists a fast recovery of the spring. As the spring tries to recover quickly the damper exerts an opposing force that grows with velocity. The 300 pounds of spring force caused by 3 inches of deflection becomes, as the spring recovers, 200 pounds at 2 inches and 100 pounds at 1 inch. The damper moves at some speed due to the 300 pounds of spring force and slows as the spring force falls off. If the system is perfectly tuned, the spring force goes to 0 at almost the same time the damper stops moving, and both are back where they started after a small amount of oscillation. A damper that does not allow a small amount of overshoot and oscillation is probably too harsh for the suspension system.

There are always exceptions. Flat-bottom racecars like IMSA WSC cars and Indy Lights Lolas are so sensitive to ride height that engineers like to tune the dampers for a lot of rebound force. These cars don't easily return to a static suspension point and are said to be "overdamped." This makes it difficult to check suspension geometry on a setup pad, and you'll see crew members jumping up and down on the car to get the suspension to settle in to a static position.

When you put springs and dampers together you have a very powerful system that is infinitely flexible. The trade-off is that spring/damper systems behave in complicated ways and are very tough to figure out. And we're lucky that's so. Racing would not be nearly so interesting if it was simpler.

Tires Are Spring/Dampers Too

When a car travels over a bump in the road, a force goes through the tire and wheel and through suspension linkages and compresses the spring and damper. How much the damper moves depends on the size of the bump, speed of the car, spring rate, damper forces, the mass of the car and the suspension components, and how much of the bump was absorbed in the tire, which is a significant spring/damper system all by itself. Each tire has a spring rate dependent mainly on internal air pressure. We showed data on that in the tire chapter. Tire damping characteristics are determined by construction and rubber compound variables.

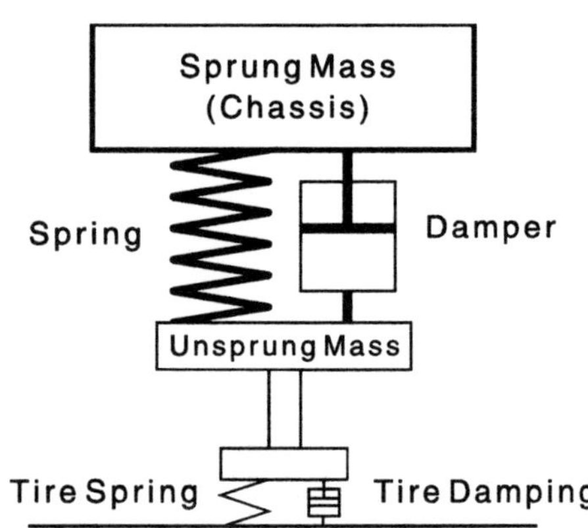

If the bump is big and fast and/or the springs and dampers are stiff, they don't compress much and the whole chassis moves up over the bump. In some cases, tire squash may be the only deflection in the suspension system. If the chassis is still moving up after the bump, it might pull the wheel and tire up with it. As the chassis pulls weight off the tire it loses traction. Even a small amount of weight removed from a tire on the edge of adhesion can cause the driver to lose control. Hopefully the suspension is tuned so as the bump goes by the tire, the spring/damper compresses and rebounds just enough to keep the tire in smooth contact with the road. Modern race teams spend a lot of time adjusting springs and shocks trying to make that happen.

That last paragraph is a very big part of all spring/shock/tire tuning. A car changes speed and/or direction because of friction between the tire and the road surface. You're trying to keep the tire at maximum grip at all times. Friction forces depend on the coefficient of friction and the vertical force: $Ff = Cf \times Fv$. If the vertical force on the tire varies widely, it can't maintain a steady lateral force. You'd like the suspension to absorb track irregularities in a way that maintains a steady vertical force on the tire. You'd also like the driver to feel what's going on with the car. The damper is a big part of making all that happen.

Aero Forces Cause Complications

As we've mentioned before, racecars that produce significant downforce—say equal to or more than the weight of the car—need high spring rates to keep that downforce from pushing the chassis right down to the track. Remember that ride height and rake are critical to optimum aerodynamic downforce, especially for flat-bottomed cars like F1 and Indy Lights. That sets up opposing goals for the suspension. You want a soft, compliant suspension to move with bumps so the tires maintain traction, but significant aerodynamic downforce dictates heavy springs to maintain optimum ride height and rake. The necessary compromise toward high spring rates means that the tires deflect significantly.

Here's the rub. If the tire has a spring rate of 1,800 pounds per inch and the racecar needs 3,000 pound-per-inch springs, then you've got two spring/damper systems in series between the ground and the chassis (as shown in the sketch above), and the most compliant component in the system is the tire, which has very little damping control. This is one of the reasons why racecar engineers try to run with the softest springs possible. As we've said before, cleverly designed and carefully tuned dampers help the spring in bump and dissipate spring energy in rebound. To some extent the shocks also influence the tire and can minimize the undamped spring lurking there.

Tire spring/damper characteristics are a great, big, hairy deal on racecars. It's one of those voodoo things that isn't talked about. I don't know if that's because people have solutions they want kept secret or just that no one has any solutions to the problem!

Single-Tube Shocks: A Big Innovation

The schematics show a single-tube damper and a double-tube damper. Single-tube dampers are usually called gas shocks, but all dampers have to have some gas in them so we're going to use the names single-tube and double-tube.

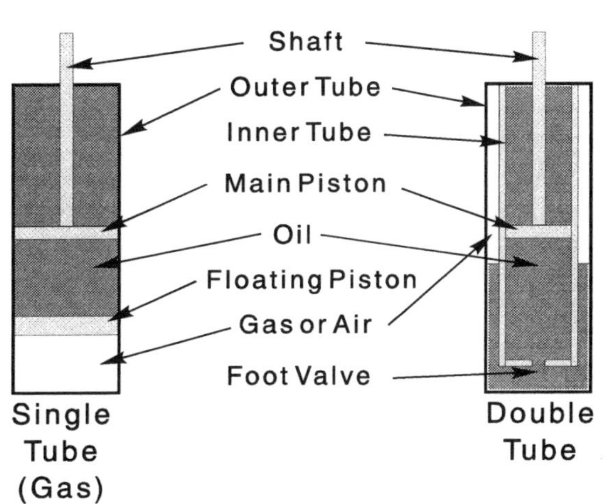

There has to be some gas—air or nitrogen—inside a damper because, as the piston moves up and down, the piston rod moves in and out of the damper. When the rod comes into the cylinder, it displaces oil and, as it moves out of the cylinder, oil has to come into the tube to make up the difference in the volume. To compensate for oil displacement caused by the piston rod, the damper needs a variable-volume reservoir for the oil.

In a double-tube shock, as you can see in the schematic, the shaft comes into the tube, fluid gets pushed out the foot valve at the bottom and moves up the space between the tubes, compressing the gas.

A single-tube shock is a little different. A floating piston separates the fluid from a variable volume of gas, and when the piston rod comes into the shock, the increase in volume inside the tube pushes the piston down and compresses the gas.

As with most choices there are trade-offs between using twin-tube dampers and single-tube dampers, but the biggest consideration is cavitation.

Cavitation

Cavitation occurs when the pressure in a fluid goes so low that air mixed into the fluid or the fluid itself expands as a gas and makes a bubble. In a damper this happens when the piston tries to move so fast that the fluid can't flow through it easily. The quickly moving piston tries to compress the fluid in front of it and tries to pull apart the fluid behind it. The piston can cause a pressure low enough that bubbles form in the oil. Oil vapor or air fills the voids in the bubbles.

The wheels on any car are jiggling up and down constantly, and that means the pistons in the dampers are moving back and forth all the time. In order to control wheel movement the piston needs to feel some resistance when it moves. When there are bubbles in the fluid they have to be compressed before the piston feels any pressure. If the piston moves back and forth fast enough it can cause a lot of bubbles in the fluid, and the piston can just jiggle back and forth with little resistance. Modern racecars don't have much suspension movement, and they can't stand any cavitation in the dampers.

If you look at the damper schematics you can see that during rebound (piston moving up in schematic) the oil can't go anywhere; it's trapped between the piston and the end of the tube. Given this description you wouldn't think cavitation would be much of a problem in the rebound direction.

Now look at what happens when the piston moves in bump (down). If there isn't much pressure below the floating piston, the main piston can push that whole slug of oil down and tries to tear apart the oil above it. This causes cavitation above the main piston, but the damper still generates damping force in the bump direction because some oil will flow through the piston and pressure builds up on the bottom of the floating piston as it compresses the gas.

The cavitation happening on top of the piston as the damper moves in bump isn't a problem until the piston reverses and begins to travel in the rebound direction. Now there are bubbles that have to be compressed before pressure builds up and oil flows through the washer stack and piston. This is the reason why cavitation is a problem mainly felt in rebound.

The solution is to pressurize the fluid inside the shock so it never gets to a low-enough pressure for bubbles to form. That's easy with a single-tube shock, because you have a floating piston between the fluid and the gas. With a high-pressure gas on the other side of the floating piston, that slug of oil below the main piston can't move down and is forced through the washer stack. In a double-tube shock the gas and fluid are in contact, and if you increased the gas pressure enough to eliminate cavitation you just force the gas into solution with the fluid at their interface and make the cavitation problem worse.

Having said that and progress being constant, low-pressure, double-tube shocks are gaining popularity on high-performance street cars. A little pressure keeps cavitation down with an acceptably small amount of aeration of the shock fluid. Double-tube shocks are still being used in street and racecars today. The Lotus Turbo Esprits competing in the SCCA's World Challenge series and IMSA's SuperCar series used production-based Monroe double-tube shocks, but they had adjustable valve stacks like any modern racecar, and the LotusSport team tweaked them a lot with help from Team Lotus suspension guru and former Lotus F1 driver John Miles.

Trade-offs

There are more trade-offs between single and double-tube shocks than just cavitation. You can see in the schematics that for the same outside diameter on both shocks, the piston inside a single-tube damper is larger and so displaces more oil for a given movement than the smaller piston in a double-tube damper. A shock is more sensitive if it's moving more oil. You can mount a single-tube shock in any position, whereas the double-tube can only be mounted the way it's shown in the schematic, because you don't want the gas to get into the inner tube. Also, in a single-tube shock, there is direct contact between the outer tube and the fluid inside, making heat dissipation more efficient. But the single-tube shock is more expensive to manufacture and has to be longer to allow room for that extra piston and the gas chamber. It's also more vulnerable to damage from external sources like flying rocks, because the outer tube is unprotected.

The trade-offs can be summarized, I think, by saying that a double-tube shock is much more easily overloaded, and damping can deteriorate from over-heating, cavitation, and/or aeration. Double-tube shocks are used on street cars mainly for cost reasons. The performance range of a street car is more predict-able than a racecar, and the dampers can be carefully designed and sized for each specific street car application. Racers, in general, need the cavitation protection, flexibility, and external adjustment capabilities of a single-tube shock.

In addition to single and double-tube dampers there are a couple of addi-tional hybrid types of dampers.

Emulsion Shocks

An emulsion shock is a single-tube shock without the floating piston. This means the gas and fluid are in contact. A charge of nitrogen gas up to 300 psi pressurizes the damper. An emulsion is what happens when small globules of a fluid are mixed into another fluid. Milk is an emulsion of fat in water. This is the wrong name to call this kind of shock because it's really a mixture of small gas bubbles in oil, not a mixture of two fluids, but why get picky?

I have trouble believing that those little bubbles don't pop up every time the wheel rebounds from a bump, but I'm told that it's analogous to a carbonated drink like a Pepsi. As long as the pressure is there, the bubbles are small and don't adversely affect shock performance.

Penske and Bilstein sell emulsion shocks, and many pro teams use them. I think this is a cost-reduction solution that lets these companies offer a lower-cost damper into a huge market. They must work or people wouldn't use them and, in fact, I've heard they're good for bumpy dirt tracks where a lot of suspension travel is needed.

Gas-Bag Shocks

This is a double-tube shock filled completely with oil. The shock is assembled with a gas-filled plastic bag inside. The bag changes in volume with shaft movements and pressurizes the fluid to retard cavitation. It's certainly cheaper to manufacture than a shock with a floating piston.

A major advantage of a gas-bag shock is you can mount it upside down. One of the advantages of a single-tube shock with a floating piston is it can be mounted with the piston shaft at the top or at the bottom. The piston and shaft are usually lighter than the oil-filled shock body, so mounting the shock upside down with the shaft connected to the suspension gives you less unsprung weight. The lower the weight of the stuff jiggling up and down, the easier it is for the spring and damper to control it.

You can't mount a normal double-tube shock upside down because the gas in the outer tube would get into the inner tube and ruin the damping action. Putting a gas bag in the outer tube during production of a mass-produced, double-tube shock solves this problem. The gas in the bag allows the damper to be fully filled with hydraulic fluid, but there's still room for fluid volume changes as the shaft goes in and out of the tube.

If gas bag shocks work for you then they're a great, inexpensive solution. In theory it sounds better than an emulsion shock because the gas and fluid don't get together, but I don't know how long the bag lasts bouncing around inside the shock and inflating and deflating at elevated temperatures. I would worry about deterioration of the damper fluid and/or the bag, if they are not totally compatible materials.

Roger Mears Introduced Single-Tube Shocks to Indy Cars

I had a chance to talk to Rick and Roger Mears in the spring of 1992. I asked Roger to tell me the story of how they began to use Fox single-tube shocks in Indy cars. He called them gas shocks.

"When was that?" I asked. "When did you first run gas shocks in an Indy car?"

"It'd be about...uh...let's see...probably about '83," was the answer.

"You were running off-road?" I asked.

"No, I was running in Indy cars also," Roger said. "And what happened was, the Indy car team I was driving for, you know, I kept feeling these shocks and complaining about the shocks, and the way the cars would change when you park them overnight, and the next day you start all over again with the setup. And so we determined that it was probably in the shocks. So we started using a gas-filled Fox shock, which eliminates the cavitation problems. And we learned from off-road racing how to tune them much better, so we put them on my car, and I ran at Atlanta Motor Speedway in an Indy car.

"At the start of the race I ran in the back, but later in the race my car got faster and faster and faster. What had been going on for years with Indy cars and a lot of other racecars is the cars would always get worse toward the end of the race. Mostly, everybody blamed it on the tires. What we proved that day was a lot of it was in the shocks. We ended up finishing fourth and, had the race been a few more laps, I feel like we could have gone better yet, because the track was very rough and very bumpy and the car got happier and happier as the race went on. Really, it was not my car getting happier, but everybody else was getting really slow. [Records show that Rick started the race on the pole and finished eighth while Roger started 22nd and finished seventh.]

"After the race, my brother [Rick] came over and said, 'Man, those shocks are great.' We talked it over and Tom Sneva and a bunch of guys came over, and they were all saying, 'What have you got on that car?' That really opened the door to Bilstein and all the other shock companies when we did that. It really turned on a bunch of lights. Penske started working with Fox directly, and they hired Ken Anderson and started making their own shocks."

Talk with Bob Fox

I visited Fox Shox in San Jose, Calif. in 1992 and met Bob Fox, founder of the company. Bob Fox is a fit-looking 40-something as he reaches over a big desk to shake hands. His large, carpeted office is hung with racing pictures. I asked about the Rick/Roger Mears connection and shock technology transfer to Indy cars. "That must have been 1983 or so," Fox said. "Roger was racing off-road and I guess he told Rick about our shocks, and, when he tried them at Indy, he went 7 miles an hour faster."

"Why?" I asked. "What was the difference between your shocks and what they were using?"

"I think they were using the usual Monroe double-tube shocks," said Fox. "They were probably fading due to cavitation and aeration. When that happens you don't get any damping at small movements. We had pressurized, single-tube shocks, and they just worked better."

Two Types of Single-Tube Shocks

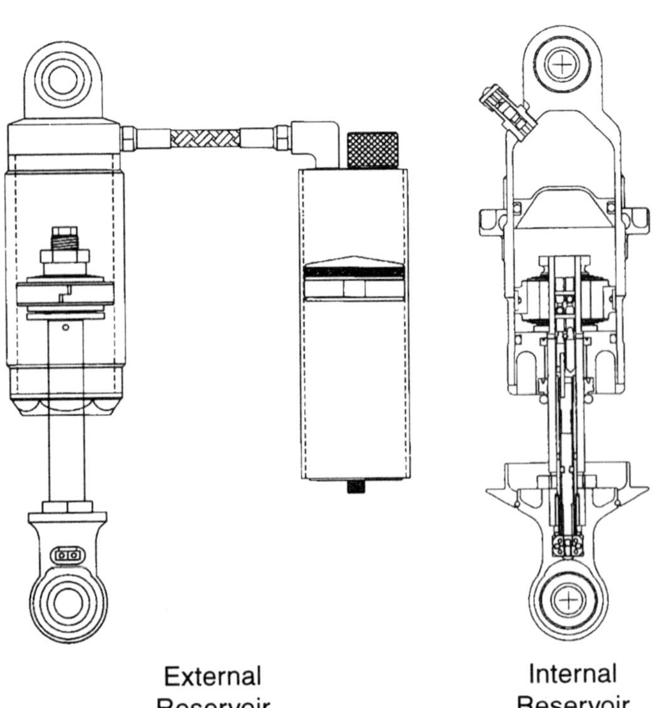

Here are drawings of two modern, single-tube shocks. The Quantum damper on the right has an internal reservoir and the Penske's reservoir is external. In both designs the floating piston and gas reservoir provide a separate gas volume to allow for fluid movement as the piston rod goes in and out of the shock. If there wasn't anywhere for this oil to go, the damper would not move; it would be hydraulically locked. As we explained earlier, the gas pressure also reduces the effects of cavitation, the formation of bubbles in a fluid when it's subjected to low pressure or violent motion.

As you see here, the internal reservoir shock is very simple and compact. Many people think this is a more elegant solution. I'm told that Penske Shocks will offer a similar product in 1995.

The external reservoir does, however, allow for damping adjustments that the internal arrangement doesn't. If you throttle oil flow into or out of the external reservoir, you can add to the damping force caused by piston movement. In fact, you can do some pretty complicated damping adjusting using the reservoir to control fluid movement caused by the piston rod going in and out of the shock. We'll see how that works later in this section.

Washer Stacks, the Heart of Modern Racing Dampers

Forces that try to move the wheel of a car act through the damper shaft and try to push the piston through the oil inside the damper. In order for the piston to move, oil has to flow through the piston in some way. There are several ways to handle that flow so the forces produced control the ride and handling and feel of the car.

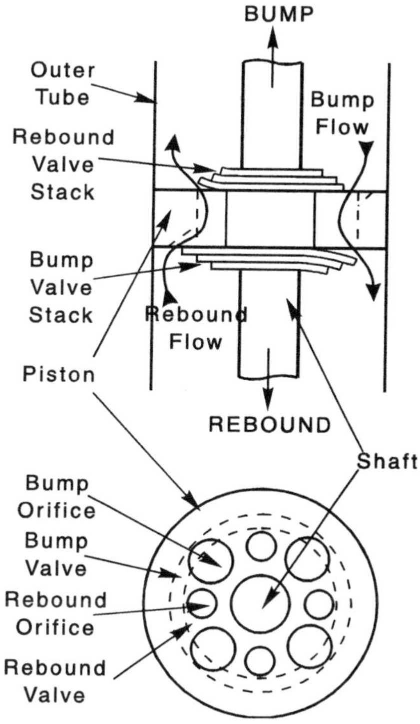

Piston and Washer Stacks

Restriction of the flow past the piston generates a pressure drop across the piston, and therefore more pressure on one side than on the other. If you measured the pressure in the fluid on both sides of the piston and multiplied each pressure times the area on that side of the piston, you would get the forces acting on each side of the piston. Pressure in pounds per square inch times piston area in inches equals pounds of force. The net difference in these two forces is the resisting force of the damper.

There are many ways to meter fluid through an orifice, but the washer check-valve stack used in most racing shocks is simple and elegant. The sketches show how each valve stack deflects and allows oil flow in one direction only.

A damper piston has holes sized and located so that they can be covered by a washer stack on each side of the piston. These washers act as one-way check valves. Dotted circles in the bottom sketch show that, in this design, the washer stacks are different diameters on each side of the piston. The piston design is such that flow in each direction is separate and has to deflect a washer stack in order to flow. When the piston reverses, the fluid can't flow backwards through that same stack, but it can flow around it and deflect the stack on the other side of the piston. Machined holes or cutouts—dotted lines in the top sketch—allow the oil to get by one set of washers and through the piston to the controlling washer stack.

The right side of the sketch shows oil flow when the piston is moving up through the oil, as when the road wheel hits a bump. The left side shows flow when the car's spring pushes the wheel back down—that's rebound. In reality, since the orifices through which the oil flows are arranged symmetrically around the piston, oil flow bends the valve stacks up all around the piston. I've drawn the schematic to show flow in both directions, but I hope it's clear that the piston is designed so that oil only flows through one set of check valves at a time.

This is not an engineering drawing, just an illustrative sketch. Real pistons may be more complicated than this. They may have oval rather than round holes, for example, and the holes may be elaborately contoured. If you think about it you can see that oil bearing on the washer at its outer diameter would have more leverage and open the washer easier than if it could only push on the washer near its inner diameter. Many people have ideas about trick pistons and, although they might buy Penske shocks, they also buy unmachined pistons and make their own.

Notice that the rebound holes in the piston are smaller than the bump holes. That means it takes more force to push the piston in the rebound direction even if the valve stacks were identical on both sides. That's because, after the bump in the road goes by, the spring is compressed and has stored energy that has to be absorbed by the damper as the wheel moves back to its normal position. Piston area taken up by the shaft is another reason why the rebound holes are smaller than the compression holes. Because the rebound side of the piston has less area than the bump side, it takes more pressure on that side to create the same force. Smaller holes restrict flow more and create extra pressure needed in rebound.

High-Speed vs. Low-Speed Damping

It might surprise you to know how quick a wheel has to move to go over a bump. If a wheel moving at 60 mph goes over a bump that moves the wheel up 1 inch as the wheel travels 1 inch along the road, the damper shaft has to move over 1,000 inches per second. That's a big bump, and, if you were in the car, you'd sense it as a loud noise and a boot in the bottom. You can calculate the shaft speed yourself. It's 60 mph times 5,280 feet per mile times 12 inches per foot divided by 3,600 seconds per hour. Even if you give the wheel 3 feet of road surface to move up a half-inch, at 60 mph you still get 15 inches per second damper shaft speed.

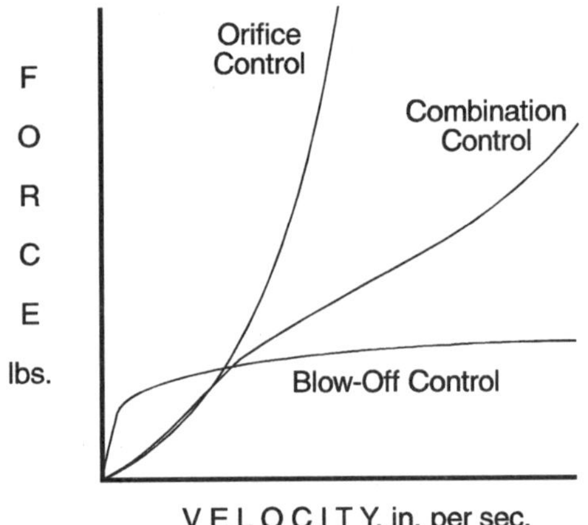

Dampers have to control wheel movements at high shaft speed and also give the driver the right feel at the lower shaft speeds caused when the car brakes, accelerates, and corners. Here's a graph that shows force vs. shaft speed for three different types of valving.

If you had a piston with a bunch of small holes in it, the pressure drop across the piston and, therefore, the damping force would be proportional to the square of the speed of the oil going through the holes relative to the piston. This is called orifice control and gives you a curve like the steeper one.

Here's why that curve shoots up so quickly. As you know, when you put your hand out the window of a moving car or try to move your hand through water, a fluid generates a resistant force when you push against it. This force is predictable when the fluid is incompressible, such as oil, and it's flowing through a hole of fixed size, like an orifice in the piston. The magnitude of the force depends on the size of the hole and the square of the fluid speed through the hole.

I'll explain a little further. You may remember that aerodynamic forces are proportional to the square of the vehicle speed—the lift and drag of a wing at 100 mph is four times that at 50 mph (100 squared is 1,000), which is four times 50 squared or 250). And a wing with double the area puts out double the lift. It's the same with an orifice control damper. When piston speed through the oil doubles, the force goes up four times and a hole of twice the area generates only half the drag (damping force in a shock absorber). The curve is steep because the force goes up with the square of piston velocity.

Where does that energy go? The oil heats up due to the viscous friction when it's forced through the piston and, as the oil passes that heat to the steel outer tube, air passing over the tube carries the heat away.

An orifice-control damper is much too harsh. Any bump but the smallest would feel like a pothole. The dampers on most street cars have pistons with orifices that are capped by a spring-loaded valve that blows off after the fluid forces overcome the initial pre-load of the spring. This configuration gives a force vs. velocity curve like the one labeled "Blow-Off Control." The "Combination Control" curve happens when you have a, guess what, combination of blow-off and orifice control.

The curve labeled "Blow-Off Control" can be achieved either with washer valve stacks or a spring-loaded valve. A small piston bypass leak hole determines the low-speed, steep part of the curve, and the washer stack or spring valve produces the linear, almost flat section.

Small holes in the piston, complicated shapes of piston orifices, washer stacks, and combinations of all these introduce viscous effects into damper performance and allow very complicated configurations. As a result, racing dampers are a rich and varied field being plowed by some very bright and innovative people.

A Real-World Damper

This graph shows a force vs. shaft velocity curve out of the Koni catalog, and you can see that in bump this damper generates about 250 pounds of force at a shaft speed of 15 inches per second. The damper force combined with the spring force might be in the neighborhood of 500 pounds, and since a street car weighs at least 3,000 pounds, the force produced by this bump would be significant and would move the whole car to some degree.

This graph is the product of a machine, called a damper dynamometer, that moves the damper shaft at different velocities and measures the resulting force. We'll describe damper dynos in detail later.

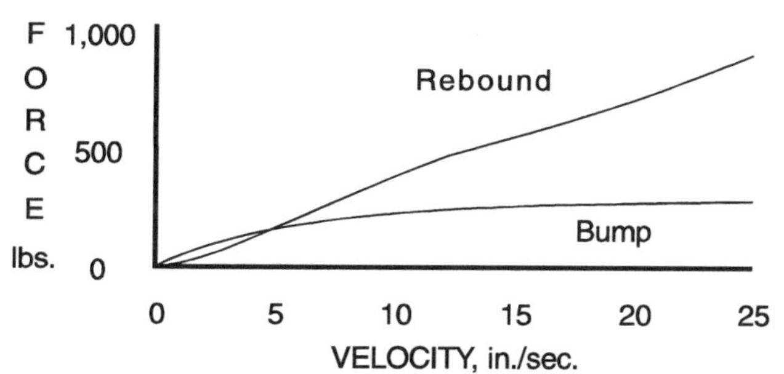

High shaft speeds are caused by bumps and low shaft speeds happen when the car turns or brakes or accelerates. Low-speed damping is what affects the "feel" of a car.

Racecar engineers use dampers extensively to tune racecar handling. These days they are paying more attention to shaft speeds in the 0- to 1-inch-per-second range. These very low shaft speeds are what matter when you're fine tuning how the car feels to the driver.

What really determines high- and low-speed damping forces is the damping characteristics of each shock as determined by the internal design and adjustments. Most dampers have a built-in leak in the piston that determines the damper's low-speed characteristics. This leak can be as simple as fluid getting by the piston seals, but a more controlled way is better. There is usually a small, 0.020 inch to 0.040 inch diameter, hole in the piston that provides a path for a small amount of fluid to bleed by the piston and bypass the valve stack. Dampers without a piston bleed hole can feel harsh; they feel very hard on small bumps. Some race engineers, however, feel a no-bleed piston is an advantage and tell the driver to get used to the harsh feel. This bleed hole can be larger or smaller by design or, if the hole is in a removable part of the damper such as a bushing, that whole part can be changed. We'll see later in the section that this kind of bypass is the primary method used to adjust the low speed characteristics of dampers.

When the main piston valve opens or "blows off," you can say the damper goes from low speed to high speed operation.

Damper Adjustments Overview

What's amazing about modern racecar dampers is their flexibility and ease of adjustment. When a racer orders a set of shocks, the manufacturer asks enough questions so that the racer gets shocks with a piston design and valving that is pretty close for that car and type of racing. The racer can send the shocks back to the manufacturer for revalving anytime, or can do it himself if the damper is field rebuildable.

Many models offered by damper manufacturers are field rebuildable. Old oil and worn parts can be replaced and different washer stacks installed. Different combinations of washers give different damping. As you might figure out for yourself more, thicker, or smaller-diameter washers will take more oil pressure to bend, and so give stronger damping. Conversely, fewer, thinner, or larger-diameter washers bend at lower pressures, giving lower damping forces. Catalogs from damper manufacturers show various valving combinations. We'll go into more detail about this subject shortly.

Put an adjustable needle valve in a piston-bypass bleed path, make it so you can adjust that needle valve from outside the damper, and you have a shock with externally-adjustable, low-speed damping. Add a ball check valve and the bleed operates only one way. Do you begin to get an idea of how complicated this gets?

Let's summarize some ways to adjust damping forces, and then we'll look at each adjustment characteristic separately and in more detail.

Internal adjustments:
- Washer valve stack—number, diameter, order, and thickness of washers.
- Size, shape, and number of orifices in the piston.
- Piston bypass bleed holes—flow area affects low-speed damping.
- Check valves—flow direction control.
- Dish in piston—pre-load on washer stack.

External adjustments:
- Adjustable internal parts—change size of orifices.
- Needle valves—adjustable bypass circuits.
- Restrictions in flow to external reservoir—variable orifices, needle valves.
- Spring-loaded washer stack—varying pre-load on spring provides adjustment.

Internal Adjustments

You have to take the shock apart to change the characteristics of the internal adjustments. While not extremely complicated, it takes long enough that these adjustments aren't done often and are used to get you in the ball park, while the external adjustments are what you work with during test sessions or during a race weekend. Well-prepared and well-heeled teams go to a race or test with several sets of dampers so they can change them quickly during a track session and rebuild them in the trailer between sessions.

Simple Washer Stacks: Fox Rebound Adjustment

The washer stack is really the heart of the modern racing damper. I think you'll see here just how flexible it can be.

The first washer in the stack, the one closest to the piston, has to be large enough to cover the orifices in the piston. This washer acts as a check valve to keep fluid from flowing back through that side of the piston. The other washers in the stack add spring rate to the stack or act as stops.

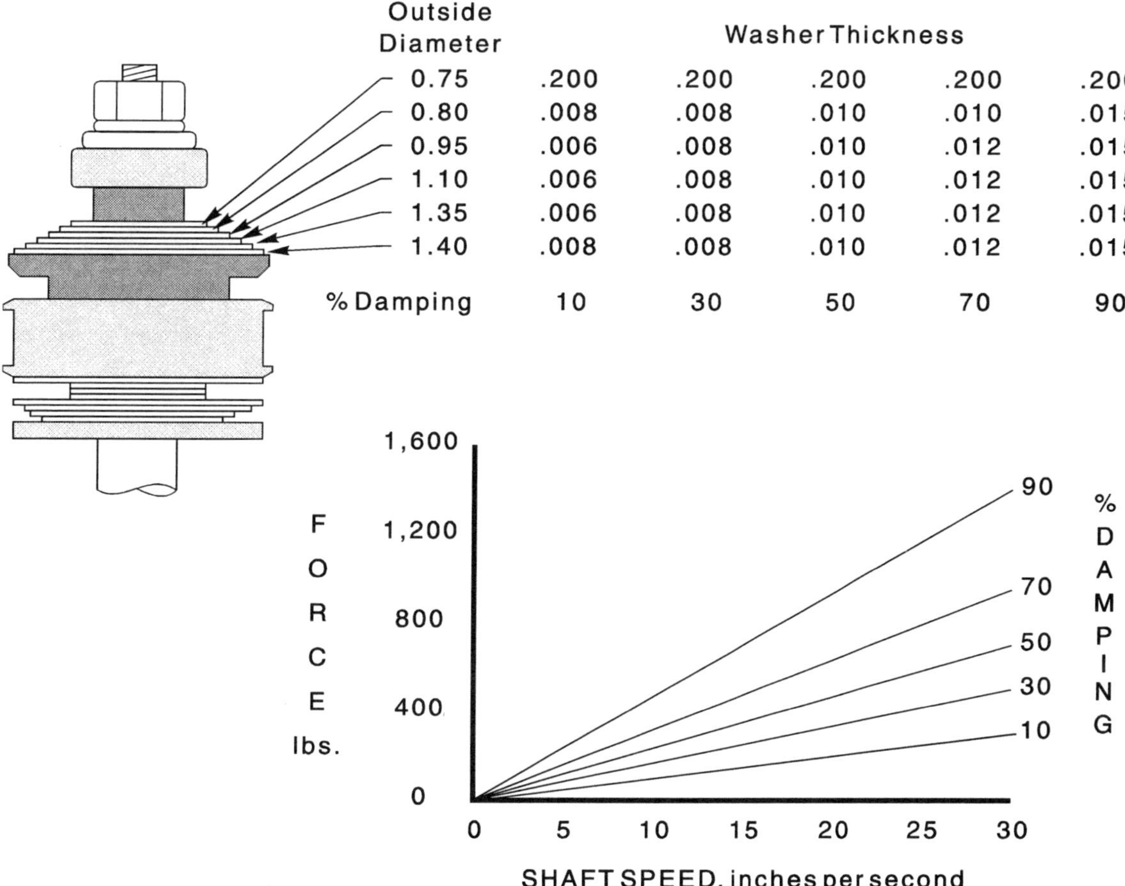

Outside Diameter	Washer Thickness				
0.75	.200	.200	.200	.200	.200
0.80	.008	.008	.010	.010	.015
0.95	.006	.008	.010	.012	.015
1.10	.006	.008	.010	.012	.015
1.35	.006	.008	.010	.012	.015
1.40	.008	.008	.010	.012	.015
% Damping	10	30	50	70	90

The drawing you see here is a cross section of a piston with washer stacks on both sides. I made the drawing, table, and graph from information in a data sheet from Fox Shox. The top stack, the one we'll look at now, is the rebound stack. The holes in the pistons, not shown here, are smaller than the holes in the other direction because, as you remember, we need more damping in the rebound direction due to the stored energy in the spring.

If you look closely you can see the washer stack is made up of six washers, and the diameter and thickness of each one can be varied to give different damping characteristics. Fox has tried to make it simple by using a percent damping number to give tuners something to talk about when developing the racecar or motorcycle. At 10% damping you've got some pretty skinny washers in there; only 6 or 8 thousandths of an inch thick. For 50% damping it takes washers that are 10 thousandths thick, and 15 thousandths-thick washers give you 90% damping. The .200 inch-thick washer is a stop that limits the travel of the other washers.

Look at the graph of force vs. shaft speed. The skinny washers used to get 10% damping flop open (blow off) pretty quickly and create about 100 pounds of force at 10 inches per second shaft speed. Even at 30 inches per second (that's recovering from a big bump), this stack only gives 300 pounds force. Thicker washers in the 70% damping stack generate 300 pounds at 10 inches per second (ips), and 700 at 20 ips.

Fox High- and Low-Speed Compression Adjustment

A more complicated stack can create a two-stage effect and allow adjustments for low-speed damping and high-speed damping in the same stack.

In this first drawing below at top left, the washer closest to the piston is thin. It will "blow off" easily and deflect until it hits the fourth washer, allowing a gush of damper fluid. This is a very "soft" low-speed damping configuration and, in this particular damper, it can be firmed up by substituting thicker washers, as in the bottom-right drawing. These adjustments only affect the low-speed damping, up to about 5 inches per second. You can see the force vs. shaft speed curve on the next page changes slope at 5 inches per second. Up to that transition speed the low-speed washer stack controls damping but, when the piston is forced to move faster, the low-speed washer pushes against the high-speed washers and opens a larger path, as in the top-right drawing. The bottom two

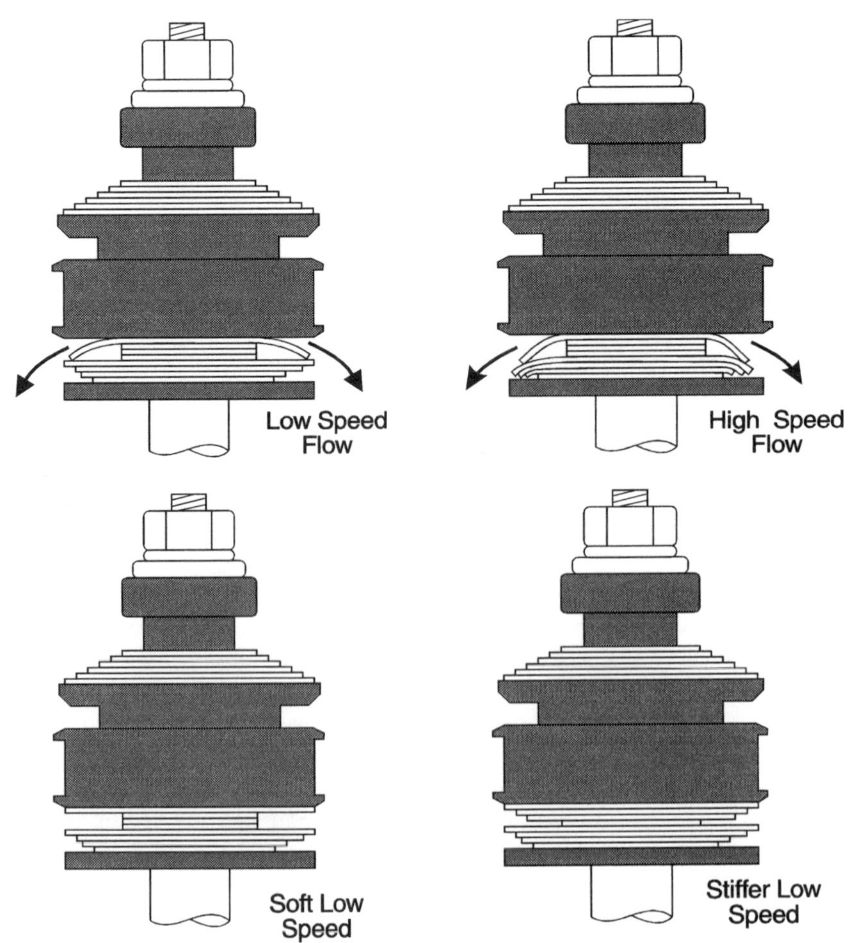

Washer Stack Adjustments

drawings show how you stiffen up the low-speed stack so it produces more damping force.

I need to stop here and point out that there is nothing magic about this 5-inches-per-second value. As I said before, many racecar engineers are concerned with tuning dampers at shaft speeds of 1 inch per second and below. Practically, in a valve-stack damper, low speed is before the washers blow off and high speed is after. Another way to look at it is that low speed is the rising, non-linear part of the curve, and high speed is the linear section of the curve. The shape of the force vs. velocity curve is a characteristic of a particular damper. For this damper the transition between low- and high-speed operation is controlled by these washer stacks. A more typical racing damper might have an adjustable bleed controlling the low-speed part of the curve, and then the washer stack opens and takes over control. Talking about low and high speed just gives us a way to discuss damper characteristics.

By now you can guess that high-speed damping is adjusted by varying the diameter and thickness of the washers below the low-speed stack in these drawings. Here's a table showing some typical washer configurations and a graph that shows corresponding force vs. shaft speed curves. In this stack there are 5 valve washers and a 0.20-inch thick "top out" washer that acts as a limit for the thinner washers. Notice also that these stacks use washers of one thickness only. Of course you can mix them up to get damping curves in between these, but using only one thickness at a time is less confusing.

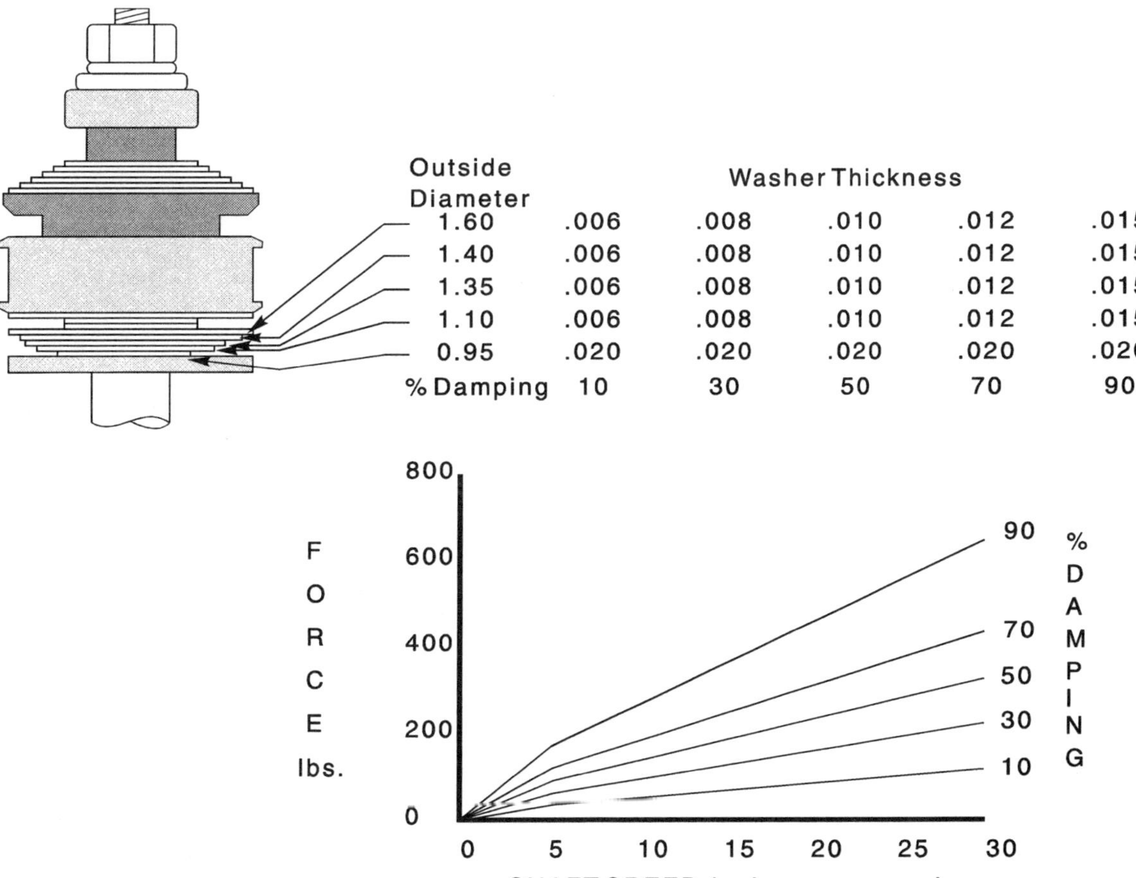

Outside Diameter	Washer Thickness				
1.60	.006	.008	.010	.012	.015
1.40	.006	.008	.010	.012	.015
1.35	.006	.008	.010	.012	.015
1.10	.006	.008	.010	.012	.015
0.95	.020	.020	.020	.020	.020
% Damping	10	30	50	70	90

Fixed-Bleed Devices

As we mentioned before, without a piston bleed hole, dampers can be very harsh at low shaft speeds. To solve this problem there are usually holes in the piston or shaft to allow some fluid flow through the piston that bypasses the valve stack. Fixed bleeds can be adjusted, but the damper has to be disassembled to do so. The hole, usually only 0.020 to 0.060 inches in diameter, can be drilled larger, the piston can be replaced with one that has a different-sized hole, or, if a bushing in the shaft is the bleed, as in the Fox shock in the section above, the bushing can be changed.

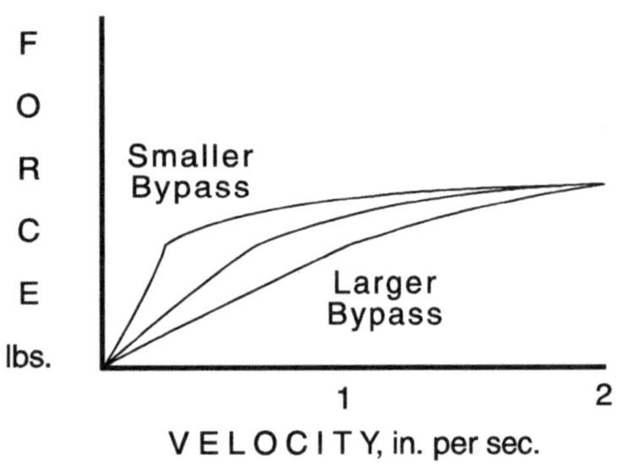

Here is a family of typical force vs. velocity curves that show how varying the diameter of the bleed hole affects the damping. The damper with the smaller bypass hole has a steeper initial section because oil flow is restricted and forces rise rapidly as shaft speeds increase. In theory, flow through the bypass hole is similar to fluid flow through an orifice, and the forces go up with the square of the velocity. When the valve stack "blows off," damper characteristics are governed more by viscous flow, and the result is a linear rise of force with velocity.

Ball-Check Valves

If you have a shock with a bleed path through the piston or shaft, that bleed allows flow whenever the piston moves in both the bump and rebound directions. If you'd like different damping characteristics for bump and rebound, you need two circuits. A ball-check valve can make sure these circuits control the flow going in only one direction at a time.

Piston Dish

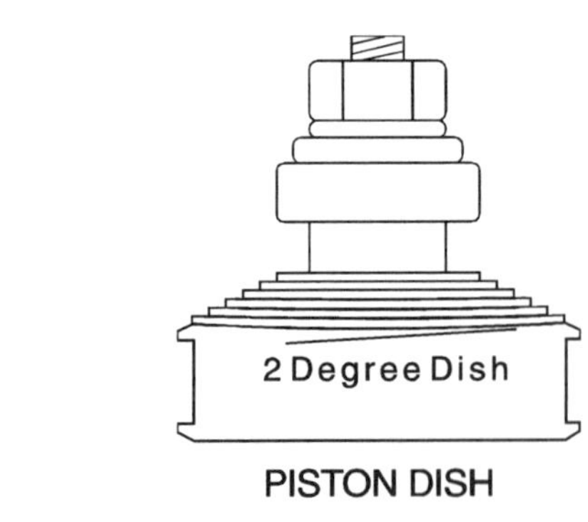

A concavity (dish) in the piston adds a preload to the washer stack. The washers are deflected slightly because they're held down tightly against the piston by a nut that captures the whole stack. Since these dished washers are now deflected from their static shape, it takes some initial fluid force to open them and "blow off" the stack. This feature slightly delays blow off, and, since the washer stack and the orifices they control have no effect until the stack blows off, piston dish allows the bypass to work at slightly higher shaft speeds.

An added benefit of piston dish is that it overcomes the tendency of washer valves to flutter just before they open. The preload prevents this flutter, and makes valve opening more predictable. A 1-degree dish is enough to accomplish this. There are shocks out there with pistons dished at angles from 1 to 4 degrees.

As shown in the aero chapter, there is an optimum ride height and rake for maximum downforce with a ground-effects car and, if the car rolls in a corner or pitches forward or backward during braking or acceleration, downforce falls off. "stabilizing the platform" is the goal, and shocks can help. Some race engineers

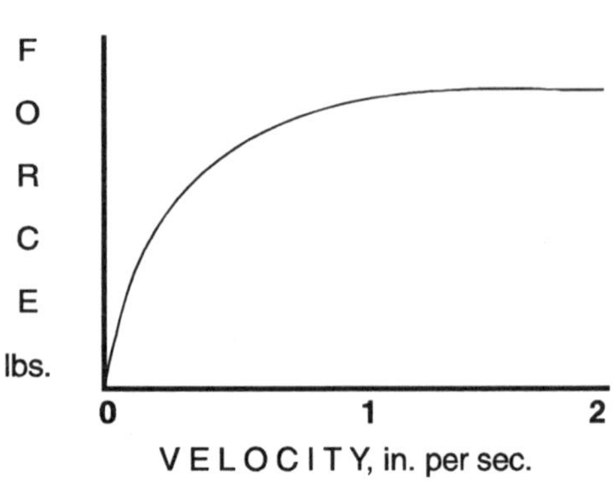

use a damper with a force vs. velocity curve that rises rapidly and falls off to a constant force. This gives the car a very responsive feel and keeps it level during cornering, but allows the wheels to deflect for bumps.

One way to do that is to use a piston with some dish and very little bleed in the piston. Ironically, this arrangement gives a force vs. velocity curve similar to a preloaded valve and spring. There's always more than one way to get the same results, especially with something as complicated as a hydraulic damper.

External Adjustments

The internal adjustments described above require that the damper must be removed from the car and disassembled. Clean, correct reassembly is important, so these adjustments can't be done in a hurry. Many dampers, however, have adjustments that are on the outside of the device and can be reached easily enough that adjustments can be made in the pit lane during test sessions or practice. If a team understands the effects of damper adjustments on the car and the driver, these external adjustments become a powerful tool.

Variable Restrictions

Many dampers have external adjustments that move internal parts and change the size of flow restrictions in the piston or some other metering orifice. Some Koni dampers use this type of adjustment to vary rebound characteristics. The way you adjust the shock is to fully extended the shock rod by pulling the shaft out as far as you can. When the shaft is fully extended a mechanism on the piston engages an external button on the top of the shock body. As you push the button and twist the rod there is a click that tells you you've advanced the mechanism one increment. From the 0 position there are 3 incremental adjustments (clicks) that change rebound forces to 120%, 150%, and 200% of the 0 value. The sketch and graph show details. The bump curve is not affected by these adjustments.

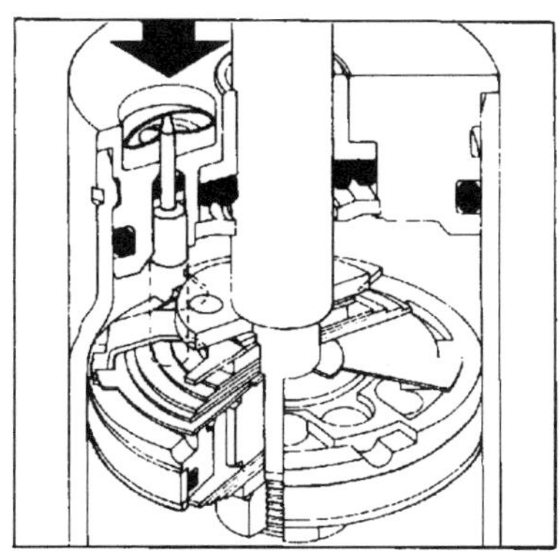

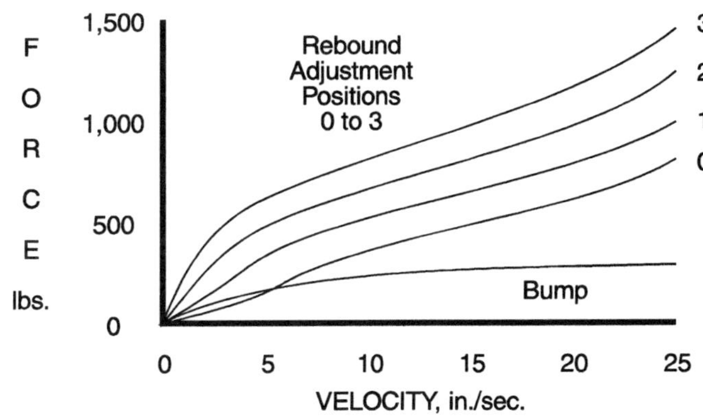

Foot Valve in Double-Tube Shocks

Here's another look at a schematic of a double-tube shock. When the shaft comes into the shock body, fluid has to move through the foot valve into the outer tube. In some dampers, the foot valve is an orifice that can be adjusted by pushing the shaft into the shock, engaging a dog on the bottom of the piston with a slot on the valve, and twisting the shaft to change the size of the orifice. Varying the restriction changes the damping forces in both the bump and rebound directions.

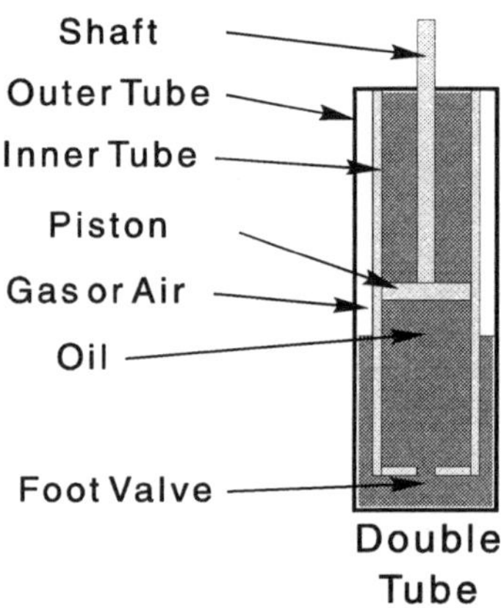

Bypass Adjustments

Many dampers, like this double-adjustable Penske, use a bolt in the shaft to engage a needle valve that allows a variable-area orifice piston bypass. This bypass circuit can be bi-directional or it can have a ball-spring check valve to control the flow in one direction only. In practice this is usually an adjustment for low-speed rebound.

The diameter of the orifice and the diameter and angle of the nose of the needle and the angle of the seat determines how the flow area varies as the needle moves.

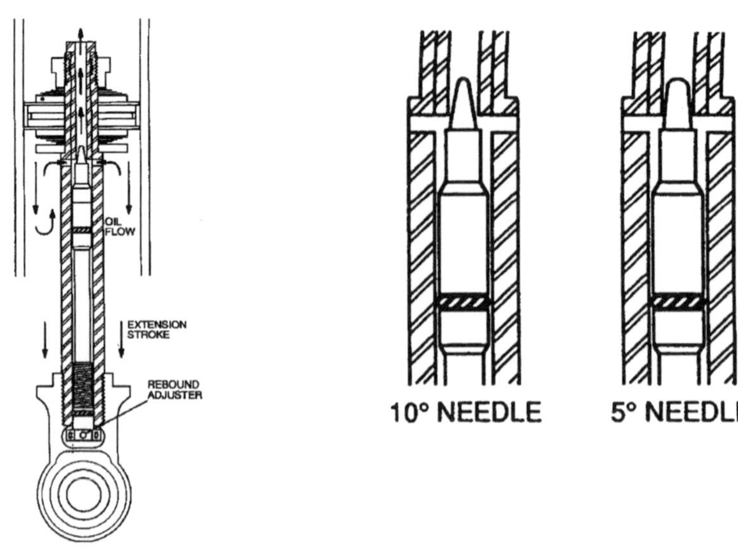

Reservoir Throttling

When a damper compresses, the shaft displaces volume inside the tube. This is why the damper design must include some extra room for the displaced fluid. Double-tube shocks have a low-pressure gas volume between the tubes and single-tube shocks use a higher pressure gas volume separated by a floating piston. In most racing shocks this second piston and gas volume occupy a second canister outside the coil-over unit that's connected to the damper body with a hose. This allows the coil-over to be compact and allows remote mounting of the reservoir. Here's a simple schematic.

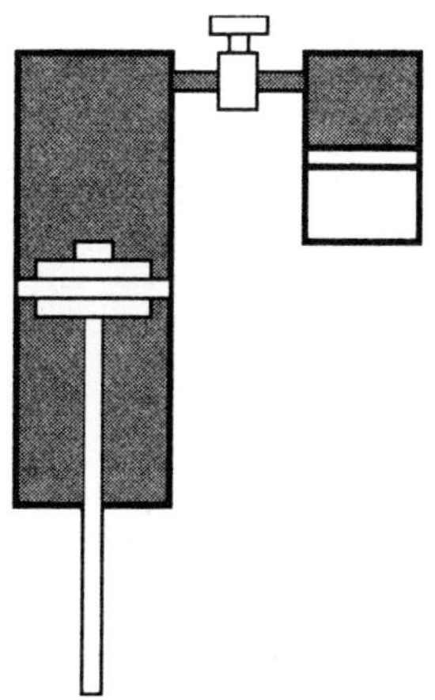

External Reservoir Bump Adjust

If there were no place for the displaced fluid to go when the shock compressed and the shaft tried to come into the shock body, you'd get hydraulic locking, and the shaft could move only if it could compress the fluid or cause leakage past the piston seals. The other extreme, unrestricted flow into the external reservoir, gives no resistance to piston/shaft movement over that generated by the valves and bleeds built in to the piston. In between these two extremes—no flow and unlimited flow—lies another opportunity to control damping forces.

There are several ways to restrict flow to the external reservoir. I show a valve in the hose from shock to reservoir but the restriction is usually in the reservoir. A needle and seat can vary flow area,and this is used widely. Several manufacturers use a disc or drum with orifices of different sizes. To adjust the flow restriction you turn an external knob on the reservoir and rotate different-sized holes into alignment with the inlet path. As you might guess, smaller holes generate higher pressure drops and therefore higher damping forces. A check valve allows free flow in the rebound direction.

Reservoir Washer Stacks

Some dampers, notably the Penske model 8500, better known as the "Penske Red Knob," use a piston and washer valve stack in the reservoir. When the shock compresses in bump and the shaft coming into the shock body forces fluid into the reservoir, that fluid has to blow off the washer stack, and so generates damping forces. The piston is dished and the external adjustment varies the pre-load of the washer stack. The benefit claimed is that of increased sensitivity at low shaft speeds.

Penske Dampers

I'm describing Penske dampers here because their designs cover almost all the ways you can externally adjust shocks, and their catalogs have drawings that show all the parts well.

The Penske Blue Knob

The 8100 series damper is also called the "Penske Blue Knob" because the knurled aluminum knob on the reservoir is anodized a bright blue color. To adjust high-speed damping in compression and rebound you have to disassemble the damper and change washer stacks.

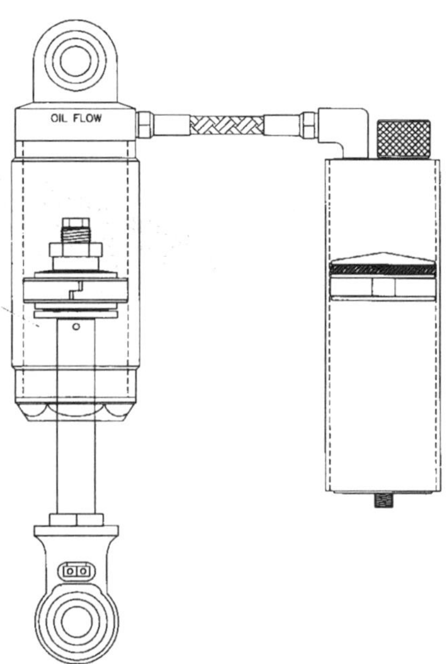

The external adjustment for low-speed rebound is a needle valve in the shaft. You use a small hex wrench or wire to rotate a bolt near the rod-end in the end of the shaft. This bolt determines the position of the needle valve, which controls the flow area of the piston bypass. As shown in the drawing on page 168, the fluid flows into holes in the shaft and through a drilled passage out the shaft end. A check valve prevents reverse flow.

Low-speed compression control comes from a rotating disc in the reservoir inlet that has different sized holes. The adjustment knob is numbered from one to six and ball/spring detents give a tactile adjustment signal. The number one setting is full soft and this rotates a large hole into the inlet path so there is little flow restriction. The number six setting gives you full hard which is no hole at all, and the only flow allowed is leakage into the reservoir or past the piston seals. Adjuster settings two through five have intermediate-sized holes that allow increments of adjustment between these extremes. A check valve allows full flow out of the reservoir in the rebound direction so that the needle valve in the shaft can control rebound flow.

The Penske Red Knob

Penske's 8500 series damper got its name from the red-anodized, knurled knob on the reservoir, and its operation is similar to the Blue Knob except that the variable-sized orifices in the reservoir inlet have been replaced by a washer stack. The red adjustment knob varies preload on the stack, which changes the force needed to blow off this stack. The claimed benefit as mentioned above is increased low-speed compression sensitivity. The curve below shows force vs. shaft velocity for low-speed compression. Low-speed rebound adjustment is the same as in the Blue Knob. High-speed compression and rebound characteristics are adjusted by changing the valve stack washers.

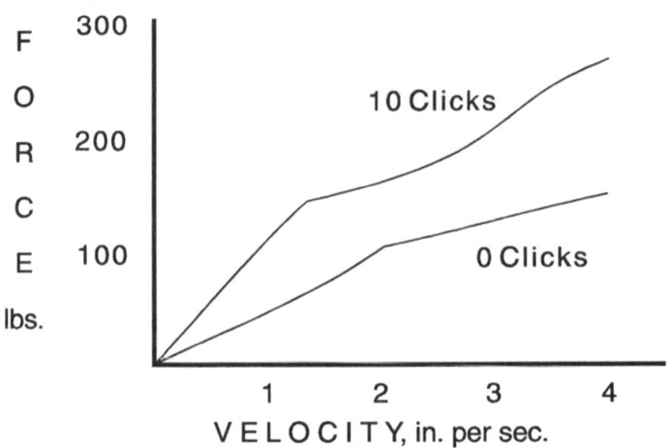

The Triple-Clicker

The Penske series 8550 and 8700 are triple adjustable, which is an evolution from the Red Knob. In addition to the washer stack in the reservoir, they have a bypass leak around this stack controlled with a needle valve that's adjusted by an external nut. As in the Red Knob, preload on the valve stack changes damping and the adjustable bypass allows another adjustment. Low-speed rebound is adjusted like the Blue Knob (nut in shaft which varies bleed past the piston), while low- and high-speed compression are adjusted using knobs on the top of the reservoir. This damper is rebuildable and has replaceable washer stacks like the other models.

The two compression adjustments are interrelated and, in practice, can be confusing. If the reservoir washer-stack bypass is fully open, the stack opens only at higher shaft speeds. With the bypass closed, the washer stack controls completely. The claimed benefit is finer control at very small shaft speeds—in the range of 1 or 2 inches per second.

The sensitivity and interrelation of adjustments makes it easy to get confused when working with these dampers. For that reason a racer using them either needs a damper dyno or the services of someone who has one. So this is a good point to take a look at a shock dynomometer.

SHOCK DYNAMOMETER: WHERE THE GRAPHS COME FROM

Dampers are the hot racecar component of the '90s. The two racing topics that were hot in the '80s, suspension geometry and data acquisition, have been absorbed by most of the serious teams. They understand, or have hired someone who understands, both these subjects and have acquired the necessary software and hardware tools. Likewise, everyone in racing acknowledges the importance of aerodynamics, and there are millions of dollars spent annually on wind tunnel and track testing of aero tweaks. The result is there are people on every pro race team who are familiar with displacement sensors, accelerometers, and laptop computers, and have data on the trade-offs of changes in roll centers, camber, vortex generators, wing angles, and ride height.

But damper performance is still voodoo to most racers, and they're scrambling to learn all they can. A shock dynamometer is the newest line item appearing in all test and development budgets. The most serious teams have one at the shop and another one in the trailer. They need a person responsible for the operation of this equipment and the associated computers, so now most big teams have a "shock guy" who's either a full-time employee or an outside consultant who's there at tests and on race weekends.

I hope I've explained things well enough so you understand by now that dampers produce a force proportional to the speed of shaft movement. If you compress a damper slowly, it generates less resistant force than if you move it faster. As mentioned before, a damper on a racecar does several very important things including providing a tunable "feel" for the driver during cornering, controlling wheel travel over road irregularities, and, most important for a ground-effects car, stabilizing the underwing of the car at optimum ride height and rake.

Since dampers are a critical component of a racecar, they should be tested periodically to make sure they are working correctly. Also, when a race engineer finds a damper set-up that makes the car faster under certain conditions at a certain racetrack, that engineer will want to have dampers set up the same way the next time the car runs on that or a similar track. As with any critical component, the race engineer would like to know more about how it works. The shock dyno is a tool used to test dampers and learn about their behavior.

What Is a Shock Dyno?

The force vs. shaft speed graphs you see in this chapter come from data generated by testing a damper in what is generally known as a shock dyno or damper dynamometer. This is a machine that compresses and expands a damper at known speeds and measure the forces produced by the damper. I'll start out by describing the simplest form of a shock dyno. This sketch shows a frame holding an electric motor with a drive belt and pulleys that spin a crank plate attached to the damper shaft through a linear bearing. As the motor spins the crank, the damper piston moves up and down just like the piston in a cylinder of an engine. Bolt holes in the crank plate allow several different stroke lengths. Different pulley diameters give different crank plate rotation speeds. The load cell measures the damper force.

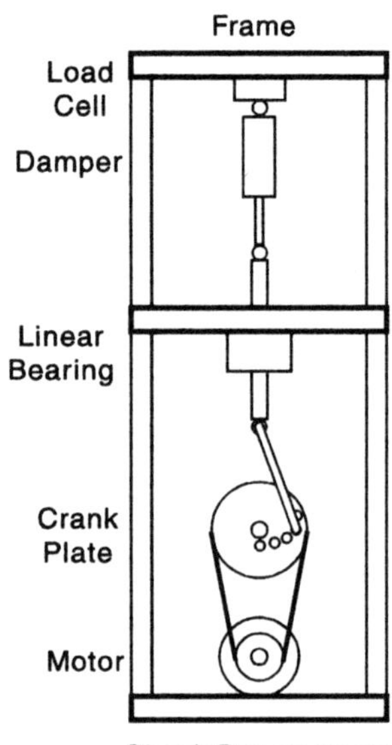

We all know that the speed of a piston connected to a crank varies continuously as the crank rotates. You might remember from high school math or physics that this type of motion is called sinusoidal because it varies with the sine of the crank angle. The piston comes to a stop at top dead center, accelerates to a maximum speed halfway down the cylinder, and slows down to a stop again at the bottom. If you have a damper attached to a crank, its piston does the same, and the force generated also varies continuously. We know, however, that the maximum speed of the piston happens only once per stroke, when the piston is halfway between top and bottom, and that's also when the damper generates maximum force. We could vary the speed of the electric motor, but motors that can do that are expensive. With our simple shock dyno we change the crank stroke to vary the maximum shaft speed and/or we use drive pulleys of different sizes.

Here's How It Works

You put a damper in the dyno, choose a stroke and pulley, and turn on the motor. The crank turns and the damper shaft moves up and down until you turn off the motor. If you know the motor rpm, the pulley ratio, and the stroke, you can calculate the maximum damper shaft speed. For example, let's say the motor turns 1,000 rpm, you've got pulleys that reduce the motor speed so the plate turns 100 rpm, and the stroke is 1 inch. 100 rpm is 1.67 revolutions per second and the length of 1 revolution is the circumference of the circle traveled by the crank bolt or Pi times the stroke. 1.67 x 3.14 x 1 inches is about 5 inches per second. This is the maximum speed of the damper piston, and it happens twice each revolution of the crank, once with the piston going up in compression and once again with the piston going down in rebound.

If we keep this example really simple and connect the damper directly to a weighing scale with a circular dial, we can stand there and read the scale pointer directly. What we'll see is the pointer cycling from 0 to some maximum rebound force as the shock expands, returns to 0, and then peaks out again at the max compression force as the piston goes back up. The needle on our scale goes from plus some number to minus some number as the damper cycles from compression to rebound and back. We can just write down the numbers at which the needle peaks as it goes back and forth. A commercially available shock dyno uses a computer to read the load cell and store the data.

Most dampers are set up to give more force in rebound than compression so, as our simple machine cranks away, we might see the scale peak at 190 pounds in compression and 250 pounds in rebound. So we know that, at a shaft speed of 5 inches per second, the damper produces 190 pounds in compression (or bump) and 250 pounds in rebound. We'd like several data points so we can draw a curve.

If we reduce the stroke to a half inch and a quarter of an inch, and also lengthen it to an inch and a half and two inches, this gives us five data points. After we make these runs and read the scale we can make a table like this:

Stroke in.	Max. Speed in./sec.	Bump Force lbs.	Rebound Force lbs.
0.25	1	75	50
0.50	3	170	150
1.00	5	190	250
1.50	8	220	350
2.00	11	250	470

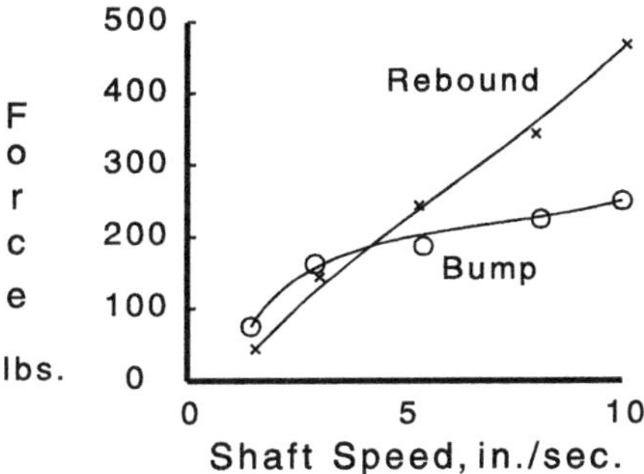

Presented as a force vs. shaft speed graph, it looks like this. We generated this data by running the crank at 100 rpm and changing the stroke to give us 5 maximum piston speeds, and we read the bump and rebound forces at those maximum speeds. Then we made a graph by connecting the dots. If we want data at higher shaft speeds we need to speed up the crank plate or lengthen the stroke. The graph shows us that the shock we tested has a pretty steep rebound curve while the compression curve starts low, rises quickly, and then levels off.

The real benefit of a machine like this comes when you test all four dampers off your racecar and find out that they all give different readings even though they are supposed to have the same valving, and you've, hopefully, set them all to the same external adjustments before you started the test. Some small difference in readings is OK, but the closer together the better. If you've got the tools and experience, you can overhaul your shocks and test them again. Maybe you'll find contaminated oil, bad seals, or worn parts. Shocks wear out like any other mechanism and need to be rebuilt periodically.

A shock dyno also allows you to see the effects of external adjustments. If the data above represents settings in the middle of the range of adjustments, varying them in increments from full-hard to full-soft will give you curves that show the effect of those changes. That will happen if your dampers produce changes big enough to be seen by your machine. If you really are just reading a scale by eye you might miss some fine points. That's why people buy dynos instead of building them.

The graph above came from data generated by looking at maximum or peak velocities. This is called Peak Velocity Pickoff, and that's the only way our simple dyno works. We varied pulley sizes and the damper stroke to give us peak velocities in our range of interest. A dyno with a variable speed motor can take peak velocity data quickly without changing the stroke.

Data from an Entire Cycle

You can get more data from a damper by taking data over a complete cycle of compression and rebound and graphing that. This is called a Continuous Velocity Plot, and there are commercially available damper dynamometers that do this.

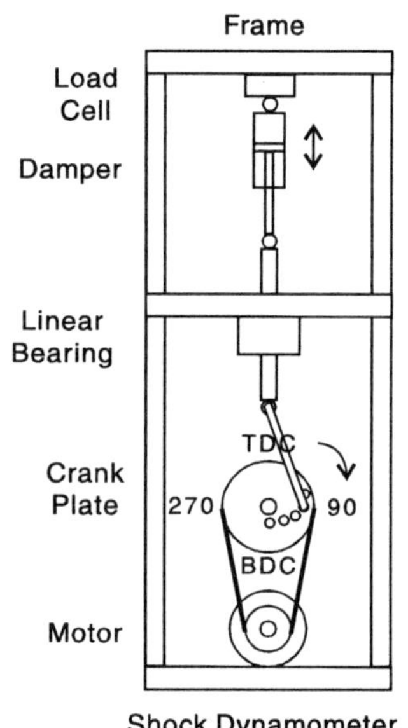

Here's another sketch of the damper dyno. I've added notations around the crank plate for Top Dead Center (TDC), 90 degrees, Bottom Dead Center (BDC), and 270 degrees. When the crank pin is at TDC the damper is compressed in bump. As the crank plate rotates clockwise (it's expanding so that's the rebound direction) from TDC, the damper piston accelerates from a stop to maximum speed at 90 degrees and then slows to a stop again at BDC. Rotation continues and the piston accelerates in compression to maximum speed at 270 degrees and slows to a stop again at TDC. The length of stroke and rotation speed depends on how you've set up your machine.

This graph shows force data taken continuously during one revolution of the crank plate. I've arbitrarily chosen shaft speed in the down direction as positive and compression force as positive. The bottom part of the curve shows shaft speed and negative force increasing as the crank plate goes to 90 degrees and then decreasing as the curve goes back up toward zero speed and force. As rotation continues, speed goes negative (compression) and force increases to a maximum again at 270 and back to 0 at TDC. The speed and force data taken to produce a graph like this comes from a velocity sensor and a strain-gauge load cell. A data acquisition system in a personal computer reads these sensors 1,000 times a second. Software processes the data and displays it in this form.

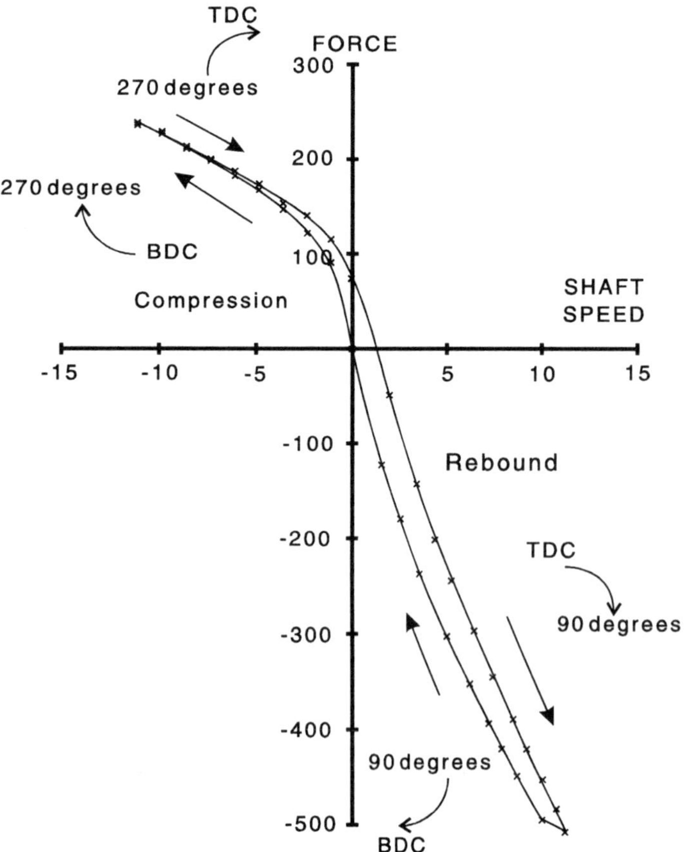

This can be confusing and you might have to look at this sketch and the graph a while before it becomes clear. The important point is the force increases with piston speed. On the lower section of the curve the piston is accelerating where the curve is headed down and slowing down as the curve swings back up. It's the same on the top part. The piston speed and damping force increase to a maximum and then slow again.

This is a lot more data than we had when we just changed the stroke and looked at the damper force at maximum piston speed. This is the same data as in the first graph, but it's presented differently. So why doesn't the damper develop the same force when it's slowing down as it did when it speeded up? I'm not certain, myself, but remember you've got a bunch of oil moving through the washer stacks and bypass paths, and it has some mass and momentum. And I don't think those washer valves necessarily close the same way they open. Also, the fact that the damper piston is always accelerating, slowing down or speeding up, may have something to do with the shape of this curve.

Data Formats

Actually there are several ways to show this data. The more complicated, S-shaped curve is the most precise way to present the data of a complete cycle of a damper. This graph would, however, get even more complicated if you overlaid data that showed the effect of internal adjustments or valving changes. To make thing simpler and easier to read you'll often see data presented with bump and rebound curves in the same quadrant, as in the graph on the left below, and everybody understands that some forces and movements are in different directions.

When showing bump and rebound data that has adjustment effects, however, it makes sense to use two quadrants, as in the graph on the right.

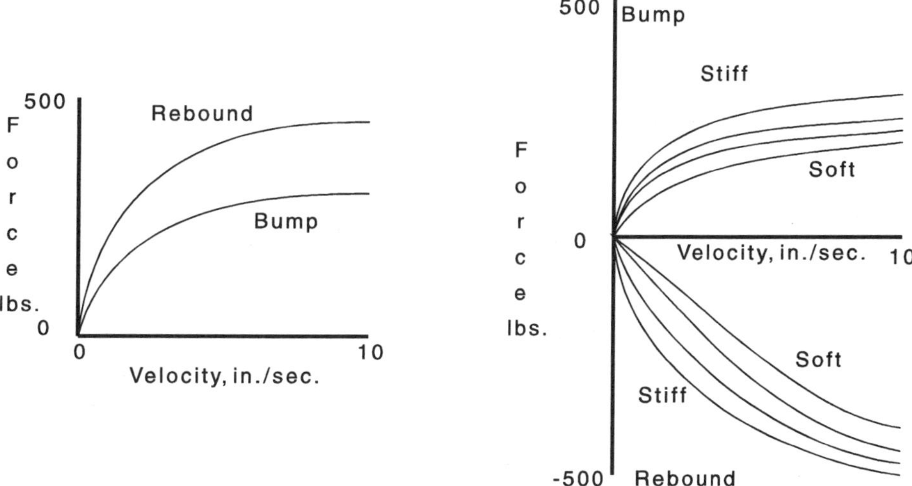

A good shock dyno generates data that you can use to test and set up dampers. But what does this have to do with what a damper does in a racecar? I don't know the answer to that question. More and more people are buying shock dynos and many of these people say they are learning more about how a shock works and that helps them make a racecar quicker.

A damper on a racecar has a very complicated behavior. It's jiggling up and down constantly in small movements caused by small track irregularities, and, at the same time, it's influencing low-speed chassis movements caused by turning and braking and acceleration; but it's also absorbing big, jolting bumps and controlling energy stored in the spring after those bumps. To make things more complicated, the tire, a largely undamped spring itself, is jiggling and squirming around between the damper and the track surface. And then, of course, there's the driver trying to go as fast as he can and get some idea from steering wheel inputs and forces on his body about whether or not he can go faster. It doesn't seem like taking force data at a few peak piston velocities can possibly tell you much about what's going on, but some data is better than no data at all.

People who think they can buy a shock dyno and immediately use data from the dyno to make a racecar faster on a racetrack are due for a disappointment. The shock just doesn't act the same in a dyno as it does in the car. There are, however, people who are running shocks in dynos and gaining experience that might help them use the dampers on a racecar to help the driver turn faster laps.

Hydraulic Damper Dyno

There is another type of damper dyno that goes one step further toward generating data at conditions closer to those a shock actually sees on a racecar. This machine is called a hydraulic dyno, and it uses a powerful hydraulic motor and fast-acting servo valves controlling high-pressure oil acting on a piston to move a damper exactly as it moves on the racecar. A computer controls the servo valves and also gathers force and speed data as on the dynos we've described.

The advantage of the hydraulic dyno is it can generate very high forces, and the servo valves can control those forces very quickly. As a result, this type of shock dyno can use information gathered by on-board data acquisitions systems on the car and reproduce, on the dyno, the same movements the shock went through during an actual lap on the track.

At least one damper dyno manufacturer is using an electric actuator to simulate on-track shock movements on a dyno. There is a demand for a way to more closely simulate actual damper movements.

JEFF BRAUN'S SHOCK DYNO SERVICE

Jeff Braun has a damper dyno at his shop in West Texas, and he does shock work for individual racers and race teams. These customers pay Jeff to do this work, and the data generated during testing belongs to them. Jeff's data comes from a Roehrig damper dyno. He sets up his tests with a specific stroke, and the variable speed motor automatically changes speeds and takes data over a range of peak velocities.

Some of the shocks Jeff gets from customers haven't been maintained well at all. Some have been modified unsuccessfully by someone trying to improve the damper's performance. He's seen pistons with passages that have been modified with a file by someone trying to change the basic characteristics of the damper. He's found piston bleed holes drilled in the wrong places, so the piston had no bleed at all. Many dampers sent to Jeff have dark, dirty oil and may have been run for several seasons without maintenance. No one would think of running an engine without routine maintenance. Dampers are just as critical as the engine and need the same kind of tuning and tweaking. Most racers are beginning to see there is a lot of potential performance in a good set of dampers, if you know how to use them.

'As-Delivered' Test

Typically, Jeff gets four dampers from the customer. He's talked to them on the phone, and he knows what kind of racing they're doing, the racecar manufacturer, what problems they're having, and what they think they want from the shocks.

The shocks are handled and tested as two pairs, front and rear. The first thing Jeff does is run them on the dyno in the condition in which he received them. He uses a standard set of external adjustment settings for this test. This first run may reveal problems Jeff can fix during the overhaul.

In the graph on the left below we see what Jeff's "as delivered" test revealed when he tested a pair of shocks that had been set up for an oval track. The right front damper is valved for higher bump forces than the left front. The left front has more rebound. The customer had been using them on road courses!

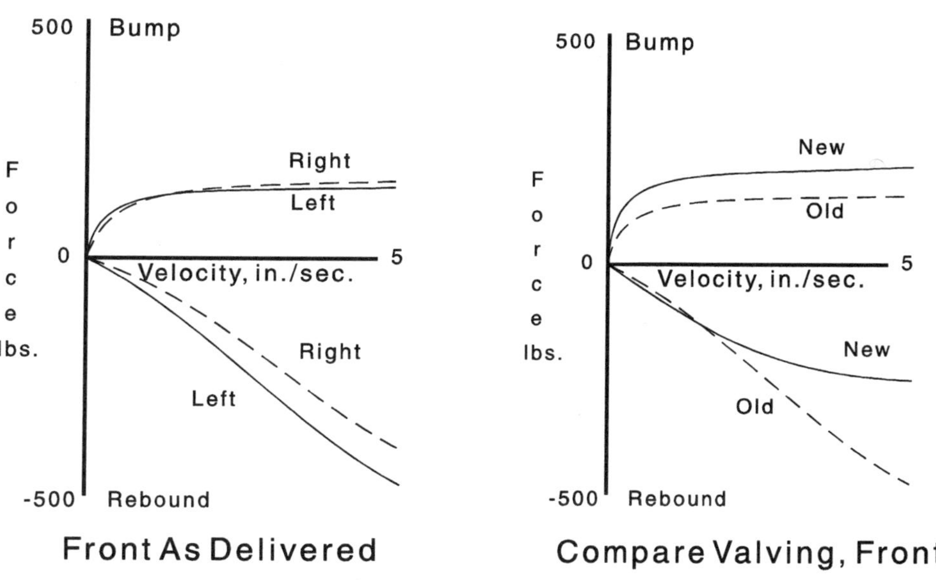

Front As Delivered   **Compare Valving, Front**

'Compare' Test

When he reassembles the shocks, Jeff will replace all the seals and he may install a new piston or a different piston design. He will more than likely use different washer valves. He might replace the hose to the external reservoir. Parts are changed or replaced as needed. Everything is cleaned up, of course, and the shocks are reassembled using new oil. Jeff documents any changes he made to the internal parts. He'll tell the customer exactly what type of piston and washer valves he installed during reassembly.

On these shocks that came to him set up asymmetrically, he installed a new piston of his own design and valved them symmetrically. He tested them again on the dyno so he had data showing shock performance before and after overhaul. This graph on the right above shows the results of that "Compare" test for one front shock.

The 'Balance' Test

Then Jeff does what he calls a balance test. For this test Jeff sets the external adjustments to what he calls base settings and tests them to make sure both front shocks produce similar results. He repeats the balance test for the rear pair.

Shock 'Profiles'

Another set of dyno runs produces some graphs Jeff calls "profiles" that show how the force vs. velocity curves vary through the entire range of the external adjustments. These graphs allow the customer to make an informed decision when considering a shock change. The graphs show the magnitude of the change magnitude of the change

Now the customer has two pairs of shocks that have been overhauled and balanced, and there are data and graphs of force vs. velocity to document how the shocks performed as delivered and after reassembly. There is performance data at some base settings and also data that shows how forces change with external adjustments. The shocks will work this way as long as they aren't damaged or worn out.

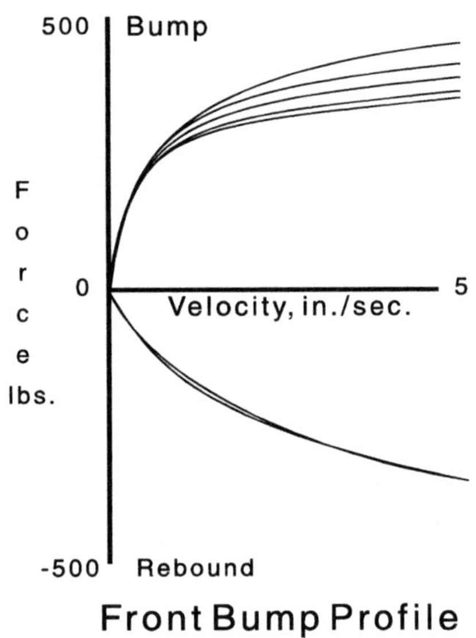

Front Bump Profile

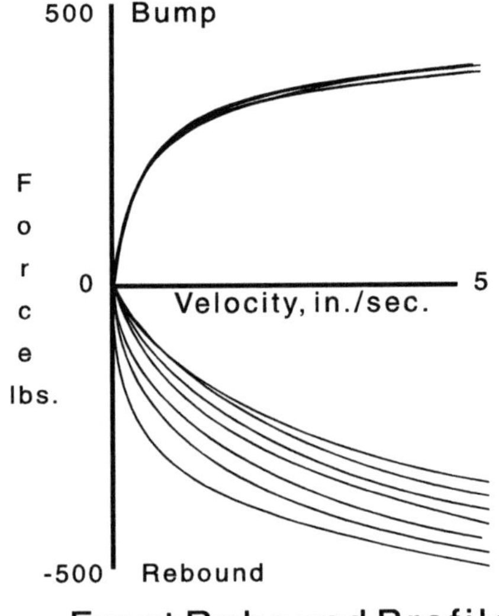

Front Rebound Profile

Shock Advice

In addition to the overhaul, repair, and testing, Jeff can start his customers in the right direction in developing this set of dampers for their specific racecar and type of racing. Here are some reoccurring comments taken from a few of the reports he sends his customers when he returns the dampers. Each comment corresponds to a specific set-up and don't apply to every shock or racecar.

- The driver can feel changes in damping at shaft speeds in the range of 0 to 2 inches per second. This is what you change if you want to change the handling of the car using the shocks.
- Bumps in the track cause high-speed inputs to the shock. To affect the way the car feels over bumps, change the shocks so the shape of the curve changes at velocities more than 2 (or 4 depending on the car) inches per second.
- Use the rebound adjustment to change the roll and pitch movements of the car.
- Use the high-speed bump adjuster to change the initial turn-in and ride quality.
- With these shocks you can go to softer springs (better mechanical grip) and still control roll with the shocks.
- The rebound adjustment is your primary method of changing the car. It will have a greater effect on the feel of the car than the bump adjustment.
- If the car feels like it is moving too much at one end, increase the rebound at that end.

- If the car is too harsh, drop the spring rate. Resist softening the internal valving to improve ride quality.
- The idea behind these shocks is to allow you to lower ride heights. You might be able to run softer springs as well.
- The shocks control the timing of corner events. You can speed up the onset of push or delay a loose exit problem by using the shocks.
- Think of the shocks as a timing device for the chassis dynamics and the springs and bars as absolute adjustments.
- Keep the pressure in the canister above 150 psi. This will prevent cavitation. Check the pressure every day before running the car.
- If you get confused, go back to the base settings as indicated on the Balance Test charts for each shock.
- These shocks have very little piston bleed so, when you put the car on the setup pad, back out the rebound adjusters all the way, or it will be difficult to get a consistent ride height.

Formula Atlantic Tips

A customer with a Formula Atlantic car sent Jeff some shocks and, after testing them, he made some changes. Here are graphs that show the changes and what Jeff told him about those changes.

"Based on discussions with the driver, I installed a different piston and valving. The idea is to run softer springs to increase mechanical grip, but give good transient response and keep the car from bottoming.

"All four shocks have a modified Penske piston that generates more damping at high and low shaft speeds. The increase in low-speed damping will make the car feel more responsive without increasing ride harshness over bumps. This will work the tires harder and give you higher tire temperatures, which is good with the hard compounds you use."

Front Shocks

"The graph shows the new configuration compared to what I tested as delivered. Be prepared to fit softer front springs. The increased rebound damping will reduce chassis roll with lower spring rates. You will have to adjust spring rate/ride height/shock settings. If the car is too harsh, drop the front spring rate. Put some laps on the car before making this change. It will feel harsh at first. Let the driver get used to it. You have to optimize the spring/shock combination. They have to work together."

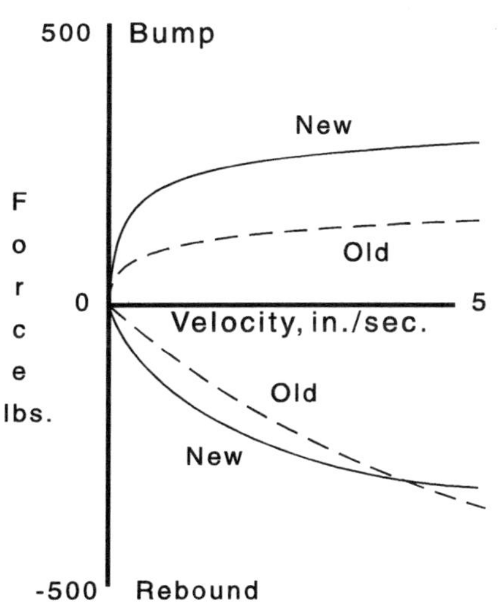

Compare Valving, Front

Rear Shocks

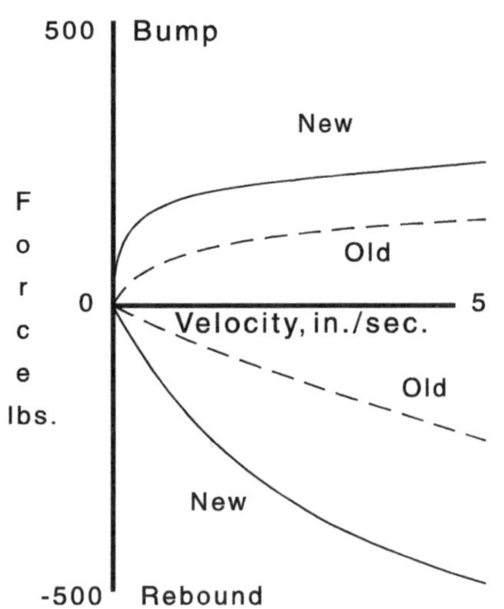

Compare Valving, Rear

"I changed the piston and valving of the rear to match the fronts. The bump valving is identical and the rebound valving gives higher forces than the front shocks. The shocks came to me with a 0.040-inch bleed hole. I changed the piston and the bleed hole diameter is smaller. This will give more damping to control the high spring rates you have at the rear.

"The car will be much more stable at the rear. This should reduce the snap oversteer you had and make the car more predictable. The increase in low-speed damping should allow you to use lower spring rates and gain mechanical grip. You should be able to lower ride height at the rear and have good transient response. Adjust spring rates as I described for the front."

IMSA World Sports Car

These Penske three-way adjustable shocks came to Jeff disassembled, with parts missing. He built them up for a specific WSC car to race at Road Atlanta. All four shocks have the same piston, piston bleed, and valving. He also suggested a test plan:

"Use the setup sheet I've provided to configure the car initially. At the start of the session put the car on the track and warm up the car and driver. I think you'll want all the aerodynamic downforce you can get. Using the nose splitters, the rear wing flap, and the Gurney size as listed on the setup sheet, and adjust the aero balance so you have no understeer in Turn 1 or in the last turn.

"While working on the balance make sure the car is as low as possible. Keep lowering the car until it bottoms out. If the car is loose, try lowering the car at the front only. Work in two-turn steps on the spring perches at first, and then go to one-turn steps when you think you're close. If the car is still loose, install the extra nose that has no splitters. Also try a 1-inch Gurney. I know that sounds big, but I don't think the wing gets much clean air.

"When the aero balance gets close to optimum, start to work on mechanical grip. Start with 400 pound/inch springs at the front and 600 at the rear. Increase the rebound two sweeps on all the shocks. See if the car pumps down and bottoms. If you like this rebound, go one more sweep on all shocks. Keep working to get as much rebound as you can without having to raise the car. Don't raise the car. Do not raise the car to make the shocks work. Add some low-speed bump damping if you need the car to feel more precise.

"If you have time here's something to try that might give you some more straight-line speed. Install 500 lb./in. rear springs. Set the rear rebound at 1 sweep, the low-speed bump at 10 and the high-speed bump at 0. This will let the car squat down at the rear under high aero loading on the back straight. This lowers the angle of attack of the rear wing and lowers the frontal area of the car. This should lower drag and increase top speed. This is a passive implementation of the button on the steering wheel of Formula 1 cars that tells the active suspension to lower the rear of the car.

"The turns that matter most at Road Atlanta are Turn 1, the Bridge Turn, and the last turn. This is where you lose or gain time. Turn 7, leading onto the back straight, is not important. Work on the front section of the track.

"The track is very smooth now. Get the car as low as you can, and use all the rebound you can. Watch for bottoming in the dip at the end of the back straight. Get enough aero downforce in the car so it's fast in the last two turns and Turn 1. Using the shocks to adjust balance is not as important here as it is at some slower tracks, but it will still work. Here are some general rules (for this car and these shocks):
- If you have push at the exit, use more low-speed bump at the rear or more rebound at the front.
- With bad power-down or skipping at the rear, use less rear low-speed bump or less front rebound.
- If you have poor grip at turn-in during braking, use less front bump or less rear rebound.
- If the car rolls too much, add rebound to all shocks.

"Priorities: Low ride height, a lot of rebound, soft springs, and max downforce. Make the car fast on the front part of the track. Good luck."

MODERN SHOCKS DEVELOPED FROM OFF-ROAD RACING

Many of the features of modern racing dampers were developed to solve problems of off-road two- and four-wheeled racecars. I had only seen Mickey Thompson Off-Road Grand Prix races on television before I went to their last event at Candlestick Park in October of 1992. I was extremely impressed by the technology in the Grand National Sport Trucks, and I got a good look at the kind of shocks they used. This series has since disappeared.

Stadium Trucks: High-Tech Racecars

You must have seen the Mickey Thompson Off-Road truck races on ESPN. There was a lot of action and the driver skill was obvious, but it looked a little like a demolition derby as the cars nudged and bumped each other at every corner, shedding fenders, doing barrel rolls, and climbing barriers. Watching on TV you really couldn't tell that these machines were real racecars. Well, one look up close was all I needed.

My first clue that these trucks were real racecars was what I saw as I entered the paddock—big semi-trailers with logos I recognized like Goodyear, Nissan, Ford, Dodge, Toyota, Chevrolet, etc. Just like an IMSA or Indy car pit, there were canopies over the pits and hospitality areas with buffet lines and rows of cloth-covered dining tables. Every truck seemed to have five mechanics swarming over it, and a peek inside a trailer revealed the usual miniature spare-parts store and machine shop.

These machines were custom-designed, hand-built, quarter-million dollar racecars with data acquisition, digital dashes, sophisticated suspensions, and electronic engine management systems. These trucks were just as technically interesting and exciting on the track as any other modern racecar.

Shock Lesson

That day at "The Stick" I talked to Charley Burton, Roger Mears' crew chief and shock expert. I told Charley I was interested in the shocks they were using, but I didn't want to know anything that was proprietary. He said, "Come on in the truck and I'll show you the parts inside the shocks. That'll make it easy to explain." I followed Charley up into the trailer. He opened up his tool box and began to pull out pistons and valve washers.

As Charley Burton explained the details of the dampers they custom make, Rick Mears (four-time Indy 500 winner for Roger Penske who had just announced his retirement) was standing at my shoulder showing a lady some photos. That was ironic because I would never get into his team's truck, since the Penske team is famous for being the most technically paranoid of all IndyCar teams. I said as much to Charley and he laughed, "There's not many secrets in off-road. We're all doing different things with the same stuff." How refreshing!

"These cars have a lot of wheel movement," explained Charley. "The shocks are important. They make the car fast or slow. We build our own because we need big shocks—3-inch diameter at the rear with a 1-inch shaft for strength. There's three-quarters of a gallon of oil in each shock. Actually, the big wheel movement works to our advantage. There's a lot of oil moving around and so it's easy to control. In the Indy cars, they restrict wheel movement and it's tougher to make the shocks work.

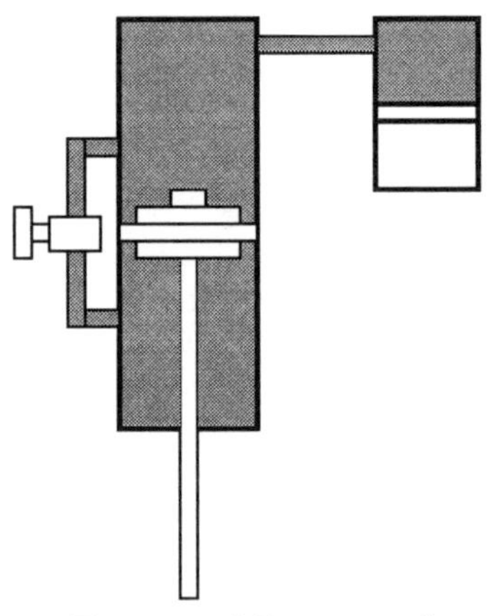

**External Reservoir
External Bypass**

"We make the shocks so they're easy to modify. We change the valves all the time. They're just round washers acting like one-way reed valves. The way you stack them up changes their spring rate and that controls the flow of the oil. We also use bypasses with adjustable needle valves to let the oil bleed around the piston. This softens the ride in between the bypass orifices. The bypasses can be one-way if we use a check valve. So the valve stacks on the piston fully control the damping only when the piston is outside of the bleed holes. In between the bleed holes the oil can go outside the tube and doesn't have to pass through the piston. We have three separate external bleeds on our rear shocks, acting in different ranges of travel.

"We don't have any data acquisition yet, but we use video cameras to show what's going on with the car. We tape the car during practice sessions and watch on a VCR in the trailer. We look at chassis vs. wheel movement and wheels vs. the ground. You can tell if the car's getting traction, or if the wheels are bouncing too much. The driver's style is important too.

"Hasn't a lot of the shock technology used now on Indy cars come from off-road applications?"

"Yeah," said Charley. "A few years ago Roger Mears told Rick about Fox shocks, and Rick tried some on his Penske. He liked them so they hired Ken Anderson away from Fox and Penske started making shocks. Now Anderson has started his own company, Quantum Suspension Technology. We use Fox shocks at the front but, as I said, we build our own rear shocks."

The Machines

Next, I went to the Toyota pit to look at the trucks of Ivan "Ironman" Stewart and Rod Millen. Millen had clinched the season championship even before this last event, and Stewart was second in points. Even from the wrong side of the usual security rope I could see the basics of a real racecar—a lot of tubing that adds up to a very stout frame with a very strong structure up front to take the hits, but I couldn't see a radiator in the usual place. I needed to ask some dumb questions about the suspension systems, so I asked a mechanic, "Who's the suspension guy?" He said, "Tom," and pointed.

Tom Morris was, at that time, the special projects manager for Precision Preparation Inc. of Rancho Santa Margarita in Southern California. He was responsible for the suspension and gearboxes on the stadium off-road trucks. For 1995 he's PPI's desert truck manager. After introductions, Tom took me behind the barrier and started talking about the trucks.

The front suspension was A-arm at the bottom and a lateral link at the top, which also actuated the sway bar. A single coil-over spring/damper unit on each side had a 2-foot-long damper, and a spring stack made up of three different springs rates in series. There were separate hydraulic bump stops for when the car landed hard on one corner. "Bump rubbers would rebound," said Tom. The steering box was a complicated custom-designed and fabricated rack and slider mechanism which helped control bump steer and maintained positive Ackerman steering angles.

At the rear Tom pointed out a conventional-looking differential and live axle setup, but the diff center section was oversized and had a custom-machined aluminum rear cover. A pair of longitudinal rocker arms located up above and to the rear of the axle (where the truck bed should have been) actuated long coil-over units mounting two different size springs.

Tom told me they think these rockers are better than the direct mounted coil-overs other teams used because they saved space and got the weight lower and further back. These rocker arms also actuate a sway bar tucked inside a rear tube. "The rockers are efficient. They use structure that needs to be there anyway," said Tom.

A separate pair of dampers that control rocking motions was mounted high in the middle of the truck and splayed back down and out to near the ends of the axle housings. Two pairs of very long trailing arms located the rear axle. Starting under the cab area, one set connected near the outboard end of each axle, while the other pair mounted to the top of that special rear cover on the diff.

Tom pointed to the radiators mounted behind the cab. "Cooling air to the radiators goes through the cockpit and is blown down by electric fans," he said. "There's no aerodynamic requirements here because the trucks don't get much over 65 mph on these cramped stadium courses. So there's no windshield." Tom began to get some questions from the crew and told me he needed to help get the car ready for the first practice session. I thanked him for the tour and moved on.

The General Is Here

In the Chevy pit area I asked one of the mechanics if I could talk to the suspension guy. He smiled and introduced me to Laurie Szczesny, an engineer from General Motor's Technical Center. Laurie is one of the growing number of female "guys" in racing. We squatted down on our heels and peered under the car as Laurie pointed out suspension features.

"The chassis is really a tube frame designed with the aid of a Finite Element Analysis computer program," she said. "We run a lot of negative camber because of tire roll. We video tape the car during track sessions. That helps us estimate suspension velocities. We look at how the wheel moves vs. the body and the track surface. Then we can go to the data from the Pi electronic system. This is the same data acquisition system and digital dashboard as used in the IndyCar Lolas and IMSA GTP and Camel Lights cars. The LED display in front of the driver shows water temperature, oil temperature, fuel pressure, oil pressure, battery voltage, and the same broad sweeping rpm indicator you've seen on TV in Indy car *Track Facts*. It's recording readings from three position sensors on the suspension; two at the front and one at the rear. The system also records front and rear wheel speed.

"Our shocks are position sensitive. That means we have bypasses built in that soften the damping at specific parts of the travel. We use long trailing arms at the rear to get rid of transient movements. We have our own proprietary suspension analysis software. There's a lot of trade-offs in suspension setup."

With such a complete presentation I didn't have any questions, so I said goodbye to Laurie and went back out into the paddock, which was beginning to fill with spectators coming to that night's event at "The Stick."

ACTIVE SUSPENSION

Here is a great quote that humorously compares the importance of active suspension with the carburetor, another great improvement in automobiles. "Without argument, 'active' suspension is the same sort of mega-leap forward as the SU Carburettor was over a bit of damp wick hanging hopefully in the inlet tract to disburse the new-fangled petroleum spirit into the entering air," said Allan Staniforth in his book, *Competition Car Suspension*. I especially like the word "hopefully" that describes that wick.

Frank Dernie, Williams Formula 1 team aerodynamicist, commented on the Williams reactive suspension (also quoted in Staniforth's book), "Our Reactive system was conceived to optimize the aerodynamic performance of the car as opposed to the suspension dynamics of the vehicle. In effect, the system is a fast load-leveling device, operating in such a way that gross changes in load due to braking, cornering, and aerodynamic effects give only relatively small body movements."

Controlled Ride Height or Active?

You're probably getting tired of hearing how important ride height and rake are to the performance of modern ground-effects racecars, so I won't repeat that. I'll try to explain the hardware that Formula 1 teams used to control ride height. This technology is still in use in some of the European Touring Car series. I'll talk briefly about the software, which is where all the creativity lies.

The Williams-Renault F1 team proved in 1992 that it could beat everyone else just by reliably maintaining the chassis rake and ground clearance in spite of track irregularities, braking, turning, and accelerating. Nigel Mansell was faster than everyone that year by one or two seconds a lap at every race. The team sacrificed the 1991 season to develop an automatic gearbox and reactive suspension, resulting in a driver's championship for Mansell and constructor's championship for Williams in 1992 and continued domination, with Alain Prost driving, in 1993.

To be precise, the 1992 Williams-Renault employed controlled ride height, not active suspension. The 1993 car might have been closer to a full-active system like Lotus created a decade before. The difference is this: active suspension uses accelerometers to sense suspension movements as they happen, and moves the wheels with hydraulic rams so that ride height and chassis attitude remain constant. As a bump moves under the tire it begins to accelerate the tire upwards, but the sensors provide this info to the computer system and the hydraulic system jerks the tire and wheel up smoothly, maintaining contact with the road, and puts it back down on the other side of the bump smooth as you please. A good analogy to active suspension is a snow-skiing human. Eyes and legs are the sensors, the brain is the computer, and the thighs are the hydraulic rams constantly adjusting many factors. To make this work on a car the sensors have to be read by the computer, and the hydraulic pressures adjusted a thousand times a second by some humongously complex and clever software.

It's Easier to Start Simple

A controlled ride height system is simpler than full-active and can work with a computer system that reads and controls only 10 times a second. The photo and schematics help show how the system works. The photo is one I took of an Indy Lights Lola at Laguna Seca in 1993. The Lola's front suspension has wide-based A-arms to link the wheels to the chassis and a pushrod to operate the coil spring/damper unit. When the wheel moves, the pushrod pivots a bell crank which moves the spring/damper unit.

All modern open-wheeled cars use this type of suspension because it gets the spring/damper out of the airstream. Packaging efficiency is the priority, and they want a slippery body shape with low frontal area. The bell crank also allows a motion ratio between the wheel and damper that amplifies wheel movement. Modern ground-effects racecars don't allow much wheel travel, but the damper needs generous piston movement to produce adequate forces.

The pushrod length can be made continuously variable if you build in a hydraulic piston as shown in the schematic. More fluid in the right side of the cylinder makes the pushrod longer, and more in the left makes it shorter. If you can control the length of the pushrod, you can compensate for wheel movements before they ever get up to the spring/damper unit. Do that a 1,000 times a second and you've got active suspension. Do it 10 times a second and you can, to some degree, control the ride height of the car. Big, fast movements still get through to the spring/damper, but that's OK.

But how do you know at what height the chassis is supposed to be? I show a displacement sensor in the schematic and represented it as a pointer that moves as the coil-over unit moves. The sensor on the racecar is actually a Linear Variable Displacement Transducer (LVDT), a telescoping, pencil-shaped device that provides a variable voltage value as it gets shorter or longer. It might read 2.5 volts when the car is at static ride height; 4.5 volts when the suspension is compressed due to a bump; and 1.5 volts when the wheel droops down. The voltage value tells you where the suspension is in its range of travel. To maintain a specific ride height you'd like the LVDT to read a constant value; that is, you'd like the spring/damper to not move at all.

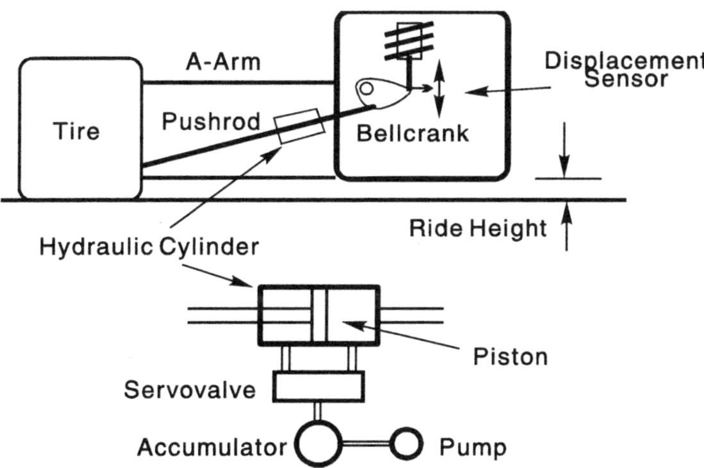

Schematic of Active Suspension and Hydraulic System

A Very Fast-Acting Valve

The other hardware component that makes controlled ride height possible is the servo valve. I understand it was provided first by Moog, but now similar units are made by several companies. The servo valve controls high pressure (3,000 pounds per square inch) hydraulic fluid at frequencies in the neighborhood of 1,000 pulses per second. The schematic shows a hydraulic pump to provide a volume of oil at that pressure, an accumulator to store fluid at high pressure, and the servo valve. The servo valve determines which side of the piston gets a squirt of 3,000 psi fluid and cycles back and forth 1,000 times a second. As long as both sides of the piston are getting an equal number of squirts, the piston just sits there. However, if the servo valve stays to one side for an additional count, that side gets an extra squirt of fluid and the piston moves.

What we have here is a control system, and we want to control ride height. If the LVDT voltage value stays the same, ride height stays the same. The software reads the LVDT voltage, and tells the servo valve to give extra squirts to one side or the other of the piston and vary the length of the pushrod so the LVDT voltage stays at the value that represents the ride height for optimum downforce.

The hardware—computer, LVDT, hydraulics, pump, accumulator, and servo valve—are all off-the-shelf industrial components. But ah, the software! That's the challenge. A real live person or group of people have to painstakingly develop computer software that reads how the LVDT voltage is changing and how fast it's changing, and decides how many squirts go to this or the other side of that piston. If the ride height is increasing at an increasing rate, the squirts have to get ahead of the change, and, when the ride height change slows down, the squirts have to slow down too or even squirt on the other side of the piston to start the chassis (LVDT voltage, really) back down to where it's supposed to be. How many squirts for what rate of change of ride height can be called a "strategy," a name for a control method. Several different strategies may be available for specific race courses (bumpy or smooth), or different conditions such as a wet track. A switch in the cockpit allows the driver to tell the computer system which strategy to use.

The software has to do its job and not make other troubles, as some software on Nigel Mansell's car did at the '91 Canadian GP. When Mansell slowed on the last lap to wave to the crowd, the car dropped below some minimum speed and the software turned off the engine, causing him to lose the race. A critical system can't just work in the shop; it has to work during qualifying and on every lap of the race.

CHAPTER 6

RACING PEOPLE

Originally I wanted an interview in each chapter, and hopefully one that would include a discussion that fit the chapter topic. But I had more opportunities to interview interesting people as the book progressed, and these three interviews all contain conversations about handling and driver/engineer communications. So I put them in a separate chapter. I also included a description of the first road-course test of AAR's Judd-engined '93 Lola Indy car. Reading about that test just after the interview with Jim Hamilton seemed appropriate. I hope you enjoy reading my conversations with these people. I learn something new and different every time I read one of these interviews.

There are many subjects mentioned here without a complete explanation. I hope that encourages you read to more about the technology of racing. As Carroll Smith says in the last interview in this chapter, "...make no mistake about it, driving a racing car properly is probably the hardest thing that the human being has yet learned how to do." There is a list of books after this chapter.

INTERVIEW QUESTIONS

When I began to get opportunities to talk to people who are experienced in the design and development of racecars, I sat down and thought about the questions I should ask. Racers continually develop racecars, and I've been told that a lot of the "trick" doodads that pop up and make one team win more races than the other teams are usually simple things or combinations of simple things. Nobody is going to explain to me the latest rash of trick stuff. It would be dumb to even ask. They've all worked hard to gain the knowledge they have and it would be silly to spread it around. Having said that, it's human nature to talk about interesting things we've learned. I've found that if you don't demand anything but ask the right question, you might be surprised at how good an answer you get.

The strategy I've evolved that seems to make people comfortable talking to me starts with a list of questions like the one below which emphasizes the way they go about their work rather than the specifics that result from that work. I usually record the conversation and transcribe it later into a text file. I send or fax the transcribed interview for approval before I publish any of it.

It's difficult to control how an interview goes. I try to keep it as conversational as possible. I try to keep the interview on track but, if the conversation gets on a side track, the results could be better than anything I could have planned. These are the questions I used in this interview with Jim Hamilton, the talk with Lee Dykstra that follows, and the conversation with Allan Mertens that appeared in the aero chapter.

1. How do you start a new project? What are your priorities? What parts of the design do you attack first? How much planning do you do?
2. What is the major source of research or feedback info? Driver? Track data? Wind tunnel? Crew and mechanics?
3. How much does the tire influence design? Springs in series?
4. How do you know when to freeze the design? Do you know the areas that need development? How do you plan development of a design in production?
5. In suspension design, what are your priorities? What geometry components do you get right first? What tools do you use? How have your ideas about suspension geometry evolved?
6. Tell me how you think about the following components when you design a racecar: tires, engine, drive train, driver, shocks, safety, wiring harness, ease of maintenance, set-up repeatability, aerodynamics, pit stops, fuel, cooling, plumbing.
7. Overall packaging?
8. How do you size components? Do you do load analysis or stress analysis?
9. How do you work? CAD or paper? Drawing board? Scale?
10. What is the most difficult component or item?
11. What people or designs have influenced your designs?
12. Trends affecting your designs?
13. L/D history and trends. When did you begin to look at that measurement? How much do you use it? At what speeds does it matter?
14. Do you consider development to be a part of design?

CONVERSATION WITH JIM HAMILTON

Jim Hamilton works for Dan Gurney at AAR in Santa Ana, Calif. Jim's business card says he's director, vehicle dynamics. As this interview shows, Jim is also a racing fan and amateur driver and an intense student of how racecars work and how drivers operate racecars. Unlike most of us, Jim has the education and experience that enable him to continue to figure out how to make racecars faster. Jim works with other people in the design team including John Ward, chief designer at AAR, and Hiro Fujimori, director of aerodynamics. These are the people who created the Toyota Eagle Mk. III which dominated IMSA GTP racing in 1992 and '93.

I had an appointment to talk with Jim at AAR in early September 1993. IMSA was going away from GTP cars so AAR was looking at getting into Indy car racing. An issue of *On Track* magazine had just reported that AAR had a new wind tunnel, an open-ended, moving ground-plane wind tunnel to test scale models as big as 40% at an air speed of 100 mph. The tunnel is small enough to fit in a 50- by 100-foot building. About that same time Swift Engineering announced it would build a state-of-the-art wind tunnel (described in the aero chapter) just south of AAR in San Clemente. Wind tunnels were a hot topic in Southern California at that time, and I started the talk with that.

Jim Hamilton

"Paul,

I'm the old guy on the left doing my best Robert Duvall. My partner on the right [Juan Fangio II] is one of the best kept secrets in world motor racing, about to lose his anonymity if our plans succeed."

PH: "You guys have a new wind tunnel?"

JH: "What we chose to do was a combination of things with experienced suppliers and some of our own ideas. It's competitive in the sense of scale and speed, without giving any numbers. It'll give us useful data, we think. We're racers, not wind-tunnel makers. On the other hand, a lot of it is customized. It seems a general rule in racing from go-karts on up, and I have a profound respect for go-karts because they're very complex little critters, and you can learn a lot from them that you can even apply to other forms of racing. I think the same is true for almost anything that you pick up and work with; the same principles apply, but sooner or later you have to do it pretty much yourself. In other words, you have to leave off with all the books and all the existing expertise and take it on from there and be creative.

"That's one of the things about this sport—there is no book. You write it week by week. In a sense there aren't many new secrets. If you harbor secrets to the point where you focus on them to the exclusion of finding new ones, you'll find that people are inventing the same thing. If you look at the history of the airplane or the history of the radio, you'll find that there were parallel independent efforts all over the world because the world was waiting for this technology to appear. If you think you're the only one to invent something, you're probably wrong. You might be the first by five minutes or five years, but if you focus entirely on that you find someone else is going to invent the thing and a bunch of follow-on products too."

PH: "The airplane is a good analogy there because there was intense activity for 100 years before the Wright brothers and some other people made it work at the start of this century."

JH: "If you go to the Deutsches Museum in Munich you'll find they think they invented the airplane.

"With our wind tunnel we start with something, call it store bought. You find that, very quickly, you're pushing its limits. You have to. The very nature of the business dictates that. It's a moving-limit business. You find that even before you can do useful development with a wind tunnel, you find yourself re-engineering aspects of it. We had to do that. You also immediately find yourself having to choose. You don't have enough money or time to do everything, so you have to choose which functions are most important. And you can't be constrained too much by what already exists. If you really need it, you have to create it. That's very vague. The wind tunnel is something that's really new for us. In very few ways is it very unique or special in the world, but the function of a tunnel is that it's a development tool unless you're in the tunnel business.

"For us, it's a tool, and we're trying to bring it up to speed as the most useful development tool we could get. That pretty much means that it goes into the background. If we have to fiddle too much with the development of the tunnel, that should only be necessary at the beginning and refined as you go on. But boy, if you can't go in there and sort of forget that you're actually in a wind tunnel because the data is so good and so compelling and because you're learning so much from it, then perhaps the tunnel isn't finished yet."

PH: "I'm not sure I get that. You say you need to forget you're in a wind tunnel?"

JH: "The tunnel should be a transparent tool. You shouldn't have to focus on the tunnel itself. To a certain extent it has to be automatic. In other words, it has to look after itself so you don't have to focus on it. It's like a measuring tool. It's like a dial caliper or something. If you have to keep calibrating the caliper, then you have to devote part of your focus to that. There's nothing unique about that. That's the mentality here. The use of the tunnel is the focus you choose. For us it's a development tool. It's not a showplace. It's got to look good because we've got sponsors, and it's an impressive piece, but, when it comes to working with it, it's a working tool.

"I think you can extend that concept to almost everything, to CAD [computer-aided design] systems, to all the different tools we use to develop a car. There's so much technology that you have to limit it,; you have to narrow it and make choices. It's easy to get caught up in the technology itself, but you don't win races if you spend too much time on it."

PH: "Your focus is different from that at Swift. They're looking at their wind tunnel as a business and profit center, and that's totally different than what you guys are doing here. That's very interesting."

JH: "Yes. That's right. They may do that. It may be a conscious choice that that will be their focus to the temporary detriment of their other programs."

PH: "What type of tunnel is your new one?"

JH: "It's not a fully closed-loop system. As I mentioned, one improvises. I guess you could call it a hybrid as far as closed loop vs. open loop. It obviously has a rolling road, and it has everything that goes with a rolling road that lets it work with high downforce cars at a very competitive speed, at a very, very respectable Reynolds number. You could almost sketch it out if you know something about tunnels. There's nothing really mysterious about it. It doesn't matter if the fan is in the front or the back or whatever. Blockage factors and that kind of thing are different strategies that exist in the market, and you make conscious choices as you're trying to gain some expertise.

"We have an expert. He [Hiro Fujimori] developed our GTP cars with a tenth-scale tunnel. It's been around here for a long time—13 years or so. It has a rolling road too. It's still here. To me it's amazing what we were able to do with what most people consider a toy. However, there aren't many people in this business, and there's a lot of networking among a very small number of people. There was a seventh-scale tunnel at Nissan (Nissan Performance Technology, Inc.), for example. It's the same in England; there's a small number of people.

"Ours turned out to be a tenth-scale open tunnel. It's affected by the Santa Ana winds [hot and dry] that blow down the street every once in a while. We always knew when that little tunnel was running because the trees would wiggle a lot more. The correlation between the results of that tunnel and full scale weren't immediately obvious. Learning to interpret the data and put in the fudge factors and so forth, even for things like balance or trying to understand what's happening in that eighth-inch or quarter-inch under the car as the air is pulled through by what's practically a sanding belt, taking what should be just garbage and making it useful was a lot of the reason for the success that we had later. The Mk. III was completely developed with that tenth-scale tunnel. So we have big ideas for this new one because it's even bigger. We did go to Japan and test at a higher scale, but the development work was done here."

PH: "I guess the trick is to figure out how the tunnel data scales to the real world. However you do that doesn't make any difference, if it works. Who's the aero guy?"

JH: "The one guy who is the aero designer is Hiro Fujimori. He lives in the wind tunnel. However, the designs, the ideas, and so forth, are partly Dan's; some of the concepts are Dan's. Discussion and refinement come from several people. The car is called the WFO92; the Mk. III is one version. That stands for John Ward, the chief designer; Hiro Fujimori; and Others. Dan is very prominent among the Others.

"If we have any secret of our success so far, I think it's very simple. It's the quality of the working relationship that we have. It's inspired by Dan. Dan attracts a lot of talented people, but there's no guarantee they'll work as a team. It's amazing to me, and I'm sure it's the same at the successful teams in England and other places, what ordinary people can do collectively, if they're really inspired and they're really working together. That's why I say the 'O' is important in that name. Ideas can come from anywhere and anybody. Not that mechanics write reports; but if you have an open and creative atmosphere, everybody feels like they can contribute in an appropriate way. And they do. Boy, what a difference it makes. I couldn't do without my tire guys, for example...or anybody. Even talking to you, I'll learn. How to think about something being forced to describe it."

PH: [laughs] "I'm glad you'll get something out of this."

JH: "Sure."

I showed Jim the book outline I had at that time. He had read the shock article I had published in my newsletter, which became the basis for the handling chapter of this book.

JH: "About off-road stuff—there's some crossbreeding, and without naming names, if you look around, there's some technology that started with off-road that has found its way into flat-pavement cars."

PH: "You said earlier there was an error in my shock article."

JH: "I'm sure other people will point it out. The nature of the business is such that those old secrets have to be replaced. I named perhaps our biggest secret, which is the teamwork we've achieved. Our approach is another secret. If you approach the problems of racing, whether it's go-karts or F1, with a certain attitude or outlook and you can maintain that, I think that's almost a secret.

"Drivers obviously do that. Ayrton Senna, gifted though he is, a lot of his gifts have to do with his approach and his commitment, what he thinks about. He started out with karts, obviously. When you start out writing a book you better be sure you want to go the whole potato. You don't want to go halfway. And yet you want to educate people. There are some good books from people who weren't even intending to educate. For example, Mark Donohue's book [Jim is talking about *Unfair Advantage*] was not intended to be an engineering treatise. And yet, because of his love of engineering involvement, it turns out to be a more useful book between the lines than the vast majority of the books that purport to be technical.

"Paul Van Valkenburg is a legitimate engineer and innovative engineer. I wrote a story 22 years ago on a new suspension that I designed. A magazine did a story. He was the editor then. Sharp guy.

"You correctly referred in that article to orifice damping as a V-squared [V=velocity] function. If you had a hole, and if it were a perfect classic hole in a perfect classic fluid, ignoring turbulence and things like that, if you put the fluid through the hole in the piston especially slowly with very little acceleration of the piston or other secondary effects, you'd find the classic V-squared dependency because you'd have fluid acceleration as the primary means of the damping forces.

"You're accelerating the damping fluid through this hole which passes the same flow rate as the piston is moving through, but through a very small hole. If you look at the simple physics involved, you find that that turns out to be a force or pressure on the piston that's proportional to the square of the speed. However, if you look at any dyno sheet, you find that that's rarely the case. You find more linear behavior. How can you get that out of an orifice? As you pointed out, the orifices are scaled differently in bump and rebound.

"Well, if you go back to classic damping, it's viscous. Viscous damping is ubiquitous in the sense that there's equivalencies of it even outside of mechanical systems. A resistor in an electrical system is the equivalent of a linear viscous damper. That means the damping goes up directly with velocity. Now we have an emulsion shock, and that's a little bit like a distant cousin at least of a viscous damper. Viscous damping is used in a lot of mechanisms, but the work that one puts into a shock means that a lot of heat is going to come out, and one principle of viscous fluids is that most of them change viscosity with temperature. There are also other factors besides temperature.

"As you pointed out, in an emulsion, if you pull it apart you get holes in there that fill with vapor or air, and you'd have cavitation. For a number of reasons, purely viscous damping isn't used that much. But there are certain aspects to damping that require that classical damping. So-called second order differential equations result when you have a spring and a mass and a damper. You want that in some places. How is that achieved with a hole? The answer is it isn't just the hole, of course. It's those strange valves called shims. Without going any further into it, those have a profound effect. They basically overwhelm the effect that you usually don't want, which is the V-squared effect.

"Now maybe that's far from the scope of what you're doing here, but [laughs] that's what I thought about when I read that."

PH: "Thanks, I'll pursue that. I'm not sure I got it."

JH: "Just a hint. The asymmetrical scaling of the holes has another purpose. The asymmetry; there's a clue there. You mentioned one of the valid reasons why shocks are asymmetrical in their damping—even the two-ways."

PH: "I'm glad the error was that esoteric [both laugh]."

JH: [Looking at the shock info already written for the book.] "This stuff on the De Carbon [single-tube] dampers is fine. The twin-tube shocks have come back; not so much in racing. They could, but they've come back into, let's say, performance street cars, with the addition of modest amounts of pressure on the top of the fluid which is simpler than a floating piston, and they need less pressure. You could consider that sort of a hybrid idea. In Europe they're pretty picky, and a number of manufacturers have gone away from De Carbon to a low-pressure twin-tube.

"The off-road guys in some cases have some dampers that are position or displacement sensitive. Certain little radio-controlled buggies with oil-filled aluminum tube shocks have the same thing. If that's considered a further development, then the off-road guys and RC buggies are ahead of us, because we don't have that in our pavement cars. It pays to keep an open mind and not be too snooty about it."

PH: "What about balance?"

JH: "Balance. Obviously, the limitation is the weak end of the car, so one seeks to at least manage—you may not always want a completely balanced car—but at least manage the differences in total cornering capability or yaw moment or however you choose to refer to it. Again, I have to invoke the milk of human kindness and stop with this statement. The ideal balance might be different under different conditions. It's extremely important, but it's not the whole story, obviously. If a race engineer approaches a given problem as a balance problem, he may be starting with the finish rather than the beginning.

"Let me speak in an analogy. I don't want to sound like Yoda, but let's assume you have a terrain of total set-up possibilities. Like a multi-dimensional engine map, you have many, many possibilities for adjustment in a race chassis, as you pointed out with the adjustment ranges in your story on two, three, and four-way adjustable shocks. And then, of course, you can reshim those, or put in different fluid or different gas pressure, or different springs, even different tires. There are many things you can do before you even get into aerodynamics. Of course the bottom of the car is a movable aerodynamic surface. There are many, many factors to look at and change. You can visualize all those possibilities as a multi-dimensional terrain. Trying to set up your racecar on any particular day, you might be on a pretty rocky part of that terrain in your expedition. You might consider that balancing the car is reaching the top or level part of the nearest terrain, and which way do you go to get there? You go up!

"If it's a rough, rocky terrain, the nearest level spot, the nearest peak, might just be a boulder on the side of a mountain, and there might be a much bigger mountain over yonder [chuckles]. The job of the race engineer is not to just balance the car, but to get the whole expedition over the crevasse. We have to do it in the dark because nobody can really see the mountains. So, to put balance in perspective, it's very important. But the maximized performance of the car in all aspects while achieving the balance is the bigger challenge. There are crew chiefs that are plenty good at balancing cars and making them extremely balanced."

PH: "Talking to people and going to more races, I'm beginning to see little bits of several things. Just the fact that there are different people at the front of the IndyCar grid from race to race means some of those teams know more about what it takes to get around a road course. They seem to know more about mechanical grip that they do aero. There's a couple of teams that know both. And then there's some teams at the back of the grid that don't have a clue compared to the guys at the front. I guess that's the same at any Formula Ford or Club Ford SCCA race. There's some guys at the front that know what they're doing, and some in the middle that will go up and some will go back, and some are just there for the hell of it."

JH: "I might be putting some milk [Jim talks about the milk of human kindness in this interview when he thinks he might be getting close to talking about something better not said.] on the table here, but some high-level teams focus on measuring the car's balance with data acquisition. They think that's a worthwhile thing to do. It can't be done. There are books out there that tell you how to do it, though [chuckles]. It goes back to priorities. If the evaluation of the balance of the car ultimately shifts to evaluating that from data, then the driver is not being trusted or doesn't know what's going on or isn't doing his job. I'm talking about evaluations from data about one order of magnitude more sophisticated than those that you may have heard about, and, still, I don't think that makes a down payment on the effort. [Formula 1 teams have made some simulation progress in the area of balance, and Jim qualified his statement later, saying it can't be done in the total, interactive sense as perceived by the best drivers using current data acquisition systems.]

"There's a lot to looking at data. Especially if you're trying to do it while two guys are coming at you at the same time. They must orchestrate it sometimes. I don't know how else they can both come in at the same second. There's one guy they want to talk to on two channels, and there's just one radio. Help! Help! That's not the time to go to the computer and do a sophisticated analysis. The data deserves a lot of time and a lot of, let's say, analytical effort, maybe mathematical. Mostly it's done in the middle of the night, when you're supposed to be in bed during race weekends, or it's done here in the office between races.

"There's always insights that come out. But often, the driver has already led you there. The driver and the relationship between the driver and the people who work with him is extremely important. It's amazing what you can achieve when you have inspired people. The driver, if he really feels comfortable saying his piece and he knows that he'll be taken seriously and he has the confidence that what he's saying is really what he's doing, I think that goes beyond data, especially in reporting things like balance.

"It's very difficult for the driver to perceive total grip, I believe, because the differences in a big grid could be as small as thousands of a second. That's about as precise as we measure, a thousand of a second, often hundreds of a second, and very often, tenths. If you look at the function of speed with lateral Gs and ask the driver to feel proportionate difference, it's very, very difficult. But he can feel balance better than any conglomeration of sensors or data or math models. He's perhaps your best indicator of balance, and the stopwatch is, of course, the integrator of all things, the best piece of data we can have [laughs].

"But you have to find other ways to evaluate the total grip that you're getting. The driver can tell you the car feels low as hell in aerodynamic grip. Are tires getting so hot that they're going away? How can he discriminate? Can he feel the car sinking down from aero forces? Yes. Does he feel the steering heavying up? Why? There's at least seven or eight reasons I can think of right now why that might happen, only two of which are aerodynamic. On-board data acquisition and analysis is necessary to truly evaluate grip."

PH: "When you start with a clean sheet of paper to design a car, are there things that you can do to make sure the driver gets feedback from the car?"

JH: "Yes. Absolutely. There's a focus that has to be there in the design stage. No question about it. [Long pause and expectant looks. Jim laughs and doles out a little more milk.] If you look in the right books, and here you have to depart from the simple books you can buy. You have to go to books that are published by the author. He's a consultant somewhere. [Jim's hinting at Carroll Smith, author of the ...To Win books. Carroll, interviewed later in this chapter, started out publishing his books himself. Classic Motorbooks published later editions.] The SAE [Society of Automotive Engineers] is a good source of information. It has to do with the way tires work. You can learn that stuff."

"Knowing the individual characteristics of tires, what the tires want, is one of the most difficult things to achieve even for those that have access to all this stuff, and yet it is right up there in importance."

PH: "Do you get good information from tire manufacturers? Do you get spring rates and slip angle vs. side force curves? Any of that stuff?"

JH: "Any of that stuff? Yes. What we really need beyond that we have to generate ourselves."

PH: "I've seen some Firestone Indy Lights info. Do you get info from Goodyear?"

JH: "Yes. Firestone is coming back. We have a historical relationship with Goodyear that goes way back between Dan and Leo Mehl. The importance of that relationship I could not overstate. It's absolutely vital to us. We try to develop a good relationship at other levels at Goodyear. Why? The tires are the only things that connect our car to the ground [laughs]. The relationship with the people is absolutely critical; you can't do anything without that. However, the relationship with the tires themselves is even more important, if you understand what I mean [chuckles again]."

PH: "Leo Mehl returns your phone calls, but those tires are there every time you run the car."

JH: "Yeah, Leo always returns our calls, but Leo doesn't connect our car to the ground. What we can learn from the tires ourselves is important. Despite the best cooperation from Goodyear, and they do cooperate, every team has to develop its own fund of knowledge."

PH: "The shocks are a big deal in giving the driver a feel for where he is?"

JH: "Especially so. There are several purposes for shocks. The ability to separate them out and report on them, while everything else is going on, is a sharp discriminator of a driver's readiness to do what you need him to do. It's very difficult and yet vital to the program."

PH: "Jim, this is great stuff. It's just what I need. People are interested in the things you're talking about here."

JH: "Well, I hope I haven't been too vague. To you there's probably no milk on the table, but to Dan it's probably spilling all over the floor [laughs]."

PH: "I don't feel that way. This is a person talking about something he knows about and cares about. That's much more important than any tidbits of information that I could wave at somebody. The people are what's important."

PH: [Looking at the list of questions.] "Personal info and background?"

JH: "I'm not an engineer. I studied physics. That gives me a little different viewpoint; maybe it doesn't [chuckles]."

PH: "Engineering is applied physics, isn't it?"

JH: "Yeah. Engineering is applied physics, and I'm trying to apply it [chuckles again] the best way I can. I was working in the aerospace business. I was lucky to go to a school that was one of the early leaders in the country in computer technology, Carnegie Tech. Way, way back in 1962 and 1963 they had a close relationship with all the big computer companies. That was Burroughs and Bendix and all these people that are out of business now. I was lucky enough to just fall into a computer science education as an adjunct to my physics degree.

"I came out to Southern California to work for TRW in aerospace writing software—simulations and modeling software. I met Bruce McLaren through Gary Knudson, who was with McLaren for many years. That meeting was an inspirational meeting. I talked to Bruce only for a very short time. He'd just arrived from New Zealand. We talked about doing computer simulation and some other computer things, including graphical ones. I had access to a big Calcomp plotter which TRW was using to draw the first maps of the world from satellite tracking. In the middle of the night, when that plotter wasn't being used, you could do your own stuff and nobody cared. It was idle time and, if you were awake enough at three o'clock in the morning, it was OK to do that.

"I did some stuff but none of it was used by McLaren because they moved to England shortly thereafter. That plotter was there and I kept fiddling with the computers and started thinking about vehicles. I had a Lotus 18 Formula Junior. I built my own engine [laughs]. I never was very good with engines. It was a good handling car. That started me on my quest for knowledge that took me through amateur racing, and then I worked for BMW in several capacities. I tuned most of their IMSA cars with David Hobbs and others driving.

"I really hadn't done this sort of business full time because I always had other responsibilities at BMW. I did work with some drivers and friends around the Northeast: Drake Olson, Chip Robinson, and others. We were all learning in Formula Fords.

"Drake got a good ride with Dyson, and I helped him kind of by remote control. He came here to drive for Dan and did great in the Group C car. He took a couple of poles and had a lap record at Lime Rock when I was still living back there. I went to see him at a race, and he introduced me to Dan. I met the Mk. II designer, Ron Hopkins. This was 1989 and I had no intention of leaving what I was doing. I met Dan and, in 10 minutes, I knew that to work for him and do this business full time would be fantastic. And, in 10 minutes, he decided to take a chance on this guy who really hadn't done much [laughs]. And the rest is hysteria!"

PH: "When did you meet Bruce McLaren?"

JH: "1965 or 1966. I think 1966."

PH: "You did some driving yourself, then?"

JH: "Yeah. I still drive go-karts. And learn a lot from them still."

PH: "I'd love to drive go-karts some."

JH: "I recommend it. There are some guys from America that have won the Paul Winfield competition in Europe, and they're kart drivers. Eddie Lawson [four-time F1 motorcycle world champion] drives out at Riverside. It's a real hotbed of kart activity."

PH: [Getting back to the question list.] "In general, in suspension design, you can't get what you want all the time so you have to make compromises. Do you have a pecking order of things you want to make sure happen?"

JH: "You have to say yes. I work with the chief designer, but you definitely have to select your priorities. One of your key criteria is what do the tires want? As you pointed out correctly, what feedback is really important to the driver? Just as important, what is less important, what don't we need to focus on because it detracts from the rest of the picture?"

PH: "In Indy cars, I notice, on low-speed corners like Turn 11 at Laguna, the inside front tire is off the ground and pointed way off somewhere, and it's got a bunch of camber. It looks like they give up on the inside tire in a slow corner."

JH: "If you look at this year's cars you might find that that's changing a little bit."

PH: "Indy cars also have a lot more camber at the front than F1 cars. I asked Greg Stucker of Goodyear Racing about that, and he said it was probably because the Indy car tires were harder and needed the camber to get heat in them. That means that 70% of the tire on the ground at 220 degrees is better than all of it at 150."

JH: "Both series [F1 and Indy cars] are constrained by dimensional specifications that are ancient, especially F1. F1 has some advantages, active suspension being the big one. The primary two goals of active suspension include some factors that make camber less necessary than perhaps what you see the Indy car guys having to do."

PH: "How do you work? Are you at a computer? Do you use commercial software or have you done your own?"

JH: "All my own software. Hard won. Hard debugged. I have no idea how other guys work. I have a lot of software."

PH: "PC-based stuff or workstation?"

JH: "It's written in programming languages like C and FORTRAN, cause I'm an old guy. Some of it's in BASIC, and one of the reasons for that is so I can share it with other guys who might not be C proficient. Or might not have FORTRAN compilers for their computers [laughs]. I'm an old fart."

PH: "How old are you?"

JH: "Fifty. You can find packaged software to do an awful lot of stuff. It's probably old-fashioned to write it from the ground up, but I believe if you do so, you've learned something important that you might not have learned otherwise. It's making you think in areas that can really expand your awareness of this stuff. Software is one of the many tools. You have to bring everything that could possibly be of use to the table—all your experience, all your intuition, even your driving experience. You have to be ready to learn from anybody or anything."

PH: "The fact that you have driven and still drive, do you think that helps you communicate with drivers?"

JH: "Absolutely! Even though, in a certain sense, it's like a kid who just experienced his first kiss trying to relate to Don Juan. There's a lot of extrapolation that goes on, 'cause you know the numbers that these guys are experiencing in terms of speeds and Gs and so forth. But driving some helps a lot."

PH: "In a philosophical way, in a very general way, if you were going to design an Indy car, and everybody seems to be doing that these days, how would you attack that, or whatever part of it you'd be responsible for? How do you go about that and prioritize that project? What do you get right first? Is the overall aero package now so important that that's got to be done first?"

JH: "Well, the first thing is you have to look at the rule book. That particular series is perhaps more constrained than it once was. As you walk along the corridor here you see a lot of pictures of old Indy cars. They've become quite constrained, and the cars look a lot alike. You can't go anywhere before you understand not only the rules, but their implications, and try to get some feeling for where they're going.

"Of course aerodynamics is profoundly important, but I guess it's a careful line there. We're trying to reverse-engineer tens of thousands or hundreds of thousands of man-hours and try to beat them. How can you do that? You need to be selective in the categories of understanding and selecting what's already been done and understanding and selecting what might be done. That's not very specific, but it's similar to the aerospace business and a lot of other businesses. You want to be at the cutting edge of any business, so you have to use your pet ideas that you've always wanted to implement. On the other hand you've got to accept that your knowledge is not ready to smoke anybody. The task, the contract or whatever, supplies a jolt of inspiration and a jolt of commitment that's going to help you somehow find answers that you don't have now."

PH: "Do you think it's a big deal that you're going from a closed-wheel design to an open-wheel design?"

JH: "Yes. The focal points will have to change in relative importance. In many respects the car that we're still campaigning is very close, in many respects very close, to the cars that we will be campaigning. With its skin off, I think you can see that."

PH: "I did see it skin-off at Laguna the first time out a couple of years ago. It does look like an F1 car with some ducts hung on the side of the tub."

JH: "Sure. I think a big difference is the intensity with which the GTP series is pursued. When we came in to IMSA, beating Nissan was an almost impossible dream. They were so dominant. We attacked it like it was F1, with every shred of our inspiration and so forth. Ultimately we did prevail, and now we feel like we're at the beginning again. Our car still holds the lap record at Portland, and, even with all the weight and restrictions they put on us, it was competitive.

"Indy cars are running at the speeds they're running partly because of their restrictions. It's severe if you look at the tunnel restrictions. So we can't pat ourselves on the back too much. We've got acres of potential downforce there compared to what they've got. We don't really know, but we are assuming that we can get the job done."

PH: "It sounds like you guys are already designing a car. Did I miss something? Has there been an announcement that there is definitely going to be an Indy car coming out of here?"

JH: "No."

PH:" It's a feasibility study? I guess I read that somewhere."

JH: "Yeah. If you're doing a feasibility study you have to act ahead of your contract. You have to act ahead of your mandate. For example, when we had absolutely nothing to do with Indy cars, it wasn't even an idea around here, I started simulating them in software. So, when I went to their races, I could learn something. Like whether their cars, by my stopwatch, are faster and slower than ours at different places, I tried to understand why with no hope at that time of doing a feasibility study in that area. It was just another racing series. But it's the closest one in terms of performance to our cars and I didn't think it was a waste of time, and it turned out not to be, to try to learn from them. I try to learn from the F1 cars. Everybody does. I watch the races and read *Racecar Engineering* and beyond that we've learned a lot through our own contacts and our own theories."

PH: "What series do you follow as a fan? What races do you go to and watch on TV?"

JH: "I love midgets and sprint cars on dirt. Perhaps because of the balance it provides to my particular area. A lot of people will say, well gee, it's guys like me and more famous guys who generate high technology that makes racing boring and too technical and gets the driver out of the picture and so forth. I don't think that's true in our series or the next one we'll get into. The rule makers are making rules to restrict that sort of thing, especially FISA. But just to enjoy racing at its purest has to include just going sideways in the dirt with a flock of cars at 130 miles an hour. Of course, I'm interested in Formula 1. Ayrton Senna is a hero of mine."

PH: "Do you get up at five o'clock in the morning to watch the F1 races on TV?"

JH: "Oh, no. I set the VCR [laughs]. Sometimes I do get up. If there's something interesting happening. The coverage is usually pathetic. You struggle through that. But if you learn one little thing there that you can file away, that just helps your understanding of the whole picture. It's well worth it. And also you can dream about stuff."

PH: "I'm running out of questions and I'm beginning to feel like I've taken up enough of your time. Thanks a lot."

The hints on tires and feedback to the driver that Jim gave me that day resulted in several hundred dollars spent on new books from the SAE as well as a thorough rereading of Carroll Smith's books. I've talked to Jim several times since and he's always the typical race fan as well as a guy who knows a lot about the technical side of racing.

ALL AMERICAN RACERS' INDY CAR TEST AT LAGUNA

As a follow-up to the Jim Hamilton interview I'll also include this report on the first AAR Indy car test at a road course. I think it gives you an idea of the resources available at AAR and the intensity and professionalism that's standard procedure among serious racers. But, even among the best, some days are better than others.

You probably read reports of the "feasibility study" being conducted in 1994 and 1995 by Dan Gurney's All American Racer organization to decide whether or not they will go Indy car racing. I talked to Gurney during a day-long AAR test March 3, 1994 at Laguna Seca Raceway near Monterey, Calif. "Racing is the best way to develop a racecar," Dan said. "We're fans and we want to race. As soon as we're doing competitive lap times I want to race. I hope we don't have to wait till '95. We're funded by Toyota, though, and it's their decision."

Dave Wilson, vice president of operations and engineering at Toyota Racing Development and head of the engine development team for that Laguna test, was a little more conservative. "We don't want to go racing until we have the capability to win. We'd rather not develop the engine during race weekends." As of May 1995 there has been no firm commitment by Toyota to fund Gurney's Indy car program.

Fangio Drove, P. J. Watched

I drove down to Laguna early and got there about 8:15 a.m. With no clouds and no wind, the temperature climbed quickly, and I was comfortable in a knit shirt and light overshirt. Juan Manuel Fangio II was in the car already and his crew was fussing around in the pedal box getting him comfortable in the car. A propane heater trained on the gearbox was loud enough that everyone had to raise their voices to be heard.

The car was a 1993 Lola and an early one at that with none of the tweaks that were developed during last season. They bought the chassis from Lola which, with John Judd's help, modified both the engine and chassis slightly to marry the two. The car was painted white, and the only writing on it was Fangio's name near the cockpit and Goodyear, TRD, and AAR logos on the rear wing end plates.

Jim Hamilton told me the car had only been to one previous test, at Firebird Raceway near Phoenix. "That was a shakedown test for the car and the engine," Jim said. "But it went real well."

At 8:50 they fired up the engine, and five minutes later the bodywork went on with a lot of fiddling around as the crew familiarized themselves with this new machine. It was a very intense, professional bunch of people.

Fangio went out for a slow lap and motored back into the pit lane. The crew took the side pods off again and there was some talk among them about what size Allen wrenches to use on what fasteners. At 9:07 somebody told Fangio to go out and do five easy laps. "Watch your temps," I heard somebody say.

Fangio's first lap was in the 1:40s and the fourth was 1:20. He came back in and the crew began to look over the car, checking everything out thoroughly.

Jim Hamilton talked about this car compared to the GTP car, the AAR-designed and built Eagle Mk. III that won two IMSA GTP championships. "This car is sprung much softer than the P car," Jim explained. "It's easier to work with. You can use the shocks to make the car handle better rather than to control pitch. [GTP cars are much more sensitive to ride height and chassis rake than Indy cars.] The P car was short wheelbase with a lot of overhang. It flowed a lot of air at the front and produced massive aero forces. This car puts out a lot less downforce and has much more compliant tires. It's real smooth and a lot easier on the driver."

About 9:15 a small twin-engined prop plane buzzed the track, and talk went around that it was probably Dan Gurney arriving from the shop 300 miles to the south. Sure enough, Gurney pulled up in a van a few minutes later. Somebody was passing out team-issue Toyota ball caps and Gurney took one, but then, spying the red, floppy granny bonnet worn by the lady operating the timing computer, asked if she had any more of those. When she came back with one he put it on and seemed pleased with it even though it looked extremely silly. He got a lot of looks and smiles, but no one kidded him. He is the boss, after all, and comfortable enough with it that it's OK to look silly around the team.

Fangio went out on the track again at 9:45 and clocked a 1:17 before he ducked back into the pit lane. For comparison, Nigel Mansell tested a 1994 Lola/Cosworth one month earlier and set an unofficial lap record of 1:10.02. On that same day Teo Fabi in Jim Hall's 1994 Reynard/Ilmor D struggled to get into the twelves. Mostly Fabi turned 1:13 and 1:14 lap times. The AAR car seemed to be doing pretty well at this point.

The crew swarmed over the car again, wiping and peering around and looking at marks on the underbody with a mirror. At 10:15 Fangio went out again and P. J. Jones arrived. I found myself standing at the concrete wall that separates the pit lane from the main straightaway leading out of the tight, left-hand Turn 11. Gurney was near and I said, "It's great to be here at a test and get so close to the car. Most of the teams don't let anyone near enough to see anything, but you guys don't have anything to hide yet." He smiled and said, "You're right, we don't. I guess that's just a part of racing. Even Colin Chapman [Lotus founder, F1 team owner, and ground-effects pioneer], when he was the champion of everything, he'd look your car over hard as it came off the trailer."

Fangio was going quicker now. I could hear him working the tires in Turn 10. But, as he came into Turn 11, the car slowed and the engine quit. He coasted to a stop right even with us on the track side of the wall. The crew went over the wall and bodywork came off. Anxious looks and questions flew around as everyone tried to figure out what was wrong.

A mustachioed guy in a Bosch shirt talked intensely in a German accent, and a few minutes later they tried to fire the engine with only momentary success. Fangio got out of the car, and one of the crew members started working behind the digital dash unit. I noticed it was getting warm and unbuttoned my overshirt. People had poured out of the two semi-trailers and everyone was out near the car as if their collective will could make it work. I counted 35 people.

Among those people were John Ward, head designer, and Hiro Fujimori, AAR's director of aerodynamics. These guys are part of the team that created the IMSA GTP dominating Mk. III, and they will design the new Eagle Indy car.

At 10:53 the car fired up and Fangio was off again. He quickly got into the 17s, but he missed some shifts accelerating out of Turn 11. After a 1:16.56 he came back in.

The crew spent some time adjusting the throttle cable, and they worked on the clutch pedal and gear shift lever. Fangio went onto the track again and turned a 16 and then a 1:15.93.

The First Tweaks

When the car came in Fangio got out, and the crew installed a "shark's teeth" vortex generator at the tunnel inlet in front of each sidepod. They safety wired it to the pod so it wouldn't vibrate and break.

"We had to make that ourselves," Jim Hamilton said. "Lola doesn't sell you any of that stuff. I don't know how close to optimum ours is. We just made it up.

We started the day with the standard Lola setup, and we've already deviated from that a little. We made some shock changes and they worked. We're going about as quick as we're supposed to. We're not going to do any 10s."

The crew continued to toil over the car. There were at least a dozen guys tweaking and wiping and tightening and doing whatever they could to urge the Lola along on the way to becoming an Eagle.

P. J. Jones said it was tough to watch Fangio in the car. "I'd like to be out there, too. I'm scheduled to do the next test. I expect to drive one of the cars next year."

"So there's going to be an Indy car program and you're going to drive one?" I asked.

"I think so," P. J. said. "I sure hope so."

Fangio, on the other hand, hated to have to go home tonight. "I want to do more testing. I'm disappointed I can't do more." Fangio is also excited about a trip to Australia, where he'll race in the Bathurst 12 Hour.

On course again Fangio turned a 1:17 and started another lap, but then the crew heard something on their radios that made them tense up. They started loading gear onto an electric cart. Fangio had missed a shift in Turn 2 and spun and stalled the engine. After the restart he drove it in, and the crew messed with the clutch pedal and the gear shift mechanism again.

During one session Fangio ran a string of 16s. You could tell he was driving the car hard because you could hear the tires in Turn 10, and the rear of the car was twitching out of Turn 11. He came in and got out of the car. The crew started several projects geared toward making the car more drivable. Dave Wilson changed the engine ignition and/or fuel map, and the crew worked on the gear shift lever. They decided to bend the lever a little bit.

Jim Hamilton spent a lot of time studying the front tires. He used a putty knife to scrape the rocks and dirt off the surface of the tire and expose the warm, dark rubber underneath.

Fangio drove the car about 15 more laps in three short sessions before the 5:00 p.m. Laguna curfew. I didn't see any lap times less than 1:16. The car just didn't seem capable of better times no matter what they tried. Finally, in an attempt to get the car to do something predictable, they dialed in a big suspension change and then, after the car didn't do anything, another change on top of that.

"Something's wrong," Jim said. "The car's not responding. There's a big problem." Just before he left to go to the airport, Gurney smiled and said, "I wonder if Carl [Haas, U.S. Lola distributor] would give me my money back?"

When I've heard about this kind of thing before, it usually turns out to be something like a chassis twisting or a bent suspension part or a seized damper. The numbers didn't turn out great for this car on this particular day. But the engine worked and the people were impressive.

A couple of weeks later I called Jim, and they'd found what was wrong with the car. He said it was kind of embarrassing. The exhaust headers had heated the underwing area causing it to deform, changing the shape of one of the ground-effects tunnels enough to drastically reduce the downforce produced under the car.

There'll be other days at the track for AAR—better and worse.

LEE DYKSTRA, INTERVIEW WITH AN ENGINEER

For many years I've heard the name Lee Dykstra associated with racecar design and engineering. I first met Lee in 1991 at the IMSA race at Laguna Seca where Price Cobb was driving the Mazda RX792P, a GTP car Lee designed. Price introduced us and later Lee subscribed to my newsletter, *TV MOTORSPORTS*. In 1994 we spoke often because we were both involved in the Indy Lights series. Lee engineered the all-conquering Tasman cars, and I worked PR for Bob Lesnett's Summit Motorsports, with Doug Boyer as driver.

We tried to get together for an interview several times at the end of the 1994 season, but it never worked out. Finally we scheduled an early morning phone call and I taped our conversation. Lee faxed me a resume and a project list, and I sent him a list of questions.

Lee Dykstra

Lee Dykstra has designed some famous and familiar racecars, including the 1981 IMSA JLP Porsche 935, 1982 IMSA GTP Jaguar XJR-5, 1985 IMSA GTP Jaguar XJR-7, 1989-'91 IMSA GTO Mazda RX-7, the aforementioned Mazda RX792P, and the ground-effects, four-wheel drive Toyota Celica that was driven by Rod Millen at Pikes Peak to an absolute record elapsed time. For this interview I used the same basic list of questions that appear at the front of this chapter. Lee's resume is impressive, and I started the conversation by acknowledging that fact.

PH: "It's obvious to me that you're one of those guys who's a real engineer. It looks like you could tackle almost anything. Where did you go to school?"

LD: "At General Motors Institute."

PH: "The resume starts in 1962, so that makes you about the same age as me. You were born in 1940?"

LD: "Yeah, in '39."

PH: "You started off at Cadillac, and then you switched to Ford and did the Trans-Am Mustang in 1968. How did you get involved in racing?"

LD: "When I was at GMI there were three of us and, when we graduated, we decided that we would build our own racecar. While we were still writing our fifth-year thesis we built a car called a C-modified, which was a space-frame car with an aluminum Buick V-8 in it. It had drum brakes from a Corvair and some other Corvair bits and pieces. I designed the car and a guy named Bob Stout did most of the welding and construction and Don Cox, who was later involved with Penske and Chevy R&D, did the drivetrain stuff. We ran that car for a year and it was absolutely terrible. [Lee chuckles.]

"If you went off the racetrack, the control arms would bend or something would fall off, and there were handling problems because of roll stiffness and roll rates, and the carburetors would cut out in the corners. But we learned a hell of a lot. We crashed it at the end of the year and built another one. That one was pretty successful. It had a Ford engine in it.

"The third car we did had a Cadillac engine in it, and we ran that at a race like the USSRC at Mosport in Canada. We qualified fifth in that car in the middle of people like Jim Hall and Bruce McLaren and John Surtees and David Piper. We got an invitation from Roy Lund of Ford's Kar-Kraft. He said anytime you guys want a job, come and see me. I went there a year later after I built the Wolverine car for Jerry Hansen. That's how I got to Kar-Kraft working for Ford. Don Cox went to Chevy R&D and was involved in a lot of the Chapparal stuff."

PH: "Who drove those cars?"

LD: "Don and Bob drove the first year, and the second year we had Glenn Lyall drive both the Ford and the Cadillac-powered cars. Glenn was pretty high up at Ford SVO. I thinks he's still at Ford."

PH: "So you did the Trans-Am Mustangs right when that series was first starting. What were some of the special problems getting those cars to go fast?"

LD: "Essentially we were taking a production Mustang and trying to fit pretty wide tires on narrow rims inside this thing, and make it look pretty close to production. There wasn't a whole lot of production pieces by the time we were done. There was a lot of competition between manufacturers at that time. We got snookered in '68 from an aero standpoint. We didn't homologate front and rear spoilers, and we had an engine problem. In '69 we picked up on that, but ended up having some reliability problems, brakewise, and the engine wasn't really responsive enough. It certainly had enough power, but it all came in a bunch at 5,500 rpm. The next year we got all our ducks in order, and the tires worked well and we were pretty well unbeatable in 1970."

PH: "I was living in LA in those years, and I remember going to Riverside to watch those races."

LD: "Did you see the 1970 race at Riverside?"

PH: "I don't know. I got laid off the middle of that year and moved back to Texas. I don't remember any specific races."

LD: "We were one-two on the grid with Parnelli Jones and George Follmer driving. And actually Parnelli's back-up car was second quickest. Parnelli went pretty far off the racetrack and bent the prop shaft and still came back and won it."

PH: "It must have been a pretty reliable car by then."

LD: "Yeah [laughing]. And he must have been pretty good too, to put up with a bent prop shaft and still win."

PH: "All this experience is the reason I wanted to talk to you. What other American designer has done as many different kinds of projects as you have?"

LD: "Well, Bob Riley [Riley and Scott] has done a lot and Trevor Harris [ex Pete Brock and Nissan] has done a lot. John Ward [All American Racers] doesn't have the diversity of experience maybe, but he's in there. Also David Bruns has done the Swift cars. That's about the list, really."

PH: "Looking over this project list, there's some pretty famous cars here. The ones that pop up for me are the GTP Jaguars. You have 'Complete Car' next to those, so you sat down and designed that whole car?"

LD: "Yeah."

PH: "That was the V-12-engined car. So that had some specific problems like a big engine in the back sitting up high. Wasn't that one of the problems?"

LD: "A long motor was the main deal. In trying to package all this in a reasonable wheelbase where the motor was 30-some inches long. And then to try to stress the thing as well, to try to minimize the structure and try to get around the engine and put big tunnels in it."

PH: "So the engine was in the way both structurally and aerodynamically?"

LD: "Yeah. A lot of the stuff we developed, the packaging we did, by the time we got to the XJR-7s, was pretty much carried over to the later Jaguars that Walkinshaw did as far as how we machined the back of the block and did the starter stuff."

PH: "The Jaguar XJR7 in 1985, was that a V-12-engined car?."

LD: "Yeah; it was a development of the other one. It had an aluminum-honeycomb monocoque with carbon-fiber panels and machined aluminum bulkheads. It was pretty trick from a chassis standpoint. The body wasn't changed much from before.

"I also did the IMSA Chevy Monza racecars. We won the IMSA championship two years in a row [1976, 1977] with those cars. That was prior to the GTP class. The cars had a complete space frame and all fiberglass body panels. That was the first sedan-type car that was essentially a real racecar."

PH: "OK, I remember that. But the most recent IMSA car you did was the Mazda GTP car with Price Cobb driving. I can remember looking over that car and being impressed. I remember telling you at the time that I didn't know there were so many things you could do to make the tunnels big. [Lee laughs.] It looked like you really got everything out of the way so you could have some huge tunnels at the rear of the car. Was that right?"

LD: "Oh, sure. With those cars the aero is first and the rest of the stuff is packaged around it."

PH: "That car had a lot of problems and never really did well. What was the deal?"

LD: "Well, the primary thing was heat. Mazda management decided that the car had to show up at the first race at Miami, and the car had never turned a wheel before it ran there. We were trying to put a muffler in this car that was 28 inches long and 11 inches in diameter, and it glowed red hot all the time. There was no way. It ran seven laps at Miami, and we had a fire. There was very little development and then the car went to Sebring and it was the same thing. After that it ran reliably the first time at Road Atlanta and every race after that the car finished the race. It was getting faster in relation to the competition. In fact, the final race we qualified fourth. It was really hurting from a horsepower standpoint. We had a little more than 600 horsepower, and we were running against the Toyota and the Nissan and the Jaguar that all had a lot more."

PH: "What other projects stand out in your mind that you're proud of?"

LD: [A long, thoughtful pause.] "Well, all those we've talked about. We also did a complete rear suspension and engine conversion in a March Indy car in 1983 for Truesports. That was when you had the Cosworth engines with a single-butterfly throttle, and they weren't very responsive on road courses. Jim Truman decided he needed a Chevy V-8 for road courses, so we did a complete redesign. Everything from the front of the engine backwards was new—the rear box, the rear suspension, all those things. The car was on the pole at Mid-Ohio and led till the first fuel stop. What happened was the doors inside the fuel cell were hanging up and we could only get 20 gallons out of the thing. It ended up not winning, but it was pretty fast and that was probably the fastest-ever stock block Indy car."

PH: "That would be a pretty difficult packaging job."

LD: "Yeah. We redid the bell housing, the suspension, the engine mounts, wing mounts, stabilizer bar, the whole deal."

PH: "Let's start on the questions. That first one is about how you start a new project, and what are the priorities and what do you do first and how much planning do you do before you start the work? How do you work?"

LD: "Well, generally there are some inputs on these things. Like Mazda says, 'OK, we want a GTP car, and this is the engine,' and the rules are such and such and the class has some tires—Goodyear or whatever. Those kinds of things you have as sort of a fixed deal. From there you're just sort of looking at it and saying 'What can I do to gain an advantage. What does this car need to have to make it competitive? More aero? Less weight? Better handling? Better brakes? Or whatever, to do the job.' It doesn't do any good to design a new car if it's not going to be more than competitive at the time you start it.

"From there you do a general arrangement trying to package all these things, where the cooling is and what the aero requirements are and such like that."

PH: "Are you working on paper?"

LD:" Paper and/or CAD [computer aided design]. We do all of our stuff on CAD now."

PH: "So when you start something like that now, you're working at a computer with AutoCad?"

LD: "Well, I do some of the stuff on a drawing board, being an oldtimer."

PH: "So you might start the initial layout on paper. Kinda draw the tires and decide the wheelbase or the track or whatever?"

LD: "Some of that stuff I can't really choose because really it's a stack-up of stuff. If IMSA says the drivers feet have to be at front-wheel centerline and the driver takes up a certain amount of space, OK, then you've got the fuel cell, the 31 gallons or whatever. That's going to take a certain amount of fore and aft space, and then the motor and then how long do you make the bell housing and such? So you don't have a whole lot of freedom as far as how much you're going do to specify wheelbase by the time you stack all this stuff up."

PH: "So you kinda start in the middle of the car?"

LD: "Actually you're taking all these things into it. The whole thing's a big compromise. You can't say this is the specific way I'm going to do it. But you end up looking at all these things and saying, 'OK, this is the best compromise here.' And we may vary a half-inch one way or the other if we need to get a clutch in or something. Weight distribution is important. All these things come in at the same time."

PH: "You just answered some of the second question. How soon would you build a wind tunnel model? Would you use data from a similar car? Or track data from something similar?"

LD: "Like with the GTP Mazda, as soon as you get an idea of a general arrangement, the size of the chassis and what kind of tunnels you can get in the thing, we do a wind-tunnel model. What we normally do is a model such that we can define the hard points, the radiator locations, wheels, rough idea of suspension, tub limitations, whatever. Then we clay an exterior shape on the thing with wings and everything. Then we can go to a simple wind tunnel, a fixed ground-plane tunnel like the one at the University of Michigan, a quarter-scale tunnel with really good boundary layer characteristics, so it's really representative as far as the exterior of the car goes. We did probably 250 tests of various shapes of clay based on airflow so we can get an idea about the exterior body shape."

PH: "So you go into a wind tunnel pretty early in the process."

LD: "Yeah. Well, you gotta define the car first, where the radiators are and all those things. So you know the basic layout of the car."

PH: "How much do tires influence the design of the car?"

LD: "As far as what?"

PH: "Do you have data on the tires when you start a design?"

LD: "You're assuming we can change things on the tires. As far as the suspension alignment goes we have an idea of what you need to run with that particular tire."

PH: "So you don't start out with any spring rate data or side force vs. slip angle data? Is that available? Do tire manufacturers give that data out to anybody?"

LD: "We have some of that. With the Mazda we used a circuit simulation program. We can plug in tire data, engine data, weight data, aero stuff, whatever, and say how does this compare with what everybody else has been running? We know going in what we have to do to make this car competitive."

PH: "And that simulation is something you've come up with yourself. We talked about that at Laguna several years ago. You've been using that long enough now that you oughta be pretty good at fudging things around so you can tell what's going on."

LD: "Yeah. It's not super detail, but when we go to a track we can tell the crew what gears to use and get a pretty good idea about the lap time it'll do."

PH: "So when do you freeze the design? Do you know the areas that still need development? Do you plan the development?"

LD: "No. You really don't say we need to develop something at that point. When we do the design of this thing we're assuming that's the very best that we can do. There's not something we know is going to break or not work right [laughs]."

PH: "OK, maybe that was a dumb question."

LD: "But you're not freezing the whole car. Essentially we're going from one end to the other. When you do the preliminary stuff you do as much as you can and say, 'Hey, this looks like everything's going to package.' And you go from there. And then you start, depending on the build sequence and what our time priorities are, trying to keep everybody that's building the car going and at the same time you're working on the complete front suspension and you haven't even looked at the rear suspension. So you're really not freezing the whole car at some point in time."

PH: "I guess the whole thing is you're working on a timetable toward the first race."

LD: "Yes. Well, to the first test."

PH: "Yeah. Hopefully you have some time to test the design."

LD: "Yeah, Well...[chuckles]. When you do get to test, then things tend to be a lot more successful. Otherwise you're showing up at the first race with no test time at all. We tested the Mazda GTO car for three-quarters of a year, and we went to Daytona and were on the pole. That's what you need to do, but, unfortunately, most of the time that time's not available."

PH: "With suspension design you always compromise. You never get it all to work like you want. What are the priorities for you? What tools do you use to design a suspension?"

LD: "We have a complete geometry, 3D geometry, program. We have the means to look at spring linkages and stuff. We have a program for every conceivable spring linkage arrangement. If it isn't available I can write it because I wrote all the other stuff anyway. So we can take our geometry data and take ball joint positions and all that and plug that into a linkage program and come out with velocities and travel ratios and all that for the complete stroke. You can go into the program and change a couple of points and come back and see the difference. It's pretty interactive."

PH: "What software language do you use?"

LD: "This is compiled BASIC."

PH: "This is graphics or numbers?"

LD: "Just numbers, but we can check it out vs. the CAD numbers for clearances and stuff like that. We also have the same kind of thing for stabilizer bars, rates, and all that. And we also have a Finite Element program where we can input the loads at the wheel and at the ground as far as braking and lateral acceleration and all that so we know the loads on the control arms so we can stress all that stuff as well."

PH: "Have your ideas about suspension geometry evolved? Did the same things matter on the Trans-Am Mustang that matter today, or have your ideas changed?"

LD: "Well, it depends. With the Mustang you're kind of trapped because you have to use production control arms. The geometry you have there, you get what you get other than what you did to lower the car, and you fudge the control arm positions a little bit on the upright. On a fully designed car like a GTP car you can do what you want, but there are still compromises because of toe-box width in the driver area or what structure you need or trying to get a unified design."

PH: "How important is the feedback the car gives the driver? Does the driver need that, so he can tell where he is vs. the ultimate grip the car can achieve? Is that something the designer worries about?"

LD: "We try to make a linear car. I think that's the main thing. Where a driver gets into trouble is if it doesn't react linearly. If he goes into a corner at X mph and the thing pushes and the next time he goes a little harder and it gets loose, then obviously he has to leave himself some margin, and you're trying to make it so he doesn't need much margin."

PH: "Is that something you feel like you've got a good handle on? When you sit down to design a car, are there things you can do to make sure that happens?"

LD: "Yeah. Obviously we try to do that kind of thing, and some of that stuff is in deflections or the amount of wheel travel or the rate of change of wheel travel or spring rates. Those kinds of things you take into account to try to make it so there's no surprises."

PH: "What are the really tough components to work with when you design a car? What do you start with and what do you leave until the end because you know you can do it?"

LD: "The big stuff goes in first [laughing]. You're packaging the driver and the cooling system and the engine and the suspension and things like that. The piping and the wiring comes in afterward. A lot of these things look like 'Wow, this guy's really a genius as far as how all this stuff fits,' but you're starting with the big stuff and working it all out."

PH: "What people or designs have influenced your work?"

LD: [Another thoughtful pause.] "When I was at GM I got everything that Maurice Olley ever wrote. He was the suspension guru at General Motors. Back in the 1930s he did a lot of work with independent suspension, and he wrote a number of papers. There were a number of things he published after he retired which are internal GM stuff about suspension, and that had a really profound influence on me. At least knowing the basics and knowing I could change roll center heights and springs and all that sort of thing but, in the end, if I go around a corner at one G and my center of gravity is 12 inches high and the track is 58 inches, I'm going to transfer this amount of weight no matter what I do. It's just a matter of how I apportion it. If you know those kinds of things then, when you go to develop the car, then there's no mystery—well there's mystery obviously [laughs], but there's no magical fix on this stuff. It's gonna do this amount, and it's just a matter of how you tune it."

PH: "So there's some things you know, and there's always some stuff you don't understand."

LD: "Well, there's 50 combinations of things. It's a matter of finding the best combination. If you're off 1% then you're 2 seconds behind."

PH: "When you say there's 50 combinations, you mean there's about 50 things you can fiddle with to tune a racecar?"

LD: [laughing] "Yeah, well that's just on an Indy Lights car. If you look at something else where you can change wing configurations and that sort of thing, then you have even more combinations.

"As far as influences, there's some Formula 1 guys—Gordon Murray and John Barnard. It's not that you necessarily copy them, but you can certainly appreciate a good design. You can look at something and say that it really looks nice—it looks right. That's what we strive for and sometimes those are more difficult to do than something that looks complex, because you make it simple. You're taking into account a lot of stuff. You can just look and you can see a design that flows, a control arm where the shape looks right. Generally, if it looks right it is right."

PH: "That sounds like there's some artistry in this."

LD: "We try to think that there is. We try to make our cars look nice on the exterior as well as go good."

PH: "What about trends in racecar design? What have you seen? You've been doing this a long time. What trends have you seen and where do you think the gains are going to be made in the future?"

LD: "Obviously the big trends have been aero stuff. When we started, like with Jerry Hansen's Wolverine I did, when he drove the car at Road America, he said it felt like the front wheels were coming off the ground on the straightaway. Obviously it had a lot of lift at the front. That's been the primary thing—to try to get some aerodynamics in the cars over the years, and making the car work with those kinds of loads in it.

"There's also been a lot done as far as shocks and active and semi-active suspension and things with differentials using electronics. Whether the rules makers allow these things is something else again, but there's certainly a big potential there."

PH: "Let's talk a little more about aerodynamics here. L over D, lift over drag, that seems to be a characteristic that engineers and designers pay some attention to. Is that something that you concentrate on? How do you use wind tunnel data to make a car actually go faster on the track?"

LD: "You're always trying to maximize your lift over drag. That's essentially your efficiency. Now, there are, what can we say here, there are certain minimums you're looking for in terms of downforce. Given that downforce, you try to minimize drag with your configuration. But, by the same token, at a street course, you still try for maximum downforce."

PH: "Let's see, the next question is about track testing. How much planning do you put into a track test, and what do you expect from a driver?"

LD: "I expect him to be consistent and at a pretty high level as far as using the car. It doesn't do us any good for him to run at eight-tenths the whole time and then at the end stand on it and say, 'Well all the stuff we've been working on, suddenly it doesn't work,' because now he's pushing it that much more and it's something different.

"As far as planning, that's going to vary with the car situation. If we have a team like a Tasman or something like that where we've had some tests prior, then we know what our weaknesses are, or what we'd like to work on so we say, 'OK, we're going to this test and we're going to test these five items or whatever.' If I go with a less than competitive team and I don't know what they've been doing, then I can't say what we need to test because I don't know where they stand."

PH: "What about shocks? How are you generating data for yourself? Do you have a shock dyno?"

LD: "No. I had one. I don't have one now. I'd like any team I work with to have a shock dyno."

PH: "So you feel like you need a shock dyno to do shock development?"

LD: "Yeah, I think so. You need to have access to the data one way or another, whatever we specify that doesn't get passed on to 5,000 other people.

"As far as the importance? It's very important. In an Indy Lights program it's one of the few things you can change, so that becomes more important in that situation."

PH: "If all of a sudden you were working for an Indy car team, and I think that's your current goal, what components would you look at to make the car better? Maybe that leads to that next question about the basic differences between the three Indy car manufacturers."

LD: "I can't really address that because I'm standing on the outside looking at those cars. Until you actually run one and compare how you do at X corner vs. the other ones you can't really say. Obviously the Penskes, because the cars can't be that much different because of the rules, then it's a bunch of little things that makes the Penskes better than the Reynard or Lola. They are just doing all the details better than the other two cars."

PH: "Can you look at those cars and see much difference? I don't know much and I look and I see a few little details that are different. I see on the Reynards a great big front wing at a great big angle, and on the Lolas I see a different front wing at a much lower angle. Other than that and maybe some differences in the engine cover, I can't really see a whole lot of difference. Just looking at them, what difference do you see?"

LD: "I see those same things. The rules are such that you really don't have a whole lot of freedom as far as what you can do. The people like Lola are also obviously in a big sales game as well. Every year March used to improve their aerodynamics 25% over the previous year [chuckles]. You know, some of that was stretching it considerably."

PH: "Are you a racing fan? Do you watch racing on TV when you're not at the races?"

LD: "To a certain extent. I don't usually go to races if I'm not working there. It's one of these things where you say I need to do this to see if there's anything that might be of some help at some time. I've got subscriptions to about 10 magazines, and not only auto racing, but maybe aircraft stuff and all this sort of thing. You just put things into your memory bank and you read something that says that the Williams F1 car had problems because the wing position in the front wasn't right, and you just sorta keep that in your mind or recorded some place, and maybe something like that will come up some time and be useful in the design of a car at some point in time."

PH: "What's the most fun about what you do? Do you ever think during a race weekend, 'Boy I'm really having fun?'"

Both of us laugh.

LD: "Usually not, [still laughing]."

PH: "Does that ever happen?"

LD: "Well, yeah. It's one of these things that if you really didn't enjoy it, you wouldn't do it for as long as I've done it."

PH: "What is it that you enjoy? What's keeping you in there?"

LD: "The thinking part of it. The thinking and the competitive part. Trying to be better than someone else by being smarter or working harder or whatever. In the design part there's a creative thing of trying to put this all together and making it work well and look nice."

PH: "What would be a dream project for you? What would you like somebody to pop in the door today and hand you?"

LD: [sigh] "Good question [long pause]. Well, there isn't any specific thing. I've always liked cars and racing, so any kind of design project with a car, there's always some challenges. So whether it's a GTP car or a World Sports Car or an Indy car or whatever."

PH: "Well, I'm running out of questions. We've covered everything I wanted. Is there anything else here? Did I miss anything? Is there some question you can think of that I should have asked?"

LD: [laughs] "No, I've talked too much already."

In June of 1995 Forsythe Racing hired Dykstra to engineer the Reynard/ Cosworth Indy car driven by Teo Fabi. The first weekend Dykstra was on the team Fabi was on the pole and finished fourth in the race at the Milwaukee Mile.

He's baaack!

INTERVIEW WITH CARROLL SMITH

Carroll Smith is the best-known racing writer in the world. His first book, *Prepare To Win*, led to *Tune To Win* and *Engineer To Win*. All are available from Classic Motorbooks and motorsports bookstores everywhere.

Carroll started out as a racecar driver, switched to race engineering, and became the first successful racing consultant. His books really provide almost all the information we need if we want to learn about racing. My copies are much-used and are beginning to fall apart. I said as much to Carroll and he suggested that I should buy new copies.

It's been fun to get to know Carroll. He tells some great stories and always has a strong opinion about anything you can think of to talk about. I've learned a lot talking to him. I asked him to read the first draft of this book in December 1994, and he took the time to do that. His comments helped a lot. I felt great relief when I got the draft back and he hadn't found a lot of dumb errors. It made me think that Jeff and I had done something we could be proud of, if it passed Carroll's inspection. That's how much respect Carroll Smith has earned with me.

Carroll recently finished writing his latest book, *Drive To Win*, which should be available in 1996. The subject is the driver and communications between the driver and the engineer. I knew about the book and built my question list around those topics. Here's the list of questions I made for the interview with Carroll:

Personal background? Where did you grow up, school, jobs, etc.
How did you get started in racing? Significant projects?
Books: How did that start? What happened because of the books?

Driver Questions
1. What is the percentage contribution of the driver to a quick lap? A race win? A series championship? Differences in percentages between F1 and IndyCar and whatever?
2. What can a racecar designer do to help the driver?
   Feedback from the car to the driver about how close to ultimate grip?
   King pin inclination, castor, camber. What's the effect of this stuff on driver feel?
3. What can a race engineer do to help the driver?
   Car tuning? Sway bars, springs, shocks, tire pressure, aero?
   What does balance have to do with it?
   Coaching?
   Interpretation of feedback?
   Cheerleading?
   Ass kicking?
   Why don't more engineers go out around the track and watch the car and driver work?
4. How should a driver best use a racecar?
   Tires?
   Engine?
   Other components?
5. How should a driver approach a track test?
   A race weekend?
   A season?
   The Indy 500?
   A career?
6. What makes a great driver? How do they get that way?
7. Why do we all love racing so much? Why do you?

Carroll Smith: Racecar Engineer, Author

PH: "Carroll, tell me where you grew up, where you went to school, and how you got involved in racing."

CS: "I grew up in upstate New York, Oswego to be exact, and, yes, the racetrack was there at that time, but it was a trotting track. I grew up in the horse business, actually jumping horses. Eventually I went to the University of Rochester and got a bachelors in mechanical engineering, and, since the Navy paid for my education, I became a naval officer.

"When I was a fairly late teenager, probably 15 or 16, maybe 17, my dad and I went to a stock car race on a local half-mile, the Sandy Creek oval. I'd never seen a motor race, and I just fell in love with it. I have no idea why. It was just, 'Wow, I gotta do that.' It took some time for me to get to do that. I did do a lot of fooling around, practicing. Being in the horse business, we followed the state and county fair circuits, and there were always dirt tracks and I could fool around on them at night. I did a lot of spinning, but never hit anything. Then in college I did a lot of fooling around in Genesee Park. I even managed to get upside down once.

"But I was trying to teach myself how to drive. I couldn't afford to race. I didn't know anything at all about road racing until my senior year in college when I read something about it."

PH: "When was that? How old are you?"

CS: "Sixty-two. I graduated in 1954.

"Anyway, when I was in Pensacola in flight training, I suddenly had enough money to buy an MG, an older MG. I started running gymkanas and time trials, and I guess we did well enough that the MG importer for whatever part of the world that was, Southeastern I guess, made a deal to supply me with a TF 1500 at importer net cost. We did real well with that, and graduated to an Austin-Healey and then a Cooper 1100. After a few years it became pretty obvious that I could either be a good naval officer or maybe a pretty good race driver, but I was doing a really bad job of trying to do both.

"So Jane [Carroll's wife, who died late last year] and I made the decision to have a go, and, since at that time it wasn't possible to make a living road racing in this country, we went to Europe."

PH: "Really? When was that?"

CS: "1960. I resigned my naval commission and went to Europe to become a racing driver. We stayed four or five years. We won some and lost some. We made a living at it, which was pretty unusual in those days, just as it is now, I might add."

PH: "What series did you run?"

CS: "I ran Formula Jr. Those were the great years of Formula Jr. And two-liter sports cars and GT cars and anything that someone would pay me to drive, basically. It was really good because you had a race every weekend, and you were usually testing two or three days in between, for somebody. You learned a hell of a lot."

PH: "You lived in England?"

CS: "Couldn't afford to live in England. The nice thing about England was, if you could have managed to beat Jimmy Clark and all those guys, they gave you a little pewter tray and a check for two pounds, ten. [We both chuckle.] Whereas on the continent you could make a living. The trouble was, it didn't lead anyplace. If you were winning on the continent, everybody said, 'So?'

"We based in Italy and lived wherever the races were. We wintered in Italy because you could test at Vallelunga, near Rome, all year long. It never got cold enough to preclude testing.

"At some point it became obvious that Jimmy Clark just wasn't losing enough sleep over me. I could probably have continued to make a decent living as a race driver for some time, but that wasn't good enough for me. I had done a little bit of work with Goodyear and had developed a bit of a reputation as a test driver. I approached John Wyer and was offered the job of becoming his understudy. That seemed like a good thing to do, so we agreed to do that.

"But, in the meantime, we came back to this country, because my parents and Jane's parents hadn't seen the baby. [Their first child, Dawn, sister to Christopher, who later followed in his father's footsteps and became a race driver.]. But, whilst here, Carroll Shelby hired me to do the Ford GT-40 program, which nobody knew he had. He actually pulled me off a bus somewhere in Pennsylvania. I told him I had already agreed to go to work for John Wyer, and he informed me that Wyer had released me which, indeed, I found he had.

"So, totally unqualified, I became the project engineer and team manager for the GT-40 program. I guess the rest is history."

PH: "So you've been a race engineer since then?"

CS: "Yeah."

PH: "What other significant projects have you worked on since then?"

CS: "Oh, boy. Sorta one a year, at least. There was the GT-40. There was Shelby's Can-Am program, which wasn't terribly successful for a lot of reasons. Then I did Milestone Racing's Formula 5000 effort, which won the championship with Tony Adamowitz driving. We actually ran it out of Shelby's shop.

"Then there was an abortive Shelby Indy program which could have been a good one but wasn't. Then, just a whole bunch of stuff for a couple of years; a lot of Formula Atlantic, a lot of Formula 5000, a lot of Can-Am. After Shelby retired, it was either go to work for somebody else or start trying to make a living as a consultant, which nobody had ever done. I really didn't want to work for anyone else, because Shelby spoils you for that."

PH: "He's good to work with?"

CS: "Oh, boy. He just gives you all the rope in the world. In many ways, even today, that was the best racing team the world has ever seen."

PH: "Why do you say that? What did it have?"

CS: "People! It's that simple. Let's face it, Shelby took on Ferrari and beat 'em! That's one of the biggest challenges the racing world has ever seen. He did it by hiring the right people and giving them a godawful amount of rope. He just said, 'Go do it.'"

PH: "Ken Miles was one of those people, wasn't he?"

CS: "Yep. And Phil Remington and Al Dowd. The best mechanics in the world; the best drivers in the world."

PH: "Al Dowd?"

CS: "Al Dowd's title was administrative assistant. Al was the guy that did all the logistics and made it all happen, so that Rem and I didn't have to worry about airplane tickets, hotel rooms, places to work, per diem, rental cars, any of that stuff. When we got real tired, Al could take over as team manager till we got some sleep. But basically, we just had the best bunch of mechanics I've ever seen. And the best drivers in the world. We could have anybody we wanted and we did."

PH: "It took a while, though, didn't it?"

CS: "Not for us."

PH: "OK, it was Ford that took a while to beat the Ferraris."

CS: "The first race we ever did was Daytona in 1965, and we won it. And we won Le Mans the second time we went there."

PH: "This was the GT-40s? Under the Shelby team banner?"

CS: "Yes. That was a great post-graduate program, and I got paid for it."

PH: "How much have things changed? What kind of stuff were you worried about then that you still worry about when you try to make a car go fast?"

CS: "It's exactly the same thing. We just didn't know as much. Nothing has changed except our knowledge has expanded."

PH: "So what are the basic things a race engineer worries about?"

CS: "Well, obviously, the first thing you're worried about is safety. The next thing you worry about is reliability. And after that you worry about balance. And after that you worry about cornering power. We used to worry about brakes, but you don't have to worry about that anymore."

PH: "There used to be a lot of emphasis on the engine. That's what everybody seemed to tweak."

CS: "We never did. I never have. I don't think you can win motor races with an engine. To me an engine is pretty much a given. You bolt that sucker in there, and, if you don't like it, you take it out and put another one in."

PH: "That's the way it is now. You did it that way in the '60s also?"

CS: "Absolutely."

PH: "How did you get started writing books on racing?"

CS: "Well, when Shelby retired from motor racing, it became necessary for me to make a living, and I wanted to do it within motor racing without going to work for another team. It took a while for the idea of a consultant to catch on. In the meantime, I approached the original Sports Car Graphic magazine with an idea, since I had developed a reputation as a preparer of racecars, of writing a series on the preparation of racecars. They bought the idea and they paid handsomely for it. They published a seven-article series which, several years later, I expanded into the first book, *Prepare To Win*. I just took a flyer to see if I could make some money at it, and, lo and behold, we did. Everything has come from that.

"It's also a question of trying to put something back. My life in motor racing has been very, very good. It isn't that motor racing has been good to us. Motor racing is inanimate. It's not good to anybody. [We both laugh.] It's just a good way to spend a life, or it's worked out that way for us. I've taken a lot out of it. I'd like to put something back. That's one of the reasons I work with young drivers so much."

PH: "My copies of your books have seen so much use they're falling apart."

CS: "Well, you should buy new ones." [We both laugh some more.]

PH: "Silly me. I hadn't thought of that.

"Your's is the only comments I've read yet of the draft of [this] book, and I saw you noticed what Jim Hamilton had to say about your books. In that interview with him he said something about a consultant out there who's written some good stuff. But what he really said was, 'There's a consultant out there who publishes his books on what looks like toilet paper.'"

CS: [laughing] "Wait till he sees the new one. It's a lot better looking than what we used to do. And it's going to start some arguments."

PH: "You just mentioned young drivers. That's question number six on my list here about what makes a good driver and how do they get that way."

CS: "Oh, boy. I've just written a whole book on that subject."

PH: "What would a young driver have to do to excite you?"

CS: [long, thoughtful pause] "He'd have to be willing to learn; he'd have to have unquenchable desire; and he'd have to have access to a reasonable budget. He'd have to be fast, and he'd have to have an attitude."

PH: "What kind of attitude?"

CS: "Real confident. Almost cocky."

PH: "Robbie Gordon?"

CS: "Yeah. Robbie could excite me. He's possibly a little more flamboyant about it than I'd like to see.

"Price Cobb—perfect race driver. He knows exactly how good he is. Robbie is a little, how to put it, I'm not going to say too cocky, but he's a little more cocky than the people I normally get along with real well.

"The people I get along with are the Ongaises, the Price Cobbs, the Bob Earls, the Christopher Smiths. They're very, very confident, but they're pretty quiet about it."

PH: "That's the people that come to mind when you think about good drivers?"

CS: "[Peter] Revson, too. Little Al [Unser]. They know how good they are so they don't have to tell the world about it. They have that total confidence. If you watch a group of drivers walking toward the grid, you can tell who came to win the motor race. And who came to carry a spear."

PH: "Just by the way they act?"

CS: "Right. Just by the way they act."

PH: "So how do they get that way?"

CS: "Part of it is, they're born that way. Part of it is a question of developing the discipline that it takes to become really good at anything that's hard to do. And, make no mistake about it, driving a racing car properly is probably the hardest thing that the human being has yet learned how to do. It's a hell of a lot harder than driving an airplane.

"It just takes a dedication and a discipline to develop whatever natural talent that God gave you. Of course they all start out the same way. They're absolutely convinced, the good ones, that God gave them talents he has never given to anybody in the whole history of humankind. And then, at some point early on in their career, somebody goes by them on the outside of a corner with 10 miles an hour in hand and gives them the finger. They figure out that, no, this isn't true. I've got the same talents that everybody else has got. I just have to learn how to develop 'em.

"The off-side of that, of course, is if a kid is good, he'll start winning right away because he's in a beginners class and most of them aren't good. So he may move up two or three classes before he finds out he's just a normal, everyday human being. Eventually he will rise to the level where there are people better than he is, and they'll beat his ass off. And then, if he's ever going to be any good, he'll sit down and say, 'Wait a minute,; I gotta learn how to do this.'"

PH: "Then how does he go about that, learning how to do it?"

CS: "Well, he asks a lot of questions, and he does an awful lot of thinking. He could read my book, *Drive To Win*, of course. If I ever get it finished. Actually I'll finish it next week."

PH: "So he's asking questions. That means he's gotta be around some people who know some answers."

CS: "That's right, and he's gotta sort out the good answers from the bad answers. You've gotta be an information sponge, obviously. But, more than that, you've gotta be an information filter.

"There are people in this, people who have a reputation, that you sure as hell don't want to listen to. And there are people in this business who haven't developed a reputation who would be well worth listening to. Most of the people in this business, if a kid asks the right questions in the right manner, they'll answer them. This business is full of very good people."

PH: "I agree. I've seen that doing interviews like this. If you ask the right question or ask a question in a sincere way that shows that you want to know, people are just likely to tell you more than they ought to."

CS: "Yeah. And even people who have a reputation for being ass holes, like Foyt. A. J. Foyt taught me more than probably anybody else ever has. And he hated himself for doing it."

PH: [laughing] "How did that happen?"

CS: "Well, he used to drive for us. He drove for Shelby. At that point, Foyt had forgotten more about racecars than anybody else in the world knew. I was pretty green, so he'd talk and he'd teach me things. He'd say, 'God damn, I don't know why I'm telling you this.' I've been very, very lucky in that I've worked with a lot of very, very, very good people. I've learned a lot from all of them, and a whole hell of a lot from a few of them. But there wasn't anybody that wasn't willing to answer the questions."

PH: "Did it help you that you had the classic mechanical engineering education?"

CS: "I don't know. I don't think it was much of any help. What the years in a university do, as you well know, is you develop a mental discipline. You learn how to attack a problem. So, in that respect, certainly, it helped. Did I get any specific knowledge in school? No. Let's face it. They don't teach you much that's going to be much good to you, when you're going to be working with vehicle dynamics and real materials as opposed to low-carbon steel, which is what they teach you about.

"But they do teach you how to approach a problem. Maybe you absorb it through osmosis. It's a lot better than it used to be, by the way. I'm one of the judges in the SAE (Society of Automotive Engineers) racecar competition, and some of the faculty advisors I wish I'd had for instructors. You would expect engineering education to get better as the decades pass."

PH: "Just having tools like spreadsheets now is great. I remember there was only one guy in my class that had a calculator."

CS: "Really? You're younger than I am."

PH: "So did the books work? Are you saying that writing *Prepare To Win* got you work? Did that make you an expert in some people's eyes?"

CS: "Yes. Definitely. Of course, one of the things about any kind of technical book, it clarifies your own thinking."

PH: "You betcha."

CS: "And that's what happened. I'd start to write a chapter and I'd realize, gee, I don't know much about this. So I had to go learn. Yeah, the book definitely enhanced my reputation. All the books have, in fact. And they have gotten me some pretty interesting jobs. They definitely got me the job with Ford of Australia."

PH: "What was that?"

CS: "I ran Ford of Australia's Touring car team during calendar year 1978, which was one of the great experiences of my life. We won all the races. No we didn't. We lost two out of 26. It was really neat because they hadn't won a race in three years. That was fun. The books got me that job. They got me the job with the Callaway Sledgehammer for sure. Which was also fun. Not so challenging, but fun."

PH: "I saw your notebook from that project when I did your seminar a few years ago."

CS: "Right, and that's something that every engineer should do is keep a project log, an informal one. Otherwise you kinda lose track of who's doing what with which to whom.

"Yeah, the books have helped. Plus they bring some money, not enough to live on, but it helps. I think, more than anything else, they've clarified my thinking on a multitude of subjects."

PH: "Yeah, writing is an interesting process. I certainly can't write about things I don't understand."

CS: [laughs] "Well, that would be very difficult."

PH: [laughing also] "But there's people who do it, I think."

CS: "Yes, I know, but we don't need to talk about that."

PH: "Let's go back to question number one. What is the contribution of a driver to a quick lap? A race win? A series championship? What differences in this is there in Formula 1 or Indy cars or whatever?"

CS: "Somewhere between 60% and 80%. And it's the same for all of them— quick lap, race win, or series championship. And I see no difference in the percentage whether it's F1 or IndyCar or anything."

PH: "So you're saying that the driver is 60% or 80% of what it takes."

CS: "I'm not saying that's all in driving skill. The driver has a great many shoes to fill, hats to wear. Number one, for a racing car to win any kind of event, including the pole, the team has to gel. It has to work; it has to spark. It has to be better than any other team present on the day. Now, the only thing available to ignite that mixture—it's like an internal combustion engine—the spark plug is the driver. Nobody else can ignite the mixture—not Carroll Shelby, not Ron Dennis, not Frank Williams, not even Enzo Ferrari. The crew will walk on burning coals for the right driver. They don't have to like him, by the way. And, if they won't do that, then success will come his way only by happenstance. So that's one of the driver's hats or responsibilities, a crucial one.

"Another is that he is the development tool. You can have all the computers in the world, and the computer can measure accelerations, and suspension travel and all sorts of things. But there's one thing it can't measure and that's balance. And balance is what makes a quick lap, a race win, a championship. It's up to the driver to achieve that balance and then, with the assistance of the engineers, to upgrade the cornering power of the car while keeping the balance. He's still the most sensitive device we've got."

PH: "You probably noticed when you read the draft of the book that I asked several people I interviewed about the relationship between ultimate grip and balance."

CS: "Yep [thoughtful pause]. The business is all about balance! [Even though this was a telephone interview I could almost see the jutting jaw and challenging eyes that always accompany a strong Carroll Smith statement.] You can have all the ultimate stick in the world, but if the driver can't control the car—perfectly— on a changing racetrack, in traffic, he ain't gonna win. So, at some level, you may well have to sacrifice some ultimate stick to give the driver a useful tool. Now the better the driver is, the less of it you'll have to sacrifice—the better, more experi- enced, more sensitive, yadata, yadata.

"In other words, if you gave, someone who shall be nameless, the same car you gave Schumacher or Senna, he couldn't drive it. Well, if you look at Schumacher right now, his teammate does have the same car. And there's three seconds difference. So, when you're playing set-up games, you have to have the driver in mind and, if you're running a middle-aged businessman in Sports 2000, you don't give him the same car you give Christopher Smith. Because he will not be comfortable and, if he's not comfortable, he can't do it. You have to bring the driver along, and, if you give him Jimmy Vasser's car to start with, he'll never develop the confidence.

"And, if you think I'm going to dissemble on the next question like everyone else did, you're right."

PH: [laughing] "Are we there yet? You were talking about hats to wear."

CS: "No, we're not there yet."

PH: "The driver has to gel the team, and he's the best development tool. What else?"

CS: "Plus, he also has to be fast, and he has to be disciplined. He has to be easy on the car or as easy as he has to be, and, most of all, he has to know how to race. You know, Danny Ongais once said in public, nice man that he is, 'Carroll Smith taught me to drive a racecar, but I already knew how to race.'"

PH: "So what's the difference?"

CS: [sigh and pause] "It's the difference between a hill-climb specialist or a drag racer and an oval-track racer or a road racer. You gotta know when to go for the hole. You gotta know when to nurse the car. You gotta know when NOT to go for the hole. You gotta know who, when you stick your front wheel in between his front and rear wheels, you can trust; and who you can't. And you have to make a whole bunch of decisions based on inadequate information—several times a lap. Some people are born with a lot of that savvy; other people develop it; and some people never develop it.

"Without naming names, we've watched for the last two years some very, very fast drivers drive into situations that anybody else would have seen a lap and a half ago.

"There's a really good book called *The Ace Factor*, as in airplane ace. It talks about situational awareness. Fighter pilots and race drivers have it—good ones. And it can be developed just like everything else.

"It's all a question of balance and discipline. Brave doesn't come into it, by the way. Bravery doesn't have anything to do with being a good driver. By definition, anybody who willingly drives a racecar in competition is brave. And that's as brave as you have to be."

PH: "Now to the magic question. What can a racecar designer do to help the driver?"

CS: [pause, sigh] "Oh, boy [pause]. Basically, if you're talking about the designer, the guy who actually pencils the car, depending on who's going to drive it...I'll give you a good example. When Derek Gardener, the guy who designed the original [Formula 1] Tyrells, came from Ferguson, he'd never seen a racecar in his life. He designed a racecar around Jackie Stewart. The car was damned near square, wide track and short wheel base. Nobody else could drive it. Stewart won championships with it. He did those cars and then, presumably, went back to designing transmissions for Ferguson. Very brilliant man.

"The designer is faced with a lot of very funny things. I should also say that there's no such thing as 'A Designer' anymore. There are no more Colin Chapmans. There are no more Ron Taurenacs. The cars have become too complex for one man to design. It's a design team like an airplane, now. But there is a design chief in each case, and it's up to him to make sure that they don't go too far out in left field and wind up with a car that doesn't work at all, like the Ferraris, for instance.

"This is an evolutionary business. I can't think, offhand, of any giant steps forward that worked right away in the history of the business. So you have to go with the wheelbase to track ratio that you know will work and the polar moment that you know will work, with geometry and aerodynamics that you have a pretty good idea is gonna work. And you have to keep the overall view, you know. You can't forget about tiny little things like torsional rigidity, like they did for a while because aerodynamics made it unimportant. Until John Barnard built a stiff car and disappeared into the distance.

"You have to design a basic balance into the car, both mechanical balance and aero balance. If you have to run the front wing stalled to get enough front download, you fell off your drafting stool, probably trying something new. Having said all that, it's basically up to the development engineer or the track engineer to work with the driver and get the damn thing to work. But if it's an evolutionary car, it'll probably work pretty well right away.

"I know you've read the statements by a lot of drivers, including Mr. [Rick] Mears, who say you know the first lap whether it's going to be a good car or not. And he's right. He better feel it's going to be a good car because, if the driver gets it in his head that it's not going to be a good car, guess what? Start over. Because you'll never convince him otherwise."

PH: "When I talked to Rick Mears at Laguna a couple of years ago, he mentioned one of the Penske Indy cars didn't give any feedback at all, and they fixed that in the next version. He said, 'The car's got to talk to you.'"

CS: "Yeah. The car's got to dance. And there are a lot of other things. And I'm going to dissemble [to conceal the real nature of, to let pass unnoticed, ignore] just like everyone else you've interviewed [both laugh]. But it has to do with those things you list in your question. It has to do with scrub radius. It has to do a little bit with kingpin inclination, a little bit with castor, a little bit with the camber curve, a lot with polar moment, a lot with spring rates, a lot with torsional rigidity [long pause]. Eeeh, that's about it, really.

"And a lot with ergonomics. You know, when you try to put a 6-foot-4 driver in a car that was made for a 5-foot-10 driver, you've got a real problem. He can't do it. Not properly. Which has been a problem with Berger all his life. The giant Berger. He's 5-foot-10 or something.

"The best racecar I ever got to drive, I couldn't, because my feet were too big. I couldn't switch my feet between the pedals. That was my fault for having size 12 feet.

"But how you load the compromise...And as I said, if you're dealing with Ayrton Senna, you can give him a less stable car with less what we'll call feedback than you would give Paul Haney. Now you hear or you read a lot about the lesser lights, particularly in Formula 1, saying these cars have no feel. They say you have to go into the corner at ever increasing speeds until you lose it, because the car doesn't tell you anything. Senna never said that. Schumacher never said that."

PH: "So what are they feeling that other people can't?"

CS: "They're more sensitive. You know what they're feeling? It's real simple. They're feeling two things. One is the slip angle of the tire, and the other is the self-aligning torque of the tires, on all four tires. And some people have honed their sense to a higher point than other people have. The press always attacked Senna, because he didn't have time for them at the race track. What he said was real simple, 'I come to the racetrack to win the race. My time is spent with my car and my engineers. If the press wants to talk to me, they can do so afterwards.'

"It's similar to...If you take a middle-aged businessman just getting into motor racing and put him in a Sports 2000, you have to give him a relatively soft car to start with. Soft tire pressures, soft spring, soft shocks—soft car, so he can feel what's happening. Well, the same thing is true at the Formula 1 level. If you put someone nameless into Schumacher's car, the car doesn't talk to him. He hasn't honed his senses or God didn't give him the senses, or both, to the extent that Schumacher has. He can't feel the car. If you soften the car for him a little bit, he'd probably be a much happier person, would stay on the road for longer periods of time, and would probably go faster.

"But, if you are the team manager or the designer working with Michael Schumacher or Ayrton Senna, you really don't want to detune the car for Mr. Nameless. It's a difficult situation. I think it helps to have driven the racecar, or driven a racecar, or lots of racecars, at a fairly high level."

PH: "You said the driver was feeling slip angle and the self-aligning torque on all four tires."

CS: "Or however many happen to be on the ground at that time."

PH: "Well, how does he feel the self-aligning torque on the rear tires? I assume he's feeling it at the front through the steering wheel."

CS: "Through his butt and through his spine."

"We don't know how the feedback loop works. Let me rephrase that. I don't know how the feedback loop works. And I've not spoken with anyone who claims to know. It's a question that interests me. I can remember, many years ago, talking to a, how to put it, a highly regarded military flight surgeon. His theory was that it was all visual, and fighter planes have either a rivet line or a seam line directly in front of the pilot longitudinally. And I pointed out that they fly these things at night. He didn't speak to me anymore."

PH: "That was rude of you."

CS: "We don't know how it works. It's the same in all sports. Why was Magic Johnson better than anybody else? He had honed the abilities that God gave him. Maybe God gave him more than most people but, mainly, he honed them. Or Willie Shoemaker or O. J. Simpson for that matter."

PH: "OK, so the car's OK and the driver kinda knows what he's doing. Then what can the race engineer do?"

CS: "He can....Most drivers don't really know very much about vehicle dynamics, and I'm not sure they should. It's the race engineer's job to take the information that the driver's giving him, and whatever information he's getting from data acquisition, if there is some, and from watching the car, and achieve a balance, which is not difficult, and then upgrade the cornering capacity of the car without losing the controllability and balance. It's all a compromise, obviously.

"As you know, you can drive a Hudson—well, OK, you can drive a Chevy Nova through a corner sideways, and no skill whatsoever is required because it's soft and floppy and has tires that develop their maximum stick at a 14 degrees slip angle or something. And you will make the car faster as you stiffen it, but there's a point when you lose more controllability and balance than you gain in stick. Now it's become fairly complex since we can adjust absolutely everything on the car, and, you know, the race engineer has to play the differential vs. the shocks vs. the springs vs. the sway bars, if any, vs. the tire pressure vs., in some aspects, camber and aero downforce vs. drag; and wind up with a better package than the other group wound up with. It helps to have a good test program. But a bad test program won't help you at all.

"It helps to develop a very efficient channel of communication with the driver. And that takes a while. It's an interpersonal relationship, if you will. There are people who are very good at it. I give you Lee Dykstra.

"I don't think anybody can lay down a series of steps and say, 'One, two, three, four.' Everybody has their own way of doing things. Lee does a lot of it from a strict engineering point of view. So does Tony Cicale [engineer on Jacques Villeneuve's Indy car in 1994 and 1995]. But then they're both very good at working with the driver, and each of them will throw away the engineering thing if it's not working and go back to gut feel."

PH: "How do a driver and engineer develop some language or way of talking about things?"

CS: "It's up to the engineer to ask the right questions. That's my way of looking at it. Debriefing should take a while. Obviously, in the pit lane with five minutes to go in qualifying, the debriefing ain't going to take long. But, if you've developed the communication skills before then, the driver can come in at that point and say, 'Give me a half an increment more front wing.' But, after the first practice session, the debrief is gonna take a long time, and you better have a good course map and a patient driver.

"My own system is to ask the driver to fill out the course map in detail before I talk to him, because I don't want to plant ideas in his head. And I want him to do that in strict privacy, without the car owner or the chief mechanic or me or without the other driver. And then, once he's done that, we'll sit down and talk, and I will ask the questions that I think I need to ask to get the answers that will allow me to make a decision—good, bad or indifferent. Or us to make a decision, actually.

"If you've done enough meaningful testing, you've almost got nomagrams—if A, then B. If you haven't then you have to kinda wing it, sort of, working on past experience and what you think oughta work. And sometimes you're right."

PH: "How much coaching should a race engineer do?"

CS: "Oh, boy [sigh]. Depending on the personality of the driver involved, as much as you can. One of the things that really amazes me about this business, every tennis pro in the world has at least two coaches and wouldn't think of leaving his hotel room without at least one of them. The best football players in the world have individual coaches. We have the back-field coach. We have the line coach. Everybody except race drivers has coaches. Jockeys have coaches. We don't have them. It's amazing."

PH: "It is amazing. Everybody thinks they already know how to drive."

CS: "Yep. I think it was Stirling Moss who said, 'There are two things a man won't admit he doesn't do well.' Stirling certainly wouldn't admit he didn't do the other one very well, indeed.

"Now, some of the very good drivers accept coaching. And some don't. In order to coach a driver, it is necessary to have either good data or be out on the racetrack, or both. Both is better."

PH: "We've talked about that before. And Jeff and I have talked about it. Why in the hell doesn't somebody in the crew go out and watch the driver on the track?"

CS: "Damned if I know. I do. I can think of no earthly good I can do sitting in the pits that I can't do from somewhere else with a radio."

PH: "I worked for Tom Rust at Sears Point 10 years ago and, when he was coaching customer drivers, he'd go out on corners and watch what they were doing and use what he saw to coach them."

CS: "Oh, yeah, and he's a heavy man who has to work to get there. Some of it you can see on data from the on-board computer. You can see if the guy is shifting properly, whether he's messing up the downshifts and snatching the rear wheels, whether he's using too much steering. You can see a lot of stuff on data. But to get a feel for what's going on, you have to be out there."

PH: "What do you look for when you're out there on a corner watching your driver?"

CS: "Oh, boy [chuckle]. You look for the driver being totally in control of his vehicle, himself, and the situation. You look for...for aggressive smoothness. How's that for a term? You look for using the tires rather than abusing them. You look for quick, clean shifts. You look for a driver who looks like he knows what he's doing. You know, if it looks right, it probably is.

"You can tell a lot watching a driver spin. Everybody spins from time to time. Prost [Alain] used to spin about twice a year. If his head is up and he's looking where the car's going, and he's fighting it all the way, you've got a guy who's in control—knows what's happening. If he, figuratively, throws his hands up in the air and says he hopes he doesn't hit anything, then you probably don't want to work with him.

"If you've got a guy who gets surprised a lot, and you can see it—he either gets surprised by traffic or he gets surprised by things the car does--if the guy's in tune with the car and the situation and the racetrack, then he puts the correction in before the car needs it. Anticipation makes you fast. Reflexes save your life when you mess up. It's hard to verbalize what you look for."

PH: "What about the cheerleading/ass kicking tradeoff?"

CS: "I don't do a lot of ass kicking [laughing]. What I find is, if I kick ass on the day, I'm very liable to spend the night fixing the car. [Both laugh at that.] I'll show him. Splat!

"I would like to think that most of the people I work with don't need cheerleading. I don't understand cheerleading. The fire in the belly comes from within. I have never been in the babysitting business, and I never intend to be. If a guy can't motivate himself, then I sure as hell can't motivate him. I will sympathize with him. And everybody gets down once in a while. I'll try to bring him back up again, but I'm not going to put on pom-poms and do the you're-the-greatest thing. This should be a game being played between adults; age doesn't matter; between mature people. It's not a place for immature people. And, maybe it's just my personality, I just don't believe that mature people respond to cheerleading.

"The ass kicking, if I'm going to do it, I'll do it at the end of the day [laughing]. When he's got all night to think about it before he splats the car.

"Now, I will say, particularly in long-distance races, there is a time, when things are gettin' tough and it's the last pit stop and you say to the driver something like, 'Look pal, an awful lot of people have given you everything they've got to give and you better pay it back right now in the next two hours.' I've done that a couple of times and it's worked very well. Both times with immature drivers, by the way [long pause]. Anyway, I guess I'm not much of a cheerleader."

PH: "Well, we're getting down here to the question about how does a driver best use a racecar, tires, engines, other stuff."

CS: "With tires, it's real simple. Use 'em, don't abuse 'em. Get 'em hot before you lean on them. Don't do a lot of steering. If you're doing a lot of steering, there's either something wrong with you or something wrong with the car.

"I think the second day Christopher was ever in a Formula Ford he said, 'That round, black thing in front of me? When I move it, it's just like pushing on the middle pedal. Fix the car so I don't have to move it.'

"Engine? Real simple. Don't over-rev it. Learn how to shift. Up and down. And don't do any throttle-jabbing. Yes, it works for Jimmy Vasser. There's an exception that disproves every rule. And Senna did some pretty incredible stuff, but that was in different situations, and it had to do with turbos and things.

"Basically, be smooth with the engine. Learn how to shift and don't over-rev it. Don't confuse noise with horsepower. And warm it up. Warm everything up. That's what the first lap is for—not the first lap of the race, obviously.

"Other components? Learn how to shift. Learn how to brake. Learn how to drive?" [We both laugh.]

PH: "And this test track question?"

CS: "How should the driver approach a test? Open mind. Absolutely determined to be the fastest person there whether it's a race, a test, a season, the Indy 500, or a career. Be ready. Be ready before every session. Let people know you appreciate the efforts they're making, particularly when you're a young driver. The young driver should never be ashamed to show that he really enjoys driving that thing. That's what's refreshing about Schumacher. The joy is visible, and it should be. Damn it, this is more fun than anything else a person can do with his clothes on. So why not show it?

"But, to me, the approach is the same whether it's a test session, a race weekend, a season, the Indy 500, or a career. You have to go there determined to do the very best that you can do, to learn everything you can learn, and to be the very best that you can be. Every day, all the time. And, you know, if you're in a racecar and it's on a racetrack, you really ought to be driving at your limit, unless you're trying to nurse the car. If there's a reason to nurse the car, that's one thing. If you've got a big lead, that's another thing. But it costs just as much to drive a car at 90% of your ability as it does to drive the car at 99% of your ability. And, if you're driving the car at 90% of your ability, you're not going to learn anything. You know how to do that. And you're not going to advance the car, because you're cruisin'. Ships are safe in port, but that's not what ships are for. After you develop some skill and you've got some experience in your bank account, you can overstep the limit a little bit and gather it right back in again. Cost you a couple of tenths. Up until you develop that skill, of course, there's liable to be a lot of noise [chuckles].

"It's a question of trying to develop the skills. And it's expensive. One of the things that Bondaurant points out in his book—words of wisdom from Bob Bondaurant, incredible—is that all the time you're driving in a street car you can be developing skills. You don't have to be driving at the limit to learn about line or shifting or left-foot braking or anticipating what's happening in traffic or being aware of what's going on around you—any of those things. You can learn a lot of it walking in traffic on a sidewalk. You just gotta think. You gotta keep the brain active. Because, let's face it, after a certain level of physical skill is learned, in motor racing or flying or bowling or golf, 98% of it is mental.

"And that, of course, answers the next question, doesn't it? The one about what makes a good driver. Determination, dedication, discipline. There have been world champions who didn't have a whole hell of a lot of physical skills. They shall remain nameless."

PH: "So Carroll, what is it about all this? About racing? Why do we love it so?"

CS: "Well, it sure isn't the women and the parties. It's the challenge. This isn't a game for people who can settle. This isn't a game for people who join unions or work an 8-to-5 job. This is a game, at every level—whether it's mechanic, engineer, driver, team owner, truck driver—for people who truly enjoy challenges.

"And, you know, it's a good way to live a life. I've been in this business for 40 years now and I hope to be in it for another 40, which is a little unrealistic."

PH: "I agree. I really enjoy the people. Right now, I'm very irritable waiting for the '95 season to start. I want to get to Miami so I can be around people who are crazy in the same direction I am. Racing people are fun to talk to; they're intelligent. And, you're right, they do enjoy the challenge.

"Well, I've run out of questions. Is there anything else we should have talked about?"

CS: "I don't think so. Oh, probably. There always is."

FURTHER READING

Smith, Carroll. *Prepare To Win*, Motorbooks International.

Smith, Carroll. *Tune To Win*, Motorbooks International.

Smith, Carroll. *Engineer To Win*, Motorbooks International.

Van Valkenburgh, Paul. *Race Car Engineering & Mechanics*, Published by the author.

Fey, Buddy. *Data Power*, Towery Publishing.

Staniforth, Allan. *Competition Car Suspension*, Haynes Publishing.

Fisher, Bill and Waar, Bob. *How To Modify Datsun 510 610 240Z* Engines and Chassis., H. P. Books.

Scibor-Rylski, A. J. *Road Vehicle Aerodynamics*, Pentech Press.

Bastow, Donald. *Car Suspension and Handling*, Pentech Press.

Gillespie, Thomas D. *Fundamentals of Vehicle Dynamics*, Society of Automotive Engineers.

Milliken, William F. and Douglas L. *Race Car Vehicle Dynamics*, Society of Automotive Engineers.

Bosch Automotive Handbook, 3rd edition, Robert Bentley.

Hucho, I. *Aerodynamics of Road Vehicles*, Butterworth Heinemann, Ltd.

Pope, Alan and Harper, John. Low-Speed Wind Tunnel Testing, Wiley.

Bamsey, Ian. *The Anatomy & Development of the Sports Prototype Racing Car*, Motorbooks International.

Incandela, Sal. *The Anatomy & Development of the Formula One Racing Car from 1975*, Haynes.

Donahue, Mark with Van Valkenburgh, Paul. *The Unfair Advantage*, Dodd, Mead & Company.